Publications of the John Gower Society

IV

FATHERS AND DAUGHTERS IN GOWER'S CONFESSIO AMANTIS

AUTHORITY, FAMILY, STATE, AND WRITING

Fathers and daughters are central to some of the most significant tales in Gower's poem. Using feminist and anthropological approaches, María Bullón-Fernández argues that father-daughter relationships, and the associated theme of incest that they sometimes suggest, enable Gower to examine authority relationships in three interconnected spheres: family, state, and writing. She suggests that Gower perceived the relationships between kings and subjects and between authors and texts as similar to paternal relationships with a daughter; and further, that Gower regarded the law of exogamy as a foundational law at the core of patriarchal society. As a father may not commit incest with his daughter and a king may not abuse his authority, so the writer (as in 'Pygmaleon and the Statue') must curb his desire to control the meaning of his creation. Thus, even as he is concerned with the limits of authority in the familial, political, and textual realms, Gower also exposes the inherently transgressive nature of such authority.

MARÍA BULLÓN-FERNÁNDEZ is Assistant Professor of Middle English Literature at Seattle University.

Publications of the John Gower Society

General editors R. F. Yeager and A. J. Minnis
ISSN 0954-2817

I

A Concordance to John Gower's *Confessio Amantis*
Edited by J. D. Pickles and J. L. Dawson

II

John Gower's Poetic: The Search for a New Arion
R. F. Yeager

III

Gower's *Confessio Amantis*: A Critical Anthology
Edited by Peter Nicholson

IV

John Gower and the Structures of Conversion:
A Reading of the *Confessio Amantis*
Kurt Olsson

Fathers and Daughters in Gower's Confessio Amantis

Authority, Family, State, and Writing

María Bullón-Fernández

D. S. BREWER

© María Bullón-Fernández 2000

All Rights Reserved. Except as permitted under current legislation no part of this work may be photocopied, stored in a retrieval system, published, performed in public, adapted, broadcast, transmitted, recorded or reproduced in any form or by any means, without the prior permission of the copyright owner

First published 2000
D. S. Brewer, Cambridge

ISBN 0 85991 578 6

D. S. Brewer is an imprint of Boydell & Brewer Ltd
PO Box 9, Woodbridge, Suffolk IP12 3DF, UK
and of Boydell & Brewer Inc.
PO Box 41026, Rochester, NY 14604–4126, USA
website: http://www.boydell.co.uk

A catalogue record of this publication is available
from the British Library

Library of Congress Cataloging-in-Publication data
Bullón-Fernández, María, 1965–
   Fathers and daughters in Gower's Confessio Amantis : authority, family, state, and writing / María Bullón-Fernández.
     p. cm (Publications of the John Gower Society, ISSN 09542817 ; 5)
   Includes bibliographical references and index.
   ISBN 0–85991–578–6 (acid-free paper)
   1. Gower, John, 1325?–1408. Confessio amantis. 2. Politics and literature – Great Britain – History – To 1500. 3. Feminism and literature – Great Britain – History – To 1500. 4. Gower, John, 1325?–1408 – Political and social views. 5. Gower John, 1325?–1408 – Views on authorship. 6. Fathers and daughters in literature. 7. State, The, in literature. 8. Authority in literature. 9. Family in literature.
   I. Title. II. Series.
   PR1984.C63 B85 2000
   821'.1–dc21   99–057065

This publication is printed on acid-free paper

Printed in Great Britain by
Antony Rowe Ltd, Chippenham, Wiltshire

CONTENTS

Acknowledgments	vii
1. Fathers and Daughters: Defining Authority	1
2. Redeeming Daughters: Thaise, Peronelle, and Constance	42
3. Fathers as Husbands, Husbands as Fathers: Supplantation and Exchange in the "Tale of the False Bachelor" and the "Tale of Albinus and Rosemund"	102
4. Limiting Authority: Leucothoe, Virginia, and Canace	130
5. Textual Fathers and Textual Daughters: The "Tale of Rosiphelee," the "Tale of Jephthah's Daughter," and "Pygmaleon and the Statue"	173
Bibliography	217
Index	235

A mi familia

ACKNOWLEDGMENTS

This book has finally reached its present form after many years of study, writing, and rewriting. Many teachers, colleagues, and friends have offered comments and encouragement along the way and it is a great pleasure for me to have now an opportunity to thank them. The first person I want to thank and the one to whom I owe my greatest debt of gratitude is Winthrop Wetherbee. He encouraged me to write about Gower and he has read, reread, and given me invaluable comments on parts of this book, even the roughest drafts, both when it was at its earliest stage as a dissertation, and, later, in its transformation into a book. I also want to thank him for his support, encouragement, and friendship, which have been fundamental not only for the elaboration of this book but also for the development of my academic career.

I owe a great debt of gratitude to Robert Yeager, editor of the John Gower Series. He believed in this project from its inception, has offered many detailed comments, and has been extremely encouraging as well as generous with his time. Alastair Minnis, also an editor of the John Gower Series, gave me a thorough critique in the later stages of development of this book, for which I am very grateful.

Special thanks also go to Carolyn Dinshaw. She has read and commented on some sections of this book and she generously sent me two unpublished papers that were directly relevant to those sections. I wish to thank Elizabeth Archibald as well for sending me one of her articles and discussing parts of this study with me.

The faculty in the Medieval Studies Program at Cornell University was very helpful in the preliminary phase of this study. I would like to thank in particular Andrew Galloway, Carol Kaske, Thomas Hill, William Kennedy, and Marilyn Migiel.

I wish to express my appreciation to the Department of English Literature at the University of Seville (Spain). Their excellent BA program gave me a solid foundation to continue my academic studies in the United States. It was actually at the University of Seville that I first encountered Gower. I still remember reading his "Tale of the King, Wine, Woman, and Truth" in Professor Fernando Toda's History of the English Language class and being very intrigued by it. I thank Rafael Portillo and Manuel Gómez Lara, who inspired me to specialize in medieval literature.

A generous Summer Faculty Fellowship from Seattle University allowed me to devote the summer of 1996 to the book. My colleagues in the Department of English at Seattle University have been very supportive and I would like to thank them for discussing Chapter One with me in a pro-seminar.

ACKNOWLEDGMENTS

At the very final stage of revising the book, I was very fortunate to have the help of my friend and colleague John Trombold. He carefully edited the manuscript, making excellent suggestions for improvement and helping me clarify my argument. Many other friends have offered great support and encouragement. They know who they are. I will mention here only three. Sharon Cumberland and Jacquelyn and Gordon Miller have been invaluable, both as friends and colleagues (they have also commented on sections of this book), since my arrival in Seattle.

Finally, this book is dedicated to my family, my parents, and my eight siblings. They have provided me not only with emotional support but also with an education, both academic and non-academic, that has enabled me to have a fulfilling personal and professional life.

Two papers of mine that were published in Spain contain early versions of arguments that I have further developed in this book: "Gower frente a las convenciones del amor cortés: el cuento de Rosiphelee y el papel social de la mujer en la *Confessio Amantis*," *Actas del XV Congreso de AEDEAN (Asociación Española de Estudios Anglonorteamericanos)*, Logroño, 16–18 de diciembre de 1991, eds. Francisco J. Ruiz de Mendoza Ibáñez and Carmelo Cunchillos Jaime (Logroño: Colegio Universitario de La Rioja, 1993): 515–19; and "Nature or Culture?: John Gower's 'Tale of Apollonius,' " *Proceedings of the VIth International Conference of the Spanish Society for Medieval English Language and Literature*, Valladolid, September 27–29, 1993, eds. Purificación Fernández Nistal and José María Bravo Gozalo (Valladolid: Universidad de Valladolid, 1995): 57–62. I thank the publishers of these volumes for permission to reuse this material.

Two sections of this book, from Chapter Two and Chapter Four respectively, have been published in slightly different forms: "Engendering Authority: Father and Daughter, State and Church in Gower's 'Tale of Constance' and Chaucer's 'Man of Law's Tale,' " in *Re-Visioning Gower: Current Work*, ed. R. F. Yeager (Asheville, NC: Pegasus Press, 1998): 129–46; and "Confining the Daughter: Gower's 'Tale of Canace and Machaire' and the Politics of the Body," *Essays in Medieval Studies* 11 (1994), 24 June 1999 <http://www.luc.edu/publications/medieval/vol.11/bullon.html>. I thank Pegasus Press, Asheville, NC, and the Illinois Medieval Association for permission to reprint the essays.

CHAPTER ONE

FATHERS AND DAUGHTERS:
DEFINING AUTHORITY

In the Introduction to his tale, Chaucer's Man of Law proclaims in a scandalized tone that he will not tell of any "unkinde abhomynaciouns" (88) such as the "wikke ensample of Canacee" (78) or the story of Apollonius and of the incestuous King Antiochus, who "Birafte his doghter of hir maydenhede" (83).[1] These famous lines have rightly been interpreted by critics as a veiled criticism of John Gower's "scandalous" work: the *Confessio Amantis*. The *Confessio* recounts the two incest stories mentioned by the Man of Law: the "Tale of Apollonius," in which a father commits incest with his daughter, and the "Tale of Canace and Machaire," in which a brother and a sister commit incest. If one reads the *Confessio* closely, though, one notices, in fact, that the Man of Law's criticism stops short. For one thing, not only does Gower tell stories of incest, but he even "fails" to condemn one of them, that between the siblings Canace and Machaire. For another, Gower tells three other short stories of incest that the Man of Law does not mention: the *exempla* of Caligula and his three sisters, Amon and his sister, and Lot and his daughters (8.199–270).[2]

Perhaps influenced by the Man of Law's reaction to Gower's use of the incest theme, few critics have looked beyond the scandal of incest in order to analyze why Gower decided to deal with such a complex and controversial topic.[3] Gower's explicit treatment of the issue of incest has a function and an

---

[1] Quoted from Larry D. Benson, ed., *The Riverside Chaucer* (Boston: Houghton Mifflin, 1987). All further quotations from Chaucer's works used in this book come from Benson's edition.
[2] Despite his disapproval of incest stories, the Man of Law himself goes on to tell a story which has a recognized father-daughter incest subtext and which Gower also tells in the *Confessio*: the story of Constance. I analyze this story in Chapter Two.
[3] Among the few studies that deal with incest extensively are a book-length study, Georgiana Donavin, *Incest Narratives and the Structure of the* Confessio Amantis, English Literary Studies 56 (Victoria: U of Victoria, 1993), and, most recently, an essay by Larry Scanlon, "The Riddle of Incest: John Gower and the Problem of Medieval Sexuality," *Re-Visioning Gower: Current Work*, ed. Robert F. Yeager (Asheville, NC: Pegasus Press, 1998), which provokingly suggests that, for critics, Gower, like incest, has become an object of repression (95).

effect that goes far beyond the scandal. Incest functions as a fundamental element in his larger exploration of father-daughter relationships, and more broadly, of relationships of authority. Thus, for instance, the fact that in the story of Canace and Machaire the act of incest between brother and sister is not condemned does not suggest that Gower had, as it were, an unusual sense of morality, but rather it suggests that he was much more preoccupied with the interaction between the father, Eolus, and his daughter Canace than with the relationship between brother and sister. Unlike the Man of Law in Chaucer's tale, Gower is not reluctant to explore the full implications of stories about authority, even if this means raising the specter of incest.

Father-daughter tales are among the longest and most complex in Gower's poem. The "Tale of Apollonius of Tyre," for instance, the last and only tale in Book 8 of the *Confessio* and the longest one in the poem, includes several pairs of fathers and daughters. These pairs have different types of relationships. At one extreme, a father, Antiochus, forcing his daughter to commit incest with him, exerts an absolute and abusive control over her. At the other extreme, another father, Apollonius, separating from his daughter Thaise shortly after her birth and entrusting her education to someone else, renounces immediate control over his daughter. Other crucial father-daughter stories are the "Tale of Canace and Machaire," the "Tale of Constance," the "Tale of the Three Questions," and the "Tale of Jephthah's Daughter," to name a few.

One of the first questions that this book aims to answer is why the father-daughter relationship occupies such a prominent place in the *Confessio Amantis*. I will argue that these father-daughter tales are crucial for Gower's project. Through them, Gower explores fundamental issues of authority. While these tales analyze the question of the father's authority over his daughter and the limits of that authority, they also become vehicles for the examination of other relationships of authority such as that between king and subjects, as most of his fathers are kings or some type of governor, and that between an artist and his work, and, more specifically, between a literary author and his text. As he examines these relationships, Gower explores the limits of the power of the authority figure over his subordinate figure. The father goes beyond the limits of his authority when he commits incest with his daughter. Similarly, the king abuses his authority when he acts like a tyrant, infringing on his subjects' private rights. And an artist, the author of a work, abuses his power when he tries to impose a one-sided interpretation on his work, trying to prevent it from producing meanings beyond his control. One of my main contentions, then, is that these father-daughter tales are fundamentally concerned with questions of power and authority in several interrelated contexts, mainly political, familial, and textual.

Even though he assigns Venus a major role in the poem, Gower's analysis of these questions is articulated within an explicit Christian framework, and thus needs to be understood in the light of the relationship between God and his daughter, the Virgin Mary. Two of the tales I analyze in Chapter Two, the

"Tale of the Three Questions" and the "Tale of Constance," use the relationship between God and Mary as the matrix that defines the relationship between father and daughter. Their parallels with the biblical story of God and Mary, I will argue, do not show that the father-daughter pair is trying to transcend their desire, as Georgiana Donavin, for instance, has argued: "In the *Confessio Amantis*' tales of transcended incestuous passion, a Marian character awaits union with her God as does the maiden in the moor: Peronelle prepares for marriage with Alphonse and Constance for identification by her father" (17).[4] The effect of the parallels with the story of God and Mary is, I suggest, quite the opposite: that is, they do not enable the fathers to transcend their desire, but, rather, they remind us of the ways in which the God-Mary relationship not only reflects the assumptions and desires of patriarchal rule, but, at the same time, also generates and articulates those assumptions and desires.

My examination of the notion of authority, the different spheres in which it is manifested, and the ways in which those spheres interact and define each other is informed by two main approaches. I read the *Confessio Amantis* in the context of the political and religious situation in fourteenth-century England as a work that is not merely a product or a reflection of its historical period, but as a work that wants to play an active role in the contemporary political scene.[5] As Judith Ferster has shown, the *Confessio* is among those late medieval literary works that "participate in the social and political conflicts within which they occur and which, by providing an appropriate language for discussion, they also enable."[6] My analysis of father-daughter relations and the incest taboo is inspired by the insights of feminist psychoanalytic and anthropological approaches.[7] These approaches provide me with a method for understanding and explaining Gower's examination of the gender dynamics that come into play within the family, within the state, and in the process of creation of a literary text, as well as the correspondences among these three realms as they are informed by the same dynamics – the male authority figure appears to negotiate between the desire for an absolute

---

[4] As I will note in Chapter Two, Donavin, like myself, sees Alphonse as Peronelle's displaced father-figure.

[5] For my analysis of the historical and political situation and its interplay with literary texts, I draw on studies by Larry Scanlon, Lee Patterson, David Aers, and Judith Ferster among others, as well as those of historians like Anthony Tuck, Chris Given-Wilson, and Richard Kaeuper.

[6] Judith Ferster, *Fictions of Advice: The Literature and Politics of Counsel in Late Medieval England* (Philadelphia: U of Pennsylvania P, 1996) 10.

[7] My feminist psychoanalytic and anthropological approach draws from the work of, among others, critics such as Judith Butler, Lynda Boose, and Carolyn Dinshaw. For my analysis of incest, gender, and discourse, I draw especially on Butler's theories about the discursive construction of the subject and about gender performativity that she develops in *Gender Trouble* and *Bodies That Matter*. I will also draw on Derrida's analysis of incest and discourse in *Of Grammatology*.

control over the female subordinate figure and the constraints imposed by social forces.

That one of Gower's main concerns in the *Confessio Amantis* is politics in its interaction with other social and religious institutions has long been recognized by critics; the notion of kingship, the values of good governance, the relations between kings and subjects are concerns apparent in many tales as well as central to Book 7 of the poem, a book modeled on the tradition of the mirror for princes.[8] With few exceptions, though, most of which are relatively recent, critics tend to view the *Confessio Amantis* in light of Gower's two earlier and highly moralistic works, *Vox Clamantis* and *Mirour de l'Omme*.[9] They thus see the *Confessio Amantis* as a work that offers a unified vision and a moralistic interpretation of Gower's contemporary problems. We would be naive, not to say anachronistic, to argue that in his last work Gower emerged as a relativistic thinker. But we would similarly miss the point if we ignored the complex problems raised by the *Confessio Amantis*.[10] While Gower's poem cannot be said to attempt to subvert the social order, neither can we say that it offers a simplistic perspective on society and the mechanisms that regulate it. On the contrary, Gower's poem explores the contradictions behind those institutions and the conflicting power relationships that regulate them. This exploration allows him to shed light on issues of power and, at the same time, to raise questions about the workings of power that do not have any easy answers. It is hardly surprising that, as I will explain towards the end of this chapter, while trying to find some kind of structural unity in the poem, those critics who argue for the poem's coherence are still puzzled by what they see as inconsistencies and contradictions in it. It is my contention that, precisely because of these inconsistencies, precisely because

---

[8] Some of the more influential studies that have focused on the political implications of Gower's poem are John H. Fisher, *John Gower: Moral Philosopher and Friend of Chaucer* (New York: New York UP, 1964), Russell A. Peck, *Kingship and Common Profit* (Carbondale: Southern Illinois UP, 1978), and Elizabeth Porter, "Gower's Ethical Microcosm and Political Macrocosm," *Gower's* Confessio Amantis: *Responses and Reassessments*, ed. Alastair J. Minnis (Cambridge: D. S. Brewer, 1983) 135–62. Two articles in a special issue of *Mediaevalia* devoted to Gower also center on the political aspect in the *Confessio*: George B. Stow, "Richard II in John Gower's *Confessio Amantis*: Some Historical Perspectives," *Mediaevalia* 16 (1993 [for 1990]): 3–31, and Judith Ferster, "O Political Gower," *Mediaevalia* 16 (1993 [for 1990]): 33–53, and *Fictions of Advice*, ch. 7. Larry Scanlon, *Narrative, Authority, and Power: The Medieval Exemplum and the Chaucerian Tradition* (Cambridge: Cambridge UP, 1994), also studies the *Confessio Amantis* in the context of fourteenth-century politics and ideology.

[9] Among the exceptions are Scanlon, *Narrative, Authority, and Power*; Theresa Tinkle, *Medieval Venuses and Cupids: Sexuality, Hermeneutics, and English Poetry* (Stanford: Stanford UP, 1996); and articles, such as Elizabeth Allen, "Chaucer Answers Gower: Constance and the Trouble with Reading," *English Literary History* 63 (1997): 627–55; and William Robins, "Romance, Exemplum, and the Subject of the *Confessio Amantis*," *Studies in the Age of Chaucer* 19 (1997): 157–81.

[10] As Scanlon, *Narrative, Authority, and Power*, puts it, "[a]ny attempt to impose a single, unified vision on the poem belies its actual rhetorical complexity" (249).

Gower raises more questions than he answers, a post-structuralist, rather than a structuralist, approach constitutes a particularly appropriate methodology for the analysis and exploration of Gower's *Confessio Amantis*.

Discourse, Incest, and the Law

As he explores the limits of authority, Gower reveals the extent to which authority depends on the discursive, that is, on the discursive definition of its own power and uses. Scanlon has argued in this sense that "[f]or Gower, all of cultural authority depends on institutional and discursive processes of historical construction. Authority must be maintained, and largely produced, from within history."[11] Moreover, Gower's exploration of royal authority's dependence on the discursive stresses also, Scanlon continues, "the interdependence between poet and prince, and the extent to which the prince's authority is always discursively constructed" (250). Thus, his interest in the relations between language and political and institutional authority is linked to the construction of his own role as lay poetic authority. In the Prologue to the *Confessio*, for instance, the poet criticizes the Church's interest in temporal power and draws attention to lay poetic authority as the appropriate moral leader of the people (Scanlon 252–56). The lay poet plays a fundamental role as the voice of the common people and reminds us that royal authority, like poetic authority, depends on discourse.

Before further elaborating on the role of discourse in shaping authority relationships within political institutions, we need to examine Gower's complex notion of the discursive construction of the individual, a central theme in a work that is fundamentally structured around an act of confession. Long before Michel Foucault foregrounded the ritual of confession as a process that plays a fundamental role in the constitution of the subject, Gower viewed confession in his own time similarly, but his use of Genius in the *Confessio* complicates Foucault's analysis of the ritual. According to Foucault, the ritual of confession is deeply linked with the creation of subjectivity and the individual: "The truthful confession was inscribed at the heart of the procedures of individualization by power."[12] The ritual of confession gives the impression that there is a hidden, private, and "true" self prior to discourse that is waiting to be discovered:

> The obligation to confess is now relayed through so many different points, is so deeply ingrained in us, that we no longer perceive it as the effect of a power that constrains us; on the contrary, it seems to us that truth, lodged in our most secret nature, 'demands' only to surface; that if it fails to do so, this is because a constraint holds it in place, the violence

---

[11] Scanlon, *Narrative, Authority, and Power* 267.
[12] Michel Foucault, *The History of Sexuality*, trans. Robert Hurley, vol. 1 (New York: Vintage Books, 1990) 58–59.

of a power weighs it down, and it can finally be articulated only at the price of a kind of liberation. (60)

The confession is supposed to be a liberating ritual in which the one who confesses liberates his/her "true self." However, this sense of liberation, according to Foucault, is a fiction. There is no true self to be discovered, because the true self is created by the ritual (60–61). As Foucault puts it, "truth is not by nature free – nor error servile – but . . . its production is thoroughly imbued with relations of power" (60). The ritual, moreover, promises the restoration of a whole self and the confessor's main function is precisely to guarantee that the promise of producing a wholeness, a stable subjectivity, is fulfilled.[13] Such a promise, though, is ultimately an imposition on the penitent by the confessor – the confessor requires the penitent to "restore" his stable subjectivity through the act of confession. The confessor, thus, is the representative authority who determines the construction of the stable self. In Foucault's words, the confession "unfolds within a power relationship, for one does not confess without the presence (or virtual presence) of a partner who is not simply the interlocutor but the authority who requires the confession . . . and intervenes in order to judge" (61).

The confessor or Father, then, is the authority figure who has control over the confessant and over the construction of his subjectivity – even to the extent of "creating" the confessant's self. In Petrus Berchorius's *Ovidius moralizatus*, an early fourteenth-century moralization of the *Metamorphoses*, the story of Pygmalion is interpreted as an act of confession. Pygmalion is compared to a confessor and his statue is interpreted as the confessant's soul: "Per istum factorem imaginum intelligo praedicatores qui animam sciunt sculpere: & pingere correctionibus & virtutibus."[14] Like Pygmalion, who shaped and constructed his statue/wife out of ivory, the confessor shapes and constructs the confessant's soul. Significantly, in the *Confessio Amantis* Genius tells his own version of the story of Pygmalion, and, as I argue in Chapter Five, this version shows that one of his functions in the poem is that of father/artist who tells stories to Amans, the soul to be molded.[15]

---

[13] Lee Patterson, *Chaucer and the Subject of History* (Madison: U of Wisconsin P, 1991), makes a similar point in his analysis of "The Pardoner's Tale": "the promise that underwrites all confession [is] that in giving himself up to the structures and language of penance the sinner will find relief from his inner torment" (385).

[14] Quoted from Petrus Berchorius, *Ovidius moralizatus*, ed. J. Engels (Utrecht: Institut voor Laat Latijn der Rijksuniversiteit, 1962) 152. ("Through this maker of images I perceive preachers who know how to sculpt and paint a soul with corrections and virtues" [translation taken from "The *Ovidius Moralizatus* of Petrus Berchorius: An Introduction and Translation," trans. William Donald Reynolds, diss., University of Illinois at Urbana-Champaign, 1971, 355].)

[15] Kurt Olsson, *John Gower and the Structures of Conversion: A Reading of the* Confessio Amantis (Cambridge: D. S. Brewer, 1992), has pointed out in this respect that "the priest comes to present an ideal of the remade man, *homo renovatus*" that he tries to use in order to "remake" Amans (195–96). Olsson then argues that "Genius does not wholly succeed in

But the ritual of confession in Gower's poem is more complicated than Foucault's explanation seems to imply, and it does not produce the promised satisfaction. The penitent Amans is frustrated by his confessor. At the end of the confession, he feels that Genius has not understood him: "Mi wo to you is bot a game/ That fielen noght of that I fiele," Amans complains (8.2152–53).[16] And more significantly, the lover also notes that, after the ritual, his self is still divided:

> Mi resoun understod him wel,
> And knew it was soth everydel
> That he hath seid, bot noght forthi
> Mi will hath nothing set therby.   (8.2191–94)

Amans's reason and will are still working at cross purposes. The confession has failed to identify, or rather, "create" his "true" self as well as to fulfill the promise of restoring his original wholeness, as the confession promises to do.[17] Of course, at the very end, Amans does feel "sobre and hol ynowh" (8.2869) and rejects courtly love, but this rejection, I would argue, does not result from the ritual of confession itself, but from his realization upon looking at himself in a mirror given to him by Venus that he was too old to love anyway (8.2820–69).

The confession thus fails to restore the penitent's whole self, and it fails to do so because Genius is a very complex figure. As Carolyn Dinshaw has argued, as confessor/father, Gower's Genius is, in fact, a more complex figure than the traditional confessor as described by Foucault, for Genius is not a representative of a single doctrine: "Gower's choice of the literary confession *and* his multiplication of authorities governing the confession are fascinating because they suggest that the confession did not and could not carry the large burden of subject formation that Foucault has ascribed to it."[18] Indeed, Genius is far from being a stable source or mouthpiece of a higher authority; his authority is paradoxically defined by at least two different discourses. Like his main predecessors, Alain de Lille's Genius in *De planctu naturae* and Jean

---

'remaking' Amans, for the lover recovers his wits only through acts of 'grace' by Cupid and Venus" (196). I argue here that Genius's failure is rather linked to the ambiguities raised by his double allegiance to the Christian God and to Venus.

16 Throughout this book all quotations from the *Confessio Amantis* are taken from *The English Works of John Gower*, ed. G. C. Macaulay, Early English Text Society, e.s. 81–82 (Oxford: Oxford UP, 1900–1901).

17 For analyses of Amans's frustrations, see Allen, "Chaucer Answers Gower," for whom these frustrations are part of the process of interpretation and self-reflection with which we as readers are meant to identify, and Robins, "Romance, Exemplum, and the Subject of the *Confessio Amantis*," for whom the frustrations have to do with the paradox of exemplarity, as it can only persuade the listener when and if the listener is ready to be persuaded.

18 Carolyn Dinshaw, "Straight is the Gate: The Heterosexual Subject of Middle English Literature," MLA Middle English Literature Division, MLA Convention, New York, 28 Dec. 1992: 13. (I would like to thank Carolyn Dinshaw for kindly sending me a copy of this paper and giving me permission to quote from it.)

de Meun's Genius in *Le Roman de la Rose*, he is a priest of Venus and a promoter of reproduction. At the same time, however, and unlike his predecessors, he is a priest who represents the moral and religious authority of the Church.[19] He thus represents a divided and contradictory self. And these contradictions are frustrating for the subject of confession, Amans, because in order to produce a stable self, the confessor himself should represent a stable authority, a requirement that Genius does not fulfill. Thus, through the relationship between Genius, the father/confessor, and Amans the confessant, Gower examines the extent to which the confessor, an unstable figure, exerts his authority over the confessant and the extent to which he determines or fails to determine the process of the confessant's subject formation.

A discussion of the constitution of the subject within the structures of ideology, as I have noted, is crucial to the *Confessio Amantis* and, more generally, to fourteenth-century England.[20] In this respect, the *Confessio* departs significantly from Gower's two previous major works, *Mirour de l'Omme*, and *Vox Clamantis*, in both of which the concern with more abstract social and moral issues overrides the concern for the individual's relationship to those issues. In the *Confessio Amantis* it is not society in the abstract but the conflicts arising in the process of the subject's constitution and interaction

---

[19] Tinkle, *Medieval Venuses and Cupids*, also stresses Genius's use of multiple discourses and she sees Genius's contradictions as "the effect of Gower's coupling of erotic fiction and moralizing commentary" (181). She continues: "[b]y translating (chiefly Ovidian) poetry as well as mythographic heremeneutics into one text, Gower foregrounds the disjunctions between them" (181).

[20] The widespread modern notion that there was no sense of self in the Middle Ages and that the Early Modern period saw the birth of subjectivity has been carefully and strongly refuted by various critics. In "A Whisper in the Ear of Early Modernists; or, Reflections on Literary Critics Writing the 'History of the Subject,'" *Culture and History, 1350–1600: Essays on English Communities, Identities, and Writing*, ed. David Aers (Detroit: Wayne State UP, 1992) 177–202, Aers develops his critique of much current Renaissance scholarship that claims that the notion of selfhood and subjectivity only started in the Renaissance. A similar critique can be found in Lee Patterson, "On the Margin: Postmodernism, Ironic History, and Medieval Studies," *Speculum* 65 (1990): 87–108. Lee Patterson has argued that "the antagonism between the desires of the individual and the demands of society provided one of the great topics for literary exploration throughout the Middle Ages" (8). Patterson situates Chaucer's exploration of subjectivity and its relation to the historical in the *Canterbury Tales* within this context, and in relation to other late Middle English literary works, like Langland's *Piers Plowman* or *Sir Gawain and the Green Knight*. It is, of course, in the same historical and political context that Gower, who shared similar concerns with Chaucer, wrote his *Confessio Amantis*. On the question of the traditional differentiation between the medieval and Renaissance periods on the basis of the notion of community versus individuality, see David Wallace, *Chaucerian Polity* (Stanford: Stanford UP, 1997), especially the Introduction and 54–62. For studies of the relationship between Gower and Chaucer, see John H. Fisher, *John Gower: Moral Philosopher and Friend of Chaucer*, especially chapter 5; Robert F. Yeager, ed. *Chaucer and Gower: Difference, Mutuality, and Exchange*, English Literary Studies Monograph Series 51 (Victoria: U of Victoria, 1991); and Scanlon, *Narrative, Authority and Power*.

with society that become the focus. In an article on the intersection of the genres of romance and exemplum in the "Tale of Apollonius," William Robins has argued that in the *Confessio* Gower examines the fundamental role of literary genres in shaping a sense of self: "in the Prologue Gower suggests that the reader's relation to society is conditioned by the possibilities of narrative" (176). Although, for Robins, "[t]his disposition of intersecting, basic modes of self-conception provokes readers to perceive that they cannot think of themselves except through these structures," he notes that Gower's self "differs from the postmodern, decentered subject for which the self is an illusion created by language, for Gower dearly holds to the belief in an interiority from which to choose between, or at least to feel and endure, competing narrative options" (178). Robins is rightly cautious to avoid any easy projections of postmodern notions of subjectivity onto Gower's work. Nevertheless, whether Gower was conscious of it or not, one can still analyze the ways in which his text raises the possibility that even the interiority of the self might fundamentally depend on its discursive construction. What Gower ultimately believed is difficult to know and the *Confessio Amantis* is not interested in providing definite answers. I will argue, though, that the poem demonstrates his interest in exploring the function of discourse in the construction of the individual, and sometimes it goes as far as raising the possibility that the self may depend fundamentally on language. Judith Butler's theories about the productive, but not absolutely deterministic, power of discourse in the construction of the self can help us understand this point.

Foucault's theory on discourse's function in determining the constitution of the subject has been seen to underestimate the possibility of subversion. Butler's elaboration on Foucault's theories leaves some space for subversion and thus will help us account for complex moments in Gower's poem. For Butler, discourse has a "reiterative power . . . to produce the phenomena that it regulates and constrains."[21] The individual who acts is not a self who has an essence upon which discourse acts. He/she is a subject in the Lacanian sense. The subject is formed and constituted by language and structures of ideology in a process of reiteration. Unlike Foucault, Butler then emphasizes that her theory does not imply that the subject is absolutely determined by those structures, for "[c]onstruction not only takes place *in* time, but is itself a temporal process which operates through the reiteration of norms" (10). Or, as she also puts it, "there is no power that acts, but only a reiterated acting that is power in its persistence and instability" (9). In this process of reiteration, then, structural gaps and fissures that can modify the construction appear. In the *Confessio Amantis*, I will argue, reiterated acting is shown to have a primary role in the construction of the self, but the need for reiterated acting will reveal gaps and fissures that open up the possibility of subversion

---

[21] Judith Butler, *Bodies that Matter: On the Discursive Limits of "Sex"* (New York: Routledge, 1993) 2.

and thus of some agency, even if the subversive possibility is subsequently closed.

Gower is interested in the incest taboo, I will argue, because of its inevitable dependence on discourse, and because of its primary role in the constitution of the subject. That Gower would put this exploration in the context of a confession is most significant, given the role of confession in the process of subject formation, noted by Foucault, and given that the ritual of confession tends to focus on sex and thus produces, in Foucault's view, the "truth" about sex (61). The law against incest and the ritual of confession cooperate to produce subjectivity.

The sin of lechery, and incest as an important subdivision of it, was, indeed, a fundamental part of the medieval penitentials.[22] The theme of incest, moreover, was prevalent in medieval literature, especially, according to Elizabeth Archibald, after the twelfth century.[23] We need to note, though, that, even though he discusses sibling incest in the *Confessio Amantis*, Gower was particularly interested in another type of incest, that between father and daughter. This book will argue that Gower's exploration of father-daughter incest is intricately connected with his exploration of authority in the *Confessio*: the law of exogamy is crucial for the definition of the limits of authority. Before demonstrating this point, we need to ask why Gower uses the figure of Genius, a figure that is part of a long literary tradition, to examine this theme. Let us discuss first Genius's analysis of incest and, subsequently, twentieth-century insights into it.

Genius devotes the first two hundred lines of Book 8 to explaining and historicizing the appearance of the incest taboo. His explanation follows Augustine's and Aquinas's own accounts of incest at the beginning of time, but was also probably influenced by other accounts.[24] Like both Augustine

---

[22] See Elizabeth Archibald, "Incest in Medieval Literature and Society," *Forum for Modern Language Studies* 25 (1989): 5–6. Pierre J. Payer, "Sex and Confession in the Thirteenth Century," *Sex in the Middle Ages: A Book of Essays*, ed. Joyce Salisbury (New York: Garland, 1991) 126–42, notes that from the time of Gratian's *Decretum*, in all theological accounts, the sin of lechery was subdivided into parts, and incest, along with adultery, fornication, sodomy, etc., always appeared as one of the subdivisions (130). These subdivisions were used in confessional manuals (130). On the importance of the penitentials for the *Confessio Amantis*, see Gerald Kinneavy, "Gower's *Confessio Amantis* and the Penitentials," *The Chaucer Review* 19 (1984): 144–63.

[23] According to Archibald, "Incest in Medieval Literature and Society," "[incest] was a frequent topic in medieval literature from the twelfth century on because it was more frequently discussed in medieval society, especially by the church, which constantly reiterated the rules about kinship as an impediment to marriage, and used cautionary tales about the monstrous sin of incest to illustrate sermons on contrition" (11). On incest in medieval literature, see also Richard Fehrenbacher, " 'Al that which chargeth nought to seye': The Theme of Incest in *Troilus and Criseyde*," *Exemplaria* 9 (1997): 341–69; and Donavin, *Incest Narratives*. The theme of incest is also very important in Arthurian literature, as Fehrenbacher notes (349).

[24] Augustine writes about sibling incest at the beginning of time in *The City of God*, 15.16, and Thomas Aquinas in *Summa Theologiae*, 2a2ae, 154.9. I analyze their positions below. For

and Aquinas, Genius starts by positing and justifying an anomaly: sibling incest was necessary and thus lawful at the beginning of time so that humanity could reproduce. Elizabeth Allen has noted that "[a]lthough the original function of brother-sister incest suggests its status as a pre-legal or pre-cultural phenomenon, both Augustine and Aquinas go to some lengths to define its parameters as lawful and regulated, located in specific times and places" (631). Christian doctrine does not consider those early incestuous acts to be sinful, because they were necessary for the reproduction of the human species. Following this line of thought, Genius remarks on the necessity of incest at the beginning of time: "Forthi that time it was no Sinne / The Soster forto take hire brother, / Whan that ther was of chois non other" (68–70). Genius's characterization of incestuous desire differs slightly but significantly from Aquinas and Augustine. In keeping with his traditional role as instinctive force, representative of the "natural" and unruly sexual impulse, Genius takes for granted the idea that sexual desire precedes any rules, that it precedes the institution of the incest taboo. Before the institution of the law, he notes, "men sein that nede hath no lawe" (75). After the Flood, when humanity needed again to reproduce regardless of kinship ties, Genius mentions that it was nature again that prompted siblings to marry each other: "as nature hem hath excited, / Thei token thanne litel hiede, / The brother of the Sosterhiede / To wedde wyves" (94–97). Thus, incest is linked to a natural force, a force that appears before the law ("nede hath no lawe").

Postulating that sibling incest was "natural" at that time allows Genius first to explain the problem of how people could reproduce then without going against the law, for there was no law against incest. Second, by arguing that the incestuous siblings were responding to a natural drive, he presents sexuality as prior to the incest taboo. Once incest was not necessary, a law against it was enacted and society began to consider incest illegitimate and irrational. Thus, from Abraham on, Genius continues, once the world was sufficiently populated, societies started to regulate marriages. Abraham himself instituted the law whereby marriage between cousins – but not

other comparisons among Augustine, Aquinas, and Genius, see Allen, "Chaucer Answers Gower": 630–33, and Donavin, *Incest Narratives* 10–11. For an analysis of Aquinas's and Augustine's notions of incest in relation to Chaucer's *Troilus and Criseyde*, see Fehrenbacher, " 'Al that which chargeth nought to seye' ": 348–51. Scanlon, "The Riddle of Incest," has argued that Genius's discussion "draws . . . from three sources, the *Historia Scholastica* of Peter Comestor, the *De Sacramentiis* of Hugh of St. Victor, and the figure of *Natura* as *doctor*, a commonplace of the canonistic and scholastic tradition that begins with the late Roman jurist Ulpian" (107). His further discussion (107–12) provides evidence of these influences, but the similarity in wording between Augustine's text, which Scanlon does not mention, and Gower's suggests that his foremost influence may have been the bishop of Hippo. Similarly, Aquinas, whom Scanlon does mention, may have been a major influence on the English author. Aquinas's preoccupation with incest in the context of social relationships and of hierarchical relationships of authority coincides with Gower's own concerns in the *Confessio*.

between siblings – was still allowed (99–141). Abraham's law was later expanded by the Church to include broader degrees of kinship (142ff). As soon as those laws appeared, committing incest – which at the beginning of time was understandable – became an act against reason: "love, which is unbesein / Of alle reson . . . spareth no condicion / Of ken ne yit religion" (153–54, 157–58). From then on, people who committed incest would be considered to be like "a cock among the Hennes, / Or as a Stalon in the Fennes" (159–60), taking anything that is at hand. The incest taboo is thus presented as a necessary law that appeared the moment "natural" sexual desire needed to be restrained. Accordingly, at the end of the short example of Amon and his sister, which Genius tells right after his discussion about incest, Gower's narrator remarks that the act of incest between Amon and his sisters was an act "ayein kinde" (8.214). Incest then became an act against nature, against human nature.

We should notice how Genius naturalizes the process. While at the beginning nature, in the sense of sexual impulse, was that which was more convenient (natural) for human society, now nature is that which goes against human society if it is not restrained by reason. We should notice, moreover, Genius's particular use of two different terms to refer to nature: "nature" and "kinde." The use of the two terms makes it difficult to pin down the meaning of "nature" in the *Confessio*.[25] As Robert Yeager has argued, "nature" seems to stand for a general force "a larger entity than 'kinde' " (121). While it refers to the urge to reproduce that humans share with animals, "nature" also appears to refer to that which is only typical ("natural") of human beings, that which is allied with reason. According to Yeager, "kinde," on the other hand, seems to stand for instinctive desire, but one controlled by reason; it is desire only for someone of the opposite sex and not too close of blood (125).

The slippage in the meaning of "natural" as it relates to incest is a slippage that accords with medieval definitions of nature, although Genius is unusual in employing two different nouns to mark the change. In the Middle Ages, there were two major definitions of the law of nature: one was that which we have in common with animals, the other, that which is exclusive of humans, the rational capacity.[26] In this respect, in Genius's explanation, incest is something natural in the sense of that which belongs to human nature. (Genius presents it as reasonable *a posteriori*: although siblings were attracted

---

[25] On "kinde" and "nature" in the *Confessio Amantis*, see Kurt Olsson, "Natural Law and John Gower's Confessio Amantis," *Gower's Confessio Amantis: A Critical Anthology*, ed. Peter Nicholson (Cambridge: D. S. Brewer, 1991) 181–213, and Hugh White, "Nature and the Good in Gower's *Confessio Amantis*," *John Gower: Recent Readings*, ed. Robert F. Yeager (Kalamazoo, MI: Medieval Institute Publications, 1989) 1–20. Both Olsson and White try to see a pattern behind Gower's use of the terms "nature" and "kinde" in the poem, but they admit the ambiguity in his use of the terms. See also Robert F. Yeager, "Learning to Speak in Tongues: Writing Poetry for a Trilingual Culture," *Chaucer and Gower*, ed. Robert F. Yeager, 121–26, and Scanlon, "The Riddle of Incest" 107–12.

[26] See, for instance, White, "Nature and the Good" 2–3.

to each other through the work of nature rather than reason, in fact, that attraction also accorded with reason, due to the need for the reproduction of the species.) Later on, Genius still defines incest as natural, but "natural" acquires a different meaning at that point; it is that which belongs to animal nature, something unreasonable. Although Genius's passage suggests that individuals have natural desires that are afterwards restrained by cultural injunctions, in historicizing the laws against incest, and in showing the shift in the notion of what constitutes incest, Gower's narrator is revealing the workings of discourse in its attempt to regulate desire by declaring what is lawful and what is unlawful.

Genius's discussion of incest and the taboo thus historicizes the appearance of sexuality *before* the incest taboo, emphasizing the "natural" (i.e., natural to humans) character of the taboo, even as he still sees sexual desire as a natural impulse as well (an impulse we share with animals). In order to understand the ideology behind Genius's discussion, we have noticed how it resembles Aquinas's and Augustine's own notions. Turning now to modern explanations of the notion of incest, we will further clarify the significance of Genius's strategy and the ideology behind it.[27] Recent analyses of the notion of incest will help us understand what is at stake in Genius's explanation of the incest taboo and what are the implications for the *Confessio Amantis*.[28]

We will see first Lévi-Strauss's explanation of the incest taboo and, second, the feminist critique of that explanation by Gayle Rubin and Judith Butler.[29] Lévi-Strauss has argued that incest transgresses the basic principles that allow for the existence and functioning of patriarchal society; the incest taboo is thus crucial for the functioning of society: "The multiple rules prohibiting or prescribing certain types of spouse, and the prohibition of incest, which embodies them all, become clear as soon as one grants that society must

---

[27] Fehrenbacher's explanation of his use of contemporary notions of incest in his analysis of this theme in *Troilus and Criseyde* coincides with my own position; his analysis, like mine, "seeks to locate and demystify a text's or a culture's foundational myths by pointing out their contradictions and examining them not as natural and authorizing origins, but rather as ideological constructs employed to justify a society's structures of power" (" 'Al that which chargeth nought to seye' ": 345).

[28] I should note that, in his account at the beginning of Book 8, it is only sibling incest that Genius initially justifies; however, when he later condemns incestuous relationships, he seems to include any kind of incestuous relationship: love, he says, "spareth no condicion/ Of ken ne yit religion... Bot takth what thing comth next to honde" (157–58, 163). And it is actually father-daughter incest that becomes the subject of Genius's last and longest tale. Father-daughter incest seems the most disturbing type of incest to Genius, and this study will attempt to explain why.

[29] In *Totem and Taboo*, Freud also relates the incest taboo to notions of nature and culture: "I should like to insist that its outcome shows that the beginnings of religion, morals, society and art converge in the Oedipus complex." (Quoted from *The Standard Edition of the Complete Psychological Works of Sigmund Freud*, ed. and trans. James Strachey, vol. 13 [1955; reprint, London: The Hogarth Press, 1957], 156.) Lévi-Strauss's explanation is more relevant to the *Confessio Amantis* because of his theory about the exchange of women.

exist."³⁰ Incest has consequences both at a familial and at a socio-political level: the exchange of the daughter represents a political act to the extent that through it the father participates in public life. It forces families to establish social bonds. Conversely, committing incest is tantamount to a rejection of society, a rejection that poses a threat to it by denying the need for the exchange of women, and thus the need for society itself.

Lévi-Strauss's theory about the incest taboo offers valuable insights into the relations of power and the function of the exchange of women within patriarchal society. It sheds light on Genius's explanation of the incest taboo in terms of nature and culture. But Genius's interest in this problem can be understood in a more complex manner if we consider the feminist critique of Lévi-Strauss's analysis of the incest taboo. Feminist critics have shown that the link Lévi-Strauss establishes between the incest taboo and the origin of society is based on at least two questionable premises. First, as Rubin has demonstrated, Lévi-Strauss's theory assumes that the only form of social organization possible is one necessarily based on the use of women as commodities for exchange.³¹ The exchange of women is thus pictured as a necessary precondition for the existence of society. Second, Lévi-Strauss's theory works on the assumption that there is a sexuality prior to the incest taboo, that men and women have a "natural" desire for the opposite sex, and thus that the taboo has the function of suppressing that desire when it is directed to one's kin. The definition of the "natural," however, as Genius's passage suggests, is more complicated than that.

Rubin's feminist critique of the theory of the incest taboo, which is based on notions of the discursive construction of sexuality, enables us to see the ideology that informs Genius's passage. Despite Genius's attempts to construct the incest taboo as a "natural" response to a natural drive, his discussion reveals that, as Butler has argued, the incest taboo is fundamentally discursive; it is not a "natural" taboo, but a taboo constituted by language and structures of ideology in a process of reiteration. Moreover, the notion that there is some prediscursive "reality" that discourse tries to shape or repress according to certain needs is itself discursive: "the illusion of a sexuality before the law is itself the creation of that law" (74).³² Incest and its

---

30 Claude Lévi-Strauss, *The Elementary Structures of Kinship*, trans. James Harle Bell, John Richard von Sturmer, and Rodney Needham (Boston: Beacon Press, 1969) 490.
31 Gayle Rubin develops this argument in "The Traffic in Women: Notes on the 'Political Economy' of Sex," *Toward an Anthropology of Women*, ed. R. R. Reiter (New York: Monthly Review Press, 1975). Dinshaw also points to the bias in Lévi-Strauss's model, and argues that this model is actually applicable to medieval hermeneutics, "because *both* modern and medieval theorists participate in the same kind of patriarchal thinking, the same ideology" (*Chaucer's Sexual Poetics* [Madison: U of Wisconsin P, 1989] 16).
32 In *Gender Trouble: Feminism and the Subversion of Identity* (New York: Routledge, 1990), Butler expands on this notion:
  The effort to locate and describe a sexuality 'before the law' as a primary bisexuality or as an ideal and unconstrained polymorphousness implies that the law is antecedent to sexuality . . . But if we apply the Foucaltian critique of the repres-

prohibition turn out to be much more slippery notions once we posit the impossibility of identifying a sexuality before the law.

That Genius, like Lévi-Strauss, would emphasize the precedence of natural desire before the law is ideologically significant. Genius's discursive construction of nature aims at constituting desire as pre-discursive, and, ultimately, at promoting reproduction by establishing heterosexuality as the only natural desire. He focuses on the incest taboo, because it plays a fundamental and originary role in the construction of heterosexuality and, consequently, of gendered subjectivity – as Butler has argued: "The incest taboo is the juridical law that is said both to prohibit incestuous desires and to construct certain gendered subjectivities through the mechanism of compulsory identification" (76). More crucially, the construction of gendered subjectivity has as its main aim the regulation of sexuality within the obligatory frame of reproductive heterosexuality:

> The incest taboo . . . repress[es] no primary dispositions but effectively create[s] the distinction between 'primary' and 'secondary' dispositions to describe and reproduce the distinction between a legitimate heterosexuality and an illegitimate homosexuality. (73)

The incest taboo then regulates sexuality and establishes heterosexuality as the only legitimate form. Similarly, in Genius's historical view of the emergence of sexuality, heterosexuality is the "primary" and only disposition. Men and women "naturally" turned to those of the opposite sex.

Genius always depicts heterosexuality as the primary disposition and "transforms" homosexuality in the *Confessio Amantis*. This depiction is significant given Genius's role in the poem. Two tales, the "Tale of Narcissus" and the "Tale of Iphis," illustrate this point. Genius's version of the story of Narcissus (1.2275–2366) differs both from his source, Ovid's version, and from most medieval retellings of Ovid's story in a significant respect: the image Narcissus sees in the water is not his own image but the image of a nymph.[33] This change is highly significant in that it tries to avoid the hints of homosexuality implicit in Narcissus's falling in love with a male image, the image of himself. Genius changes the gender of the image to circumvent the problem, but of course his solution raises new questions. The incongruity of Narcissus seeing an image of a woman (who is a different person) as a reflection of himself cannot be easily ignored. In the "Tale of Iphis" (4.451–505),

---

sive hypothesis to the incest taboo, that paradigmatic law of repression, then it would appear that the law produces *both* sanctioned heterosexuality and transgressive homosexuality. Both are indeed *effects*, temporally and ontologically later than the law itself. (74)

[33] See Ann Tukey Harrison, "Echo and Her Medieval Sisters," *Centennial Review* 26 (1982): 324–40. Among the different medieval retellings of the story analyzed by Harrison, the twelfth-century "Lay of Narcissus" is the only one in which the image Narcissus sees in the water is, as in Genius's version, a female.

on the other hand, he again tries to circumvent the problem of a homosexual relationship. Iphis, a girl, falls in love with another girl with whom she has been sharing a bed. Cupid intervenes to change Iphis's sex so that their relationship can be "possible." But if, in Genius's view, a homosexual relationship would have been "ayein kinde," one wonders why his definition of "kinde" does not consider a change of sex to be "ayein kinde" too (even if it is effected by a divine figure).

Even though homosexual desire is apparent in his sources, Genius, as it were, "heterosexualizes" it in these two tales. He thus uses these stories to show heterosexuality as the only imaginable alternative. But, why is Genius so interested in suppressing any hints of homosexuality? Genius's interest in discarding homosexuality as a possible form of sexuality is linked to his role as promoter of reproduction and to his explicit treatment (unlike the Man of Law's) of the question of incest. The incest taboo is crucial for the affirmation of heterosexuality as the primary disposition. Given Genius's traditional role, his investment in defining the incest taboo becomes clear, for no one could be more interested in heterosexuality than Genius, the priest of Venus and representative of procreative sexuality.[34]

In addition to his investment in procreative sexuality, there is another significant reason why Genius is interested in the incest taboo. As I will argue in Chapter Five, following the allegorical tradition of other Geniuses, Gower's Genius represents the poetic principle. Writing about Alain de Lille's Genius, one of the predecessors of Gower's Genius, Winthrop Wetherbee has argued that Genius is a creative principle both in the sexual sense and in the literary sense: "Genius's posture is that of a lyric poet, his yearning constrained by sin but capable of lyric expression."[35] The notion that Genius stands for the creative poetic principle returns us to the link between the incest taboo and language. Although I will explain this point at greater length in Chapter Two, it is necessary to note here that Genius's treatment of incest in the "Tale of Apollonius" anticipates Lévi-Strauss's coupling of the exchange of women and the exchange of words as effects of the law of exogamy. It also anticipates Rousseau's theory about the origin of society in his *Essay on the Origin of Languages*, which Jacques Derrida has analyzed in depth. Before the incest taboo, Rousseau argues, "there were families, but there were no nations. There were domestic, but not popular languages . . . Each family was self-sufficient and perpetuated itself exclusively by inbreeding."[36] In Rousseau's analysis, as Derrida explains, "[s]ociety,

---

[34] I will argue later that his investment in heterosexuality is also dependent on, and responds to, his gendered notion of artistic creation, whereby the text is imagined as feminine and the author masculine.

[35] Winthrop Wetherbee, "The Theme of Imagination in Medieval Poetry and the Allegorical Figure 'Genius,' " *Medievalia et Humanistica*, n.s. 7 (1976): 50.

[36] Quoted in Jacques Derrida, *Of Grammatology*, trans. G. C. Spivak (Baltimore: Johns Hopkins UP, 1976) 263.

language, history, articulation, in a word supplementarity, are born at the same time as the prohibition of incest" (265). Language and the incest taboo are intricately connected. Genius, producer of words, has a profound investment in a law that cannot be divorced from language.

The law against incest becomes the first law and the origin of laws; as Derrida puts it, "[t]he origin of laws must be law" (265). We should recall here that for Genius incestuous desire is a natural desire ("as nature hem hath excited," 94) that precedes the law ("nede hath no lawe"). The productive law against incest produces other laws that regulate social exchange, such as the relationship between kings and subjects. In the same way that a feminist and deconstructive critique of Lévi-Strauss's theory uncovers the assumptions behind it, and more importantly, the ways in which those assumptions shape and generate his conclusions, a feminist and deconstructive critique of Genius's own theory about the origins of the incest taboo can uncover the assumptions behind it and, also more importantly, the ways in which those assumptions specifically shape his treatment of fathers and daughters, of the question of kingly authority in the *Confessio Amantis*, and, finally, of the relationship between an author and his work.

Fathers and Daughters, Kings and Subjects: Familial and Political Authority

Genius devotes an entire book, Book 8, to explore and to ultimately establish the role of incest in the foundation of patriarchal society and the maintenance of the heterosexual norm. Book 8, the last book in the poem, is about the sin of incest. More significantly, even though his preliminary discussion justifies sibling incest at the beginning of time and does not present any examples of father-daughter incest, and even though he includes two short stories of sibling incest right after his discussion, those of Amon and Caligula, his major focus in the final book is on father-daughter incest. Indeed, in addition to the short exemplum of Lot and his daughters, the only lengthy tale in the book and by far the longest tale in the *Confessio* as a whole, the "Tale of Apollonius," is about father-daughter incest.

Gower had very significant reasons for illustrating the sin with the example of a father-daughter, rather than a sibling or mother-son, incestuous relationship. Towards the end of his elaborate discussion on consanguinity, marriage, and natural law in his *Summa Theologiae*, Thomas Aquinas argues that by natural law both the father and the mother are debarred from marrying their children, *but*

> *magis* etiam mater quam pater, quia magis reverentiae que debetur parentibus derogatur si filius matrem, quam si pater filiam ducit in uxorem, cum uxor viro aliqualiter debeat esse subiecta.[37] [my emphasis]

[37] Thomas Aquinas, *Summa Theologiae*, suppl. 54.3, vol. 5, Biblioteca de Autores Cristi-

Aquinas's passage calls attention to a crucial element in father-daughter incestuous relations, namely, authority and power. In father-daughter incest the dynamics of power are similar to those in traditional husband-wife relations – the male, according to the norm, possesses and has authority over the female. Since in father-daughter incest there is no inversion of male-female power relations, for it reproduces the accepted structures of authority, this kind of incest is less scandalous than mother-son incest, or less against nature, as he puts it later in the same article: "homo naturaliter abhorret cognoscere non solum matrem, sed etiam filiam, quod est adhuc *minus* contra naturam, ut dictum est" (my emphasis).[38] Unlike Aquinas, though, Gower stresses the unacceptability of father-daughter incest more than that of sibling incest. Moreover, although he condemns mother-son incest in his discussion of Venus and Cupid in Book 5 (1406–20), and, although mother-son incestuous desire becomes an important part of some tales, most notably the "Tale of Constance," mother-son incest does not seem to concern him as much as father-daughter incest. What, then, is wrong with father-daughter incest according to Gower? Why is he interested in this type of incest?

The father who commits incest with his daughter abuses an established relationship of authority sanctioned by society in order to deny the very need of society. A fundamental difference between father-daughter relations and husband-wife relations is that the latter is a public act, an act that signifies an alliance with society, acknowledging its existence, while the former denies the existence, or the individual's need of, society.[39] It takes place in private. For the system of exchange to work in patriarchal society, the father has to give up his daughter and turn her over to society. As Lévi-Strauss puts it, "marriage is an arbitration between two loves, parental and conjugal" (498). Father-daughter incest is the negation of the social and public act of marriage, even the negation of society itself. It is, therefore, the worst sin against the foundations of patriarchal society and its system of exchange.

Father-daughter incest is also subversive in another sense: it recognizes the father's desire for the daughter and thus the possibility that the father could be seduced by the daughter. It threatens, therefore, the very foundation of the social structure; as Jane Gallop has noted, "[i]f the father were to desire his daughter he could no longer exchange her, no longer possess her in the

---

anos 87 (Madrid: Editorial Católica, 1958) 260. The passage can be translated as follows: "... the mother still more than the father, since it is more derogatory to the reverence due to parents if the son marry his mother than if the father marry his daughter; since the wife should be to a certain extent subject to her husband." (Translation comes from *The Summa Theologica of Saint Thomas Aquinas*, trans. Fathers of the English Dominican Province, vol. 3 [New York: Benziger Brothers, 1948] 2759).

[38] *Summa Theologiae* 260. "... [M]an naturally abhors carnal knowledge not only of his mother, but also his daughter, which is, however, less against nature, as stated above" (*The Summa Theologica* 2760.)

[39] As Lévi-Strauss, *The Elementary Structures of Kinship*, remarks, "[m]arriage is . . . a dramatic encounter between nature and culture, between alliance and kinship" (489).

economy by which true, masterful possession is the right to exchange."[40] Moreover, because, as Gallop remarks, "[p]atriarchy is grounded in the uprightness of the father" (75), father-daughter incest suggests the possibility that the father may not uphold the law. That is, it suggests the threatening possibility that the system may be subverted by he who is supposed to be its main source of stability. It is indeed illuminating to think of Gower's poem in this context. That Gower, unlike Chaucer's Man of Law, or any society that is reluctant to raise the specter of incest, is interested in entertaining such a threatening possibility, that he does not avoid looking into the foundations of the law, reveals his critical and questioning attitude towards those in power – whether the head of the household or the head of the state. Gower allows for the possibility that the ruler might subvert the system. Hence, the ruler needs to be warned about the limits and extent of his own power. If a father commits incest or if a king abuses his power in a tyrannical manner, the father and the king should be divested of their power. The larger system needs to prevail.

One of the significant limitations on paternity is its dependence on discourse. Due to what Marc Shell has called "the ultimate indeterminability of biological paternity," kinship relationships depend fundamentally on discursive and social agreement.[41] A father is a father when social discourse recognizes him as such. The importance of the discursive and social definition of fatherhood, even beyond biological ties, can be seen more clearly in the cases of godchildren and of adopted children: the incest prohibition also applies to godfathers and to fathers of adopted daughters.[42] Paternal power is enabled through the performative power of language. And, as paternity is defined primarily by discourse, so is the incest taboo, as we have seen. The

---

40 Jane Gallop, *The Daughter's Seduction: Feminism and Psychoanalysis* (Ithaca, NY: Cornell UP, 1982) 76.
41 Marc Shell, *The End of Kinship: Measure for Measure, Incest, and the Idea of Universal Siblinghood* (Stanford: Stanford UP, 1988) 5. Shell further explains that
> the societal need to determine paternity . . . requires us social beings either to maintain distinctions by accepting the fiction of biological paternity as the literal truth of things (as we do in this culture) or by establishing persons to be *thought* of 'as of a father' (HAM[let] 1.2.108) – as figural or sociological fathers. (5)
42 See Shell on the canon laws and the prohibition against marriage with relatives by legal adoption (51), and with godchildren (9). On this same question, see also James A. Brundage, *Law, Sex, and Christian Society in Medieval Europe* (Chicago: U of Chicago P, 1987), esp. 191–95. Writing about the canonists' regulations of marriage, Brundage notes:
> Closely linked to restrictions on consanguineous marriages was a battery of canonistic prohibitions against marriage with affinal, or fictive, relatives. Marriages with relatives by marriage or adoption had long been forbidden, and the major canonists included numerous earlier pronouncements on this topic in their collections. The reform canonists place much greater emphasis than had their predecessors on other and more tenuous affinity ties, notably the relationship between godparent and godchild or between co-godparents. (193)

taboo, as Butler notes in *Gender Trouble*, is primarily a law that both creates and represses the desire for the mother or father: "The taboo might be understood to create and sustain the desire for the mother/father as well as the compulsory displacement of that desire" (76). Hence the importance of language for the definition of the extent and limits of the father's relationship of authority with his daughter.

Most father-daughter tales in the *Confessio Amantis* reveal that paternal authority and the incest taboo depend on the discursive. This dependence becomes especially evident in the tale in which the father's abuse of his authority becomes literal when he commits incest with his daughter, that is, in the "Tale of Apollonius." As I argue in Chapter Two, Genius's version of the story of Apollonius manifests the importance of the discursive for the definition of the extent and limits of the father's authority over his daughter. Throughout the tale, Gower emphasizes the importance of language, or the use of words, to define kinship relations, thus to establish who can marry whom and maintain the incest taboo.

Father-daughter relationships, therefore, are especially relevant for a study of the limits of authority. They can become a vehicle for manifesting the subjection of the person who holds authority to the larger institution of society. When the daughter marries, the father suffers a loss. As Boose has noted, "the daughter's movement to cross the threshold and move out of the father's house, whether into the house of another man or into the world of paternal institution, threatens the father, familial or cultural, with loss."[43] But while this is a loss for the father, it is also a gain for society. The father has to negotiate his possession with society and has to give in to social rules. Although he has authority over the daughter within the house, and she is, as Boose argues, not just material property but also his sexual property (46), that authority over her is limited by the social rules of exchange. Hence, the daughter is an ideal site for the exploration of the negotiations between self and society as well as for the exploration of the extent and limitations of fatherly authority in all its aspects.

Gower's exploration of the limitations of fatherly authority extends to the patriarchal head of the state: the monarch. The theme of incest, as Gower uses it in the *Confessio Amantis*, is a powerful and meaningful metaphor in the context of English fourteenth-century politics. The analysis of the discursive character of the definition of incest and the justification of the taboo as regulator of sexual relationships in the *Confessio Amantis* informs Gower's exploration of the discursive character of political relationships as well. It was noted above that the *Confessio Amantis* is especially interested in examining the extent to which royal authority depends on the discursive. It explores, in Scanlon's words, "how monarchical and other forms of political and institu-

---

[43] Lynda Boose, "The Father's House and the Daughter in It: The Structures of Western Culture's Daughter-Father Relationship," *Daughters and Fathers*, eds. Lynda E. Boose and Betty S. Flowers (Baltimore: Johns Hopkins UP, 1989) 46–47.

tional authority both enable and are defined by the performative power of language" (256–57). Royal authority, like paternal authority, is defined and enabled by discourse. An analysis of the concerns of Gower and his contemporaries with King Richard II's rule, and with issues of kingship and governance that his rule raised, sheds light on Gower's project and on his use of the theme of incest and father-daughter relationships.

Historians have shown that one of the main criticisms against Richard II, especially in the articles of deposition and in the chronicles written immediately after his deposition, was that he ruled in a tyrannical manner.[44] He was accused of disposing arbitrarily of the property of his subjects, which was seen as a tyrannical act. In the articles of deposition, Tuck observes, "the essence of the charges against him was that he had violated his oath to rule in accordance with the laws and customs of the realm, and had sought instead to rule according to his own will."[45] These accusations of tyranny referred to events that took place between 1397 and 1399 when Richard was deposed, that is, several years after Gower's completion of the *Confessio Amantis* around 1390. Nevertheless, the controversies around Richard's manner of rule started much earlier and the events in the last years of the fourteenth century confirm what many were already criticizing in the 1380s.

As early as 1382, there was a first hint of friction between the court and the nobility when Richard dismissed his chancellor Sir Richard Lescrope for refusing to draw up charters that would grant lands to "knights and esquires of low degree" (Tuck 88–89). The next year, the Commons began to be concerned about questions of finance and foreign policy (Tuck 89–91). Similar confrontations continued during the following years and culminated in the second major political crisis that Richard had to face after the Peasants' Revolt of 1381: the so-called Wonderful Parliament of 1386. The nobility criticized his choice of advisers and the favor shown to those close to the king, while the Commons resented the king's financial mismanagement (Tuck 87). Problems and confrontations continued to arise and 1388 saw the third major political crisis at the Merciless Parliament, in which the Lords Appellant managed to rid the country of the king's favorites as well as to reverse the direction which patronage had taken since the early 1380s (Tuck 127).

The incidents that led the nobility and the Commons to question and be hostile to the king were various, but they were generally related, or were seen

---

[44] The following studies inform my analysis of the reign of Richard II: Anthony Tuck, *Crown and Nobility, 1272–1461: Political Conflict in Late Medieval England* (Totowa, NJ: Barnes & Noble Books, 1985) and *Richard II and the English Nobility* (London: Edward Arnold, 1973); Chris Given-Wilson, *The Royal Household and the King's Affinity: Service, Politics and Finance in England 1360–1413* (New Haven: Yale UP, 1986); Richard H. Jones, *The Royal Policy of Richard II: Absolutism in the Later Middle Ages* (New York: Barnes & Noble, 1968), and Harold F. Hutchinson, *The Hollow Crown: A Life of Richard II* (New York: John Day, 1961).
[45] Tuck, *Richard II* 222.

to be related, to two features in Richard's form of rule: first, the increasing number of favorites at his court and the resultant difficulty for those outside the court to have some influence on binding decisions; second, Richard's own understanding of his rule in a manner that was close to the absolutism that later characterized Renaissance monarchies.[46] Tuck has argued that during the first four and a half years of his reign Richard used the power latent in the king and his household to the point that it was seen as virtually impossible to control it permanently from outside (57). Between 1382 and 1386, Richard developed the "machinery of household government to a degree unparalleled since the reign of Edward II" and he relied in counsel upon certain officers who benefited from royal favors to the detriment of other prominent noblemen (58). This led to a concentration of power in the court, which made it more difficult to exert any influence from outside, and which was a major reason for the hostility of the nobles against Richard.[47]

In the *Confessio Amantis* the metaphor of incest not only alludes to the king's abuse of his power over his subjects, but also is used by Gower in a different sense – to suggest the king's refusal to interact with others and comply with the law. The absolutist king who concentrates his power in the court and does not interact with the outside is like the father who, in committing incest with his daughter, refuses to interact with society. The incompatibility of the concepts of exogamy and absolutism, and thus the parallel between incest and absolute rule, have been analyzed by Bruce Boehrer in relation to Early Modern English politics:

> From the social standpoint, the rule of exogamy poses an ever-present threat: when practiced rigidly over a great length of time, it leads any ruling elite to admit new members . . . [F]rom the psychological standpoint, the prohibition of incest forces any absolute monarch to belie his or her own absolutism by relying upon external factors – a foreign wife or husband, an elaborate marriage treaty . . . – to maintain the royal lineage and the royal myth.[48]

The power dynamics behind the act of incest thus resemble those behind

---

[46] See the chapter titled "Ricardian Absolutism" in Jones, and also David Wallace, *Chaucerian Polity*, on Richard II's attempts to become an absolutist monarch like some of his contemporary Italian princes. Wallace, for instance, remarks that "Richard II, who styled himself 'entier Emperour de son roiaulme d'Engleterre' in 1397, might be described as a monarch with *entieriste*, if not absolutist, pretensions" (xv), even if such claims as Wallace notes, "were repudiated two years later" by those who disagreed with Richard.

[47] In *Chaucer and the Subject of History*, Patterson similarly notes:
> [T]here was not only a gradual concentration of the business of government in the *camera regis*, but the royal household came to function less as the focus of the aristocratic community as a whole than as the king's *privata familia*. And under Richard this concentration of power in the court, and the parallel development of a specifically courtier nobility, became a matter of royal policy. (50)

[48] Bruce Thomas Boehrer, *Monarchy and Incest in Renaissance England: Literature, Culture, Kinship, and Kingship* (Philadelphia: U of Pennsylvania P, 1992) 13.

absolutism. The act of incest by the father is tantamount to a rejection of society insofar as it represents a refusal to comply with the laws of exchange, laws that are over and above the father's power. The absolute king also uses the law according to his own will and regardless of the will and interest of his country. In a sense, *he* becomes the law.

As the incest taboo regulates sexuality and the social exchange, the political system also regulates the king's authority through the law, in order to prevent him from abusing it and concentrating power in himself. Precisely the relation between the king and the law was a highly controversial issue during the reign of Richard II.[49] In *Richard II*, Tuck notes, for instance, that "[Richard's] tendency towards secretive and arbitrary action . . . created insecurity and called in question the whole basis of the relationship between the king and the law" (95). Since the king was the embodiment of the law, he was not supposed to use secretive methods, because his secretiveness suggested that he was trying to circumvent the very law he represented. As the embodiment of the law, the king was supposed to be the first one to uphold it. This, then, suggested that there was something over and above the king, i.e., the law, and that the law which the king represented marked at the same time the limits of his authority. Thus, in October 1386, Gloucester and Bishop Arundel gave a speech in front of parliament in which they reminded the king "that the community had the right to depose a king if he refused to be governed and ruled by the laws of the kingdom and the advice of the lords" (Tuck 103). These worries surfaced again during the Merciless Parliament in 1388 and so the king was made to renew his coronation oath while the lords renewed their homage, "a symbolic reaffirmation of the accepted relationship between the king and the law, and a means of removing the taint of disloyalty and deposition" (Tuck 126). Richard had to be reminded that the king's will alone was not granted the power to change the law.[50] Gower himself makes this point explicitly in the *Cronica Tripertita*, his last major work, written after the *Confessio Amantis*. At several points in the *Cronica*, he deals with the king's relationship to the law, accusing Richard of subverting the law of the land. For instance, in Part I Gower writes: "Dum stat commotus Ricardus amore remotus, / Principio Regis oritur *transgressio legis*" (my emphasis).[51]

---

[49] The definition of the relationship between the king and the law in the late Middle Ages was extremely complex. See Kantorowicz, *The King's Two Bodies* (Princeton: Princeton UP, 1957), for an examination of the seemingly contradictory statement that the king is both above and under the law as it was formulated in England (142–64).

[50] Richard was accused of having said that everyone's life, goods and chattels were at the king's will. Tuck notes that, whether Richard had actually said this or not, "he behaved as though he believed it was true" (204). Such a view of the relationship between the law and the king's will, Tuck continues,

> was a view of government which no English king could hope to sustain, for it was bound to seem a threat to the lives and property of his subjects, whose security was founded upon the king's observance of due process of law in his dealings with them. (204)

[51] *Cronica Tripertita, The Complete Works of John Gower: The Latin Works*, ed. G. C.

Gower's use of the metaphor of incest in relation to monarchy anticipates the use of the notion of incest in Renaissance England. Boehrer has argued that the Renaissance saw a shift in power from the Church to the monarch and that this shift had much to do with incest laws:

> Throughout the Middle Ages, incest both within and without matrimony remained the exclusive province of church courts ... Henry VIII's divorce [from Catharine of Aragon], however, changed all of this by defining the king as the supreme head of both the secular and sacred legal regiments. One immediate result was that Henry used Parliament ... to determine what is and what is not incest; and while matrimonial cases remained within the purview of the church courts throughout the Renaissance, it was clear from Henry on that church law did not have exclusive authority over such matters. (152)

This argument needs some qualification in the light of Gower's poem. Even if cases of incest and their punishment remained the exclusive province of the Church courts, Gower's *Confessio Amantis* shows that in the Middle Ages incest was not seen as an exclusively religious matter, and that Gower himself did not see incest as an exclusively religious concern, a sin of the individual against God. As Scanlon puts it, "[i]ncest for Gower is both a penitential category and a complex social reality."[52]

Indeed, Gower was not the only medieval author to see the political and social implications of incest. We will see below Walsingham's use of the metaphor. Both Augustine and Thomas Aquinas also saw these implications. Augustine argues that the purpose of the law against incest was "that one man should not comprise many relationships in his one self but that these connexions should be severally distributed among individuals and in this way serve to weld social life more securely by covering in their multiplicity a multiplicity of people."[53] In similar terms, Aquinas justified the Fourth Lateran Council's prohibition of marriage to the fourth degree of consanguinity on social, besides moral and religious, grounds. Incest, according to Aquinas, "would hinder a man from having many friends."[54] Gower similarly saw the social and political implications of incest and especially the issues of

---

Macaulay, vol. 4 (Oxford: Clarendon P, 1902) I.4–5. "When the turbulent Richard forsook loving-kindness, there arose a trangression of the law, originating with the king." (Translation comes from *The Major Latin Works of John Gower*, trans. Eric W. Stockton [Seattle: U of Washington P, 1962] 290.)

[52] Scanlon, "Riddle of Incest" 99.

[53] Augustine, *The City of God*, ed. and trans. Philip Levine, vol. 4 (Cambridge: Harvard UP, 1966) 503. I quote the original Latin, also from Levine's edition: "nec unus in uno multas haberet sed singulae spargerentur in singulos ac sic socialem vitam diligentius conligandam plurimae plurimos obtinerent" (502).

[54] Thomas Aquinas, *Summa Theologica* 2a2ae. 154. 9, trans. Fathers of the English Dominican Province, vol. 2 (New York: Benziger Brothers, 1947) 1824. The original Latin reads as follows: "[incestus] imperidetur multiplicatio amicorum" (*Summa Theologiae*, vol. 3, Biblioteca de Autores Cristianos 81 [Madrid: Editorial Católica, 1956] 955).

authority raised by it. Committing incest represents more than a religious or moral sin; it is also a sin against society and the state because it ignores fundamental laws that regulate society and that are over and above the king himself. Gower uses the theme of incest to suggest that the way Richard (or any other king who would act like Richard) wanted to conduct government was potentially subversive against the basic laws of the community. Gower's warning seems especially appropriate when we notice that, later, Henry VIII decided to define those laws that, according to Gower, the king should also respect. Henry VIII's shifting of incest laws from the religious to the secular realm turns out to be less unexpected when seen in the context of medieval views on incest, and especially of Gower's treatment of the theme of incest as a social and political issue in the *Confessio Amantis*.

David Wallace has recently shown that a metaphor used by medieval authors to refer to the relationship between the king and his subjects or his country was that of husband and wife.[55] Gower uses this metaphor at some points in the *Confessio Amantis* (e.g., when referring to the relationship between Apollonius and his city, as will be seen in Chapter Two). Amans himself associates his lady with his homeland and with his own domestic affairs when he argues with Genius about a knight's duties. Genius says that a knight should first fight abroad ("Somtime in Prus, somtime in Rodes, / And somtime into Tartarie," 4.1630–31). Once he gains fame, he will win his lady; his fame will:

>   ... to his ladi Ere bringe
> Som tidinge of his worthinesse;
> So that sche mihte of his prouesce
> ...
> The betre unto his love acorde
> And danger pute out of hire mod.   (4.1636–38, 1640–41)

Amans, by contrast, believes in paying more attention to the lady, who is at home, than to foreign wars: "What scholde I winne over the Se, / If I mi ladi loste at hom?" (4.1664–65), he asks. Or, similarly, "What scholde I thanne go so ferr / In strange londes many a mile / To ryde, and lese at hom therwhile / Mi love?" (4.1706–09). In Amans's opinion one should take care of what one has at home rather than fight in foreign lands.

Nevertheless, the most recurrent metaphor used in the *Confessio Amantis* to imagine the relationship between the ruler and his subjects is that of father and daughter.[56] In fact, it is no coincidence that Gower uses both metaphors,

---

[55] David Wallace, *Chaucerian Polity*, esp. 295–98.
[56] Imagining the king as a father was common in the Middle Ages. Kantorowicz, *The King's Two Bodies*, has argued that "as opposed to the earlier 'liturgical' kingship, the late-medieval kingship by 'divine right' was modelled after the Father in Heaven rather than after the Son on the Altar" (93). We should note that Kantorowicz even remarks that "[i]n medieval England, the marriage metaphor seems to have been all but non-existent" (223). According

because, as I show in Chapter Three, he is interested in exploring the similarities between husband-wife and father-daughter relationships. By using both metaphors and exploring their implications, Gower enters a complex debate about the parallels between the rule over the family and the rule over the state. The rule of the *paterfamilias* was compared to that of the monarch, but medieval political theorists, following Aristotle, often distinguished between the husband's rule over the wife and the father's rule over his children, comparing conjugal to political rule and paternal to regal rule.[57] James Blythe distinguishes between these two types of rule as follows: "Political and regal rule are over a free people; in the former the citizens rule and are ruled in turn, in the latter one person with full power rules alone" (11). But he cautions that "[n]o medieval writers used the terms *regal* and *political* rigorously; no matter how strict a definition they give, they all go on to apply the words loosely to kingship and republican government respectively" (94). Gower, I argue, also uses the concepts loosely, because in fact he is interested in the similarities between the two. And thus if in the relationship between a husband and a wife theorists note that the husband's power over the wife is limited by certain laws, while in the relationship between the father and his children the father rules according to his will, Gower attempts to show that the father's power over his daughter should also be limited by certain laws.[58] The father-daughter metaphor allows Gower to stress that the subjects may be subordinate to the king but that they are still separate from him; they are a different "self," and thus there are limitations to the king's power over them. A father does not have complete ownership over his daughter, because he has to exchange her eventually.

What then, we should ask, is the significance of this new assertion of the political relevance of incest and father-daughter relationships? In the context of this new assertion, moreover, what are the implications of Gower's turning the sexuality of daughters into an important narrative subject? After Joan Kelly-Gadol's "Did Women Have a Renaissance?" numerous studies about women and gender in that period have argued that women's sexuality and lives did not enjoy a "Renaissance," primarily because of the changes in the familial and political structures of the time. The Renaissance saw, as Lawrence Stone has shown, "[a] reinforcement of the despotic authority of husband and father – that is to say, of patriarchy."[59] This reinforcement was

---

to Kantorowicz, the marriage metaphor seems to have been less common than Wallace's examples imply.
[57] See James M. Blythe, *Ideal Government and the Mixed Constitution in the Middle Ages* (Princeton: Princeton UP, 1992), esp. 18, 62–67, 94–95, 180.
[58] Blythe, *Ideal Government*, notes that Giles of Rome stresses the limits of the husband's rule over his wife, while he argues that the father rules his children according to his will (63–65); William of Ockham makes a similar distinction (180–83).
[59] Lawrence Stone, *The Family, Sex, and Marriage in England 1500–1800* (New York: Harper & Row, 1977) 151. See also, Jonathan Goldberg, "Fatherly Authority: The Politics of Stuart Family Images," *Rewriting the Renaissance: The Discourses of Sexual Difference in*

actively supported and theoretically justified by both Church and state; for Stone, "[t]he growth of patriarchy was deliberately encouraged by the new Renaissance state on the traditional grounds that the subordination of the family to its head is analogous to, and also a direct contributory cause of, subordination of subjects to the sovereign" (152). As a result of this reinforcement of patriarchy in the house and in the state, women were confined to playing a more limited, domestic role than they had played before.[60] Moreover, the confinement of women's sexuality and roles to the domestic sphere paralleled the emphasis put in the Renaissance on the significance and meaning of a woman's body in relation to the state. In Elizabethan England such an emphasis was certainly linked to the fact that the head of the state was a woman.[61] Like the body of the Queen, the body of the woman is often figured in Renaissance texts as a closed area that itself is to be kept confined.[62]

My analysis of Gower's *Confessio Amantis* suggests that the identification of woman with the state as it is linked with the reinforcement of patriarchy is also traceable in the late Middle Ages.[63] While Gower's tales do not reinforce the father's "despotic authority" – on the contrary, he is very interested in marking the limits of that authority – they do suggest that the daughter's sexuality, and, more generally, women's sexuality, is also a matter of state, not only of a particular family. In some of his tales we can see how the woman is identified with the nation/country. For instance, in the "Tale of Galba and Vitellius" (6.537ff) a land and its people are compared to a woman. Genius tells the story of two powerful Spanish princes, Galba and Vitellius, as an example of "glotonie and drunkeschipe" (543). According to Genius, through their drunkenness, they "Oppressede al the nacion / Of Spaigne" (568–69). More importantly, this oppression is manifested through the rape of the women: "Ther was no wif ne maiden there, . . . Whom thei ne token to defoule, / Wherof the lond was often wo" (572, 574–75). The rape of the women stands for the oppression of the land, which is therefore put in the feminine position.

Early Modern Europe, eds. Margaret W. Ferguson, Maureen Quilligan, and Nancy Vickers (Chicago: U of Chicago P, 1986).
[60] See Ferguson, Quilligan, and Vickers, Introduction, *Rewriting the Renaissance*. These critics point out that "Renaissance women of all classes were increasingly (although by no means universally) confined to a private sphere" (xxvi).
[61] See, for instance, Peter Stallybrass, "Patriarchal Territories: The Body Enclosed," *Rewriting the Renaissance* 123–42. Stallybrass has shown how contemporary representations of Queen Elizabeth suggest an analogy between the body of the Virgin Queen and the integrity of the state so that, "[t]he state, like the virgin, was a *hortus conclusus*, an enclosed garden walled off from enemies" (129).
[62] See Stallybrass, "Patriarchal Territories" 126–30.
[63] This is a link that medievalists need to explore further. For an example of a study of this link, see Paul Strohm, *Hochon's Arrow: The Social Imagination of Fourteenth-Century Texts* (Princeton: Princeton UP, 1992), esp. ch. 6.

Thus, Gower's stories about fathers and daughters are also about King Richard II and England and about any king and his country.[64] I would like to emphasize the equation implied by the verbal phrase "are also" in the preceding sentence. In the *Confessio*, the family is not a mere excuse for writing about politics. Neither are the daughters in the tales interesting only because they may stand for England. Family and state have a relation of interdependence; the definition and stability of the one depends on the definition and stability of the other. Indeed, as Paul Strohm has argued, the family, one among other "ostensibly non-political institutions," does have a political character, for "the master in his shop and the husband in his household and the priest in his parish participate analogically and symbolically in the regality of the king" (125). Strohm continues, "the attempt to protect masters, husbands, and priests results not just from a sudden perception of similitude, or a sudden deference to localized interests, but from a more broadly couched defense of a cluster of sites vital to the reproduction of monarchic and patriarchal practices" (125). Thus, if by writing about fathers and daughters Gower is writing about the king and his country, by writing about the king and his country he is also writing about fathers and daughters. In other words, in line with Stone's observation cited above, we need to note that the crucial point is not just that family and state resemble each other, but that they resemble and depend on each other *because* they share the same dynamic as products of the same historical moment, of the same predominant ideology. In Gower's tales of fathers and daughters what is at stake in the control of daughters' sexuality is not *only* the survival of a certain family, but *also* the survival of the whole nation. Gower's tales both reflect and contribute to emphasizing the important political role ascribed to women's sexuality.

In imagining the king-subject relationship as a father-daughter relationship and raising the specter of incest, Gower uses sexual metaphors. The use of sexual metaphors for political purposes was not new to him, nor to other fourteenth-century writers, as Sylvia Federico has shown.[65] Analyzing sexual metaphors in political tracts and narratives of the late fourteenth century, Federico argues that in *Vox Clamantis*, "Gower's attempts to link political behavior to sexual behavior show the wide availability of sexual metaphors for political uses" (133). Even more important, Federico gives an example

---

64 Gower's later rededication of his poem to King Henry IV has been the object of great controversy. I see Gower's rededication as a sign of his political independence, for if there is a political critique in the poem, this critique can be seen as an immediate warning to King Richard, and also as a forewarning to Henry as well as to any other king. For a study that argues for Gower's political independence from Richard II and Henry IV, see V. J. Scattergood, "Literary Culture at the Court of Richard II," *English Court Culture in the Later Middle Ages*, eds. V. J. Scattergood, J. W. Sherborne, and J. A. Burrow (New York: St. Martin's Press, 1983) 29–43.
65 Sylvia Federico, "A Fourteenth-Century Erotics of Politics: London as a Feminine New Troy," *Studies in the Age of Chaucer* 19 (1997): 121–55.

from Thomas Walsingham's *Historia Anglicana* in which the sexual metaphor of incest is used for political purposes. She quotes the following passage: "Alii peccatis dominorum ascribebant causam malorum, qui in Deum erant fictae fidei . . . vivendo incesti, violatores conjugii."[66] Even though Walsingham is referring here to incestuous lords, not kings, it is still significant that he uses the metaphor of incest to refer to political evils.

Gender, the Private, and the Public

The identification of women with the nation or the land is not, of course, new in the history of Western culture. It is evident, to mention only two famous cases, in the story of Helen of Troy or in Livy's account of the Rape of Lucrece, which the Roman author presents as the crisis that gave way to the overthrow of the monarchical system of government in Rome. What we should note is that these stories, in which women's sexuality is central as it becomes the site for political contests, receive a renewed attention in fourteenth-century England and particularly so in Gower's *Confessio*.[67] The question, then, is not so much what is the relation between woman and the state, but rather why is there a renewed interest in constructing this relation in late medieval England. The answer, I argue, is intricately connected to the contemporary political scene. Richard's concentration of power in the court and the conflicts he raised by attempting to subordinate the law to his own will worried those who saw in this an absolutism that both undermined the basic social laws of the community and threatened their own power. The abuse of authority by the incestuous father is similarly threatening for the community; for incest signifies the rejection of basic rules that allow for the functioning of society. Thus, the growing emphasis on the political dimension of women's sexuality and on the dangers of fathers' abuse of their power over their daughters in Gower's *Confessio Amantis* is inextricably linked to the questions raised by Richard's attempts to centralize and consolidate the nation-state in his own person in fourteenth-century England.

The identification of woman with the state and of public affairs with

---

[66] Quoted in Federico 133. I reproduce the quotation more fully below as taken from Thomas Walsingham, *Historia Anglicana*, ed. Henry Thomas Riley, vol. 2 (London: Longman, 1864): "Alii peccatis dominorum ascribebant causam malorum, qui in Deum erant fictae fidei . . . Erant praetera in subditos tyranni et in pares tumidi [sic], invicem suspecti, vivendo incesti, violatores conjugii, Ecclesiae destructores" (12). ("Others ascribed the cause of the evils to the sins of the lords, who feigned their faith in God . . . They were, moreover, tyrants against their subjects, and cowardly towards their peers, suspicious of one another, living in incest, violators of their spouses, destroyers of the Church" [my translation].)

[67] Chaucer also paid considerable attention to such stories. To mention only two, in "The Physician's Tale," he narrates the story of the sacrifice of Virginia, and in *Troilus and Criseyde*, he tells the story of Criseyde, a woman whose sexuality becomes the symbolic site on which the Trojan wars are waged.

domestic affairs also raises questions about the public and private domains, questions that the *Confessio Amantis* explores in depth. The words "prive" and "priveliche," on the one hand, and "open" and "openliche," on the other, recur with great frequency in the *Confessio Amantis*.[68] But before analyzing these concepts in the poem, I would like to echo Dorothy Helly's and Susan Reverby's call to rethink and, more specifically, "to historicize our notions of public and private and to link them to other hierarchies of power and social relations."[69] Too often, as these critics note, by imposing our own constructed notions of public and private, we have "impos[ed] a structure on history that obscured rather than revealed the past" (2). It is in the spirit of these considerations that I examine the notions of public and private in Gower's *Confessio Amantis*, for as Helly and Reverby also note, we need to "plac[e] the division betwen public and private in the realm of culture and politics, not nature" (9).

Modern notions of privacy differ from medieval notions of privacy, as Sarah Stanbury has argued, in that they are intimately tied to the concept of private rights: "Recent work on private life in the Middle Ages has argued that privacy was not invested with the sense of bodily or spatial right that it has come to assume in twentieth-century Western culture."[70] The sense of "pryvetee" in Chaucer's poetry, she notes, reveals some ambivalence about the concept, especially as it relates to women: "women in Chaucer's fictions could indeed claim privacy as a territory of the person – even though we are to understand that the very claim of privacy as a right is somehow a wrong" (279). In Gower's poetry there is a similar ambivalence about the word. Privacy can acquire very different meanings, both positive and negative, in the poem, as it does in other fourteenth-century texts.[71] The meanings can range from 'personal,' and 'familial' in a positive sense, to, more negatively, 'selfish,' 'secret', 'hidden.' It also fluctuates between two meanings that are intimately connected: the notion of a private self, of a private space, and the notion of private property.[72] The ambivalence towards privacy in the late

---

[68] A look at *A Concordance to John Gower's Confessio Amantis*, ed. J. D. Pickles and J. L. Dawson (Cambridge: D. S. Brewer, 1987), shows that "privite" and cognates such as "priveliche" and "prively" appear more than one hundred times, while "open" and cognates such as "openli" and "openliche" appear more than forty times bearing the connotation of publicness in the majority of instances.

[69] Dorothy O. Helly and Susan M. Reverby, *Gendered Domains: Rethinking Public and Private in Women's History* (Ithaca, NY: Cornell UP, 1992) 7.

[70] Sarah Stanbury, "Women's Letters and Private Space in Chaucer," *Exemplaria* 6 (1994): 278.

[71] See Thomas J. Farrell, "Privacy and the Boundaries of Fabliau in 'The Miller's Tale,'" *English Literary History* 56 (1989): 773–95. Throughout the article, Farrell identifies several meanings for the word "prive" and its derivations in "The Miller's Tale" which correspond to the meanings that also coexist in Gower's *Confessio*.

[72] It is not suprising that "privite" fluctuates between these two meanings for there is a profound link between privacy and property. This link, as well as its consequences for women, was most famously identified by Friedrich Engels in *The Origin of the Family, Private*

Middle Ages and in Gower's and Chaucer's poetry may have to do with the increasing convergence of these two notions. On the one hand, although, as Stanbury notes, "autonomous acts were most often viewed as inimical to the social good" (278), there are signs, like women's letters, that indicate a recognition of "a zone of female 'pryvetee' that prefigures modern territorial private rights" (280). On the other hand, the close link between privacy and property ensured the gradual valorization of privacy. It is significant that English common law developed from the twelfth century on a great interest in private property to the point that one scholar has called this interest a "property fetish."[73] Thus in the second half of the fourteenth century, King Richard's lack of respect for his subjects' property could only conflict with such a "property fetish." I would even argue that Gower's and Chaucer's interest in defining the meaning of privacy may be a response to Richard's abuse of power; his attempts to violate privacy created an urgent need to define more precisely the notion of privacy in order to limit the king's power.

In the *Confessio*, then, Gower is in a process of exploring the notions of public and private, notions that are linked to his own preoccupations about authority as well as to fourteenth-century notions of privacy. The public and the private do not constitute a binary opposition with clear boundaries in Gower's work and, partly for this reason, because he does not imagine them as a binarism, he does not privilege one notion over the other.[74] It is now a commonplace among critics that as, for instance, Elizabeth Porter has written, for Gower "good governance of others depends on ethical self-

---

Property, and the State in 1884. While critical about the documentation used by Engels, feminist critics have developed Engels's major thesis regarding privacy, property, and the status of women. See, for instance, Eleanor Leacock's introduction to Engels, *The Origin of the Family, Private Property and the State* (New York: International Publishers, 1972), or Leacock's application of Engels's thesis in her study of egalitarian societies in a chapter titled "Women's Status in Egalitarian Society: Implication for Social Evolution," in her book *Myths of Male Dominance* (New York: Monthly Review Press, 1981). Joan Kelly-Gadol, "The Relation of the Sexes: Methodological Implications of Women's History," *Signs* 1 (1976): 809–23, draws a similar link between private property and gender. For recent comments on some of these studies and their implications for the notions of private and public spheres, see Helly and Reverby, *Gendered Domains* 11ff.

[73] See Donald R. Kelley, *The Human Measure: Social Thought in the Western Legal Tradition* (Cambridge: Harvard UP, 1990) 171. Kelley argues that "[w]hat distinguished English from French society (at least before the French Revolution) was above all the respect for property, expressed, for instance, in the prohibition of the billeting of troops and of arbitrary taxation without consent... Property, indeed, was the subject of the greatest legal treatise of that age – 'Littleton on Tenures' " (170). Gower's *Confessio* can thus be seen as an exploration of such a property fetish and its various ramifications.

[74] Gayle Margherita, "Historicity, Femininity, and Chaucer's *Troilus*," *Exemplaria* 6 (1994): 243–69, makes a compelling analysis of some of the consequences of seeing the public and the private as a binary, whereby one becomes privileged over the other and, in psychoanalytic terms, one, the public, becomes the real and historical, the other, the private, becomes the realm of fantasy, and, therefore, of the apolitical, that is, of that which is not to be taken very seriously (see pp. 243–49).

rule."⁷⁵ The private and the public are thus interdependent and mutually reinforcing. And they do so in very complex ways that do not necessarily correspond with our notions of public and private, as I hope to demonstrate in this book.

These two realms, as feminist criticism has made clear, are inevitably bound up with notions of gender. However, there is not a one-to-one correspondence between private and female and public and male in the *Confessio*.⁷⁶ The female is used to explore the notion of a private self, but her actions are not simply limited to the private sphere.⁷⁷ While women are not on an equal footing with men in the public sphere, they may still peform a public role. Indeed, in the *Confessio*, not only can women perform public functions, but it is when they do so that the system works well. An important part of Gower's political world is constituted by something akin to what Wallace has identified as a unique feature in Chaucer's polity: wifely eloquence.⁷⁸ In the case of Gower, though, it is not just wifely, but also daughterly eloquence that can play a role in his polity. I would then adopt the term 'female eloquence' (a term also used sometimes by Wallace) to account for Gower's own sense of the public role of women.

In her article on women's letters and private space, Sarah Stanbury has noted that privacy and the notion of property become in Chaucer's poetry "the site of extraordinary anxieties about issues of control."⁷⁹ More specifically, his poetry reveals "anxieties about female control within the house" (283). Issues of control are, of course, first and foremost issues of authority and power, and it is for this reason that the notions of private and public are so central to Gower's *Confessio Amantis*.⁸⁰ They relate, moreover, to issues of

---

⁷⁵ Elizabeth Porter, "Gower's Ethical Microcosm" 135.
⁷⁶ As Jean Bethke Elshtain, *Public Man, Private Woman: Women in Social and Political Thought* (Princeton: Princeton UP, 1981), has put it:
> [T]he way in which determinations about the public and the private and the role and worth of each is evaluated will gear a thinker's attitudes towards women. That is one way to put it. Another might be: a thinker's views on women serve as a foundation that helps to give rise to the subsequent determinations he makes of the public and the private and what he implicates and values in each. It is not easy to decide which way the vectors of personal and theoretical exigency move. (4–5)

⁷⁷ Judith M. Bennett, "Public Power and Authority in the Medieval English Countryside," in *Women and Power in the Middle Ages*, eds. Mary Erler and Maryanne Kowaleski (Atlanta: U of Georgia P, 1988), has argued that we need to make a distinction between power and authority, when we analyze medieval women's public roles: "All women, regardless of rank or class, were effectively excluded from formal political activity in medieval England ... All these women, however, could aspire to public power, not only as heads of households, but also as controllers of the economic resources left by their husbands" (29). And she concludes that "[m]edieval Englishwomen ... were often powerful, but they were never authoritative" (29).
⁷⁸ See Wallace, *Chaucerian Polity*, esp. Introduction and ch. 12.
⁷⁹ Stanbury, "Women's Letters" 278.
⁸⁰ As Stanbury, "The Voyeur and the Private Life in *Troilus and Criseyde*," *Studies in the Age*

power over the private sphere raised by Richard's attempts to have absolute power over his subjects, including rights over their property, as explained above. One of the questions Gower asks in his narrative poem is a question about boundaries. Referring to Chaucer's female letter writers, Stanbury has argued that these women raise an important question: "what are the boundaries of women's private space – and as a territory, what are its protections and vulnerabilities in a patriarchal domestic empire?"[81] A similar question is central to Gower's poem but, in his case, this question generates also a set of parallel and interdependent questions: what are the boundaries of the subjects' own private space vis-á-vis a king's power?; and, a question we will examine in the following section, what are the boundaries of an artist's power over his work? The development of a notion of privacy, then, was intimately connected with the notion of women, and in the *Confessio Amantis* women are used to help men imagine and define what it means to have a private self, even as, at the same time, the poem raises questions about whether there is an interior self that is independent from the outside.[82]

Textual Authority

While the relationship between fathers and daughters assumed a new salience as a political metaphor, it also became a concern for Gower as a lay poet who saw himself playing a fundamental political and authoritative role but who was also critical of this role. In this respect, Gower's examination of different forms of authority in the *Confessio Amantis* also includes the examination of his own authority. If the stories of fathers and daughters in the *Confessio Amantis* raise the question of the limits of the authority figure over the subject of that authority in both political and familial contexts, they also shed light on another type of relationship of authority, that between Genius and his tales, that is, between an author and his text. Genius's contradictions, mentioned above, have been the cause of major disagreements among critics over the meaning and significance of his role.[83] Some critics have seen his

---

of Chaucer 13 (1991), puts it, the opposition between private and public is "a matter of power, and especially *kinds* of power" (141).
81 Stanbury, "Women's Letters" 279.
82 Gayle Margherita, "Historicity, Femininity, and Chaucer's *Troilus*," has arrived at a similar conclusion through a psychoanalytic standpoint: "The medieval association of textual 'privitee' with the secrets of the feminine body is encrypted in [the] critical insistence on a correspondence between femininity and an apolitical private self; both are symptomatic of a male fantasy of feminine interiority, a fantasy that allows masculinist poets and critics to imagine for themselves an extra-textual and extra-semiotic speaking position" (247).
83 For a detailed summary of the different interpretations published up to 1989, see Peter Nicholson, *An Annotated Index to the Commentary on Gower's* Confessio Amantis, Medieval & Renaissance Texts and Studies 62 (Binghamton, NY: Center for Medieval and Early

incongruities as a manifestation of Gower's incompetence and hence as a failure of the poem; others have argued that one of Genius's sides (usually, either his venereal or his Christian side) triumphs over the other. Yet others have seen Genius as the manifestation of the reconciliation between the two sides. Finally, more recent critics have tended to stress that Genius's incongruities are precisely the point. Olsson notes the struggle of different ideologies in his character: "The point is that the counsel is unsure: what 'truths' he voices in one aspect of his character may be challenged by what he voices in another aspect. He represents divided counsel, or unresolved 'consail on alle sides.' "[84]

Instead of analyzing Genius's incongruities to see whether in the end he is consistent or not, I suggest here that we look beyond the character himself and ask why the ultimate author of the *Confessio*, Gower, created such a divided figure or why this figure "represents divided counsel." In order to answer this question, we need to look at the other major role, apart from that of father confessor, that Genius plays in the *Confessio Amantis*, his role as narrator. As narrator of the tales, Genius also has a relationship of authority with his own text; he tries to exert control over his stories in an attempt to reduce their meaning to his own purposes. Significantly, as the author and authority behind the tales, Genius is often seen as a mouthpiece for Gower himself. For instance, in his study on the medieval notion of *auctoritas*, Alastair Minnis argues that in the *Confessio Amantis* Gower makes "a claim to a limited *auctoritas*."[85] Minnis sees Gower's *auctoritas* speaking through Genius, and although he avoids identifying Genius with Gower, he finds that the disagreements between these two voices is ultimately subordinated to "the singleness of the writer's purpose and the essential unity of his materials" (190). Although, unlike Minnis, Scanlon does not see a singleness of purpose in the *Confessio*, like Minnis, he does see Genius as a mouthpiece for Gower's authority. To Scanlon, Genius's use of the two doctrines is evidence of Genius's capacity to see beyond his own moral *and* narrative authority, but he ultimately ascribes to Gower this capacity to see beyond authority and lay poetry: "As a figure, like Venus, for Gower's own authority, [Genius] demonstrates the capacity of lay poetry to generate from within its own limitations an authority that transcends them."[86] In Scanlon's argument, then, there is not a fundamental difference between Genius and Gower.

And yet, Genius is a contradictory figure whose authority is sometimes

---

Renaissance Studies, 1989) 11–13, and 97–101. In the pages below, I will refer to other, more recent, interpretations.

[84] Olsson, *John Gower and the Structures of Conversion* 23–24.

[85] Alastair Minnis, *Medieval Theory of Authorship: Scholastic Literary Attitudes in the Later Middle Ages* (Philadelphia: U of Pennsylvania P, 1984) 188. See also Yeager, *John Gower's Poetic: The Search for a New Arion* (Cambridge: D. S. Brewer, 1990) 93–113, for an illuminating discussion of Gower's notion of poetic authority vis-á-vis French courtly poets, especially, Machaut and Deschamps.

[86] See Scanlon, *Narrative, Authority, and Power* 277. For a similar view, see also Rita Cope-

questioned by Amans and by the contradictions themselves. Amans's disagreements with Genius, I would add, disallow any direct identification between Genius and Gower. These disagreements as well as Genius's incongruities, in fact, are used by Gower to explore the question of textual authority. Because he cannot be identified with Genius, Gower can question Genius's authority (and thus ultimately his own authority and that of any author). While Genius serves Gower to explore the notion and workings of authority – in a sense the priest is Gower's *alter ego* – it is also fundamental to note that Gower maintains a distance from his priest. As Rita Copeland has argued, "even while he is a projection of *intentio auctoris*, Genius is also an actor in the narrative. He serves therefore as a rhetorical sleight of hand, as a disguise for the author's auto-exegesis."[87]

In addition to making Genius an actor in the narrative, Gower creates such a distance between himself and Genius also by including another main character in the frame of the *Confessio*, Amans. We know from the poem itself that Gower takes on Amans's *persona* – at the end of Book 8, Venus discloses Amans's identity by addressing him as John Gower. This identification, though, cannot be taken to mean that Amans represents Gower's voice, for as Minnis has demonstrated in another discussion, Amans is a role Gower takes on, and throughout the poem "there is a considerable distance between *persona* and *auctor*."[88] Even at the end when we are told Amans is 'John Gower,' he "moves quite close to the *auctor* envisaged by the commentary" (56). Amans and Gower are "quite close" at the very end but not so close that we would identify Amans with Gower. But even though we cannot identify Amans with Gower, taking on Amans's *persona* allows Gower to reflect on Genius's authority. Indeed, the authority relationship between these two characters is evident. Amans assumes a subordinate position from the very beginning of Book 1, when he pleads with Venus for help, and when Genius, sent by Venus, assumes the position of authority in relation to Amans. Genius assumes this position not only by virtue of being the confessor, but also by virtue of narrating the tales, organizing the material, and extracting the morals from them.

From his subordinate position, however, Amans makes some comments that give us a different angle on Genius's tales and morals, sometimes questioning the narrator's authority and drawing attention to Genius's own use and abuse of his authority over his own tales. For instance, as I point out in Chapter Five, Genius acts like a tyrannical father when he blames Jephthah's daughter for not having married before her own father sacrificed her, and when he also presents Rosiphelee with a terrifying vision of the fate that

---

land, *Rhetoric, Hermeneutics, and Translation in the Middle Ages: Academic Tradition and Vernacular Texts* (Cambridge: Cambridge UP, 1991) 205.
[87] Rita Copeland, *Rhetoric, Hermeneutics, and Translation in the Middle Ages* 205.
[88] Alastair Minnis, "De Vulgari Auctoritate: Chaucer, Gower and the Men of Great Authority," *Chaucer and Gower*, ed. Yeager, 56–57.

awaits her if she does not marry. Amans himself notes Genius's harshness, pointing to him that he has noticed how, "ye the wommen have noght spared / Of hem that tarien so behinde" (4.1600–1601). Gower's assumption of the role of Amans thus allows him to distance himself from Genius. Through Amans, he can maintain a critical detachment in his exploration of the workings of authority.

Gower's detached viewpoint and his examination of authority is also enabled by the very layout and organization of the *Confessio Amantis*. The use of Latin verse at the beginning of each section as well as the use of Latin glosses that sometimes conflict with Genius's interpretations also question Genius's authority.[89] Thus Gower, who had positioned himself as a moral authority through literary creation in *Vox Clamantis* and *Mirour de l'Omme*, raises questions about his own authority through Genius. In this sense, Genius's use of the Pygmalion story not only points to his role as confessor/Father and shaper of Amans's soul, as mentioned above; it also points to his role as narrator/creator of his tales. The priest's identification with Pygmalion suggests that he sees himself as the artist/*auctor* who creates his tales and characters. Significantly, as narrator/creator of the tales, his relationship of authority with his tales as depicted in the *Confessio Amantis* resembles that between a father and a daughter. Like a father, he has authority over his own creation, but that authority is limited by the interaction with society – when the tales circulate, the author has to lose some control over their meaning. The incestuous father wants his daughter to obey him in every respect and mirror his desire; the "abusive" author wants his text to mirror his intention; he tries to control its meaning. But such a desire for control cannot be fulfilled once the text circulates. In my analysis of the story of Pygmalion, I argue that this myth reveals an anxiety about the incest-like relationship between an artist and his creation and thus that Gower uses the story to explore the question of the boundaries of artistic power.

What then are the implications of Gower's interest in these two types of relationship, that between fathers and daughters and that between an author and his text? Gower's interest in the notion of authority in the *Confessio*, as Scanlon has argued, should be understood as part of an attempt by lay authors in fourteenth-century England to emphasize the precedence of lay political authority over clerical authority in issues of government.[90] It should also be

---

[89] See Siân Echard, "With Carmen's Help: Latin Authorities in the *Confessio Amantis*," 95 (1998): 1–40, for a thorough and provocative analysis of the conflict among the different voices in the poem (Latin glosses, Latin verse, and English poem) based on an analysis of most manuscripts of the *Confessio*. Echard's analysis, like my own, emphasizes the conflict among the voices: "Gower's Latin problematizes the question of authority in the Confessio by presenting the reader with several competing authoritative voices, Latin and vernacular, none of which seems capable of taming the text" (7). Patricia Batchelor, "Feigned Truth and Exemplary Method in the *Confessio Amantis*," *Re-Visioning Gower*, ed. Yeager, 1–15, makes a similar argument on the basis of other types of evidence.

[90] Scanlon, *Narrative, Authority, and Power*, ch. 9.

understood as an effort by lay poetic authors to appropriate clerical authority. Through his *Confessio*, Gower not only claims but also enacts his own authority. In this way he also gives a renewed importance and assigns a new function to literature in the vernacular. For Gower, literature in the vernacular is not a mere form of entertainment or an ideological vehicle for particular local families or interests, but it plays a major political role as it tries to influence and define royal authority. Literature partakes of major political interests, of the interest of the "comune profit" of the whole state. In this sense, as Anne Middleton has shown, Gower shares with other fourteenth-century authors a clear sense of literature's political role.[91] But Gower's sense of his political role, I would add, has another fundamental dimension: as the English author explores and defines the limits of kingly and paternal authority, he also explores and defines the limits of his own poetic authority. Gower's examination of the notion of incest, of absolute control over something or someone created by oneself, reveals his anxiety about his relationship with his own creation, the text, about his desire to have his text mirror his own will and his own meaning, unambiguously.

The preceding analysis further suggests a significant analogy. We do not know much about the circumstances in which King Richard commissioned Gower to write the *Confessio Amantis*, except for Gower's reference to Richard's commission in the Prologue to the first recension of the poem (ll.34–53*). We do not even know if Richard actually commissioned Gower to write his poem. Whatever the circumstances, whether this happened or not, we can bring the notion of exchange and authority in the poem to bear upon the (real or fictional) exchange of the poem between Gower and the king in the first recension.[92] The *Confessio* suggests that the text can be compared to a daughter whom the author/father exchanges with his most immediate audience: King Richard. The text then performs a feminine role, specifically the role of daughter in the process of exchange. That a text would be imagined as feminine was not, of course, unusual in the Middle Ages. Dinshaw has demonstrated this point clearly in her analysis of patristic

---

[91] See Anne Middleton, "The Idea of Public Poetry in the Reign of Richard II," *Speculum* 53 (1978): 94–114.

[92] Dhira B. Mahoney, "Gower's Two Prologues to *Confessio Amantis*," *Re-Visioning Gower*, ed. Yeager, 17–37, discusses the three recensions and questions very persuasively modern editors' privileging of the second and third recensions, rededicated to Henry IV, to the detriment of the first one. I am focusing on the first recension here both because, like Mahoney, I think there are no valid reasons to neglect it and also because I agree with Mahoney that it presents a more vivid and personal representation of the relationship between author and patron (19). Nevertheless, I will also point out that even if they are less vivid and personal, this notion of exchange also functions in the second and third recensions. In a more abstract sense, Gower's implied audience in the later recensions are both Henry and England – he now claims to write the poem "for Engelondes sake" (24), rather than "for king Richardes sake" (*24). The exchange of the poem is thus an exchange not so much with the king as with the nation.

notions of the Biblical text, a notion later adopted by medieval authors.[93] In Gower's poem the gendering of the text as feminine is seen most clearly in the story of Pygmalion, as I will argue in Chapter Five.

Such a gendered notion is also behind Gower's act of exchange of his text with the king. This act of exchange of the text, moreover, is an ambiguous moment. It is a moment in which Gower exerts authority, but it is a moment that is recounted right at the beginning of a text in which the limitations and problematic aspects of relationships of authority (including textual ones) are going to be analyzed in all their complexity. On the one hand, then, Gower shows that his text/daughter is worthy of being offered to the king in exchange not for immediate material rewards but for exerting some influence, or wielding some authority in the socio-political structures of power governed by the king. In the act of offering his poem, Gower affirms and enacts his own authority and power. On the other hand, though, this act of exchange is also a recognition of the limitations of his own authority and power. Accepting the need for the traffic in women and the traffic in texts assumes that the authority figure gives up absolute control over his subordinate figure. The anxiety of committing incest with the text, that is, of desiring the text's perfect compliance with its author's will, is a fundamental aspect of Gower's exploration. Thus, as he asserts the need for the traffic in women, Gower is also asserting the need for the traffic in texts.

It is because of this anxiety that Gower creates a narrative which refuses to identify an authoritative voice. The *Confessio Amantis* has no single authoritative voice, but many different voices. Gower is more interested in the contrast among these voices than in the hegemony of one over the others. This point can be better understood, I will argue in Chapter Five, by comparing the *Confessio* to Jean de Meun's *Roman de la Rose*, where the authorial voice, as various critics have shown, is also unlocatable. Gower's *Confessio Amantis*, like Jean's poem, recognizes the illusory and problematic nature of the belief in, and desire for, absolute, indeed, incestuous, authorial control.

The chapters in this book are arranged thematically. Each chapter analyzes either two or three father-daughter tales that share a major common theme. Chapter Two, "Redeeming Daughters: Thaise, Peronelle, and Constance," analyzes three tales in which the main daughters help their fathers comply

---

[93] See Introduction and Ch. 4 in Dinshaw, *Chaucer's Sexual Poetics*. The notion of the text as feminine is also apparent in early humanist conceptions of philology, an ideology that applied the notions of chastity and purity to politics and the practice of philology (see Stephanie Jed, *Chaste Thinking: The Rape of Lucretia and the Birth of Humanism* [Bloomington: Indiana UP, 1989]). Jed has argued that in fourteenth- and fifteenth-century Florence the story of the "Rape of Lucretia" was used to promote this new ideology. Gower's own notion of the text as feminine and at the same time as a participant in politics parallels contemporary humanist notions which were developing in Florence.

with the injunctions of patriarchal society, cooperating with their own exchange and with their separation from their fathers. Even though these tales show daughters who ultimately reinforce the system of exchange, they also reveal the unstable points in the system. I start with the last tale in the *Confessio*, the "Tale of Apollonius," because it is a kind of microcosm of most of the issues that will be discussed in the book: it deals with several father-daughter pairs and analyzes them from familial, sexual, and political viewpoints; there is a case of father-daughter incest as well as a case of complete physical separation between father and daughter. Moreover, in my analysis of this tale, I expand on the theoretical considerations I outline in this first chapter and argue, not only that the definitions and limits drawn by the incest taboo are used by Genius to generate other definitions and limits, but also that the discursive character of these definitions and limits turn out to be their major weakness. In the "Tale of the Three Questions" the daughter not only redeems her father but participates as an agent in the process of her own exchange. She does so by using humility, traditionally considered a feminine virtue, as a masquerade. While Peronelle's actions do not prove to be subversive, they do point to the fissures in the system of exchange. In this tale, moreover, we see Genius interpreting the daughter's actions in ways that are not necessarily self-evident. This is not the only time that he does so; we will see other instances in which Genius uses the daughters to prove his points, ignoring certain complications raised by his tales. Chapter Two ends with the "Tale of Constance." This tale has fundamental political implications for the debate about the distribution of power between State and Church in the late Middle Ages. The underlying incestuous motif in this tale, which Gower does not suppress, is used to examine the complex struggle for power between lay and clerical authority in the fourteenth century. The limits drawn by the incest taboo once again help generate other limits, but such limits turn out to be difficult to stabilize. Finally, my analysis of the parallels between the father-daughter relationships and the relationship between God and Mary in the "Tale of the Three Questions" and the "Tale of Constance" demonstrates that one of the reasons why those limits are difficult to stabilize is that the transgression of boundaries, the father's desire for his daughter, is at the heart of patriarchal rule.

Chapter Three, "Fathers as Husbands, Husbands as Fathers: Supplantation and Exchange in the 'Tale of the False Bachelor' and the 'Tale of Albinus and Rosemund,' " analyzes two tales that reveal that the process of exchange is a form of supplantation in which the supplanter, the bridegroom, is fundamentally (and, from the point of view of authority, structurally as well) the same as the supplanted, the father. In the process of the exchange of women, fathers and husbands relate to the exchanged woman in similar ways, that is, as authority figures. In other words, for the exchange to take place father and son-in-law must be interchangeable. Genius's examination of the theme of supplantation in the "Tale of the False Bachelor" reveals that supplantation is not only the False Bachelor's sin, but also the "sin" of the system of exchange.

This theme is also evident in the "Tale of Albinus and Rosemund" where Albinus takes the place of (supplants forcefully) his wife's father and also supplants him as king of the Gepids. The interchangeability of father and husband explains Genius's difficulty in delimiting the father's authority and constitutes one of the weaknesses in the system of exchange. Moreover, I will further argue, both tales reveal that father and husband are interchangeable also because they are primarily defined as men. Masculinity, particularly masculinity as defined by chivalry, depends on performativity and this dependence on acting produces what, borrowing Butler's terms, we may call the "gaps and fissures" in the construction of gender.[94] As in the "Tale of the False Bachelor," in the "Tale of Albinus and Rosemund" Albinus's final demise is linked with chivalry's excessive dependence on performance. But the latter tale goes even further than the former in also showing how, resembling the self-absorption typical of incestuous desire, chivalry's self-absorption makes chivalric ideology an inappropriate ethos for the ideal ruler.

"Limiting Authority: Leucothoe, Virginia, and Canace" is the title of Chapter Four. In this chapter I focus on Genius's attempt to mark the limits of patriarchal authority by defining a public and a private sphere. This definition proves to be complex because the definition of the private is fluid: it is inherently dependent on the definition of the public. In the "Tale of Leucothoe" the private body is defined in terms of property: it belongs to the father – no other male, not even someone with more authority than the father, has a right over it. In the "Tale of Virginia," the daughter's body is also presented as the father's private property, but this private space becomes the site for a public struggle. In the "Tale of Canace and Machaire," by contrast with the other two, the daughter's body is more clearly defined as the daughter's private space, not the father's. Thus while these three tales are about three fathers' abuse of their authority over their daughters, only one of them, the "Tale of Canace and Machaire," focuses on and condemns explicitly the father's abuse of his authority. Genius's failure to condemn the same abuse of power and in effect to draw the limits of the father's authority over the daughter's private body in the other two tales, the "Tale of Leucothoe" and the "Tale of Virginia," suggests, on the one hand, that private and public cannot be delimited by fixed boundaries, and thus that authority cannot be delimited by fixed boundaries either. On the other hand, it also suggests that Genius himself is also tempted to use his authority as the narrator of the tales in a way that may be seen as abusive, for he tries to fix, to control, the meaning of his

---

[94] See, for instance, *Bodies That Matter*, where writing about the notion of "sex," Butler argues that "[a]s a sedimented effect of a reiterative or ritual practice, sex acquires its naturalized effect, and, yet, it is also by virtue of this reiteration that gaps and fissures are opened up as the constitutive instabilities in such constructions, as that which escapes or exceeds the norm, as that which cannot be wholly defined or fixed by the repetitive labor of that norm" (10).

tales. This discussion leads into the final chapter, which analyzes Gower's examination of the relationship between an author and his work.

The final chapter, "Textual Fathers and Textual Daughters," discusses three tales from Book 4, the "Tale of Rosiphelee," the "Tale of Jephthah's Daughter" and "Pygmaleon and the Statue." My main aim in this chapter is to show that Gower's reflection on authority relationships within the family and the state also entails a reflection on the relationship between an author and his text (I use "his" here advisedly, because of the distinctly gendered character of this relationship in the poem). More significantly, the metaphor that Gower employs to define this relationship is the father-daughter relationship. Two of the three tales, the "Tale of Rosiphelee" and the "Tale of Jephthah's Daughter," show Genius imposing his authority very explicitly and revealing that he sees himself as an *auctor*. Genius's transformations of the tales reveal that he is also a father of sorts and that the daughters in his tales become, in a sense, his daughters. They are his own creation, and, in trying to control their meaning, he abuses his own narrative authority. That Gower uses the father-daughter relationship as a model to analyze textual relationships of authority becomes even clearer when we look at his version of the myth of Pygmalion. In "Pygmaleon and the Statue" Gower hints at the problematic incestuous connotations involved in the nature of artistic creation. I finish the book with this tale, because it points to Gower's awareness of his own role as author, thus casting a new light on the other tales (as well as on the whole *Confessio*), and suggesting, first, that the discussions about authority in the father-daughter tales have significant implications for an understanding of Genius's textual authority, and, second, that they also reveal Gower's own anxieties about his relationship of authority with his own text.

This book asks why Gower raises the specter of incest, but, more crucially, it also asks why fathers and daughters are so central to some of the most significant tales in his Middle English poem. While incest is a fundamental theme in the *Confessio Amantis*, we need to ask why it is primarily one kind of incest, father-daughter incest, that interests Gower. Due to the hierarchical and gendered character of this relationship, this type of incest enables Gower to explore the boundaries of power and authority in different, though interrelated, spheres, and to raise questions about power, subordination, and the limits of the authority figure. The law against incest, and specifically against father-daughter incest, in Gower's *Confessio Amantis* is examined as the foundational and originary law at the core of patriarchal society.

Chapter Two

REDEEMING DAUGHTERS:
THAISE, PERONELLE, AND CONSTANCE

Introduction

In the "Tale of Apollonius," the "Tale of the Three Questions," and the "Tale of Constance," the protagonists are fathers and daughters who have very close relationships, but who always avert the possibility of incest. In the "Tale of Apollonius," though, the main father-daughter pair, Apollonius and Thaise, is fundamentally defined through the explicit incestuous relationship that takes place at the beginning of the tale between another father, King Antiochus, and his daughter. Although they do not become the major focus of the tale, Antiochus and his daughter constitute the force that drives the plot and casts its shadow over all the later father-daughter relationships we see in the story. Nonetheless, in the three tales Genius focuses on daughters, Peronelle, Constance, and Thaise, who play crucial roles in complying with the system of exchange and in helping their fathers when they are in potentially dangerous or socially problematic situations. All three daughters become queens either during or at the end of their tales, and they act as intercessors for their fathers, an intercessory role that, according to Paul Strohm, became the major role of queens in the late Middle Ages.[1] No violent coercions, social, cultural, or religious, are explicitly imposed on the daughters; no father chastises his daughter or imposes his will against his daughter's own will. The daughters know and perform the role assigned to them by society.

These three tales, though, do not simply show socially compliant daughters and fathers but reflect on the structure and organization of familial and political relationships. While, ultimately, the potentially dangerous moments tend to be contained, this reflection lets us see the unstable points in the system, its gaps and fissures. Thus, it is true, for instance, that in the case of Peronelle, by displacing her biological father with her political father, this daughter ultimately confirms and reproduces the structures of authority and gender relationships. However, by taking power into her hands and arranging her own exchange, she also reveals the existence of points of instability in the patriarchal system of exchange. Similarly, in all three tales the potentially

---

[1] See Strohm, *Hochon's Arrow*, ch. 5.

dangerous intimacy between the pairs of fathers and daughters is displaced and rearticulated within the system, but these displacements are far from being unproblematic. Incest is never committed by the main father-daughter pairs in the tales – Peronelle and Petro, Constance and Constantine, and Thaise and Apollonius – but the shadow of incest always looms large in the close relationship between these fathers and daughters. This is, of course, especially true of the "Tale of Apollonius," where one father-daughter pair does commit incest. It is significant, therefore, that at times Genius defines the intimacy between father and daughter as a love relationship, which reminds us of traditional courtly love scenes. In the "Tale of the Three Questions," for instance, the exchange between Peronelle and her father in their garden, as Donavin has noted, is reminiscent of the garden where *l'Amant* longs for his rose in the *Roman de la Rose*.[2] In the "Tale of Constance," the heroine refers to her thoughts about her father as her "querele," a word also used in the *Confessio* to refer to the crises produced by sexual desire. And in the "Tale of Apollonius," during the recognition scene in which Apollonius and his daughter, Thaise, meet after a long separation, the verbal exchange between father and daughter is charged with some sexual innuendoes before they recognize each other.

When I allude to the daughters' desire in this chapter, I am not arguing that they have a "natural" desire for their fathers that language has the function of diverting. I interpret the daughters' desire in these tales not as some kind of natural desire that precedes the law against incest, but as a creation of the law itself. For, as I explain in Chapter One, following Butler's analysis of the incest taboo in *Gender Trouble*, the taboo does not only prohibit the desire; it also effectively creates that desire. In Butler's words, "[t]he taboo might be understood to create and sustain the desire for the mother/father as well as the compulsory displacement of that desire" (76). It is thus significant that the three main daughters in the tales have a powerful command of language. This control of language, their power of speech, is a crucial element in connection with the incest prohibition. Language both manifests the displacement of desire *and* creates the desire. The daughters' control of speech manifests their perfect acculturation into the social system.

By defining what constitutes incest, the law creates and delimits incestuous desire and the taboo. It creates the desire and at the same time, through the taboo, marks the boundaries of that desire. Moreover, the incest taboo, according to Butler, is a fundamental and originary law of discourse that delimits and constructs other oppositions:

> [the incest taboo] effectively produces heterosexuality, and acts not merely as a negative or exclusionary code, but as a sanction and, most pertinently, as a law of discourse, distinguishing the speakable from the unspeakable (delimiting and constructing the domain of the unspeakable), the legitimate from the illegitimate. (65)

---

2 Donavin, *Incest Narratives* 54.

The taboo becomes an originary law that produces other laws. Exploring the limits of the law and of authority (the lines between the legitimate and the illegitimate) both within the family and within the state, as this book argues, is a major concern in Gower's *Confessio Amantis*. In the three tales studied in this chapter, the exploration of the delimitations established by the incest taboo generates other delimitations, like those between the speakable and the unspeakable, between the legitimate and the illegitimate, between male and female, or between private and public. Thus, Gower's focus on father-daughter relationships in these tales is intricately linked with his concern with social and political order and with delimiting kingly authority. Peronelle, Constance, and Thaise prove crucial in helping to define and delimit both kingly and paternal authority. All three daughters show the kind of "female eloquence" that I mentioned in Chapter One. By answering the questions, Peronelle manages to prevent the king from capriciously abusing his power and killing her father. Constance's eloquence is the reason she has a suitor – the sultan – and thus is separated from her father, helping her father comply with the social injunction to separate from his daughter; her eloquence is also the reason she marries her husband Alla. Finally, Thaise helps her father to avoid committing incest with her and assists him to come to life again through the power of words.

It was noted in Chapter One that in some of the tales in the *Confessio Amantis* cities and countries are depicted as feminine and that even Amans's lady stands for England at one point. This gendered relationship between the king and his country is stressed in the "Tale of Apollonius," in which Apollonius's city mourns its prince's absence like a lover (8.472–94). By presenting the political relation between king and country as a gendered relation in which the country is depicted as feminine, Gower is suggesting a further parallel between king-country and husband-wife and, by extension, father-daughter relations. (In Chapter Three I explain why I equate husband-wife and father-daughter relationships.) But the role of gender in these relations (unlike in other tales) is not simply established along an active/passive or a public/private axis in which the king and the father are the only ones who act or who perform a public role. On the contrary, the three tales I discuss in this chapter emphasize that the interaction between king and country, and between father and daughter, as well as their role in maintaining social order, does not just depend on the king and the father but rather on the active and public role of both king and country and both father and daughter. Daughters then have a public role to perform, even though it is a limited public role that ultimately confirms their subordination.

This chapter also reflects on Genius's investment in the issues raised by his tales, as well as on Genius's understanding and interpretations of the daughters' actions. I argue that his moralizations reveal a limited approach to his own stories. There are discrepancies between Genius's single-minded interpretation of the daughters' actions and the more complex interpretation to which those actions lend themselves. These discrepancies reveal that, by using and abusing his own authority, Genius attempts to control the meaning of the tales by imposing a moral on them.

The destabilizing moments in the "Tale of Apollonius," the "Tale of the Three Questions," and the "Tale of Constance" discussed in this chapter become evident not only when we analyze the tales themselves, but also when we consider them vis-à-vis the tales analyzed in the next three chapters. The discussion about problematic fathers and daughters in other tales will make it evident that the tales with happy endings and "ideal" characters, like the ones discussed in this chapter, are more complex when read in the context of other tales, as I believe the *Confessio Amantis* invites us to do. For even as these tales try to delimit clearly the roles of fathers and daughters as opposed to husbands and wives, they also suggest their instability. The boundaries between husband and father and between daughter and wife are fluid and can destabilize the system of exchange. The limits of the authority figure, therefore, prove difficult to mark.

This major argument – that the limits of authority prove difficult to mark because the boundaries are defined as fluid – becomes especially evident in light of the parallels we see in the "Tale of the Three Questions" and in the "Tale of Constance" between the fathers and daughters, on the one hand, and the biblical story of God and Mary, on the other. I will argue that the riddle of the relationship between God and Mary – who is at the same time, mother, daughter, and wife of God – manifests the ambiguity at the heart of the patriarchal system of exchange, and, in a sense, even generates the ambiguity as it becomes the matrix for the understanding and articulation of father-daughter relationships in medieval Christian culture.

The Tale of Apollonius of Tyre

According to Gower's organization of the *Confessio*, Book 8 should have dealt with the sin of *luxuria*; instead, it treats of a branch of this sin: incest. The "Tale of Apollonius of Tyre," the only tale in Book 8 and the longest one in the *Confessio Amantis*, tells about an incestuous act. One other tale in the *Confessio*, the "Tale of Canace and Machaire" (3.143–336), also concerns an incestuous relationship (between siblings in this case); but, with the exception of the brief *exemplum* of Lot and his Daughters narrated also in Book 8 (223–46), the "Tale of Apollonius" is the only tale in which incest is committed by a father and a daughter. The incestuous act, moreover, is committed only at the beginning of this longer tale and is not mentioned explicitly again until the very end.[3] While it illustrates the sin of incest, the

---

[3] This structural imbalance has given rise to very different views about the tale. For a summary of criticism on the "Tale of Apollonius," see Yeager, *John Gower's Poetic* 216–17. Yeager notes that earlier critics like William G. Dodd and G. C. Macaulay found the tale rambling and diffuse and, years later, Runacres judged the tale uninformative, confusing,

"Tale of Apollonius" is much more than a counterexample to the sin; it achieves much more than just teaching Amans about one more type of dishonest love that he should avoid. The tale deals with some of the major questions that previous tales have already raised; and while it shows how those problematic issues are to be contained, it also points to the gaps and fissures in the system. As the tale unfolds, Apollonius learns how to handle issues raised by relationships of authority, like those between fathers and daughters, and between kings and subjects, but his need to learn reveals the ways in which these hierarchical relationships are constructed through a process of reiteration and thus depend fundamentally on acting.[4]

Let me first outline the plot of the tale. After his wife died, Antiochus committed incest with his daughter and tried to keep her to himself by challenging his daughter's suitors to solve a riddle that disclosed his incestuous relationship. Apollonius of Tyre solved the riddle and had to leave Antioch. Fearing the king's revenge, he also fled from Tyre and went first to Tarsus, where he stayed with Strangulio and his wife, Dionise. He then took to the sea once more and, after suffering a shipwreck, he landed on the shores of Pentapolis, where he met King Artestrathes. Artestrathes's daughter fell in love with him, and Apollonius married her. After Antiochus died, Apollonius decided to sail back to his people with his wife, who was pregnant. His wife gave birth to their daughter, Thaise, in the ship and seemed to die after giving birth. She was therefore put in a coffer and thrown into the sea. Apollonius decided to entrust Thaise's education to Strangulio and he himself went to his city, Tyre, where he mourned his wife's death. Thaise grew up and Strangulio's wife felt jealous of her because she thought Strangulio treated Thaise better than his own daughter. She tried to have her killed, but Thaise escaped from her murderer and was then kidnapped by some pirates who brought her to a brothel in Mytilene. There she managed to convince her

and poorly chosen for the lesson. More recent criticism, though, tends to view the tale in a more positive light. Yeager himself, for instance, sees it as a compendium or summary of the whole work: " 'Apollonius' reflects and completes the entire poem" (218). Yeager argues that incest in this tale is considered in its "broad meaning," and that "[t]he tale is offered as a counterexample" (218). See also Robins, "Romance, Exemplum, and the Subject of the *Confessio Amantis*," for whom the alleged confusion in the tale has to do with Gower's interest in contrasting the genres of romance and exemplum in order to "prompt his readers to recognize their situation at the intersection of two discursive modes" (159).
[4] Allen, "Chaucer Answers Gower," has argued that "Apollonius continually reshapes his role in relation to both his political subjects and his closest subject, his daughter" (637). While Allen also acknowledges the close resemblance between incest and its avoidance (639), my reading is more skeptical than hers in that it stresses the instability that derives from that resemblance, rather than the resolution of the problems raised by the resemblance. My reading is in this sense closer to Scanlon's in "The Riddle of Incest." Scanlon argues that "the tale enacts the return of the repressed" and that it raises the question of "whether [the father's] protective desire [for the daughter] doesn't give way to a desire for dominance ultimately indistinguishable from the illicit sexual desires the father's protection is meant to prevent" (118).

pimp to let her preserve her virginity by offering to make money for him by teaching women. When Apollonius went to Tarsus to seek his daughter, he was told she was dead. He took to the sea again, and, full of sorrow, he hid in his ship's cabin and refused to see anybody. His ship arrived in Mytilene. The king of Mytilene, Athenagoras, heard about Apollonius's grief and sent Thaise to comfort him. Apollonius did not recognize her initially and refused to be comforted by her. He even slapped Thaise in the face. This violent reaction made Thaise tell him who she was, which, in turn, led to their recognition. Apollonius was full of joy and, after Athenagoras's request, he gave him Thaise in marriage. They all intended to go to Tarsus to take revenge but Apollonius had a dream in which he was told to go to Ephesus. There he found his wife, who had not actually died. Apollonius made his daughter and her husband king and queen of Tyre. Following Artestrathes's death, he himself was proclaimed king of Pentapolis.

While in the other two tales studied in this chapter the daughters are the main characters, the story of Apollonius places a strong emphasis on the roles of the fathers. The three main fathers in the "Tale of Apollonius," Antiochus, Apollonius, and Artestrathes, are all kings as well as fathers; thus, their behavior raises questions about the limits of authority both within the state and within the family. At the beginning of the tale, Antiochus, blinded by lust ("with lustes blente," 295), commits a dark sin against the basic law that prohibits incest. Apollonius's trip to Antioch constitutes a journey into the dark side of patriarchal society (Antiochus's sin). During that trip, he uncovers a foundational patriarchal sin, the father's desire for sexual union with his daughter. From that critical moment on, Apollonius, the major father in the tale, tries to travel away from this dark sin and comply with the law that prohibits father-daughter incest. He then goes through a process of education during which he learns how to define himself in opposition to Antiochus and to follow the example of Artestrathes both in his relationship with his daughter as a father and in his relationship with his own country and the law as a prince. If Apollonius shows that he complies with social rules by separating from his daughter, he also learns how to be a good prince and avoid becoming a tyrant in his relationship with his city. Thus, this tale shows how a prince and a father should behave ideally. At the same time, though, it raises many questions about this behavior.

In the process of following Apollonius's education, Genius touches on very complex issues, which, like incest itself, are at the heart of the structure of authority relationships. In fact, incest, I will argue, is the vehicle that allows Gower to arrive at those deeper issues, for incest is imagined as a foundational and originary law that generates other laws. Incest and the taboo enable Gower to explore the limitations of authority by looking at other fundamental notions that are also defined on the basis of a notion of authority, such as the relationship between the public and private spheres, male and female, father and daughter, husband and wife. Defining authority in these realms, though, proves to be difficult because of the fluidity of these notions.

Thus, for instance, Gower's narrator associates Antiochus's incestuous world with the exclusive attention to the private, which is also initially identified with the feminine world. By contrast, he defines Apollonius's role as father and king as the ideal balance between family and country, private and public, feminine and masculine. Nevertheless, family-private-feminine do not constitute one side of a binarism and country-public-masculine the other. In fact, the tale suggests the fluidity of these notions and their dependence on discursive construction. The notion of the private and the public is under constant negotiation in the tale and it has a complex relationship to gender. In fact, the major daughter in the tale, Thaise, plays a crucial role in this exploration. She is the intercessor for her father in both the public and the private realms, questioning the exclusive identification of the private with the feminine. In the process of his education, then, a process that Thaise herself also needs to go through, Apollonius learns how to define these terms and thus ultimately how to enact his authority in a manner that does not disrupt the system of exchange.

In the following pages, I will discuss first both Apollonius' and Thaise's gradual learning, focusing on how they learn to negotiate between the private and the public. Second, I will analyze the recognition scene between Thaise and Apollonius as the moment that reveals the very constructedness of the incest taboo, its dependence on the discursive.[5] In order to avoid incest, a discursive definition of the differences between fathers and husbands in their relationships with their daughters and wives needs to be articulated. But this dependence on language, rather than on some "natural" definition, proves to be the taboo's major weakness, its fundamental source of instability. Third, in connection with the constructedness of the taboo, the tale raises the question of whether Apollonius has a moral, inner self, or whether his is an intersected subject whose behavior depends fundamentally on how others interact with, and define, him. Although Genius seems to try to persuade us that Apollonius's and Thaise's roles are stable and grounded in some inner moral self, his constant reminders about the fluidity of the different definitions that he uses undermines the sense of stability that he would like to create. Genius's final mention of the role of God and Fortune in Apollonius's life amounts to a recognition of the difficulty of knowing the extent to which Apollonius can be seen as an agent, and even of determining whether there is a self prior to language.

Genius's account starts by focusing on King Antiochus, the one father who commits incest with his daughter in the tale and lays a special emphasis on Antiochus's seclusion from the public world. Even though Antiochus is a king, at the beginning Genius describes him mainly in his private world, a world that is presented at this point as a feminine one. Antiochus is surrounded only by his wife and daughter. No men appear in his world until

---

[5] Scanlon, "The Riddle of Incest," has similarly noted the tale's "heightened awareness of the essentially discursive status of familial categories" (125), and hence of the incest taboo.

later on (352ff), when his daughter's suitors approach the court. Moreover, Genius does not mention anything about Antiochus's kingdom, i.e., about his public side, except for the fact that the city of "Antioche tok / His ferste name" from him (275–76), a significant observation since it suggests a complete (even absolute) identification between king and city. When Antiochus's wife died, he "made mochel mone" (283), and instead of looking for consolation outside, in the public world, he turns to his private world, to his daughter "which in hire fadres chambres duelte" (291). After raping her, the father goes out ("Out of the chambre goth the king," 313), while she stays within the chamber and also within herself ("Withinne hisself such sorghe made," 315). The only other person who knows about the rape is the daughter's nurse, but this does not make a significant difference because the nurse herself is also part of the limited private world of the king.

Privacy and staying inside are also equated with ignorance and secrecy in the Antiochus episode. The king of Antioch, Genius says, felt concupiscence "Withoute insihte of conscience" (294). He was ignorant of any moral conscience. They are also equated in a subtle way when Genius says that the daughter "couthe noght hir Maidenhede / Defende" (302–03). The auxiliary "couthe" plays on two meanings: she could not physically defend herself, and she did not know how to (she did not have the knowledge to) defend herself. This double meaning becomes more evident when we compare her inability to defend herself with Apollonius's daughter's self-defense in the brothel in a later episode. Genius observes that when men entered Thaise's room in order to sleep with her, she would cry and make "wofull pleintes" (1442), so that "Was non of hem which pouer hade / To don hire eny vileinie" (1430–31). Moreover, incest is equated not just with ignorance but also with secrecy; it can keep being performed as long as it is kept private, i.e., as long as "Ther was non other which it wiste" (341).

Even though he tries to hide his sin, Antiochus cannot avoid the fact that he is a public figure and that society (especially the male world) will demand that he exchange his daughter. Even if he has managed to become one with his city and his family, he cannot prevent his city from interacting with the outside world, the world that Apollonius comes from. Thus, "fame, which goth every weie, . . . / The grete beaute telleth oute / Of such a maide of hih parage" (348, 350–51). He tries, though, to keep his secret by laying out his own law of exchange ("his lawe he taxeth," 361). Antiochus's transgression of the law that forbids father-daughter incest results in his creation of a new law in the realm according to which a suitor can only obtain his daughter's hand if he answers a riddle. Suitors have to solve a riddle that, as Apollonius puts it, "toucheth al the privite / Betwen thin oghne child and thee" (425–26). Apollonius is the only suitor who solves the riddle. He, however, knowing that he has uncovered a dark secret (their "privite"), cannot make it public. Once he shares the knowledge of the secret, Apollonius also has to act secretively, in order to save his life. As Genius puts it, after his return to Tyre, he has to leave this city "priveliche" (467) without telling his subjects. He too is stigmatized by the secret.[6] Therefore, he will be able to reunite with his city as a good king only after he has gone through a process of education that prepares him to avoid the danger of incest, or to restrain himself from any incestuous desires.

After visiting Antiochus, Apollonius needs to redefine the meaning of private. In his process of learning and education, Apollonius finds in King Artestrathes the perfect balance between the private and the public. Apollonius thus goes from the "private" world of Antiochus to King Artestrathes's balanced world in Pentapolis. He arrives at Artestrathes's kingdom when attempting for the second time to escape from Antiochus, and after suffering a shipwreck off the shores of Pentapolis (666ff). King Artestrathes's openness and public life, as well as the masculine world he moves in, contrast markedly with Antiochus's privateness and secrecy, as well as the feminine world with which he surrounds himself. Genius shows Artestrathes participating fully in the masculine world of exchange. The first time we see King Artestrathes, he is at a public game. The game has homoerotic connotations: it is restricted to men and they all play naked, in Artestrathes's "sihte" (692). In the Latin prose version, *Historia Apollonii*, which Gower probably knew, the game takes place in a gymnasium and Artestrathes himself plays against the other men and against Apollonius.[7] Gower's version is quite different. The game does not take place in a gymnasium, but in a "large place" (689). In the opinion of G. C. Macaulay, Gower changed the account, because "[he] did not understand the Greek customs."[8] I do not see any reason why we should make such an assumption. Rather, Gower modified his source to emphasize two main points about the game. First, as Russell Peck points out, the game emphasizes Artestrathes's public-mindedness.[9] Second, it shows Artestrathes acting as the king. By not participating in the game, but just observing, he is above any kind of competition. Indeed, one is reminded of the tournament that Theseus presides over in the "Knight's Tale." In both the tournament in Chaucer's tale and the game in Gower's, men gather to compete publicly in front of the king. A major difference, though, is that in the "Tale of Apollonius" women are

---

[6] Allen, "Chaucer Answers Gower," has similarly noted that, "Apollonius's willingness to entertain the subject of incest implicates him in the incest system, much as the Man of Law suggests Gower is implicated in his own subject matter" (637). Scanlon, "The Riddle of Incest," also makes this point: "Apollonius must atone for so long because Antiochus' guilt is ultimately also his own" (126–27). In my reading of the tale, I emphasize that Apollonius's adventures represent not so much an atonement for the sins of patriarchy, but a process of education, thus presenting Apollonius's avoidance of the sin not as a natural but a learned (discursive) reaction. Rather than providing him with an opportunity for atonement, Apollonius's adventures teach him to escape from the possibility of commiting incest and, as I will argue later, from death.

[7] See *Apollonius of Tyre: Medieval and Renaissance Themes and Variations*, ed. and trans. Elizabeth Archibald (Cambridge: D. S. Brewer, 1991) 124.

[8] Macaulay, note to l. 679.

[9] Russell Peck, *Kingship and Common Profit* 169–70.

excluded from the game; and, thus, the game serves mainly as a homosocial bonding event.

But Artestrathes's world is not only masculine and public. There is also a private and a feminine side to it, a side that is defined differently than in Antiochus's world. The supper that follows the game shows him combining both aspects of his life. He eats with his lords and in the company of his wife and daughter, as well. The events at supper also confirm that Artestrathes, unlike Antiochus, is willing both to establish bonds with men and to exchange his daughter. A significant difference between the way his daughter falls in love with Apollonius in the Latin version and in Gower's illustrates this point. According to the Latin version, when she entered the room, she saw Apollonius and then asked her father who he was.[10] In Gower's version, the father sends her to Apollonius before she even notices him, and she functions as the intermediary between the two men. She is controlled and guided by her father, going back and forth between him and Apollonius. First, Artestrathes sends her to ask Apollonius about his "hevynesse" (729). When Artestrathes sees that Apollonius is weeping as he tells his story to the daughter, he sends again for her and asks her to play the harp for the shipwrecked man. Once again she obeys her father and goes back to Apollonius, thus working as the instrument through which Artestrathes woos Apollonius, as it were. Only after the king himself has established the bond with Apollonius and has shown he is ready to give his daughter away, does she fall in love with Apollonius.

Genius describes how Artestrathes's daughter falls in love in terms that echo the Antiochus episode, but with significant variations that entail a redefinition of the notions of private and public. Once she falls in love with Apollonius, she restrains herself and keeps her love "Withinne hir chambre, and goth not oute" (863). Antiochus commits his sin, because after his wife's death he is "al him one" (284) and because his daughter dwelt "in hire fadres chambres" (291). Unlike Antiochus, even though she falls madly in love, Artestrathes's daughter is aware of the public: "Sche wolde hire goode name kepe / For feere of wommanysshe schame" (854–55). Antiochus acknowledged the shame of his sin only after Apollonius solved his riddle. Moreover, this daughter cannot remain in private, apart from the public world, because society requires her exchange and because her father is ready to comply with the law. Initially, the daughter herself refuses to go out. Using terms similar to those Genius used previously to describe Antiochus's incest, the daughter says that her "schame" cannot be "unloke" (894–96) in speech, but at least it can be in writing.[11] Apollonius had used the same word "unloke" to describe the act he would perform were he to reveal the solution to the riddle: "The

---

10 *Apollonius of Tyre*, ed. Archibald, 126.
11 Compare this "schame" with Virginius's "schame" and Canace's lack thereof, discussed in Chapter Four. The meaning of "schame" here is also associated with a sense of the public and the private; Artestrathes's daughter has such a sense.

question which thou hast spoke, / If thou wolt that it be unloke, / It toucheth al the privete" (424–26). Moreover, when Artestrathes reads the letter, he tells the suitors very "prively" that they have not been chosen. And later on in the "chambre," Artestrathes tells Apollonius "al the private" (918) of his daughter. In sum, the scenes and vocabulary are parallel to the story of Antiochus, but in these instances privacy, secrecy, and being inside do not acquire negative connotations.

Quite to the contrary, privacy and secrecy are ultimately handled wisely and for public purposes. The wedding celebration shows the openness of the relationship between Apollonius and Artestrathes's daughter:

> Thei wedde and make a riche feste
> And every thing which was honeste
> Withinnen house and ek withoute
> It was so don, that al aboute
> Of gret worschipe, of gret noblesse
> Ther cride many a man largesse
> Unto the lordes hihe and loude. (957–63)

When Apollonius and Artestrathes's daughter get married, they manage to combine both the private and the public, the inside and the outside. The adjective "honeste" conveys this sense of openness.[12] One of the meanings of "honeste" according to the *Middle English Dictionary* is moral uprightness and purity. Unlike Antiochus, neither Apollonius nor his wife have anything shameful to hide because their behavior is morally upright. Hence, their wedding can be proclaimed loudly.

Apollonius's behavior in King Artestrathes's court shows that he has found a new meaning for the notions of the public and the private. Nevertheless, the fact that his subsequent behavior is the exact opposite of Antiochus's suggests that he cannot escape the prior meaning, that is, that the prior meaning shapes his subsequent behavior. Thus when he later becomes father to a daughter and has to go through the same experience as Antiochus, i.e., the loss of his wife, Apollonius's response to the experience is the opposite of Antiochus's response: Apollonius separates from his daughter as soon as his wife dies. Entrusting her education to his friend Strangulio, he promises that he will grow his beard, "Til it befalle that I have / In covenable time of age / Beset hire unto mariage" (1304–06). He will look "wild" until he manages to exchange her. Furthermore, unlike Antiochus, Apollonius goes back to his city and shares his mourning with the lords of his realm, turning his mourning into a public event, a highly significant gesture.

---

[12] Later in the tale, "honeste" is applied explicitly to the love relationship between Apollonius and his wife. As will be seen below, Apollonius is praised for loving "honesteliche." For an analysis of the concept of "honeste love" as a love relationship realized within the boundaries of Christian marriage, see J. A. W. Bennett, "Gower's 'Honeste Love,' " *Patterns of Love and Courtesy: Essays in Honor of C. S. Lewis*, ed. John Lawlor (London: Edward Arnold, 1966) 107–21.

REDEEMING DAUGHTERS: THAISE, PERONELLE, AND CONSTANCE

Before analyzing the mourning scene, let us first consider the deep connection between mourning and melancholia. Genius had established this connection, a connection I will further analyze in Chapter Four, in another tale about incest, the "Tale of Canace and Machaire" (Book 3). Such a connection is also hinted at in "Apollonius" and needs to be examined in order to understand the significance of Apollonius's separation from his daughter as well as his public mourning. Typically, as Freud has argued in "Mourning and Melancholia," the person who mourns denies the absence of the loved object; hence, as he puts it, sometimes "the existence of the loved object is psychically prolonged."[13] At the beginning of the tale, Antiochus had prolonged that existence not psychically but physically by substituting the daughter for the mother. Apollonius, by contrast, avoids doing so by leaving his daughter. Moreover, writing about the correlation of mourning and melancholia, Freud has argued that, "[m]ourning is regularly the reaction to the loss of a loved person, or to the loss of some abstraction which has taken the place of one . . . In some people the same influences produce melancholia" (243). Already in Antiquity and the early Middle Ages, as Mary Wack has noted, melancholia was most often associated with lovesickness.[14] Genius's fathers are linked by a similar sense of loss of their daughters. As we will see in Chapter Four, in the "Tale of Canace and Machaire" another father, Eolus, commits what Genius classifies as the sin of melancholia when he learns about his daughter's pregnancy, that is, when, in a sense, he loses her. In the *Confessio Amantis*, melancholy, as Allen has observed, even affects Amans, and this melancholy turns him into a tyrannical figure with a self-destructive impulse:

> [I] am so malencolious,
> That ther nys servant in myn hous
> Ne non of tho that ben aboute,
> That ech of hem ne stant in doute,
> And wene that I scholde rave
> For Anger that thei se me have.   (87–92)

Allen also notes that, in the "Tale of Canace and Machaire," through the wrath of Eolus, "Genius politicizes household wrath" (634). I would argue that a similar politicization can be seen in the case of Antiochus and Apollonius.

Antiochus's mourning and consequent incest turn into a political problem. Apollonius manages to avoid creating a similar political problem by escaping from his own daughter until his mourning period is over and by

---

13 Sigmund Freud, "Mourning and Melancholia," *The Standard Edition of the Complete Psychological Works of Sigmund Freud*, ed. and trans. James Strachey, vol. 14 (London: Hogarth Press, 1957) 245.
14 Mary Wack, *Lovesickness in the Middle Ages: The 'Viaticum' and Its Commentaries* (Philadelphia: U of Pennsylvania P, 1990) 162.

sharing his mourning publicly with his subjects, rather than turning inwards. Genius remarks that, "For he som confort wolde gete, / He let somoune a parlement, / To which the lordes were asent" (1550–52). Similarly, he also decides to celebrate a "feste" with a "sacrifice" in memory of his wife (1562–63). This public mourning, we should note, also reinforces the bond with the men, "the lordes," of his community.

Only after he has gone through the period of mourning does Apollonius decide to go back and seek his daughter, Thaise. His decision to wait until then avoids repeating Antiochus's mistake. Notice how Genius had previously linked Antiochus's period of mourning with his act of incest:

> The king, which made mochel mone,
> Tho stod, as who seith, al him one
> Withoute wif, bot natheles
> His doghter, which was piereles
> Of beaute, duelte aboute him stille. (283–87)

The king is mourning, making "mochel mone," when he turns to his daughter, who is still at home. Apollonius avoids the temptation to turn to his daughter by separating from her while he is mourning. He does not try to reunite with her until after the funeral for his wife has been held:

> Whan this [the funeral] was do, thanne he him thoghte
> Upon his doghter, and besoghte
> Suche of his lordes as he wolde
> That thei with him to Tharse scholde,
> To fette his doghter Taise there. (1567–71)

These lines show that Apollonius has begun to learn how to relate to his daughter and his country in a way that markedly distinguishes him from Antiochus.

The daughter, like the father, also has to go through a process of education before she can see her father again and before she can redeem him. As Scanlon has remarked in "The Riddle of Incest", the tale draws constant parallels between father and daughter, not only through the "repetitions of plot motifs" but also through "a set of characterological repetitions" (117). While her father mourns, Thaise receives a good education in Tarsus, an education that makes her wise like her father, and that also teaches her, as it teaches Peronelle and Constance, to participate actively in the system of exchange. Genius emphasizes Thaise's education:

> Sche was wel tawht, sche was wel boked,
> So wel sche spedde hir in hire youthe
> That sche of every wisdom couthe,
> That forto seche in every lond
> So wys an other noman fond. (1328–32)

As part of her education, moreover, Thaise, like her father, also has to go

REDEEMING DAUGHTERS: THAISE, PERONELLE, AND CONSTANCE

through the experience of a destructive father-daughter relationship, although in her case the relationship becomes destructive not because of the father, a figurative father, but because of the mother, also figurative, who is envious of her. Thaise's tutor, Strangulio, replaces her father so well that his wife comes to hate Thaise and tries to have her killed. She thinks that he prefers Thaise to his own daughter. Full of "fals envie" (1334), like Constance's two mothers-in-law, Strangulio's wife orders her slave ("hire bondeman") to kill Thaise, because "The comun vois, the comun grace / Was al upon that other Maide, / And of hir doghter noman saide" (1342–44). Thaise, though, manages to escape unharmed from this attempt to murder her. Like Apollonius, she also has to escape from a destructive parent-child relationship.

But before Thaise is prepared to confront her biological father successfully, we see that she has also learned how to define the private and public in an "appropriate" way. After she escapes from her murderer, she is abducted by some pirates and brought to a brothel. This episode reveals that Thaise has learned to perform a public function. More crucially, it also points to the link between women's sexuality and language. Her pimp Leonin sets her "Clos in a chambre be hireselve, / [where] Ech after other ten or tuelve / Of yonge men to hire in wente" (1425–27). However, she makes such sorrow that "Was non of hem which pouer hade / To don hire eny vileinie" (1430–31). Her situation parallels that of Antiochus's daughter, but her reaction is very different. The "chambre" (1425) becomes again a central image, but this time the daughter knows how to get out of that private space. While Antiochus's daughter "couthe not" defend herself, Thaise's education helps her defend and preserve her virginity. She tells one of Leonin's men that she would like to strike a deal with Leonin:

> Bot soffre me to go mi weie
> Out of this hous wher I am inne,
> And I schal make him forto winne
> In som place elles of the toun.   (1452–55)

She offers to earn money by teaching other women. Notice the opposition between "hous" and "toun" in this passage. Thaise wants to leave the house and perform a public function in the "toun" as a teacher. Thaise thus manages to use language in a public way, instead of her sexuality, in order to make money (even though her public action here is limited to women). Antiochus's daughter, by contrast, stayed within the chamber and did not do anything about her situation. She only talked to her nurse, but the nurse was an "inside" character as well. Thaise's time in Mytilene shows that she is ready to comply with social rules. Language as a social act displaces the threat of illegitimate sexuality.

Apollonius, by contrast, still needs to learn. After some years, he decides to recover his daughter from Strangulio, but Strangulio tells him that she is dead. Her supposed death, as well as his coming close to suffering another shipwreck, makes Apollonius turn inward, hiding in the "Caban" of his ship and letting nobody talk to him.[15] Apollonius's reaction to this second loss tests the limits of his learning. This time he cannot avoid mourning only in private. The "Caban" is an enclosed and private space, a space dangerously cut off from the outside, from public interaction. He does not even want to see the light (1600ff). He goes into a darkness, a moment of mourning, that recalls Antiochus's moment of darkness and mourning, a dangerous moment that led the latter to commit incest. Unlike Antiochus, though, Apollonius comes out of this darkness, out of this private enclosed space. He manages to do so through his daughter; as Scanlon puts it, "Thais is Apollonius's way out of abjection" (117).

The encounter of this father and daughter pair is a dramatic moment of uncovering, of bringing to light what remained private. In this dramatic moment, words, language, become the means that bring about the recognition and that work to avert incest.[16] We should note with Olsson that Gower has rewritten this particular scene in a subtle way.[17] Unlike the Thaise in his source, the *Historia Apollonii regis Tyri*, Gower's Thaise, Olsson remarks, "is perfectly secure in herself, and she betrays no need to make . . . an opening speech in defense of her honor" (219). In the scene, Thaise's confidence is emphasized by Genius through her command of language. When she sees that Apollonius does not respond to her songs,

> Sche falleth with him into wordes,
> And telleth with him of sondri bordes,
> And axeth him demandes strange,
> Wherof sche made his herte change,
> And to hire speche his Ere he leide
> And hath merveile of that sche seide.   (1675–80)

---

[15] There is a significant parallel between this scene and the scene in which Apollonius's wife gives birth to Thaise. Apollonius's wife is also in a "Caban" (1051), when she gives birth. Apollonius recovers his royal status inside a "Caban" (1744). It is as if Thaise gives birth to a new Apollonius.

[16] It is interesting to mention here that there is a recognizable fear in this story of early Christian origins. John Boswell, *Christianity, Social Tolerance, and Homosexuality* (Chicago: U of Chicago P, 1980), has noted the relation between the sexual exploitation of minors, or child prostitution, and the fear of incest in early Christian writers:

> Christian writers were profoundly disturbed by the possibility of accidental incest presented by this aspect of the slave trade . . . Tertullian argues against exposing or offering for adoption children who may ultimately engage in incestuous relations with parents they cannot recognize; and Clement laments 'the countless unknown tragedies occasioned by casual sexual encounters. How many fathers, forgetting the children they abandoned, unknowingly have sexual relations with a son who is a prostitute or a daughter become a harlot?' The public sale of children as slaves clearly persisted for centuries after the Roman world had become Christian. (144)

A similar fear underlies the story of Apollonius.

[17] See Olsson, *John Gower and the Structures of Conversion*, esp. 219–20.

Despite her words, he falls again into silence. Then she touches him. He responds by slapping her; at this point, Allen has noted, "Apollonius's rage and physical violence echo that of Antiochus" (638). But, rather than passively enduring his rage, Thaise responds to Apollonius's action with a further outpouring of words, which she uses to defend herself. Her words this time construct the story of her life and, thus, create the connection of consanguinity with Apollonius. As in the brothel episode, Thaise uses language to displace the threat of illegitimate sexuality. Indeed, once the connection with Apollonius is discursively constructed, once both of them "know," incest can be avoided. Language, in this way, fulfills the main function of deterring any possibility of incest between father and daughter. By contrast, it should be remembered, the absence of language marked Antiochus's incest with his daughter.[18] Genius relates no exchange of words between father and daughter either before or after the first time he forces her to commit incest with him. Neither do they talk to each other later. Language diplaces incest; silence acquiesces with it.

These two scenes, when Antiochus commits incest with his daughter and when Apollonius avoids incest with Thaise, become very significant when read in the light of Derrida's and Butler's theories on the relationship between incest and language. As Bruce Boehrer notes, Derrida, in his analysis of Rousseau's *Essay on the Origin of Languages*, "couples language to the incest taboo, describing both as parallel constituents of social consciousness"; and, Boehrer continues, "[t]he moment of the prohibition of incest – a prohibition that can only be articulated *between* families and hence in 'popular language' – thus presupposes and comprises the extension of language, too, as a generalized social construct."[19] To Rousseau, the prohibition of incest coincides with the moment human beings become aware of themselves as social rather than primarily familial beings: before the prohibition, "there were families, but there were not nations. There were domestic, but not popular, languages ... Each family was self-sufficient and perpetuated itself exclusively by inbreeding."[20] Languages thus develop when humans start to interact socially. As Derrida puts it, "[s]ociety, language, history, articulation, in a word supplementarity, are born at the same time as the prohibition of incest. That last is the hinge [*brisure*] between nature and culture."[21] By talking to

---

[18] Olsson, *John Gower and the Structures of Conversion*, has dismissed any possible connotation of desire in this scene: "A modern might read this as betraying a repressed desire, but Gower makes no such connection" (221). However, Thaise's answer to Apollonius's slap does suggest a sexual connotation. For one thing, Apollonius dares strike her because he thinks she is a prostitute. For another, Thaise makes him see the wrong he has done by claiming "I am a Maide" (1696); she is a virgin. Scanlon, "The Riddle of Incest," recognizes, like my reading does, the sexual connotations and the specter of incest in this scene; he also highlights the importance of the discursive at this point (147ff).
[19] Boehrer, *Monarchy and Incest in Renaissance England* 136.
[20] Quoted in Derrida, *Of Grammatology* 263.
[21] Derrida, *Of Grammatology* 265.

each other, by re-creating the bond of consanguinity between them through language, Apollonius and Thaise avoid the possibility of committing incest. The invention of language and the prohibition of incest coincide.

The familial relationship, indeed, is finally established (or, rather, constructed) through the fiction of words. Marc Shell has pointed out that, "[t]o call any particular child some man's son or daughter – or any particular man someone's father – is a fiction insofar as all paternity is inevitably indeterminable."[22] Apollonius and Thaise do not "know" that they are father and daughter until they put it in words. It has been argued that Genius suggests that Apollonius had some non-linguistic awareness that she was related to him, when the narrator remarks that Apollonius felt that "he hire loveth kindely" (1706).[23] But "kindely" is a problematic word which, as pointed out in Chapter One, is ambiguous, and which thus manifests very appropriately the ambiguity of the situation. "Kindely" could mean 'sexually,' a meaning "kinde" has in other instances in the *Confessio*.[24] And even though it seems that "kindely" in this sense is only associated with love between those of opposite sex who are not too close of blood (see Chapter One above), the line immediately following ("yit he wiste nevere why," 1707) suggests the ambiguity of the moment: Apollonius does not know how to interpret his feeling. He can know only what his "kindely love" means when she tells the story, when she verbalizes her past.[25] Once they construct their relationship, he

---

[22] Marc Shell, *The End of Kinship* 5. See also my discussion in Chapter One above.

[23] Götz Schmitz, *'the middel weie': Stil- und Aufbauformen in John Gowers* Confessio Amantis (Bonn: Bouvier Verlag Herbert Grundmann, 1974), for instance, has remarked that Apollonius's feeling is genuinely fatherly though he does not yet know that Thaise is his daughter (152–53). Peter Goodall, "John Gower's *Apollonius of Tyre: Confessio Amantis*, Book VIII," *Southern Review* 15 (1982): 243–53, has remarked that, "the whole reunion scene testifies in a most powerful way to the almost mystical ties of kinship" (247). Robins, "Romance, Exemplum, and the Subject of the *Confessio Amantis*," echoes Goodall's words and argues that there is an "internal predisposition" that moves Apollonius to recognize the ties of kinship "not because it offers an *analogy* to his own predicament, but because it is a *part of his own story*" (171).

[24] See Olsson, "Natural Law and John Gower's *Confessio Amantis*," esp. 182–86. See also Chapter One above. In *John Gower and the Structures of Conversion*, Olsson himself, though, discards the possibility that "kindely" could mean "sexually" in this particular scene in "Apollonius" (222–23). The line "yit he wiste nevere why," I argue, suggests that there is more ambiguity in the scene than Olsson recognizes. If Apollonius does not know why he loves her "kindely," why are we to assume that "kindely" has a definite meaning in this episode, especially since "kinde" is such an ambiguous term in the *Confessio*?

[25] Allen, "Chaucer Answers Gower," interprets this scene differently than I do. She sees the moment of recognition as a moment that reveals the process of learning how to read: "The resolution of incest comes within a hair's breadth of incest itself; the distinction depends on a series of subtle acts of reading ... Thaise can teach her father to read because she herself reads his silence and rejection as temporary aberration rather than unshakable prerogative" (639). Allen then argues that "the language of natural kinship and resolution encourages us to read [the threat of incest] like the generous Thaise and thus ... to insist that Apollonius 'wolde noght be so salvage' " (639). My reading focuses on precisely that act of choice in reading. That we have the possibility of choice suggests that our reading, and

REDEEMING DAUGHTERS: THAISE, PERONELLE, AND CONSTANCE

(re)interprets that "kinde" love as the love a father has for his daughter, rather than sexual love. The recognition scene thus emphasizes the role of words and fiction in the construction of the father-daughter relationship.

Returning to Derrida and to the beginning of the tale, we can see now why Antiochus's sin is described as "derke" and has to be necessarily private, i.e., not known to society. We can also see why Genius says that Antiochus was "Withoute insihte of conscience" when he committed the sin, and why Antiochus formulates his sin through a riddle whose meaning is barely comprehensible. Since the prohibition and language are seen as having appeared simultaneously, as Boehrer puts it, "the moment of incest . . . constitutes our only access to what lies *before* public utterance" (137). By committing incest, Antiochus goes back to the moment before socialization, that is, to the moment "*before* public utterance." His incestuous act is thus represented as a regression to a moment before language. Antiochus's daughter does not utter a word to her father when he rapes her. Unlike Thaise, she does not (and "couthe not") defend herself with words, and is thus unable to avoid the regression to a moment before language. Apollonius and his daughter Thaise, on the contrary, with their wealth of culture and education, cannot and would not go back to that moment before public utterance.

So far, this analysis of the moment of incest might seem to have assumed a nature/culture opposition, or an opposition between the pre-linguistic and the linguistic, the pre-linguistic being defined as a dark, instinctive, and natural moment. However, our discussion should be inserted within the broader theoretical frame of Derrida's discussion of Rousseau's theory on incest, society, and language. Derrida's analysis of incest points to the fundamental problem of any notion of incest that assumes that incestuous desire is pre-cultural, a problem also examined by Butler, as mentioned in Chapter One of this book. Such an assumption postulates the existence of an original, "natural" state that culture acts upon. It is impossible, however, as Derrida argues, to go back to that origin, because the concept of origin is but a function of the system of signification; that is, the moment we try to conceptualize an original moment, a moment before language, we must use language: "Is the concept of origin, or of the fundamental signified," Derrida asks, "anything but a function, indispensable but situated, inscribed, within the system of signification inaugurated by the interdict?" (266). His own answer to this question, namely, no, leads Derrida to conclude that "[l]anguage is neither prohibition nor trangression, it couples the two endlessly" (266). Thus, in the recognition scene, when Thaise constructs her relationship with her father through language, language displaces incest, as I noted above; at the same time, though, it also creates the possibility of trangression.

Derrida's theory also helps us to understand Genius's strategy in his reading of Antiochus's incest. Genius's use of the word "unkinde" to refer to Antio-

---

Apollonius's reading of Thaise's story, is not the only "natural" reading. Genius, of course, presents Apollonius's reading as if it were the only natural possibility, rather than a choice.

chus's desire for his daughter reveals how Genius is attempting to postulate the existence of an original, natural, and pre-legal state that the incest taboo tries to tame. But other instances in his description of Antiochus suggest that the incestuous king has not reverted to a natural, pre-legal state. Apollonius, I noted above, feels "kinde love" for Thaise before he recognizes her as his daughter. By contrast, Antiochus's desire for his daughter is repeatedly characterized as "unkinde." At the beginning of the tale, Genius refers to the first time Antiochus rapes his daughter as an "unkinde fare" (312), and in the moral to the tale, he insists on the "unkinde" quality of this father's own love for his daughter: Antiochus "sette his love unkindely" (2005), and he died suddenly, "Set ayein kinde upon vengance" (2007). That his love is "unkinde" seems to suggest, as I have pointed out, a return to a pre-cultural stage. However, can we say that Antiochus is ignorant in the same way as his daughter may have been? Does committing incest in his case represent an un-learning while in the case of his daughter it is a lack of learning? Or, does it represent, as Scanlon argues, a moment of regression to an infantile stage (119)? In fact, Antiochus's elaboration of a clever riddle in order to keep his daughter to himself suggests that he is not ignorant or instinctive or even fundamentally childlike; he is not simply forgetting what culture has taught him or going back to a moment before discourse. Quite to the contrary, he conceives of his sin discursively, as he knows very well what he is doing and creates a riddle to hide it – when Apollonius tells him he knows the answer to the riddle, Genius says Antiochus was aware of the shame of it: "The king was wonder sory tho, / And thoghte, if that he seide it oute, / Than were he schamed al aboute" (428–30). That he knows that his act of incest is shameful suggests that he understands the moral and socially transgressive implications of it. Indeed, even more crucially, he knows very well he is transgressing the law, so much so that he creates his own "lawe" (361) – i.e., solving the riddle as a requirement for a suitor to obtain his daughter's hand – in order to try to bypass the culturally sanctioned law against incest. Antiochus uses cultural parameters, he uses language and the law (his own law), in order to cross the line and fulfill his desire. He is able to create a new law that challenges the law against incest. His actions are thus not pre-legal or pre-linguistic; rather, they change the existing law and they produce a new type of discourse, the riddle.

We can understand the prohibition of incest and Genius's construction of it when we set it in this context. The prohibition of incest, as presented in the "Tale of Apollonius of Tyre," tries to create a line of separation between the cultural and the natural, or, in epistemological terms, between knowledge and ignorance, between the rational and the irrational, the speakable and the unspeakable. Thaise avoids incest because her knowledge and education have taught her to avoid it. Antiochus's daughter, however, is depicted by Genius as someone who does not know how to respond to her situation, and in this sense she is seen as ignorant. By presenting incestuous desire as that which culture has not tamed, that which is dark and unspeakable, Genius, like Rousseau, is presenting it as an originary desire, a desire that precedes culture. In this way, Gower's narrator is establishing the definitions and oppositions that, as Butler has pointed out, are generated by the incest taboo:

> [T]he repressive law effectively produces heterosexuality, and acts not merely as a negative or exclusionary code, but as a sanction and, most pertinently, as a law of discourse, distinguishing the speakable from the unspeakable (delimiting and constructing the domain of the unspeakable), the legitimate from the illegitimate. (65)

Genius constructs incest in precisely these terms, as the speakable versus the unspeakable, the legitimate versus the illegitimate (what goes against the laws of "kinde"). By doing so, he is effectively delimiting certain cultural parameters. However, Antiochus's behavior suggests that binarisms are discursive constructs, and, significantly, that the incest taboo, the foundational and originary law, is fundamentally discursive. The prohibition fails in its attempt to identify a pre-linguistic state, for the pre-linguistic state must be constructed through language.

By dealing with the theme of father-daughter incest, Genius explores the "heart of darkness" of patriarchal society. If language is a creation of the father, of a male-dominated society, incest, then, constructed as a rejection of language, as a desire to go to some "original" moment before language, is the worst sin against the law of the father. And this sin becomes even more subversive because the person who commits it is someone who, due to his role as father and as king, is supposed to be the main upholder of the law.

Gower is concerned in the *Confessio Amantis* with delimiting authority and human forms of power, particularly royal, paternal, and authorial power. The "Tale of Apollonius" ends with an affirmation of Apollonius's "ideal" behavior as king, lover/husband, and father. Despite his troubles and tribulations, Apollonius's adventures end happily. And they end happily, Genius assures Amans, because Apollonius's intentions and behavior were always honest:

> Lo, what it is to be wel grounded:
> For he hath ferst his love founded
> Honesteliche as forto wedde,
> Honesteliche his love he spedde
> And hadde children with his wif. (1993–97)

The word "grounded" is a masterstroke in this passage. Genius seems to mean that Apollonius has shown moral "groundedness" throughout the tale.[26] His

---

[26] The *Middle English Dictionary* notes several meanings for "grounden," including the two meanings I point out in this passage: the physical meaning of "To lay the foundation for (a building, wall); *fig.* fix (mountains or plants on or in earth)"; and the spiritual sense of "To establish (sb. in grace, goodness, charity, bliss, manhood, etc.)," or as a past participle "learned (in a branch of knowledge)."

love was honest, as proved by his marriage, and he fulfilled his love honestly by having children, in perfect accordance with Genius's doctrine. Notice how "honesteliche" can be seen as having connotations of openness and publicness. But there is also irony in the word "grounded." We know that, from a physical point of view, Apollonius has been far from being "well grounded" in the tale, due to his constant sea voyages. He was continually moved back and forth either by others or by natural elements like sea storms.

In fact, in the tale Apollonius is far from being grounded also in a sense other than just a physical one. The fundamental role of external circumstances in the story raises questions about Apollonius's self. Even though Apollonius's deeds are morally upright, his process of learning suggests that perhaps there was not a self that was morally upright from the very beginning, or, at the very least, that we cannot really identify an originary self that preceded discourse, for his self was constructed through the interaction with others. My argument then differs from that of Robins, who argues that, even though Gower explores the role of language in shaping the subject, he "dearly holds to the belief in an interiority from which to choose between, or at least to feel and endure, competing narrative options."[27] Perhaps Gower believed in an originary self that is later molded by discourse, perhaps one can see this belief in other tales, but the story of Apollonius raises questions about this belief. We do not know whether Apollonius behaved the way he did because he had a morally upright self from the beginning or if his morally upright self was a product of the different situations in which he found himself, or, most importantly, a product of his discovery of Antiochus's incest. We should note that, for Apollonius, incest and death are coupled from the very beginning. He learns about the stigma of incest at Antiochus's court, and he learns that he will die if he uncovers the dark secret. We do not know what is his moral reaction to the incestuous relationship. We do know that he is aware that his discovery has put his life in danger. Thus, rather than a conscious flight from an immoral act, his flight from incest is actually a flight from death. Later on in Artestrathes's court, he is restored to life and at the same time learns about the appropriate behavior of a figure of authority. For Apollonius the appropriate use of authority becomes associated with the preservation of life. Thus again his behavior has to do with self-preservation rather than with social or public concerns.

Significantly, Apollonius's dependence on others in the process of construction of his self is emphasized by Genius also in a political sense. As a king, he uses his power and authority appropriately because his actions do not depend mainly on his will, but also on the people's consent. Indeed, Genius makes frequent references to Apollonius's relationship with his people, stressing their harmonious interaction and common interests. When Apollonius is forced to leave Tyre secretly after he has returned from Antioch, the

---

[27] Robins, "Romance, Exemplum, and the Subject of the *Confessio Amantis*" 178.

REDEEMING DAUGHTERS: THAISE, PERONELLE, AND CONSTANCE

city is very sorry for his disappearance, because, among other reasons, he had left " 'Withoute the comun assent' " (493). Similarly, Genius also draws attention to the fact that, when Apollonius goes back to Tyre after Antiochus is dead and recovers his power, it is his people who tell him the news and who ask him to return. The lords of Tyre write to him, "in name of al the lond, and preie, / That left al other thing to done, / It like you to come sone" (1004–06). His people help mold and determine his actions.

The harmonious relationship between Apollonius and Tyre is described in terms that suggest an intimate relationship. When Apollonius left Tyre trying to escape from Antiochus, his city mourned him like an abandoned lover:

> They losten lust, they losten chiere,
> Thei toke upon hem such penaunce,
> Ther was no song, ther was no daunce,
> Bot every merthe and melodie
> To hem was thanne a maladie.   (476–80)

A similar loving relationship is suggested when Apollonius returns to Tyre after the apparent death of his wife. His subjects are first filled with joy at his return ("Was nevere yit in no cite / Such joie mad as thei tho made," 1316–17), and then mourn with him the death of his wife ("For he som confort wolde gete, / He let somoune a parlement," 1550–51). The intimacy of the relationship and the understanding between ruler and subjects plays on the metaphor of familial relationships. As Apollonius was honest in his relationship with his wife, and as he was honest in his relationship with his daughter, he is also honest in his relationship with his city. The city for its part also takes the initiative in ensuring a good relationship with its ruler, thus behaving like the good daughters in the tales analyzed in this chapter, i.e., Thaise, Constance, and Peronelle. These are active daughters who, like the city, not only comply with social rules, but also help their fathers comply with those rules.

The "Tale of Apollonius of Tyre" thus shows that the ideology that informs the power structures within the family and the ideology behind political power structures are not only similar but also mutually reinforcing. If one fails, the other fails. As I remark throughout this study, and as Genius presents them, family and politics, fathers and daughters, kings and subjects, are governed by similar and intricately connected dynamics. When a king and father like Apollonius, a people like Apollonius's subjects, and a daughter like Thaise work harmoniously in the interest of the common good rather than on behalf of their own personal advancement, there is peace and harmony, according to the intrinsic logic of the system. Indeed, Genius keeps reminding us, although the king is the fountain of the law, he is also subject to his own people. And, ultimately, both the people and the king are subject to a higher power.

Nevertheless, although Genius tries to "ground" Apollonius, his final words about him problematize the suggestion of an originary self that is afterwards molded by the circumstances. Notice Genius's words when Apollonius becomes king of Pentapolis at the request of his people:

> ... thei alle of on acord
> Him preiden, as here liege lord,
> That he the lettre wel conceive
> And come his regne to receive,
> Which god hath yove him and fortune. (1971–75)

Genius notes that the people ask him "alle of on acord," a politically charged term, as we will see in Chapter Four, that he assume this new power. But, more significantly, Genius mentions God (along with Fortune) as the ultimate source of power and authority ("Which god hath yove him and fortune"). Rather than his own moral groundedness, it is the intervention of God and Fortune that finally "ground" Apollonius.

Apollonius thus learns to become a good father and a good king, and he does so primarily because of external circumstances, such as God, Fortune, his subjects, his daughter, and, more fundamentally, his encounter with incest at the beginning of the tale. He becomes, rather than "is," a centered self through repeated actions. Similarly, Thaise "becomes" a redeeming daughter and, with her female eloquence, helps her father to avoid incest. In the next tale under discussion, the "Tale of the Three Questions," another daughter, Peronelle, cooperates with the system, playing a public role in order to mediate between her father and her king and preventing the latter from committing some excesses. But, again, the threat of instability lurks behind Genius's attempts to define roles clearly and delimit authority in stable ways.

The Tale of The Three Questions

The "Tale of the Three Questions" (1.3067–3402) starts in the masculine world of the court of King Alphonse, a proud king. Alphonse is surrounded by wise men who try to answer the questions he asks them. One of his knights, Petro, always gives the correct answers. Annoyed at this, King Alphonse, who wants to show that he is the wisest man in his country, issues the ultimate challenge to Petro. The knight has to find the answer to three obscure questions, and, if he fails, King Alphonse states, "he schal be ded / And lese hise goodes and his hed" (3114–15). A conflict of authority between a king and a subject in the public world, then, is the starting focus of the plot. The focus changes when Petro goes from the public setting of the court to his own private house. The younger of his two daughters, Peronelle, meets him in their garden and convinces him to let her answer the questions. Back in the court, Peronelle impresses the king by giving the correct answers. The king then says that he would marry her if she were of noble stock, and he offers her anything she wants. Peronelle asks him to make her father an earl. When the king does so, she argues that since her father is an earl, she is noble herself and, thus, the king should keep his word and marry her. The king, impressed by her wit, gives his consent and they marry.

If we follow Genius's own interpretation, the "Tale of the Three Questions" serves as an example of the virtue of humility. Throughout the tale, Genius repeatedly portrays Peronelle, the female protagonist, as a very humble character. For example, when he introduces her, he notes that she approaches her father "With humble herte" (3146). He also repeatedly describes her as kneeling both before her father, when she asks him to let her know what worries him (3145), and again before the king (3346 and 3359). Humility is also the virtue Peronelle herself praises when she answers the king's second question, while pride is the one she derides in her answer to the third question. Genius's moral explanation of the "Tale of the Three Questions" emphasizes again the value of humility:

> Bot Humblesce is al otherwise,
> Which most is worth, and no reprise
> It takth ayein, bot softe and faire,
> If eny thing stond in contraire,
> With humble speche it is redresced. (3413–17)

This emphasis on humility has led some critics to read the tale primarily in terms of the virtue.[28] But humility is also the traditional virtue of the Virgin Mary, and Peronelle's own invocation of the Virgin in lines 3275–80 as well as her repeated acts of kneeling, a traditional Marian gesture, remind us of the Virgin.[29] Patrick Gallacher and Georgiana Donavin have emphasized the link between Peronelle and Mary.[30] Both suggest that the parallels enable the

---

[28] Fisher, *John Gower*, dismisses the tale as merely "a general illustration of the virtue of Humility with neither romantic nor political implications" (195). Emphasizing the tale's didacticism, Yeager, in both his article "John Gower and the Exemplum Form: Tale Models in the *Confessio Amantis*" (*Mediaevalia*, 8 [1982]: 325–30), and his book, *John Gower's Poetic*, argues that it shows four interconnected illustrations of the virtue of humility, Peronelle being one of them. In Yeager's view, Peronelle is an allegory of humility (*John Gower's Poetic* 143).

[29] For kneeling as a typical gesture of the Virgin Mary in medieval iconography and, generally, for the association of the Virgin Mary with the virtue of humility, see Marina Warner, *Alone of All Her Sex: The Myth and the Cult of the Virgin Mary* (New York: Vintage Books, 1983) 177–85. Warner argues that this association started to become popular around the middle of the fourteenth century due to "[t]he impact of the friars' new ethic on the cult of the Virgin Mary" (182). Warner goes on to observe that "[i]t was a logical development of Franciscan piety that the Virgin should kneel in adoration before her newborn child: one icon of sublime humility before another" (183).

[30] For the association of humility and the Virgin with Peronelle in the "Tale of the Three Questions," see Patrick J. Gallacher, *Love, the Word, and Mercury: A Reading of John Gower's Confessio Amantis* (Albuquerque: U of New Mexico P, 1975) 37–40. Gallacher has analyzed the religious allusions and has concluded that the tale is a kind of allegory of the Annunciation (37–40). Peronelle, in his interpretation, represents Mary, and "the kinges word" (3369), invoked by Peronelle, evokes "the connotations of the *Verbum*" (40). More recently, Donavin, *Incest Narratives*, has further expanded on the allegorical reading, identifying both the king and Petro with Jesus (142–49).

characters in the tale to transcend their reality. To Donavin, for instance, there is a hint of an incestuous passion in the relationship between Petro and Peronelle, but this passion "is providentially transformed to a yearning for human salvation, much as Mary and Jesus in the exegesis on the Song of Songs allude to an ineffable desire that results in the conception of the Savior" (55). Like Genius's own reading, though, such readings gloss over crucial political aspects of the tale.[31] Moreover, rather than emphasizing a transcendental and allegorical meaning, rather than transcending incestuous desire, as Donavin argues, the father-daughter pair, I suggest, reveals the extent to which the relationship between God and Mary articulates father-daughter relationships in medieval Christian culture. The God-Mary model, nevertheless, does not absolutely determine the construction of the relationship. Peronelle's complex role in the tale, her repeated enactment of Mary's role, points, if only briefly, to gaps and fissures in the construction of patriarchal rule.

Peronelle, indeed, plays a very active role in the tale, a role that Genius himself, in his desire to convey a single moral, ignores. From the moment she appears in the tale, Peronelle takes control of the plot and its outcome. Like Thaise, she uses her female eloquence to redeem her father and also to mediate between two men, her father and her king, thus preventing male violence from disrupting public life.[32] As soon as she knows about her father's plight, she persuades him to let her take charge, thus saving his life (preventing the king from killing him) and not only restoring his goods, but even making him a peer of the kingdom. Moreover, she arranges her own marriage with no less than the king, thus refusing to become a mere object of exchange between her father and a male suitor, and positioning herself as an agent in her own exchange – she becomes in a sense both the exchanger and the person exchanged. (This tale, more than others, emphasizes the economic nature of the system of exchange.) Peronelle reaches such a position by using humility. Her outwardly humble behavior allows her to empower herself without raising any suspicions. The fact that critics, and Genius, see her primarily as an example of the Christian ideal of feminine virtue, whose paragon is the Virgin Mary, proves the success of her strategy. Humility, we will see, becomes Peronelle's "masquerade" (in the sense Joan Rivière has used this term). She uses her humility as a masquerade with which she hides her use of power.

Her use of power, though, does not prove to be subversive but is ultimately

---

[31] Peck, *Kingship and Common Profit*, is the only critic who stresses the political significance of the tale and thus recognizes an aspect other than the religious one (55–58). Although at times, Peck argues, the tale suggests the "potentiality of self-destruction," it also shows "Gower's version of an ideal community" (58). Peck, however, also focuses on the exemplary nature of the tale.

[32] In this sense, she is like the wife in Chaucer's "Melibee," who, according to Wallace, *Chaucerian Polity*, "prevent[s] masculine violence from disrupting the public domain" (5).

contained, as it reproduces the political and social structures of exchange and the hierarchical relationships of authority between father and daughter, king and subject, God and Mary. As mentioned before, Strohm has argued that the late Middle Ages emphasized queens' roles as petitioners and intercessors, modelling them after the Virgin Mary and Esther and emphasizing "queenly access to mercy or compassion, personal experience of abjection or sorrow, and deference to established authority."[33] This role was not necessarily very powerful:

> This regrounded role promised women a particular kind of power, but power premised on exceptional vulnerability. It credited women with spiritual faculties but conditioned these faculties on an exclusion from the centers of mundane authority . . . It invited women to correct male judgment, so long as that judgement was modified or supplemented rather than overturned. (96)

In my analysis of Peronelle's actions, then, I share Strohm's "personal skepticism" (96) about the extent of her "feminine" power.

Peronelle does not ultimately subvert the hierarchical structure in which she is immersed. Her relationship with her father is replicated in her relationship with the king. As she persuades her father to tell her about his plight, she also persuades the king to spare her father's life by giving the right answers to the king's questions. Eventually too, she marries the king, thus substituting the king for her father as the authority figure over her. It is no surprise to find this structure of replication (or of supplantation), because both Petro and the king are father-figures for Peronelle and because she defines herself as a Mary-figure. Her desire to marry the king is a displacement of her relationship with her father from the father onto the king, her political father. In this sense, the "Tale of the Three Questions" bears an interesting resemblance to other stories of fathers and daughters, like the "Tale of Jephthah's Daughter" or the "Tale of Virginia," in which a father's conflict with an authority figure is solved by means of the daughter's sacrifice. In the case of the "Tale of the Three Questions" the daughter is not killed, but, giving herself up to the king, she mediates in the conflict between him and her father. Although the daughter's "sacrifice" in this case proves advantageous for herself, we can hardly ignore that this tale reproduces the same pattern whereby a daughter mediates between two male authority figures through some form of sacrifice. What is more, Peronelle's "sacrifice" not only serves to assuage the conflict between her father and her king, but it also serves to restrain the king's attempt to abuse his own authority. King Alphonse's threat to kill Petro if he cannot answer his questions represents a capricious abuse of his authority. Peronelle's action prevents the king from following his capricious decision to its utmost consequences. While her manipulation of humility serves her personally, as it certainly advances her own social position, it also confirms

---

[33] Strohm, *Hochon's Arrow* 96.

and supports the established structures of authority and the system of exchange. She ultimately becomes a redeeming daughter.

My analysis will start by examining the significance of Peronelle's female eloquence and arguing that her role is not subversive. I will, nevertheless, also contend that even though Peronelle's actions are not ultimately subversive, they do show gaps and fissures in the system of exchange and in the definition of father-daughter and king-subject relationships. Even as it contains it, the tale shows the potential both for female power and for the disruption of the system of exchange. Peronelle takes on an active public role and suggests the possibility that a woman can take control of language and thus of the system of exchange, even as she herself does not ultimately take advantage of that possibility.

The relationship between Petro and Peronelle is set in highly ambiguous terms from the very beginning. The first time father and daughter meet, in the garden scene, it becomes clear that they enjoy a certain intimacy that is tinged with incestuous overtones, overtones suggested by the courtly love connotations and the parallels with the "Tale of Apollonius." Donavin has fittingly compared this scene and the setting to the lover's garden in *Le Roman de la Rose* (54). In their conversation, courtly love vocabulary and behavior predominate. This is especially true in the case of Peronelle, who acts as lover and seductress, trying to persuade her father to let her take charge of the situation. When she sees her father in the garden, he is alone and, Genius notes, "sorwe and sike" (3140), because he cannot find the answers to the questions. But notice also the resemblance to the recognition scene in "Apollonius," when Apollonius is feeling sad and is consoled by his daughter Thaise – even though initially they do not recognize each other. Peronelle, then, kneels in front of Petro and asks him to tell her why he has such "hevy chiere" (3148). In order to persuade him, she recalls times when he would tell her his "privite" (3157), a word that, as we have seen, is charged with ambiguity in the *Confessio Amantis* – most significantly, it is used by Apollonius to refer to Antiochus's incestuous relationship with his daughter (8.426). In these lines, as Donavin notes, Peronelle alludes "to a world in which there is 'non other' but her father and herself . . . describing the exclusionary microcosm of the Court of Love" (54). Peronelle then starts weeping and even cries "merci" like traditional (usually male) courtly lovers. She finally succeeds in persuading her father not only to tell her his "privite," but also to let her take charge of the situation. Like Thaise, Peronelle is an eloquent and wise daughter whose words create incestuous desire through her courtly love language, and, at the same time, as I will argue later, her words also displace that desire as she uses them later to seduce the king.

Peronelle's wisdom can also be seen in her acute awareness regarding her own situation within her family and thus as an object of exchange. When Genius describes Petro's family, he merely remarks that he had a wife (3130), and "children ek also, / Of whiche he hadde dowhtres tuo" (3131–32). Genius does not specify whether among his children Petro also had any sons.

Significantly, Peronelle herself gives us more details about her family. When she tries to convince her father that he should tell her his "privite," she mentions the existence of a brother and a sister:

> ... ye such trust have on me leid,
> That to my soster ne my brother,
> In al this world ne to non other,
> Ye dorste telle a privite
> So wel, my fader, as to me.   (3154–58)

It is significant that, unlike Genius, Peronelle does not forget about her brother and sister. Unlike other daughters in Gower's tales, e.g., Constance, Thaise, or Rosiphelee, Peronelle is not the only heir to her father. And she is very aware of her position within her family, within their private world – she is the "yongest" child.

This position has fundamental economic implications for her, which the tale does not ignore. In fact, the economic factor plays a major role in the tale and references to it recur throughout. Petro's life is consistently equated with his goods from the very beginning of the tale. When the king challenges the knight, he says that if he fails, he shall "lese hise goodes and his hed" (3116). Petro's potential loss of his goods would certainly affect Peronelle. As the younger member of the family, and a daughter at that, Peronelle is already at a disadvantage from an economic point of view. Being the youngest of Petro's children, Peronelle's value as an object of exchange would not be very high, especially since her father is a mere "Bacheler" (3373).[34] But if her father were to fail to answer the king's questions, Peronelle's situation would be even worse, since Petro would lose not only his life, but also, as he himself tells her, "al my good" (3181). If her father lost his goods she would lose her dowry and any chance of making an advantageous marriage. Peronelle's mention of her brother, moreover, further shows that she is aware of her own economic position. This awareness can also be seen when she tells her father that she wants to save not only his life but also his goods: "For yit par chaunce I may pourchace / With som good word the kinges grace, / Your lif and ek your good to save" (3203–05). (Notice here the verb "pourchace," which suggests an economic exchange.) Genius echoes Peronelle's words when he notes that Petro, about to reply to her offer, "betre him thoghte in aventure / To put his lif and al his good" (3212–13).[35] Thus, his life is as important as his goods,

---

[34] The Middle English Dictionary defines "bacheler" first as a "young man" or "an aspirant to knighthood." But "bacheler" can also refer to a rank within knighthood. He can be "a knight in service of another knight, a nobleman, or the king" or "a knight in the social scale, ranking just below the hereditary nobleman; a knight belonging to the lower of the two ranks of kinghts." On ranks within knighthood, see Maurice Keen, *Chivalry* (New Haven: Yale UP, 1984) 168ff. Keen notes that the rank of knight bachelor was below that of knight banneret (168).

[35] The word "aventure" suggests a parallel with the "Tale of Florent" (1.1407–1861), a famous tale in which a knight finally decides to put his life in the old hag's hands. Petro puts

and Peronelle takes charge not only in order to save her father's life, but also to save his goods, which ultimately will ensure her own exchange value.

Peronelle's ambition goes beyond merely ensuring her own value as a gift, though. Refusing to become a passive "gift" in the system of exchange, she even increases that value when she arranges her own exchange in order to become a queen. Peronelle's wisdom empowers her to choose her own husband, thus breaking the bipolar relationship whereby two men (the father and the male suitor) exchange a woman (the daughter). Bypassing her father's patriarchal prerogatives over her future, she becomes one of the exchangers herself. It is significant that, as noted above, she exerts her power to exchange herself through words. In Lévi-Strauss's theory of kinship, words are like women in that both are means of communication, signs that men exchange; quoting from W. I. Thomas, he states that " 'exogamy and language . . . have fundamentally the same function – communication and integration with others.' "[36] Lévi-Strauss further adds that, "the relations between the sexes can be seen as one of the modalities of the great 'communication function' which also includes language" (494).[37] But Lévi-Strauss acknowledges a major problem in his theory and makes a caveat as regards his equation of woman and sign: "woman could never become just a sign and nothing more, since even in a man's world she is still a person, and since in so far as she is defined as a sign she must be recognized as a generator of signs" (496). Peronelle shows that woman is not simply a word, but a user and manipulator of words too – a generator of signs. More importantly, entering the masculine and public world of exchange, she uses language to displace incestuous desire.

Peronelle enters this world by subtle means. Her aspirations to marry a king, being as she is the daughter of a "Bacheler," is at odds with the humble Peronelle that critics describe to us. If Peronelle does not have the right to marry a king, and if she is so humble, why does she trick King Alphonse into marrying her? It is also at odds with Gower's own definition of humility in *Mirour de l'Omme*. In his description of the virtue of humility, Gower uses Gregory's *Moralia* as his authority:

> Gregoire dist en son Moral,
> Trois choses par especial
> D'umilité font demoustrance:
> C'est le primer et principal,
> Ses sovereins en general
> Obeie sanz desobeissance,
> En fait, en dit, en contenance;
> Puis n'appara par demoustrance

---

his life in a female figure's hands too, his own daughter. Once his life is saved he does not have to marry her, but the man she marries is a socially acceptable substitute for himself.
[36] Claude Lévi-Strauss, *Elementary Structures of Kinship* 493.
[37] See my discussion of the feminist critique of Lévi-Strauss's theories in Chapter One.

>   Q'a son pareil soit parigal,
>   Ne des soubgitz vaine honourance
>   Requiere.... ³⁸

Peronelle fails especially with regard to the second requirement explained in this passage: she manages to ascend the social scale and appear equal, not merely to her neighbor, but to her king. Moreover, by marrying the king she will not be able to comply with another feature of those who are humble:

>   Om dist auci q'abitement
>   En terre basse seurement
>   Valt plus q'en halt, u l'en cherra:
>   Pour ce cil qui vit humblement
>   Se tient en bass si fermement,
>   Qe d'orguil monter ne porra.   (12535–40)³⁹

As a queen, Peronelle would be in the highest position, from where she might fall ("u l'en cherra").

As I noted above, and as critics have amply demonstrated, not only does Peronelle use the humility *topos*, but she also draws parallels between herself and the Virgin Mary during the Annunciation scene.⁴⁰ However, although there are definite and significant allusions to the Virgin and to the Annunciation, the traditional interpretation of the tale as a parallel to the Annunciation cannot account for some significant differences between the two daughters. The parallel does not just show an unproblematic re-enactment of that scene in which Christian values, and especially the association of Peronelle's apparent humility with the humility of God's Daughter, go uncontested. Mary did not actively attract God or ask Him to choose her; neither did she trick God into "marrying" her, but passively obeyed Him. Peronelle, by contrast, takes control of the situation by manipulating the humility *topos*

---

38 Quoted from *The Complete Works of John Gower: The French Works*, ed. G. C. Macaulay, vol. 1 (Oxford: Clarendon Press, 1899): 12433–43. In *John Gower: Mirour de l'Omme*, trans. William Burton Wilson (East Lansing, MI: East Lansing Colleagues Press, 1992), the passage is translated as follows:
> Gregory says in his *Moralia* that three things especially demonstrate Humility. The first and principal thing is to obey one's sovereign in deed, in word, and in appearance; next, not to try to appear equal to one's neighbor; and finally not to require vain honor from one's subordinates.

39 Wilson translates this passage as follows: "It is also said that living in a low place is better than living in a high one, where one might fall. Therefore, he who lives humbly holds himself down so firmly that he cannot mount up in pride."

40 Gallacher, *Love, the Word, and Mercury* 37–40, and Donavin, *Incest Narratives* 142–49, for instance, have analyzed these Annunciation motifs. Peronelle's kneeling in front of her father and in front of the king parallels the Virgin's kneeling before her son and before Gabriel at the Annunciation. The daughter also plays an intercessory role for her father. She mediates between her father and the king and allows him to regain the king's "grace." Moreover, in her response to the second question, Peronelle alludes to the Virgin's "humble entente" as what made God choose her to bear Jesus (3275–80).

and the parallel that she draws between herself and the Virgin Mary. Even if Peronelle is Genius's character and Gower's ultimate creation, it is still significant that Genius has Peronelle herself, in her own speeches, with her own words, draw those parallels. Peronelle also kneels repeatedly, enacting Mary's role. But why does Peronelle draw these parallels and, more importantly, why is it significant that at least for a moment we can entertain the possibility that Peronelle is independent from her male creators?

Peronelle uses language, or her female eloquence, to draw the parallels, and it is by means of language (her three answers) that she saves her father. It is also by using language that she arranges her marriage; she takes advantage of the value of a king's word in order to make King Alphonse fulfill his promise: "And this wot every worthi lif, / A kinges word it mot ben holde" (3368–69). Language appears to be another form of economic exchange, a form of communication. Peronelle takes language out of male control and uses it to exert control over her two fathers – her biological father, Petro, and her political father, King Alphonse. Her control over her father and the king is manifested in her seduction of them by means of words. In a sense, she is also taking control over Genius's own language. Although, on the one hand, this language is ultimately the language of the father in a Lacanian sense and thus manifests her subordination – it is even literally the language of father Genius – on the other, *pace* Butler, in taking control of it and in using mimicry to manipulate it, as we will see, she is pointing to the gaps and fissures in the system of exchange; for a moment, her mimicry and her manipulation of language open up the possibility of female agency.

Indeed, Peronelle's manipulation of humility resembles the manipulation of femininity by certain women that Joan Rivière has analyzed in her essay "Womanliness as a Masquerade," despite the historical distance between these examples.[41] Rivière undertook a study of a woman who was very succesful in her profession. She was an academic woman who spoke in public and who manifested a tendency to exaggerate her femininity and to seek the approval of men. Women like the one Rivière studied, she notes, "may put on a mask of womanliness to avert anxiety and the retribution feared from men" (35). The mask, in other words, helps them cover their desire for power, which to Rivière is ultimately a desire to take the place of the father (41). Like "womanliness," Peronelle's humility functions as a masquerade. Her manipulation of humility resembles Rivière's woman's use of femininity to hide her desire for, and her use of, power. The comparison between womanliness and humility proves to be even more pertinent when we remember that humility is often represented as a feminine virtue, and, especially in the "Tale of the Three Questions," that the epitome of humility is also the epitome of femininity, the Virgin Mary. In the end, Peronelle obtains what she wants and is still seen as a perfectly humble and virtuous woman.

---

[41] Joan Rivière, "Womanliness as a Masquerade," *Formations of Fantasy*, eds. Victor Burgin, James Donald, and Cora Kaplan (London: Methuen, 1986) 35–61.

Butler has developed some of Rivière's suggestions establishing a link between power and words.[42] In the case of the particular woman Rivière has analyzed, Butler remarks,

> the rivalry with the father is not over the desire of the mother, as one might expect, but over the place of the father in public discourse as speaker, lecturer, writer – that is, as a user of signs rather than a sign-object, an item of exchange. This castrating desire might be understood as the desire to relinquish the status of woman-as-sign in order to appear as a subject within language. (51)

In the "Tale of the Three Questions," I would argue, rather than competing with her father for her mother, Peronelle also refuses to become a mere sign, something spoken about. When she answers the questions, Peronelle is literally taking the place of her father, in order to enter public discourse and take control over her own exchange, assuming an active part within the masculine play of power. After persuading her father in the private realm, Peronelle enters the public world, the court, where she succeeds in persuading her other father, the king.

Although Peronelle's actions do not ultimately prove to be subversive, her self-empowerment suggests that in the system there are unstable points that a woman can manipulate to her own advantage; without subverting the system, she does open up a space for subversion. It will be useful to mention here Susan Crane's use of the concept of masquerade in her analysis of some of Chaucer's romance female characters in the *Canterbury Tales*.[43] One of the uses of masquerade Crane describes is what she calls "vocal mimicry," that is, when characters use courtly *topoi* against themselves in their "attempts to resist the scripted roles of courtship" (60–61). Crane argues that Dorigen in the "Franklin's Tale" and the falcon in the "Squire's Tale" make such a use of vocal mimicry. In Gower's tale, Peronelle also uses vocal and gestural mimicry in her imitation of the Virgin Mary. However, unlike Chaucer's Dorigen or Canacee, she is not so much resisting the scripted roles of, in her case, the Christian religion, as she is manipulating them.

Nevertheless, as she advances her position, Peronelle does not ultimately undermine the system. Although she manages to position herself as a speaking subject, a "generator of words," she does so to participate and reaffirm the system of exchange. It is not coincidental, in this sense, that she decides to marry the king. While this manifests her ambition to move up the social scale, it also suggests a displacement of her desire for her father onto the king. Such a displacement is far from being subversive. For one thing, the king is in a sense a father for his subjects, as I argue in this book, and thus another father for her. For another, as Donavin has pointed out, the king is a

---

[42] Butler, *Gender Trouble* 50–54.
[43] Susan Crane, *Gender and Romance in Chaucer's* Canterbury Tales (Princeton: Princeton UP, 1994). See ch. 2, "Feminine Mimicry and Masquerade."

God-figure (57), which suggests that ultimately Peronelle still responds to the scripted role of God and Mary. In this sense, Peronelle just displaces her desire for her biological father onto her political father and thus allows the reproduction of patriarchal structures of authority. Her potentially subversive empowerment through words ultimately works to sustain and repeat the accepted structures of kinship. To quote Strohm again, the new intecessory role of queens "invited women to correct male judgement, so long as that judgment was modified or supplemented rather than overturned" (96). Peronelle's action modifies but does not overturn the system. In fact, it improves significantly her father's social status and wealth and also provides a wife to a bachelor king, thus ensuring the continuation of the royal line and the enactment of the law of exogamy.

Genius's reading of the tale is significant. There is a discrepancy between Genius's narrative and the moral he imposes on it. In order to make his point, Genius glosses over Peronelle's ambition and focuses on her apparent humility. This emphasis on her outward humility ignores her show of power when she arranges to be married to the king himself. The limitation of Genius's own interpretation reveals the workings of moralistic literature. In order to make one point and support a clear model of conduct, *exempla* have to simplify the human psychology. Linda Burke, for instance, cites the story of Judith as an example of the discrepancy between an original story and the moralists' reading of it.[44] In the *exempla* Judith is "commended for her chaste widowhood," while much more active traits like her "military courage," and, I would add, her defeat of male power, are simply ignored (54).[45] Similarly, Peronelle's actions question the final religious lesson that Genius, as well as the critics, want to draw from the tale; the potential subversiveness of her own ambition and desire and of her control of language is "tamed" by Genius's moral. More clearly than Thaise, Peronelle points to the gaps and fissures in the system of exchange, but both her final submission to the system and Genius's interpretation of her behavior close the gap opened by her show of power.

In the "Tale of Constance," analyzed next, female eloquence cooperates again with the system of exchange. Constance, another daughter, uses language as "wisely" as Petro's daughter, avoiding incest and complying with social rules. Although, unlike Peronelle, Constance does not take a direct, active role in her own exchange, she does facilitate the process through her wisdom and words. But the "Tale of Constance," unlike the "Tale of the Three Questions," takes the implications of incestuous desire a step further. After performing her social and religious role, Constance is allowed to go

---

[44] Linda Barney Burke, "Women in the Medieval Manuals of Religious Instruction and John Gower's *Confessio Amantis*," diss. Columbia University, 1982, 54.

[45] For similar but later interpretations, see also Elena Ciletti, "Patriarchal Ideology in the Renaissance Iconography of Judith," *Refiguring Woman: Perspectives on Gender and the Italian Renaissance*, eds. Marilyn Migiel and Juliana Schiesari (Ithaca, NY: Cornell UP, 1991) 35–70.

back to her biological father, and in this way she confirms the desire created by the incest taboo. The "Tale of Constance," moreover, reveals more explicitly very specific fourteenth-century English political concerns. The theme of incest is used to raise questions about the struggle for power between lay and clerical authority in the fourteenth century.

The Tale of Constance[46]

The importance of the father-daughter relationship and the underlying but inexplicit incest motif in the "Tale of Constance" (2.587–1603), as well as in Chaucer's version of the story in the "Man of Law's Tale," is now generally recognized among critics.[47] Gower's source, Trivet's version of the legend in *Les Chroniques*, avoids alluding to the incest motif in the original sources, but critics agree that Gower must have also known versions other than Trivet's in which a daughter has to escape her father's incestuous desires.[48] Although in Gower, as well as in Trivet and Chaucer, this relationship is pushed to the margins of the story (it is mentioned at the beginning and at the end), it is crucial as it envelops Constance's life. In highlighting the father-daughter relationship, Gower brings the "Tale of Constance" closer to the "Tale of Apollonius." Peter Goodall has noticed that the two stories have many struc-

---

[46] The following section has been adapted from my "Engendering Authority: Father and Daughter, State and Church in Gower's 'Tale of Constance' and Chaucer's 'Man of Law's Tale,'" *Re-Visioning Gower*, ed. Yeager, 129–46. Used by permission of Pegasus Press, Asheville, North Carolina.

[47] The first critic to make this point was Margaret Schlauch, *Chaucer's Constance and Accused Queens* (New York: New York UP, 1927) 133. More recently, Elizabeth Archibald, "The Flight from Incest: Two Late Classical Precursors of the Constance Theme," *Chaucer Review* 20 (1986): 259–72, has expanded on Schlauch's suggestions. Among the few Gower critics who have analyzed the incest motif are Donavin, *Incest Narratives* (esp. 57–63), and Allen, "Chaucer Answers Gower" – my reading differs from theirs, as I will explain below. The function of the incest motif has been more frequently analyzed in the past years by critics of Chaucer's tale. See, for example, R. A. Shoaf, "'Unwemmed Custance': Circulation, Property, and Incest in the Man of Law's Tale," *Exemplaria* 2.1 (1990): 287–302; and, especially, Dinshaw's chapter, "The Law of Man and Its 'Abhomynaciouns,'" in her book *Chaucer's Sexual Poetics*. Dinshaw's feminist analysis of the father-daughter incest subtext of Chaucer's tale partly informs my own analysis of Gower's tale. See also, Elizabeth Scala, "Canacee and the Chaucer Canon: Incest and Other Unnarratables," *Chaucer Review* 30 (1996): 15–39.

[48] We do not know the exact dates of composition of Chaucer's and Gower's versions. However, we know that Gower must have written the first recension of the *Confessio Amantis* in the 1380s and must have finished it by 1390. Critics generally agree that Chaucer wrote his "Man of Law's Tale" around 1390 and thus that Chaucer knew Gower's "Tale of Constance" when he wrote his version of it. For a discussion of the dates of composition of the two tales, see Patricia J. Eberle's introduction to her explanatory notes on "The Man of Law's Tale" in *The Riverside Chaucer* 856–57. For an analysis of the date and circumstances in which Trivet's *Chronique* was produced, see Ruth Dean, "Nicholas Trevet, Historian," *Medieval Learning and Literature: Essays Presented to Richard William Hunt*, eds. J. J. G. Alexander and M. T. Gibson (Oxford: Oxford UP, 1976) 339–49.

tural and thematic similarities: "[I]n both [stories] the father-daughter relationship is especially significant and the reunion of husband and wife is overshadowed by the reunion of father and daughter – indeed it is the reunion which completes the structure of the work."[49] Both Gower and Chaucer are aware of these similarities. But Gower's version of the legend of Constance does the opposite of what Chaucer's Man of Law's version tries to do: while the Man of Law explicitly differentiates the Constance story from a story like that of Apollonius of Tyre, Goodall notes, Gower links them closely (96). Gower, I further argue, is interested in exploring the father-daughter relationship and its implications, while the Man of Law tries to suppress those implications. As Allen has observed, in Gower's version there are constant reminders that this was originally a story of father-daughter incest: "Gower breaks down the heroine's saint-like immunity from violation and calls up threats that evoke or resemble the secret tyranny of incest" (646). In this way, Allen continues, "our initial assumption that Constance experiences no threat of incest becomes increasingly less comfortable" (646).

Constance, the only daughter of the Emperor Constantine, shares many features with Peronelle, Petro's daughter, and Thaise, Apollonius's daughter. Like these daughters, Constance is articulate, she has female eloquence, and she uses her command of language to exert a certain form of power, a power that goes beyond the private sphere. One of the first things Genius notes about her is that she converted the men of "Barbarie" with "hire wordes wise" (606). Just as Peronelle seduced the king with both her "wordes wise" and her humility, Constance persuades and converts the sultan's men, the sultan himself, and Allee, with her religious speech.[50] Constance's religious function, though, is as important as her social role. Her speeches, whether rendered directly or indirectly, tend to be geared towards both religious and social functions. Whenever she speaks, or whenever Genius decides to render her speech directly, she prays, asks for God's help, or shows her sense of social duty. Although Constance does not utter many speeches in the tale, unlike Peronelle or Thaise, Genius emphasizes that she does speak, and that her speech exerts a definite power, since she uses it to convert people.[51] Her language thus has a markedly public function.

Gower's Constance, Winthrop Wetherbee has argued, not only plays an important role but her helplessness is not portrayed in such a pathetic tone as that of Chaucer's Custance.[52] Even though Constance is not as pathetic as Custance, however, Genius's heroine, I will argue, is constrained and pathetic

---

[49] Peter Goodall, " 'Unkynde Abhomynaciouns' in Chaucer and Gower," *Parergon*, n.s. 5 (1987): 97.
[50] Gallacher has pointed out that, "[t]he persuasive speech of Constance on behalf of the Christian Faith generates the events of the story" (93).
[51] In this respect, Gower's Constance is also very different from Chaucer's Custance, whose speech is often rendered directly by the Man of Law.
[52] Winthrop Wetherbee, "Constance and the World in Chaucer and Gower," *John Gower*, ed. Yeager, 65–93.

to the extent that her active role in the tale is mostly conditioned by her social and religious functions. Only at the very end does she act according to what Genius presents as her own desires. Constance's public role, therefore, is as problematic as Custance's, since it stems from a sense of duty that puts the social and the religious before the individual, in a way denying and suppressing her desire for the sake of society. In the following analysis, I will argue, first, that Gower's Constance is denied her individuality and desire, but only to an extent. This denial is geared towards facilitating her exchange and avoiding the threat of incest. As in the cases of Peronelle and Thaise, Constance's use of speech shows her compliance with the social injunction to avoid incest. Thus the theme of the tale does not revolve around a confrontation between the daughter and the patriarchal system of exchange, as is the case in other tales that I will anayze later on, but, quite to the contrary, on a daughter's perfect compliance with the demands of the system. These demands, moreover, are articulated through her father's commands to Constance, which she obeys dutifully.

Constance, nevertheless, is denied her individuality and desire only to an extent. This is particularly significant given the incest theme in the tale. Arno Esch has remarked that "Constance always retains something cool, strange, impersonal," qualities that he attributes to her saint-like character.[53] Esch is certainly right to note that the tale draws from the genre of saints' legends, but Constance's "mystery" comes from reasons more complicated than her saintliness. Gower's tale is not a saint's life, and his heroine is more complex than the typical saint. That "mystery" comes from her silences. Her silences suggest that Genius is trying to depict Constance as an individual with some agency. As Allen has put it, "Gower raises the question of where [Constance's] own agency might, or should, begin" (642). Constance thus can be seen as an example of the "intersected subject" that Robins has found to be typical of the *Confessio Amantis*. She is defined by certain types of discourse, religious and social; she becomes the voice of those discourses. But the tale still presents her as retaining a certain sense of individuality, a sense of choice. In this sense, the tale seems to show us that, as Robins has argued, Gower still believes in an interiority from which we make choices (178). However, as I mentioned before, I do not think that we can determine whether Gower believed in an interiority or not. I will be more concerned, therefore, with examining why Gower creates this sense of choice and individuality.

At certain points in the tale there are details, primarily her silences, that take the Lévi-Straussian link between words and women a step further than other tales. During her stay in England and in Rome with Salustes and his wife, she remains silent about her past and about her true identity. For Schlauch, those silences are evidence that the tale was originally a tale about

---

[53] Arno Esch, "John Gower's Narrative Art," trans. Linda Barney Burke, *Gower's Confessio Amantis: A Critical Anthology*, ed. Nicholson (Cambridge: D. S. Brewer, 1991) 106.

the flight of a daughter from her father (133). The daughter has to remain silent about her past, so that her father will not be able to find her. In Gower's tale, though, those silences serve a further purpose. Allen contends that they reveal that Constance does not yet have a stable social role. Dinshaw argues about Chaucer's heroine that "Constance's limited self-consciousness serves patriarchy."[54] In the following analysis I will argue first that they help construct Constance's desire and thus characterize her as an individual, a self. Second, taking Schlauch's suggestion a step further, I will demonstrate that they are also significant in the context of Gower's exploration of the theme of incest in the tale.

The "Tale of the Three Questions" and the "Tale of Apollonius" hint at the incestuous overtones in the relationship between Peronelle and Thaise, on the one hand, and their respective fathers, on the other. In the case of Constance, Gower not only hints at the incestuous implications of the father-daughter relationship but even follows those implications through to the end. After her second husband dies, Constance and her father are finally allowed to reunite for good. In this sense, her use of silence becomes significant. While Constance, like Peronelle and Thaise, uses language to comply and promote a certain social and religious ideology, she alone also uses, in significant ways, the power that comes from the control over the flow of words, that is, from silence. Thus, even though her silence subjects her to others' misreadings, as Allen has argued (642), they also manifest her control over her own destiny. Constance's silences are unlike those of the daughters who escape from their fathers in the folk tales. Her silences are not evidence that she tries to hide from her own father; rather, they suggest that she does not want to reveal her past and her desire to others, that she does have some control over it.

Moreover, while those silences protect her as an individual, protect her own desires, they also mark a boundary between two realms. They are significant because they show Genius constructing the realms of the speakable and the unspeakable and delimiting boundaries between them. Thus, her conscious use of silence becomes fundamental as it helps construct those domains. The construction of such an opposition, as I argue in this book, is intricately connected to the construction of the incest taboo as a law of discourse, as Butler puts it, "distinguishing the speakable from the unspeakable (delimiting and constructing the domain of the unspeakable), the legitimate from the illegitimate."[55] Indeed, if Peronelle and Thaise manifest the Lévi-Straussian parallel between women and words as objects of exchange, as examples of "the great 'communication function'" (494), then the absence of words, silence, indicates the refusal to communicate, and, hence, the refusal to exchange. Throughout most of the tale, Constance "commu-

---

54 Carolyn Dinshaw, *Chaucer's Sexual Poetics* 112.
55 Butler, *Gender Trouble* 65.

nicates," but there are also significant moments when she refuses to do so. I will return to this point later.

In the following analysis I will explain first Gower's exploration of the theme of father-daughter relationships and the incest taboo in the "Tale of Constance." I start by examining the religious and social aspects of Constance's role, particularly the fulfilment of the demands of the system of exchange whereby Constantine has to exchange his daughter. Despite her compliance, Constance performs a role that is more active and public than critics usually concede. This role suggests that she will comply with the incest taboo, but her silences also suggest that she has a desire (an unspeakable desire) which, nevertheless, she controls. Second, I will argue that Gower uses the theme of father-daughter incest to explore a political theme in the tale, namely, the question of the relationship between lay and clerical power, or the distribution of power between State and Church. The relationship between Constantine and Constance enables Gower to explore and define the relationship between State and Church, between temporal and spiritual power. Such a relationship is defined within the matrix of familial relationships and along gender lines, as Constance figures as mother and wife, as well as daughter, of the emperor. Through this particular story, Gower presents the Church in a subordinate role to royal power, but he also suggests at the same time that lay power defines its relationship of authority with the Church in a manner that is charged with incestuous overtones.

Genius focuses at first on Constance's religious side. He introduces her as the only child of the Emperor Constantine and his wife Ytalie, and he hastens to add that she was devoted to God. At first, Gower's priest does not leave room for any aspect other than the religious one in Constance. She is unlike most of Genius's other female protagonists whose physical and spiritual attributes he describes as soon as he introduces them. For example, Peronelle is introduced as the "yongest" (3133) of Petro's children and, he adds, "of visage / Sche was riht fair, and of stature / Lich to an hevenely figure" (3134–36); while he introduces Rosiphelee, another daughter, as a woman "of gret renomee / For sche was bothe wys and fair" (4.1250–51). Constance, by contrast, is Constantine's only daughter; he and his wife,

> No children hadde bot a Maide;
> And sche the god so wel apaide,
> That al the wide worldes fame
> Spak worschipe of hire goode name.   (593–96)

Genius does not provide any other description of Constance until we are told that the sultan fell in love with her "beaute and ... grace" (622), as described, interestingly enough, by his own men. Trivet also focuses on her devotion when he introduces Constance, but the Man of Law describes her beauty and spiritual qualities from the very beginning: "A doghter [Constantine] hath that, syn the world bigan, / To rekene as wel hir goodnesse as beautee, / Nas nevere swich another as is shee" (157–59). Immediately afterwards, one of the merchants expands on her qualities, stressing her beauty, virtue, humility, courtesy, and holiness (162–68).

Soon enough, though, the overlap between the religious and the social becomes evident; the two are equally important in defining Constance and cannot be distinguished. Her religious conversion of the pagan merchants brings about her social exchange, while her social exchange brings about the conversion of the sultan. Throughout most of the tale, without voicing any complaints whatsoever, Constance is moved back and forth by others, according to her social and religious roles. First, her father sends her to "Barbarie" where she performs her two roles: by marrying the sultan she complies with the social necessity of her exchange, and by converting him she performs her religious function. Later on, once again someone else decides her destiny. Her first jealous mother-in-law kills Constance's husband and puts her on a ship. She reveals that she does so, as Wetherbee notes, for social reasons: "Gower's 'Sarazine' fears only the loss of secular status ('astat' [II.649]) that Constance's marriage to her son would entail."[56] Social reasons, thus, seem to determine Constance's new trip; but this trip also turns out to have a religious function: she introduces Christianity into England as a result of it. Finally, the second mother-in-law also determines her third trip, although we do not know her reasons for doing so; Genius only tells us that she forged her son's letter in order to send Constance off to the sea.

Constance's religious and social functions are highlighted even the first time she sleeps with Allee, her second husband. Genius describes the conception of their son Moris in terms that suggest that, like Peronelle, she is playing the role of the Virgin Mary:

> The hihe makere of nature
> Hire hath visited in a throwe,
> That it was openliche knowe
> Sche was with childe be the king.   (917–20)

The social and the religious work together at this moment. It seems to be God rather than Allee who makes her pregnant, alluding to the conception of Jesus and making her thus a Virgin-figure. On the other hand, her pregnancy is proclaimed "openliche," i.e., publicly; she is providing an heir for the king. By contrast, Trivet only mentions that Constance "conseut del rey [vn] enfaunt madle."[57] And the Man of Law makes sexual relationships a necessary evil, ignoring the social or the religious aspects of reproduction:

> For thogh that wyves be ful hooly thinges,
> They moste take in pacience at nyght

---

[56] Wetherbee, "Constance and the World" 71.
[57] Quoted from Margaret Schlauch, "The Man of Law's Tale," *Sources and Analogues of Chaucer's Canterbury Tales*, ed. W. F. Bryan and G. Dempster (Chicago: U of Chicago P, 1941) 172. All further quotations from Trivet's version of the Constance story are taken from the same edition.

> Swiche manere necessaries as been plesynges
> To folk that han ywedded hem with rynges
> And leye a lite hir hoolynesse aside. (709–13)

By stressing the idea that sex is opposed to holiness, the Man of Law divorces the moment of conception from any form of divine intervention. Likewise, he avoids the association of sex with the social need for reproduction.

Constance's sense of public duty overrides her own thoughts and feelings, even in the dramatic moment when she is set adrift with her son. This constitutes one of the few moments in which Genius renders directly a relatively long speech by his heroine. But in this case too, as her own words show, she does not reveal much about herself as an independent individual who has her own desires. The entire passage is worth quoting:

> 'Of me no maner charge it is
> What sorwe I soffre, bot of thee
> Me thenkth it is a gret pite,
> For if I sterve thou schalt deie
> So mot I nedes be that weie
> For Moderhed and for tendresse
> With al myn hole besinesse
> Ordeigne me for thilke office,
> As sche which schal be thi Norrice.' (1068–76)[58]

She reacts as the "perfect" nurturing mother, who only worries about her son not about herself. But the words she uses to describe her situation reveal an impersonal sense of duty. Words like "mot I nedes be," "besinesse," or "office" suggest that her mothering role is an injunction by society, a duty she has to perform, rather than her own individual choice.[59]

What Constance feels about her husbands also remains vague. We do not know what she thinks when she marries the sultan; and, when he is killed, we do not know if she is sad for having lost him. Although Genius does tell us that she made "many a wofull mone" (703), her "mone" is provoked by the massacre of all those who were at the wedding banquet – "hem [who] deie on every side" (701). Again, when King Allee falls in love with her, Genius tells us clearly what he feels, and only obliquely what she feels. When she marries him, Gower's priest remarks that "for no lust ne for no rage / Sche tolde hem nevere what sche was" (910–11). In general, we only know in a very indirect

---

[58] This passage is quite different from its equivalent in the "Man of Law's Tale," in which Constance does voice her anguish in a pathetic tone (451–60).
[59] Commenting on Genius's depiction of the moment when the sultan decides to marry Constance, Esch has noticed that "Gower's narrative manner resembles an impersonal report" (100). The same sense of impersonality tinges Constance's own words in the passage I have quoted. Esch notes that, unlike Chaucer's depiction of this scene, which "borders on sentimentality ... Gower aims at a typical and conventional picture" (104).

and vague manner about her reactions to the events that affect her, i.e., through Genius's reports rather than through her own direct speeches.

While speech, whether it is rendered directly or indirectly in the tale, constitutes a major defining feature of Gower's Constance, she also has significant moments of silence. One of the intriguing questions that the tale raises, as noted above, is why Constance hides her identity when she arrives in England and, later on, when she stays in Rome with the senator. In Genius's version, those silences acquire an added significance in the context of his tale and in view of Constance's final reunion with her father. Her production of "wise wordes" is a sign that Constance has learned to perform her religious and social duties, actively contributing to her exchange and separation from her father. But her silences suggest that despite her dedication to her religious and social mission, Constance also knows how to protect herself as an individual, and how to keep unspoken certain "non-social" aspects of herself that pose a threat to the system of exchange. In this way, to borrow Butler's terms, Contance's silences contribute to delimit and construct a domain of the unspeakable. The unspeakable is the refusal to "communicate" in Lévi-Strauss's sense, that is, both the refusal to speak and the refusal to comply with the laws of exchange.

Constance's remaining silent about her past and her identity is striking in view of Genius's notion of public and private in the tale, because her silences are associated with the notion of privacy, and privacy, as in the "Tale of Apollonius," sometimes carries negative connotations. In fact, it carries such negative connotations even within the tale itself. Thus, the "sinners" in the "Tale of Constance" always act privately. For instance, when the first mother-in-law learned about her son's wedding, envy started working inside her, Genius points out, "So prively that non was war" (642). By contrast, the public stands for positive qualities, like openness and truth. Thus, Constance and her religion are open, i.e., true and public. For example, after Hermyngheld performs the miracle of the blind man, Genius says that the miracle was an "open thing" (776). And when Constance conceives Moris, "it was openliche knowe / Sche was with childe be the king" (918–19). Constance, however, is not always "open" and public, and the negative connotations of doing things privately cast some shadows over her behavior in England and especially later in Rome.

The passage that relates the encounter between Senator Arcenne and Constance is particularly significant. The senator wants to know who she is, but she tells him in only vague terms, without revealing her identity, that her lord set her adrift with her son for reasons that escape her. Then she says she is a Christian and refuses to say anything else. Genius repeatedly remarks on her refusal to reveal more: "Bot forthermor for noght he preide / Of hire astat to knowe plein, / Sche wolde him nothing elles sein" (1164–66); and some lines later,

> Bot of Constance hou it was,
> That cowthe he knowe be no cas,

> Wher sche becam, so as he seide.
> Hire Ere unto his word she leide
> Bot forther made sche no chiere. (1187–91)

Constance's silent behavior during her stay with the senator is also significant for another reason. Not only does she control her past and her individuality by withholding some information, but she also uses language in two instances to avoid telling the truth. This fact is even more intriguing in view of Genius's concern in the tale with the opposition between true and false speech. Genius's tale is supposed to teach Amans that he should leave "wicke speche" (571), and thus we find that the sinners of the story are notorious for their "wicke speche." For instance, the sultan's mother "feigneth wordes in [her son's] Ere" (654), pretending that she is glad about his marriage. Or, the knight who kills Hermyngheld accuses Constance of murdering her, "He sclaundreth there in audience / With false wordes whiche he feigneth" (864–65). Surprisingly, later on we find out that Constance, the heroine of the tale and supposed model of true speech, of "wise wordes," can also feign. When she tells her name to the senator she says it is "Couste," and Genius, using again the verb "feign," remarks that "hire name . . . sche feigneth" (1167). Constance "feigns" a second time when she hears that her husband Allee has arrived in Rome. At the news, she swoons in front of the senator, and, in order not to reveal that Allee is her husband, Genius says that she "*feigneth* seknesse of the See" (1351). Constance's feigning suggests that there is more to her behavior than "true speech" and public actions.

The senator does not know the true reason why she swoons, but neither do we, nor, in a sense, does even Genius himself. The only reason Genius offers is that "it was for the king Allee, / For joie which fell in hire thoght / That god him hath to toune broght" (1352–54). But this is just Genius's interpretation, which evidences his own interested reading of the heroine of the story he is retelling. We have some good reasons for reading Constance's behavior differently. For instance, when Constance and Allee actually reunite, Genius tells us that Allee is very happy (1439–45), and comments briefly on her reaction. Constance, he says, "hadde a gret part of [Allee's] wille" (1447). This reaction, defined in terms of Allee's will, contrasts with the joy she manifests, as we will see, when she reunites with her father. Thus, while the heroine is supposed to be a model of true speech, it is striking that that same heroine also uses speech, or rather non-speech, silence, to keep some things private.

Genius's treatment of the father-daughter relationship reveals a different side to Constance, a side that remains unspoken. When father and daughter reunite for the first time after her wanderings about the world, Constance uses a significant word, "querele," to describe what she feels about her father:

> And of this time that I se
> Youre honoure and your goode hele
> Which is the helpe of my querele,
> I thonke unto the goddes myht. (1514–17)

The noun "querele" is sometimes associated with love in the *Confessio*. In Book 1, for instance, Amans asks Venus: "Behold my cause and my querele" (134).[60] When Rosiphelee starts to feel love, Genius says: "And so began ther a querele / Betwen love and hir oghne herte" (4.1302–03). Moreover, Constantine's reaction also suggests more than paternal love: "Was nevere father half so blithe / Wepende he keste hire ofte sithe, / So was his herte al overcome" (1521–23). Nevertheless, father and daughter cannot reunite for good until her husband is dead, because the social and religious bond between Constance and Allee still has to prevail.

It is only when her husband is dead that Constance has fulfilled her social and religious duties, and that thus she can finally follow her desire, make her own decisions about her life, and return once and for all to her father. Significantly, Genius describes Constance's decision to go back to Rome after Allee's death as a personal one, offering an interpretation that differs from those of Trivet and the Man of Law. Trivet provides a "good" reason for her to go back: "pur la nouele qe ele oy de la maladie son piere" (181). She goes back because she has heard that her father is ill. The Man of Law remarks that when Alla died, Custance had "greet hevynesse" (1145), and simply mentions, "dame Custance, finally to seye, / Toward the toun of Rome goth hir weye" (1147–48). No specific reasons are given. In Genius's version, however, her reasons for returning to Rome and to her father are significantly personal. As Genius puts it: "And therupon hire herte drowh / To leven Engelond for evere / And go wher that sche hadde levere" (1580–82). This time her reasons are not social or religious, no "bessinesse" or "office" determine her decision, but are personal; "hire herte" decides. This is the first time, we should note, that Constance decides all by herself to follow her own desire, the first time she does what "sche hadde levere."

By going back to her father, Constance closes the circle of her relationship with him. The sense of closure is conveyed and underscored by the final image of Constantine dying in Constance's arms: shortly after Constance returns, "deth of kinde hath overthrowe / Hir worthi fader, which men seide / That he betwen hire armes deide" (1588–90). It should be remarked that this image comes from Trivet, and that, while Gower retains it, Chaucer's Man of Law ignores it. The Man of Law, though, makes an interesting remark at the end whose resonance is worth commenting upon. He states that father and daughter lived together "Til deeth departeth hem" (1158). The verb "departeth" in this context emphasizes the idea of separation, of parting, rather than reunion, thus suggesting the Man of Law's anxious tendency to omit any incestuous implications in his tale. However, we should also note that "Til deeth departeth hem" also echoes the formula used in marriage vows when

---

[60] Other examples of Amans's use of "querele" in the same sense can be found in 8.2173, where he asks Genius to intercede with Cupid and Venus for him and "Be frendlich toward mi querele," and in Amans's "Supplication" to Venus when he complains that Cupid "somdiel is cause of mi querele" (8. 2272).

the couple promises to be married until death separates them.[61] The Man of Law's remark, then, ambiguously emphasizes their separation and at the same time alludes to the special character of their final reunion. Genius's image, by contrast, unambiguously emphasizes the bond between father and daughter.

The final reunion of father and daughter marks a major difference between the "Tale of Constance," on the one hand, and the "Tale of Apollonius" and the "Tale of the Three Questions," on the other. While the latter tales focus exclusively on the socially necessary father-daughter separation, the "Tale of Constance" starts by dealing with the separation, but focuses finally on the bond between father and daughter, in spite of the problematic implications of this bond. The return of Constance to her father Constantine, and their death, marks the end of the story itself and gives a sense of closure to the father-daughter relationship. Genius mentions that Constance's son, Moris, will be the heir to Constantine, but there is a sense that Moris's is another story, different from the completed story of the father and the daughter. In the "Tale of Apollonius" and in the "Tale of the Three Questions," however, after the father and daughter reunite, the daughters are married off; thus, they still have another life to live, separated from their fathers and from the threat of incest. In the "Tale of Constance," even though in the end father and daughter do not actually commit incest, the fact that Moris inherits from Constantine suggests a kind of incest. Indeed, by becoming Constantine's heir, Moris is like his son, and this son is at the same time Constantine's own daughter's son. Both father and daughter, thus, displace their attachment to comply with society and religion, but do finally reaffirm their bond.

Genius can emphasize the bond between father and daughter, because it does not interfere with the daughter's social exchange and thus with her reproductive function, and, more significantly, because it suggests that there is a "natural" desire between father and daughter. Like Peronelle and Thaise, Constance has a powerful command of language, and that command enables her social exchange. Fulfilling her social function in the system of exchange and her religious function, spreading the word, Constance uses language to participate actively in public life. Her "wordes wise" bring about the sultan's desire for her; her power of conversion also attracts King Allee. In emphasizing the father-daughter bond, Genius's version has an even more important effect. By suggesting Constance's desire, Gower's narrator implies that daugh-

---

[61] See, for instance, the "Ordo ad facienda Sponsalia" from a printed early fifteenth-century ecclesiastical manual from York, which reproduces a fourteenth-century manual in manuscript form, of which we have four extant manuscript copies. The phrase that both bride and groom have to pronounce during the ceremony is the same that the Man of Law uses: "Here I take the N. to my weded wyfe [or husbande], to haue and to holde ... in sekeness and in hele, *tyl dethe us departe*" [my emphasis]. Quoted from *Manuale et processionale ad usum insignis ecclesiae Eboraciensis*, ed. W. G. Henderson, Publications of the Surtees Society 63 (Durham: Andrews, 1875) 27. Dinshaw, *Chaucer's Sexual Poetics*, has also noticed the resonance of the verb "departeth" as a verb used in late-medieval wedding ceremonies (102).

ters have a natural desire for their fathers that social laws, and particularly the incest taboo, have the function of repressing. This establishment of a natural desire, or sexuality, prior to culture rests on the assumption that there is some prediscursive "reality" that discourse tries to shape or repress according to certain needs, as discussed in Chapter One. Like Rousseau, Genius sees incest as a desire that precedes the institution of language and thus in a sense sees language as the incest prohibition itself. But if we posit with Derrida that "[l]anguage is neither prohibition nor trangression, it couples the two endlessly" (266); that is, if we posit that the incest taboo does not only repress but also creates the desire, then the daughter's desire turns out to be a creation of the law itself. Genius's strategy in the "Tale of Constance" is crucial for our understanding of his discussion of incest in the *Confessio Amantis*. By suggesting the natural and unspeakable origin of the desire, Genius effectively validates the daughter's desire and confirms the need for the law against incest.

At the beginning of this discussion, I mentioned that, according to Butler, one of the functions of the incest taboo is to delimit the speakable from the unspeakable, the legitimate from the illegitimate. Constance's command of language, unlike Peronelle's or Thaise's, goes beyond the production of words and focuses on the control of that production as well. She alone also uses silence in significant ways, to protect herself as an individual, to protect her own desire – the incestuous implications of her bond with her father, that which is prohibited, has to remain in silence. Thus Constance's command of language can be seen to mark boundaries between the speakable and the unspeakable, between incest and its prohibition, between the legitimate and the illegitimate.

This reflection on father-daughter relationships also serves Gower to comment on the crucial political theme in the "Tale of Constance." As in most of Gower's father-daughter tales in the *Confessio Amantis*, the father is the head of a state – he is the emperor of Rome – and his daughter is his only child. Unlike other daughters, though, Constance, the woman who converts the sultan and the English, the woman who spreads the word, has a clearly religious and redeeming function in the tale. She is both saint-like, and an active preacher; in this sense, like the Man of Law's Custance, she represents the Church and its power to convert and spread its spiritual ideology. Her father, Constantine, on the other hand, as the emperor of Rome, represents political and lay power.

Around two thousand lines after the "Tale of Constance" and in the same book, Genius tells the story of another emperor, also named Constantine, the "Tale of Constantine and Silvester." The similarity between the names in this tale and in the "Tale of Constance" goes beyond the anecdotal, suggesting fundamental common themes. Peck has observed that one tale explains how England became a Christian nation, the other how the Roman empire became Christian.[62] But both tales, I would argue, focus less on how

---

[62] Peck, *Kingship and Common Profit* 63.

the English and Roman peoples converted to Christianity than on how the political powers in those nations converted to Christianity.

The centrality of the story of the Donation of Constantine as a foundation myth, a myth that tries to define the relations between lay and clerical powers, has been pointed out by Scanlon: "As an historically authentic figure embodying the seamless interweaving of the clerical and the monarchical, of *auctoritas* and *potestas*, Constantine was important to both sides in the institutional struggles between the papacy and lay monarchy."[63] As Scanlon argues, in his version of the story, Gower gives his own definition of clerical versus lay power. The monarchy is "inherently self-regulating" and Christianity's main role is to reinforce that self-regulation: "divine authority enters the social to empower monarchical self-restraint, removing any material cost such self-restraint has to pay" (266). Thus Gower foregrounds the "moral integrity of the secular" to confine the role of the Church to a purely "spiritual sphere" from which the secular draws its authority (266). The "Tale of Constance," we will see, also confines the Church to a purely spiritual role.

The "Tale of Constance" functions as a kind of foundation myth. In a recent essay titled "The Question of Authority and The Man of Law's Tale," Patricia Eberle has argued that Chaucer's "Man of Law's Tale" and Gower's "Tale of Constance" are both stories of "origins," but differ in their questioning of types of political authority.[64] Following Brian Tierney's definition of a story of origins, Eberle explains that, "[this] is a story told in order to lend legitimacy to a particular view on the question of authority" (124). This type of narrative is "related to a tendency in medieval political thought to found a theory of political authority on a hypothesis about its beginnings in a primitive state" (125). Using Walter Ullmann's definition of authority, Eberle distinguishes between two views of authority: 'ascending' and 'descending.' According to the 'ascending' view, power ascends from the subjects to the king. Hence, the subjects have the power to depose a king who does not comply with the law (116–17). According to the 'descending' view, power descends from the monarch. Chaucer's tale, Eberle argues, questions this view: "[it] rewrites the view of the heroine found in his sources in order to offer a reexamination of the 'descending' view of the question of authority that she represents" (125). Unlike Chaucer's "Man of Law's Tale," Eberle further argues, Gower's "Tale of Constance" supports the descending view.

Eberle's essay represents an important new approach to the Constance narrative, but its exclusive focus on state politics ignores the crucial role of the Church in the tale. Indeed, Eberle's study points to a fundamental aspect of the story to which critics have paid little attention: its political dimension.

---

63 Scanlon, *Narrative, Authority, and Power* 263.
64 Patricia J. Eberle, "The Question of Authority and The Man of Law's Tale," *The Centre and Its Compass: Studies in Medieval Literature in Honor of Professor John Leyerle*, eds. Robert A. Taylor, et al., Studies in Medieval Culture 33 (Kalamazoo, MI: Medieval Institute Publications, 1993) 111–49.

In doing so, she departs from traditional criticism of both tales, which has often centered on the religious aspect of the story, whether to analyze it from the point of view of religious skepticism, or, as Kolve or other critics like Morton Bloomfield have done, to analyze it from a more orthodox Christian viewpoint.[65] Eberle rightly demonstrates that an exclusive focus on the role of the Church in the tale leaves out a fundamental dimension of the story. Nevertheless, her focus on the examination of authority in a strictly lay context in turn suggests that the Church only serves as a backdrop to this examination, that Church politics itself is not part of the subject of the story. The Church, however, does play a fundamental role in the legend of Constance, whichever version we examine. It is, indeed, significant that the two major authority figures in the story are the respective representatives of the State and the Church, an emperor and the pope. Thus while the analysis of the religious dimension needs to take state politics into account, the analysis of state politics also needs to take Church politics into account. More specifically, any analysis of the tale, whether Chaucer's or Gower's version, needs to situate it within the context of the power struggles towards the end of the Middle Ages between the emperor and kings, on the one hand, and the pope, on the other.[66] Because it does not recognize this context, Eberle's analysis simplifies Gower's complex tale.

The tensions and struggle for power between State and Church are more evident in Gower's version, which fully examines these issues, than in Chaucer's Man of Law's, which only hints at them. That the Man of Law's version only hints at the conflict, or, to put it more accurately, that his version suppresses it, is probably one of the reasons why critics have neglected to study the State-Church relationship in the story. Since critical studies have usually focused on Chaucer's version, while discussing Gower's only as it mirrors, or fails to mirror, Chaucer's, these studies have themselves failed to notice the relevance of the conflict in the story. However, if we start from Gower's tale, we are able not only to illuminate his version in new and insightful ways but also to open up new possibilities in Chaucer's version. My

---

[65] See V. A. Kolve, *Chaucer and the Imagery of Narrative: The First Five* Canterbury Tales (Stanford: Stanford UP, 1984) 297–98, and Morton W. Bloomfield, "The Man of Law's Tale: A Tragedy of Victimization and a Christian Comedy," *Publications of the Modern Language Association of America* 87 (1972): 384–90.

[66] As R. N. Swanson, *Church and Society in Late Medieval England* (Oxford: Basil Blackwell, 1989), has noted, "[t]he debates between 'papalists' and 'royalists' in the thirteenth to fifteenth centuries were essentially about the structure of Christendom and the relations between the various fragments (the kingdoms) and its religious head (the pope)" (91). Some of the most influential studies of Church-State relationships in the Middle Ages, studies which inform my analysis, are: Walter Ullmann, *Principles of Government and Politics in the Middle Ages* (London: Methuen, 1961); Brian Tierney, *The Crisis of Church and State, 1050–1300* (Toronto: U of Toronto P, 1988); Michael Wilks, *The Problem of Sovereignty in the Later Middle Ages* (Cambridge: Cambridge UP, 1963). On these struggles in fourteenth-century England, see also, W. A. Pantin, *The English Church in the Fourteenth Century* (Toronto: U of Toronto P, 1980), esp. ch. 5.

analysis will show that the depiction of Christian religion and its representative institution, the Church, in Gower's "Tale of Constance" carries significant political implications. Gower's version offers a complex comment on State-Church relationships. It uses the story as a 'story of origins' in Tierney's sense, that is, to describe the myth of an origin: that of the political subordination of the Church to the State. Gower does so neither to justify this subordination, nor to defend the opposite form of subordination – that of the State to the Church – but to question the royal absolutist implications of this particular story of origins.

The following analysis, moreover, will show how lay power uses gender to articulate its vision of State-Church relationships.[67] Gower's "Tale of Constance" examines the uses of gender in the institutional conflict between State and Church at the end of the Middle Ages. The political implications of the tale, I will show, are imbricated in the tale's father-daughter theme. Indeed, Gower's version of the Constance story uses the father-daughter relationship as a metaphor for the relationship between State and Church, the Church representing the feminine in its relationship with State masculine power.

It is no coincidence that Gower uses a woman to represent the Church. In "Custance and History: Woman as Outsider in Chaucer's 'Man of Law's Tale,'" David Raybin has argued that Chaucer's tale treats Constance as an outsider, as someone ahistorical.[68] During her voyages, according to Raybin, "[s]he is exiled from the temporal world and thus unconstrained by time, bound to her faith and thus spiritually free, existing in an emblematic position largely outside human contact, outside history" (69). And, when she is ashore, "it is to live in the margins, both spatially and, in spite of her royal birth, socially" (69). Raybin sees Constance's ahistoricity as a positive feature: "The tale . . . demonstrates the insufficiency of patriarchal history, the limitations of institutionalized religion, the more positive values in femaleness and sexuality, and ultimately the necessity for a woman's spiritual power in the context of such a world" (65). I have no contention with Raybin's argument that Chaucer's tale emphasizes Custance's timelessness, her ahistoricity. In fact, an emphasis on Constance's timelessness is also evident in Gower's version. However, Raybin's suggestion that Chaucer's version ultimately demonstrates the value and necessity of women's spiritual power does not recognize the subordinate status of such power. In both

---

[67] While several recent studies of the Man of Law's version have focused on issues of gender from various viewpoints, none of them has analyzed their intersection with State politics. See, for instance, Dinshaw, *Chaucer's Sexual Poetics* 88–112; the chapter titled "Womanliness in the Man of Law's Tale" in Sheila Delany, *Writing Woman: Women Writers and Women in Literature, Medieval to Modern* (New York: Schocken Books, 1983); and, more recently, Susan Schibanoff, "Worlds Apart: Orientalism, Antifeminism, and Heresy in Chaucer's Man of Law's Tale," *Exemplaria* 8.1 (1996): 59–96.

[68] David Raybin, "Custance and History: Woman as Outsider in Chaucer's Man of Law's Tale," *Studies in the Age of Chaucer* 12 (1990): 65–84.

Chaucer's and Gower's versions, Constance is divested of power, of self-willed influence on historical and political events. I should qualify this assertion by noting that I am not denying that Constance influences history, that she does take an active part at times. Her influence, however, is always an act of obedience to male authority, whether to the authority of her biological father or of her Divine Father. Constance's limited self-consciousness stresses not just women's subordination but also the Church's subordination to the State, to royal power.

The question of the distribution of power between State and Church was a major source of political debate and tension throughout the Middle Ages. Where does the power of the pope end and where does that of the king begin? In his influential study, *The Problem of Sovereignty in the Later Middle Ages*, Michael Wilks has analyzed the debates that arose around the struggle for power and sovereignty between State and Church toward the end of the Middle Ages. Significantly, in order to define the distribution of power, theorists and those in political positions of authority frequently resorted to familial metaphors. The pope was the great father, the patriarch who, as representative of God, ruled over his children, the whole of Christian society, including kings and emperors.[69]

Of course, kings and emperors did not like such a role and tried to minimize the extent of the pope's power. One of the ways in which they did this was by redefining the traditional distinction between temporal and spiritual power to their own advantage. Traditionally, in drawing the distinction between temporal and spiritual power, popes did not renounce legislative and political authority. As Wilks has put it, "[t]he famous 'Render unto Caesar' text, the allegories of the two swords, or the sun and the moon, are for the papalists simply means of expressing this distinction of functions, but they do not deny the overriding papal right to exercise both himself" (267). Lay rulers, though, tried to counter this conception of papal rights by redefining the limits of the spiritual realm. They sought to limit the pope's authority, Wilks observes, "by making a rigid separation between the provinces of pope and lay ruler, to create in effect autonomous spheres of temporal and spiritual in which emperor and pope could reign supreme" (70–71). Thus, lay rulers tried to relegate the pope to a confined and strictly spiritual role. The pope was the father for spiritual matters, he was the one to consult on spiritual concerns, but he would have no power in terms of practical and immediate political decision-making (285ff).

---

[69] Wilks, *The Problem of Sovereignty* 159. See also Alexander de S. Elpidio's remarks in *De ecclesiastica potestate*: "Et secundum hanc acceptionem ecclesia Romana est ... universalis ecclesia prima ... Et sicut eius episcopus pater est et pastor omnium pastorum, ita Romana ecclesia mater et caput est omnium ecclesiarum" (quoted in Wilks 397). ["And in this sense, the Roman church is ... the first universal church ... And as its bishop is the father and the shepherd of all shepherds, so the Roman church is the mother and the head of all churches" (my translation)].

Several critics have demonstrated the importance of the conflict between State and Church in fourteenth-century England.[70] One of the voices that expressed its opposition to the Church's temporal power was that of Wyclif and, later, the Lollards.[71] Gower's views on the subject, though, cannot necessarily be seen as having been directly influenced by Wyclif. For Wyclif and the Lollards, according to Hudson, in their desire to divest the Church of temporal power, did not show a strong opposition to excessive royal power: "It is notable ... that most Wycliffite texts are far more prepared to countenance resistance to spiritual authority wrongly exercised than to a secular tyrant" (366). Gower, as the "Tale of Constance" shows, was concerned about any form of tyrannical power, whether ecclesiastical or royal. His anti-clericalism thus probably had more to do with, in Scanlon's words, "the general anti-clericalism that was widespread in English society in the last decades of the fourteenth century."[72]

The "Tale of Constance" relegates the pope to a strictly spiritual role, but this is not the only tale in Gower's *Confessio Amantis* which does so. Scanlon has argued that two crucial tales in Book 2 of the *Confessio Amantis*, the "Donation of Constantine," mentioned above, and "Pope Boniface" also examine this theme (256–57). These two tales, according to Scanlon, show Gower delimiting and reducing the power of the Church over temporal matters to the benefit of kings. The story of Pope Boniface, especially, manifests "a particularly extreme version of the royalist position" (258). In this story, Scanlon observes, "Gower disenfranchises clerical power by making it entirely spiritual" (262). It is this disenfranchisement, this confinement of the pope and the Church to a purely spiritual role, that is also working in the "Tale of Constance," a tale included in Book 2 of the *Confessio*, as well. But there is also something quite distinctive about the "Tale of Constance," something that one does not find in the stories of Pope Boniface or of Constantine and Sylvester. This tale illustrates, in significantly gendered terms, the proper relation of lay and spiritual power through the use of a father-daughter relationship.

Throughout the "Tale of Constance," the father and daughter pair turn metaphorically into a husband and wife and a mother and son. I noted above that the metaphor of father-daughter relations is pushed much further in this tale than in other father-daughter tales. In the end, father and daughter reunite, suggesting an emotional attachment between the two that other tales problematize. I have observed that the reunion of Constance and

---

[70] Pantin, *The English Church in the Fourteenth Century*, for instance, has written that the period of Anglo-papal relations from 1360 to 1399 "consisted of negotiations, serious attempts to reach an agreement, interspersed or accompanied by protests and conflicts" (87).

[71] On Wyclif's and the Lollards' ideas about the extent of the Church's power, see, for instance, Anne Hudson, *The Premature Reformation* (Oxford: Clarendon Press, 1988), esp. 334–46.

[72] Scanlon, *Narrative, Authority, and Power* 8–9.

Constantine hints at a kind of incestuous love, and that Moris's inheriting from Constantine suggests that he is the offspring of the father and the daughter. Yet Genius uses another familial metaphor in the tale, a metaphor that is the more remarkable because it is completely original with him. Neither Trivet nor Chaucer's Man of Law use it. When Constantine recognizes his daughter at the end of the tale, Genius remarks:

> For thogh his Moder were come
> Fro deth to lyve out of the grave,
> He mihte nomor wonder have
> Than he hath whan that he hire sih. (1524–27)

Peck has noted that in this passage it seems that "[t]o the emperor, reclaiming his daughter is like a resurrection," a resurrection of Constance, her husband and child, and of himself (69). I would argue that what is remarkable about this unparalleled passage is that it points to Constance's third familial, and Marian, role vis-à-vis her father: Constance also becomes her father's mother.[73]

Throughout this tale, then, Constance becomes at the same time daughter, wife, and mother of the emperor in a mysterious riddle that reminds us of Antiochus's riddle in the "Tale of Apollonius." In addition, the simultaneous roles of mother, wife, and daughter also remind us of the Virgin Mary's relationship with Christ. Julia Kristeva has argued that, "[t]he highly complex relationship between Christ and his Mother served as a matrix within which various other relations – God to mankind, man to woman, son to mother, etc. – took shape."[74] The Virgin Mary, moreover, was sometimes identified with the *Ecclesia*. The Church was thus also seen as bride, mother, and daughter of God, or of the Christian community.[75] I suggest that the relationship between Christ and His Mother is also the matrix that in the "Tale of Constance" defines the relationship between Constance and Constantine

---

[73] Allen, "Chaucer Answers Gower," has made a similar point. She notes what she calls "[t]he emperor's vaguely incestuous equation of daughter with mother" (645). Donavin has also remarked on this Oedipal moment, but I differ with her interpretation of it as evidence of Constantine's "hope in the resurrection" (61).

[74] Julia Kristeva, "Stabat Mater," in *The Female Body in Western Culture*, ed. Susan Rubin Suleiman (Cambridge: Harvard UP, 1985) 104.

[75] On the identification between the Church and Mary as mother-wife-daughter, see Marina Warner, *Alone of All Her Sex*, esp. 17–18, 105–11. Warner, for instance, notes that,

> [i]n iconography of medieval Christendom and later, she often holds the centre stage, both at the Ascension and at the gift of tongues; a towering figure, she becomes the very embodiment of *Mater Ecclesia*, brimming over with the grace and power of the Spirit, and before whom the apostles sometimes kneel in awe. (18)

This identification between *Ecclesia* and Mary is also particularly evident in commentaries on the Song of Songs in the Middle Ages, like those of Bruno of Segni in the late eleventh century. See Ann W. Astell, *The Song of Songs in the Middle Ages* (Ithaca, NY: Cornell UP, 1990), especially the second chapter, titled "The Exemplary Bride: *Ecclesia* and Mary."

and, figuratively, State and Church. Furthermore, Gower's use of such a matrix points to the problematic aspects of those relationships. Of course, throughout the Middle Ages, the Church was also conceived in other terms, as, for instance, *corpus Christi mysticum*.[76] But what I would like to stress here is that, of all the different metaphorical interpretations of the function of the Church from which he could have drawn, in the "Tale of Constance" Gower represents the Church as the feminine mother-wife-daughter.

To suggest the Church's proper role, Gower stresses the importance of Constance/the Church as feminine spiritual leader rather than as a patriarchal and political institution and reduces the pope's role in the tale. This telling characteristic also distinguishes Gower's from Trivet's rendering of the story of Constance, and, to a lesser extent, from Chaucer's. In Gower's version, the pope is pushed to the margins of the events, playing a strictly spiritual role. He is only mentioned three times, and those three times he is always scarcely more than a point of reference, a symbolic representation of power who does not exert power himself. It is the emperor, the father, who takes the initiative and makes decisions. In Nicholas Trivet's version, before the marriage of Constance to the sultan is decided, the pope is consulted along with "the other great ones of Holy Church" (6). Moreover, the sultan sends letters indicating his desire to marry Constance to the emperor, to Constance herself, and, we should note, also to the pope. Thus, the pope and other officials of the Church are present and play a role almost as important as that of the emperor. In Gower's version, by contrast, the pope is mentioned only briefly. When he learns about the sultan's intentions, Genius notes,

>... the fader in himselve
>Was glad, and with the Pope avised
>Tuo Cardinals he hath assissed
>With othre lordes many mo.   (634–37)

It should be noticed that the "he" in line 636, the one who sends the cardinals, as well as the lords, is the emperor rather than the pope, while the pope is consulted only once.

In Trivet's version, the institutional presence of the Church is also more salient during Constance's stay in England. When, after the miracle of the blind man, Constance converts Hermingheld and Elda, the bishop of Bangor is immediately called upon to sanction their conversion by baptizing them. In Gower's version, however, Hermingheld is considered to be fully converted without the intervention of the bishop (751–78). The bishop appears only later when he is to marry Constance and the king, and it is during that trip that he baptizes the king and many others (903ff). Another significant example of the limited role of the institutional authorities of the Church in

---

[76] On the Church as *corpus Christi mysticum* and other similar metaphors, see, for instance, Francis Oakley, *The Western Church in the Later Middle Ages* (Ithaca, NY: Cornell UP, 1979), esp. 159–63.

Gower's version occurs towards the end of the tale. In Trivet's *Chroniques*, when the Emperor Tiberius decides to appoint Maurice as his heir, he needs "the consent of Pope Pelagius and all the senate of Rome" (50). In Gower's tale, the pope has nothing to do with this decision. Only the Parliament is consulted:

> A parlement er that thei wente,
> Thei setten unto this entente,
> To puten Rome in full espeir
> That Moris was apparant heir. (1549–52)

Chaucer's version, we should note, departs here from Gower's in a significant way. His Man of Law does not mention the emperor's and the Parliament's deliberations, but mentions and foregrounds the pope's role by remarking, "This child Maurice was sithen Emperour / Maad by the Pope" (1121–22).

The function of the pope in Gower's tale, moreover, is even problematized textually. Unlike the Middle English verse, one of the Latin glosses to the tale represents him as playing an authoritative role. I mentioned before that in Gower's tale the emperor is the one who actually makes the decision to marry his daughter off to the sultan. The first Latin gloss to the tale disagrees on this point; after noting that the sultan had promised to convert to Christianity, the gloss remarks: "cuius accepta caucione consilio Pelagii tunc pape dicta filia vna cum duobus Cardinalibus aliisque Rome proceribus in Persiam maritagii causa nauigio honorifice destinata fuit."[77] It is remarkable that the gloss, unlike the tale itself, does not even mention the father and that it gives more relevance to the pope by specifying his name. The discrepancy between the Latin gloss and the vernacular tale thus reproduces textually the tension between clerical and lay power. It enacts the struggle for sovereignty between pope and emperor, or between Church and State. As Echard has argued, "Gower's Latin problematizes the question of authority in the *Confessio* by presenting a reader with several competing authoritative voices, Latin and vernacular, none of which seems capable of taming the text."[78] The "Tale of Constance" shows an example of such a competition.

Gower uses the metaphor of father-daughter relations to suggest the subordination and dependence of the Church on paternal, royal power. The additional ascription of the roles of mother and wife to Constance in her relation with Constantine has a further effect. Commenting on Dante's line "Vergine Madre, figlia del tuo Figlio" as a line that "perhaps best captures the combination of the three feminine roles – daughter-wife-mother – within a whole," Kristeva argues that "[t]he nexus of these three functions is the basis of immutable and atemporal spirituality: 'the fixed term of an eternal design,' as *The*

---

77 "The pledge being accepted by the counsel of Pelagius, who was Pope then, the said daughter with two cardinals and other Roman officials was sent to Persia with honor in a ship for marriage" (my translation).
78 Echard, "With Carmen's Help" 7.

Divine Comedy magisterially puts it" (105). The "mystery" of Constance puts her in an atemporal, ahistorical plane that divests her of immediate, independent power and confines her to a fundamentally spiritual role.[79] Of course, this does not mean that she does not influence and exert power over others in other immediate ways that do affect history. We have seen her active role in the tale, a role that is not only religious, but effectively political as well. Her conversions have definite politically advantageous consequences for Rome. Thus, for instance, Constance's marriage with Allee not only brings about the conversion of England, but also unites eventually, through the inheritance of her son, Moris, two political powers: England and Rome. The political uses of Constance's power, though, are always subordinate to lay political power and work for it. Constance obeys the authority of her father, the authority of Rome, and her obedience provides Constantine and Rome with an heir who brings about the political advancement of the Roman empire. Thus, as daughter and figurative wife, Constance, and the Church, are subordinate to the authority of the monarch.

Furthermore, Constance's roles as daughter and figurative mother also constitute a comment on the authority of English royal power. As noted above, I agree with Eberle's interpretation of the "Tale of Constance" as a "story of origins," even though I disagree with the implications she draws from this interpretation (she sees the Constance story as a comment on the descending versus the ascending view of authority). Like Eberle, I see this story of origins as an attempt to legitimize a certain form of authority. Constance and the Church are figurative mothers that represent the origin of political authority. Constance is represented as Constantine's mother as well as England's mother. She is the one who, according to the tale, brought Christianity to England. She is in this sense the origin, the spiritual mother who gave birth to the authority of the Christian monarchs of medieval England, and the one who thus validates royal authority. It is significant, of course, that a woman sent by an emperor, a lay political authority, should function as the symbolic origin of the Christian English state, rather than a man sent by the pope (as was historically the case with Saint Augustine's conversion of the English). No imposition from the pope turned England to Christianity but the faith of an obedient daughter who had less to do with the institutional and political power of the Church than with secular authority. Moreover, Constance not only validates royal authority, but, as a woman, also affirms the subordination of the Church to the male king. Constance's

---

[79] This effect is similar to the effect that the competing discourses of misogyny and courtly love have on women; as Howard Bloch, *Medieval Misogyny and the Invention of Western Romantic Love* (Chicago: U of Chicago P, 1991), has pointed out: "essentialist definitions of gender [whether positive or negative] are dangerous not only because they are wrong or undifferentiated but ... because historically they have worked to eliminate the subject from history" (6). And Bloch continues, "the denial of history to women entails an abstraction that also denies the being of any individual woman, and is therefore the stuff of a disenfranchising objectification" (11).

contradictory familial roles, like those of the Virgin Mary and the Church, are always defined in relation to, and as subordinate to, political and male power.

Thus in the "Tale of Constance," familial relationships function as the matrix, not just for the examination, but also for the definition and delimitation of power relationships. Gower's tale offers a complex comment on the relationship between State and Church. His version de-emphasizes the role of the patriarchal figure of authority, the pope, and, through Constance, foregrounds the Church's feminine role in its relationship with lay power. By "feminine," though, I do not simply mean submissive and passive. Constance's role in the tale is more complex than that, as the roles of other women, and particularly daughters, in the *Confessio Amantis* cannot be simply classified as passive either. Through Genius, Gower uses the father-daughter relationship in the "Tale of Constance" as a matrix not just for the examination but also for the definition and delimitation of power relationships between State and Church.

Nevertheless, Genius's use of the father-daughter relationship to define the relationship between State and Church is highly problematical, given his critical examination of father-daughter relationships and his warnings against the abuse of power by paternal authority in other tales, such as the "Tale of Apollonius." I want to return now to the incest subtext in the tale to articulate my final argument about the tale and its ultimate implications. Swanson has observed that, "[t]he slow development towards a lay – but not secular – view of the state, with the emphasis on royal power proceeding directly from God rather than being mediated through the church, challenged, and then shattered, the church's hold on the succession, and on the legitimization of regimes" (121). The emphasis on royal power proceeding directly from God and circumventing the pope's power, as I have shown, is clear in Gower's version. The one who institutes the beginning of Christian monarchy in England is Constance, a woman sent by the emperor, not by the pope himself. The pope's authority is thus circumvented. Swanson has also pointed out that in emphasizing, "the prince's duty as *rex Christianissimus* . . . [Christian monarchs had] purely practical aims[;] the most important political theorizing was propounded for a very specific end: effective royal control over Parliament" (93). The tensions between the two powers as articulated in different treatises tended to justify lay power on the basis of its Christian origins and this justification was used to control parliament. If, as Swanson argues, at least one of the purposes of political theorizing in late medieval England was the establishment and justification of effective royal control over Parliament, then a fundamental question inevitably arises: is Gower's purpose in the tale to give English monarchs the necessary justification, based on a myth of origins, for ruling over Parliament?

My analysis of the incest theme in the tale and in the *Confessio Amantis* as a whole suggests that we should not hasten to answer this question in the affirmative; in fact, when one examines the suppressed incest theme in the tale and compares it to the explicit condemnation of father-daughter incest in the story of Apollonius, the answer is, instead, negative. In this story, as we have seen, Genius depicts father-daughter incest as a most horrible and unnatural act: "The wylde fader thus devoureth / His oghne fleissh" (309–10). He also describes it as an "unkinde fare" (312), a "horrible vice" (317). As I argue in Chapter Four, Genius also uses incest in other tales as a metaphor to condemn other fathers' oppressive and, in a sense absolutist, relationships with their daughters, most notably in the "Tale of Canace and Machaire." These fathers tend to be rulers with significant political power. In these cases, as in the case of the actual incestuous relationship between Antiochus and his daughter in the story of Apollonius, Genius condemns the father as well as the ruler. The metaphor of incest thus serves to denounce absolutist political power.

Incest does not occur in the "Tale of Constance" as it does in earlier versions of this narrative studied by Schlauch. However, as I have tried to show, the incestuous connotations in Gower's version of the story are far from being suppressed. In fact, the links between the narratives of Constance and Apollonius, as well as Genius's condemnation of father-daughter incest elsewhere in the *Confessio*, cast a very dubious light over the "Tale of Constance" and its fantasy of self-reproducing, in other words, incestuous, royal power. Scanlon has shown that in its reappropriation of clerical power one of lay power's most important strategies was to sacralize itself.[80] He notes that, initially, in the Carolingian period, as it became part of the ruling class, clerical power produced conceptions of power for lay rulers. It did not do so without reaping its own benefits: "There is no doubt this process involved an ecclesiastical appropriation of major proportions, as clerics invested pre-existent lay political forms with sacral and ecclesiological significance" (86). And, Scanlon continues: "The laicization of the later period should . . . be seen, at least in part, as a reappropriation rather than a simple act of resistance, as the growing power of royal courts enabled them to take fuller control of the legitimating functions that had earlier been provided by the Church" (86). In the "Tale of Constance," lay power, or more appropriately royalist ideology, as defined by Swanson, that is, the ideology that tries to establish effective royal control over Parliament, appropriates the God-Mary relationship as a matrix to explain the relationship between Constantine and Constance, thus reappropriating sacral images and stories for lay purposes.

But the question still remains: does the tale show this reappropriation uncritically? Because of its use of familial metaphors, the God-Mary-Christ riddle represents in a sense a symbolic and religious story of incest – God the Father conceived a son through his own daughter. While this relationship, as I have argued before, is indicative of patriarchy's desire for the daughter, it is rarely understood to be incestuous, because, among other reasons, it tries to

---

[80] Scanlon, *Narrative, Authority, and Power* 86.

situate itself in a different, supra-human plane. Nevertheless, it becomes a model, or a matrix, for the articulation of literal, human father-daughter relationships. It is thus significant that in the case of Constance and Constantine, their relationship, even though it may have some religious overtones, is fundamentally human. Their father-daughter relationship, unlike the relationship between God and Mary, is literal, rather than metaphorical, and human, rather than divine. Donavin has argued that we are encouraged to see the Constance and Constantine relationship as a relationship that transcends the human. Constance and Constantine, she argues, "providentially transcend the negative effects of actual incest and metaphorically enact the soul's arrival in Heaven" (61). I would add that Gower's Constance also sometimes seems like a supra-human heroine and the tale encourages us to compare her to the Virgin Mary. However, it is not apparent that Gower's story tries to make, or is even interested in making, Constance exclusively saintly or supra-human, and reading her exclusively in those terms ignores crucial aspects in Gower's version. Throughout the tale, Constance is driven not just by a sense of religious duty, but also by a sense of social obligation. She is not just a saint. As Wetherbee has argued, Gower's version "emphasi[zes] . . . Constance's active, public role," by contrast with Chaucer's version in which the Man of Law has "a tendency to fetishize her helplessness and underplay her normal social relations."[81] Her role goes beyond the religious function of converting others. It is also social and political as she becomes a mother and provides an heir for her father.

Furthermore, Constantine himself does not seem a figure for God, as Donavin argues (63), someone with supra-human or divine qualities. Constantine is very 'human' and political when he arranges a convenient match for his daughter by marrying her to the sultan. The marriage ensures the advancement of his religion, but this advancement also has obvious political and economic advantages for Rome. Constantine's humanity is further emphasized at the end. When he dies in his daughter's arms, we are reminded of a pietà scene: Mary/Constance has the dead Christ/Constantine in her arms. However, even here the parallel between the Jesus-Mary and the Constance-Constantine pietàs brings us back to the human dimension. The son/father in the Constance-Constantine pietà scene is all too human. Notice how Genius emphasizes Constantine's natural death: "*deth of kinde* hath overthrowe / Hir worthi fader, which men seide / That he betwen hire armes deide*" (1588–90). Thus Gower's depiction of their appropriation of the God-Mary relationship as a matrix to articulate their relationship cannot

---

[81] Wetherbee, "Constance and the World" 69. Olsson, *John Gower and the Structures of Conversion,* has made a similar argument. He has argued that Gower's tale is "less vertical in orientation" than Trivet's or Chaucer's versions (97). Gower, Olsson continues, stresses the importance of the natural and of human law, rather than the supernatural: "[u]nlike the Man of Law, who responds to weakness by pointing to a transcendent justice, Genius . . . hopes to find a goodness and strength in *kinde.*" In this way, "Gower rehistoricizes the tale." Gower, then, makes the tale more secular and social.

be considered purely and uncritically allegorical. For one thing, the relationship between God and Mary, couched in familial terms, cannot avoid the connotations of incest. For another, foregrounding the incestuous connotations of their relationship, the human dimension in the case of Constance and Constantine is even more insistently there and reminds us that, rather than transcending their blood relationship, they remain literally and biologically father and daughter.[82]

If one examines the incest theme, then, the ultimate political implications of Gower's tale do not necessarily entail the uncritical support of royalist aspirations. As I have argued, Gower uses the father-daughter relationship in the "Tale of Constance" as a matrix not just for the examination, but also for the definition and delimitation of power relationships between State and Church. But he does so not in order to justify royalist absolute power. Quite to the contrary, Gower's version questions the model of self-reproducing, incestuous, royal power that the Constance story presents. This further suggests that, *contra* Eberle, he is not supporting the 'descending' view of authority, according to which the king has absolute power over his subjects. Rather, in questioning the self-sufficiency and incestuous character of a power concentrated in royal families, Gower questions the ideology behind the mode of the royalist appropriation of papal power. The incestuous character of the relationship between Constance and Constantine suggests an absolutist model that Gower did not support.

It needs to be emphasized that Gower's questioning of this appropriation does not imply that he supports clerical power over *temporalia*. Gower makes explicit his disapproval of clerical appropriation of lay power through the prophecy mentioned at the end of the story about the Donation of Constantine. Genius says that he read in a chronicle that as soon as Constantine made his donation of *temporalia* to the Church,

> A vois was herd on hih the lifte,
> Of which al Rome was adrad,
> And seith: 'To day is venym schad
> In holi cherche of temporal,
> Which medleth with the spirital.' (3488–92)

According to Genius, the donation had been a well-meaning mistake – "[Constantine's] will was good" (3482), he remarks. But this mistake became the source of a host of problems, which Genius hopes "God mai amende it, whan he wile, / I can ther to non other skile" (3495–96).

There are significant links between the story of the Donation of Constan-

---

[82] This emphasis on the king's humanity is perhaps surprising given medieval notions of divine kingship. Wyclif himself stressed the king's divinity; as Hudson, *The Premature Reformation*, observes, "Wyclif developed a strongly regalian position . . . The pope in the true sense of the man most perfect on earth, might only claim to be the Vicar of Christ in his humanity, but the king was the vicar of God, the vicar of Christ in his divinity" (363).

tine and the "Tale of Constance" that further illuminate Gower's complex analysis. Even though the Constantine of the Donation is not the same Constantine as Constance's father, the coincidence in the names as well as the proximity of the tales within the *Confessio* encourage us to see links between them. I mentioned above that both tales are foundation myths. Moreover, both are in Book 2, the book about the sin of envy; one illustrates an example of a branch of envy, backbiting, the other an example of the opposite of envy in a general sense, charity. And, most important, the Donation of Constantine was one of the best known narratives representing clerical appropriation of lay power. As noted, the story was used by the Church to justify its supremacy over lay rulers. It is thus significant that the "Tale of Constance" presents the opposite move, that is, the reappropriation of clerical power by lay rulers. Illustrating this parallel, nevertheless, is not meant to delegitimize this reappropriation of power.

There is no condemnation of the reappropriation of clerical power by lay rulers in the "Tale of Constance." As the prophecy in the "Tale of Constantine and Sylvester" suggests, and as Scanlon has amply illustrated, Gower definitely condemned the Church's use of temporal power. But Gower's criticism of the Church's use of temporal power does not lead him to a blind support of any form of royal power. What the "Tale of Constance" does, I suggest, is question the model used to justify the appropriation. The tale hints at the dangers of using a model that, in suggesting the incestuous, self-reproducing character of a power concentrated in royal families, carries absolutist political implications. Gower's condemnation of father-daughter incest, and his use of it as a metaphor to condemn absolutist use of royal power in other tales, suggests that his support of royalist reappropriation of *temporalia* in the "Tale of Constance" is not an uncritical acceptance of royal pretensions to power, but points at the same time to the need to delimit those pretensions.

The attempt to delimit those pretensions, though, faces a major obstacle, for, as the "Tale of Constance" shows, the notion of family in medieval Christianity – a notion, I would add, that still underlies Western conceptions of the family – carries a fundamental structural weakness: as the God-Mary riddle suggests, even as families depend on the clear definition of the familial roles men and women assume within them, the boundaries between those roles are fluid and thus become a cause of instability. The three tales studied in this chapter present us with three daughters who seem to perform their social roles perfectly, responding to the demands and needs of their fathers and without explicitly questioning the system, even as, at the same time, Gower does not suppress the potential dark side of these ideal daughters and fathers and their happy-ending stories. The tales I will analyze in the next chapters, most of which have some kind of tragic outcome, bring up those disturbing moments more explicitly and illuminate even more clearly the complexity of Gower's treatment of Thaise's, Peronelle's, and Constance's redeeming function. Gower even seems to insist again and again on bringing up disturbing moments and problematic associations in order both to explore the specter of incest in a familial setting and to use the implications of the metaphor of incest to examine other forms of authority relationships.

The fluidity of familial roles is the subject of the next chapter. The "Tale of the False Bachelor" and the "Tale of Albinus and Rosemund" show how husbands and fathers perform similar roles in their relationship with either their wives or their daughters. In this sense, the system of exchange appears to be just a form of supplantation. Supplantation is a dangerous crack that threatens the system, because, for a system that depends on the clear delimitations of the roles of fathers, husbands, daughters, and wives, the possibility of supplantation suggests that those roles are far from being stable.

CHAPTER THREE

FATHERS AS HUSBANDS, HUSBANDS AS FATHERS:
SUPPLANTATION AND EXCHANGE IN THE "TALE OF THE FALSE BACHELOR" AND THE "TALE OF ALBINUS AND ROSEMUND"

Introduction

The two tales I analyze in this chapter, the "Tale of Albinus and Rosemund" and the "Tale of the False Bachelor," suggest that, historically, father-daughter and husband-wife relationships share the same structure and power dynamics and are therefore interchangeable. The theme of supplantation in the "Tale of the False Bachelor" hints at the dynamics of supplantation in the system of exchange. In this tale the sultan of Persia designates a Roman knight as his replacement, that is, as the masculine authority figure over his daughter (this Roman knight is, in turn, treacherously supplanted by another knight who tries to marry the sultan's daughter in his stead). The same dynamics play a major role in the "Tale of Albinus and Rosemund." By defeating his enemy and then marrying his daughter, Albinus replaces Rosemund's father both at a familial and at a political level. Gower's insight concerning the similarities between husband-wife and father-daughter relationships explains in part why – although, as Wallace has argued, the husband-wife metaphor was commonly used in the later Middle Ages to imagine and explain the relationship between king and subjects – the father-daughter metaphor is used by Gower to explore this political relationship.[1]

In the hierarchical relationship of authority between father and daughter and husband and wife, gender, rather than the individual's specific familial role, determines who has authority over whom. We can recall here Aquinas's distinction between mother-son and father-daughter incest mentioned in Chapter One. According to Aquinas's explanation, the former is more against natural law than the latter because in the latter, at least, the "appropiate" relationship of authority between the man and the woman, as dictated

---

[1] Wallace, *Chaucerian Polity* 295–98.

by natural law, is maintained. Playing an active role, the man is expected to be the figure of authority over the woman, while the woman is defined as a subordinate and passive figure. We have seen in Chapter Two that Genius does not always define men's and women's roles in such clear-cut, opposite ways, and thus that women are not always defined simply as passive objects in the *Confessio Amantis*, even if their actions do not ultimately pose any threats to the ideal system envisioned by Gower's priest. However, in the two tales studied in this chapter, men and women are sharply differentiated along gender lines. Thus, masculinity is defined rigidly and becomes a central concept that defines a knight's identity, while the women are passive objects whose main role seems to be to prove the knights' masculinity.[2] The only roles women are allowed to play are defined by men. The sultan's daughter submits totally to the authority of the father (to his "wille"); she does what he commands her. Rosemund obeys Albinus after her father is defeated; although eventually she does act on her own initiative, even then her behavior significantly mirrors that of her husband.

The theme of gender, then, is fundamentally connected to a major theme in these tales: chivalry and the construction of knightly identity. Gower examines the construction of chivalric (and masculine) identity within the world of politics. His treatment of chivalry becomes especially relevant when we take into account the political scene contemporary to Gower's poem, in particular, King Richard II's inclination to chivalric self-display. In the "Tale of Albinus and Rosemund" Genius stresses the incompatibility of kingship and chivalric ideology, an incompatibility that also has consequences at the familial level. In the "Tale of the False Bachelor" he uses his examination of the dependence of chivalric identity on performance to point to the social instability this dependence brings to the functioning of the structures of replacement within the family, as well as within the royal system of succession. The two tales show how the chivalric ethos can be destructive for the men and women ruled by it as well as for the community as a whole.

In his critique of chivalry, Gower points to what Butler would call the gaps inevitably opened by chivalry's dependence on the repetition of acts, on performance, in order to construct the identity of the knight. In the "Tale of the False Bachelor," the Roman knight chosen to replace the sultan as authority figure over his daughter and as sultan of his country is easily supplanted by another knight, because the identity of the Roman knight is primarily, even exclusively, defined on the battlefield. Chivalry is an ideal site for the examination of the performative character of gender, not because gender functions only performatively in the world of chivalry, but rather

---

[2] As David Aers, "Masculine Identity and the Courtly Community: The Self Loving in *Troilus and Criseyde*," *Community, Gender and Individual Identity: English Writing, 1360–1430*, ed. David Aers (London: Routledge, 1988), has put it, "the female is the spoils of male victory, the proof of masculinity in the community" (127).

because chivalry's fundamental reliance on performance, on ostensible and exterior action, makes the performativity of gender more evident. Precisely this dependence on performance is the weakest point in the construction of chivalric identity. For performance is something patently exterior, not an essential, ontological feature. In this context, we can also see the weakest point in the system of exchange: it relies primarily on a rigid gender distinction between male and female. Thus, if masculinity is the primary defining attribute of the one who holds the position of authority, whether as husband or father, then father and husband are to an extent indistinguishable, and, thus interchangeable, in their relationship with the woman – if the husband becomes the father, the father can also easily become the husband. This supplantation suggests that the system of exchange itself creates the possibilities for its own subversion. The "Tale of Albinus and Rosemund" and the "Tale of the False Bachelor" point to the dynamics of supplantation inherent to the system of exchange, and thus to the inherent ambiguity in the system – for the daughter to be exchangeable, father and son-in-law need to be interchangeable. Such an ambiguity complicates Genius's attempts to define and delimit the role of the father vis-à-vis his daughter.

The Tale of the False Bachelor

In a time of peace in his land, the son of the emperor of Rome wants to fight in order to prove his chivalry. Without his father's permission he goes to Persia with a knight of his to participate in the war between Persia and Egypt. He fights for the sultan of Persia and falls in love with his daughter. One day the sultan has to leave his daughter in order to fight a major battle. Before leaving, he takes a ring from her and tells her that if he dies she should marry the man who will bring back her ring. The sultan is mortally wounded in the battle, and, before dying, he gives the ring to the emperor's son. Subsequently, the emperor's son tells his companion about the ring. The latter decides to steal it and supplant the former. He goes back to Persia and marries the sultan's daughter. The emperor's son cannot prove that his knight is supplanting him and that he was the one chosen by the sultan to marry his daughter. He falls sick with grief, and before dying, he reveals his identity. Thus, the treachery of the false bachelor is discovered. The dead emperor's son and the false bachelor are sent back to Rome, where the false bachelor will be judged.

The "Tale of the False Bachelor" is one of the three stories in Book 2 of the *Confessio Amantis* that illustrate the sin of supplantation, a branch of envy – the other two are the "Tale of Geta and Amphitrion," and "Pope Boniface." The Latin verse introducing the section on supplantation explains the sin by means of a plant metaphor and a wordplay on the basis of the Latin word "planta." The supplanter plows underneath the supplanted's plant uprooting it: "Inuidus alterius est Supplantator honoris, / Et tua quo vertat culmina subtus arat."³ In his discussion of the sin following the Latin verse (2327–2458), Genius uses a similar wordplay in Middle English:

> ... thei that worchen be supplaunt,
> Yit wolden thei a man supplaunte,
> And take a part of thilke plaunte
> Which he hath for himselve set. (2368–71)

And, some lines later: "Supplant . . . / Fulofte happneth forto mowe / Thing which an other man hath sowe" (2374–76). The use of the plant metaphor in both cases may seem to characterize the act of supplantation as an unnatural act against the plant; the supplanter cuts the plant's "natural" growing process. However, the plant itself does not just grow naturally either, that is, without human intervention, but it is planted and grown by its owner (Genius notes that the owner "hath for himselve set," and "hath sowe" the plant).

The metaphor of the plant serves to introduce the theme of identity in the tale. Genius's explanation of the sin of supplantation raises questions about identity and the self. In the Latin verse, the plant seems to stand for honor ("alterius... honoris") or, more vaguely, just "quod" ("what"): the supplanter "capit occulte, quod nequit ipse palam."⁴ In Genius's version, it stands for "worschipe" (2331) – the supplanter appropriates another person's "worschipe" and stands "with his slyh compas / In stede there another was" (2341–42) – or, vaguely, for that "Thing which an other man hath sowe" (2376), or that thing "that an other man schal lese" (2345). In the following pages, I will first argue that these different "things" refer to parts that constitute the identity of the supplanted, and thus that the "Tale of the False Bachelor" is about the constitution of an individual's identity, and, more broadly, about the construction of identity, not only in connection with knighthood, but also with the family and political structures of authority.

Knightly identity is, indeed, a major theme in the "Tale of the False Bachelor." Establishing his identity as a knight constitutes the motive that drives the emperor's son to war. He wants to fight, even though his country is not at war with any other country, because he needs to establish his knightly identity, and he can only do so through the constant repetition of knightly feats of prowess. For, as Marshall Leicester has pointed out regarding Chaucer's "Knight's Tale," the estate of knighthood "is not a preexisting entity but an institution and an *activity*."⁵ Dinshaw has established a similar

---

3 "The envious man supplants another's honor; / He plows beneath to fell what you've raised up." (Translation taken from *The Latin Verses of the* Confessio Amantis, ed. and trans. S. Echard and C. Fanger [East Lansing, MI: East Lansing Colleagues Press, 1991] 39).
4 "[He] seizes on the sly what he can't claim." (*The Latin Verses*, ed. and trans. Echard and Fanger 41.)
5 Marshall Leicester, Jr., *The Disenchanted Self: Representing the Subject in the* Canterbury Tales (Berkeley: U of California P, 1990) 372. Leicester argues about Chaucer's tale that it is

connection between knighthood and performance in the case of *Sir Gawain and the Green Knight*.⁶ Dinshaw has argued that "[k]nighthood is a performance – is indeed a performative, conventional and iterable, not freely chosen but constrained by birth, class status, and other structures of the normative – and Gawain is always *in production* in this poem" (213). The knight's chivalric identity, moreover, constitutes a fundamental element that defines him as a man. Thus, during the temptation scenes, "[w]hen his active role is usurped by the lady here, when he is not *doing*, [Gawain] has no proper, courtly masculine identity" (213). Following a similar line of argument, I will examine knighthood in the "Tale of the False Bachelor" as a constituent of masculine identity that grows on the basis of the repetition of certain acts, on the basis of performativity, like watering the plant repeatedly to make it grow.⁷ It is the repetitiveness of his actions that constitutes the knight's identity. But it is also this repetitiveness that opens gaps and fissures in the construction of knightly identity.

The themes of supplantation and the construction of identity and gender are further explored in the context of the father-daughter relationship in the tale. The "Tale of the False Bachelor" is also about a father's search for his replacement, a replacement that needs to be both familial and political. Since the sultan of Persia's only child is a daughter, his son-in-law will replace him, not only as the authority figure over his daughter, but also as sultan. The "Tale of the False Bachelor" suggests that the replacement of the father is also a form of supplantation. I will show that the tale's treatment of the knight's supplantation by the False Bachelor draws attention to the instability in the construction of gender. Moreover, I will argue that by suggesting parallels between this supplantation and the system of exchange, the tale also draws attention to the interchangeability of familial roles. If one knight can easily replace another knight and a son-in-law can easily replace his father-in-law, then it is suggested that the two individuals who can replace one another are

---

"not only an image of knighthood and the noble life but also an exemplary instance, consciously and deliberately presented, of the *doing* of knighthood" (372). The "Tale of the False Bachelor" is about the *doing* of kinghthood too, but also about the consequences of the *doing*.

⁶ Carolyn Dinshaw, "A Kiss Is Just a Kiss: Heterosexuality and Its Consolations in *Sir Gawain and the Green Knight*," *Diacritics* 24 (1994): 205–26.

⁷ My notion of performativity follows Butler's as she explains it in *Bodies That Matter*:
> Performativity is neither free play nor theatrical self-presentation; nor can it be simply equated with performance . . . [P]erformativity cannot be understood outside of a process of iterability, a regularized and constrained repetition of norms. And this repetition is not performed *by* a subject; this repetition is what enables a subject and constitutes the temporal condition for the subject. This iterability implies that 'performance' is not a singular act but a ritualized production, a ritual reiterated under and through constraint, under and through the force of prohibition and taboo, with the threat of ostracism and even death controlling and compelling the shape of the production but not, I will insist, determining it fully in advance. (95)

fundamentally the same and thus, more troublingly, that the father could also easily replace his son-in-law in his relationship with his daughter. The parallels between both forms of supplantation, moreover, are further emphasized by the fact that the sultan chooses the Roman knight as his successor on the basis of the knight's performance rather than of some other distinctive feature. The sultan chooses him, not because he is an emperor's son – since he does not know this – but because he performs well on the battlefield; in other words, he likes him for his knightly deeds, not for what he may "be." What the Roman knight does constitutes his identity.

A comparison with the source for the tale highlights Gower's particular interest in the theme of identity and shows once again his independence from his sources. The "Tale of the False Bachelor" is based on the story of "Annulus" in *Le Roman de Marques de Rome*, a French prose romance from the thirteenth century.[8] In the French romance, the wife of the Roman Emperor Diocletian tells the story of the false bachelor to her husband as an example of how even the most trusted servant can cheat his lord.[9] For this reason, her story finishes with the death of the Roman knight; with that she has proved her point. The theme of identity is implicit in *Le Marques de Rome*. None of the characters in it has a name; they are identified by their political or social role. Similarly, in the "Tale of the False Bachelor" none of the characters has a name, but they are identified as the emperor of Rome, the emperor's son (also known as the "Romein kniht"), the "kniht" who betrays the emperor's son, the sultan, and the sultan's daughter. What they do or represent socially defines their identity rather than any individualizing traits. Gower, we will see, develops this implicit theme of identity, deftly adapting his source to his own purposes.

Genius starts the tale by noting that Rome was going through a peaceful time, which "To some it thoghte for the beste, / To some it thoghte nothing so" (2510–11). One of those who did not like the peace was the emperor's son, who wanted to be a warrior, "As he that was chivalerous / Of worldes fame and desirous" (2517–18). Chivalry was one of the major constituent elements in the construction of masculine identity in fourteenth-century English courtly culture; knighthood is a form of realizing one's masculinity and thus a crucial part of a man's identity. This tenet of the masculine code of chivalry is clearly suggested by Genius. He notes first that those "Whos herte

---

[8] See Lewis Thorpe, "A Source of the *Confessio Amantis*," *Modern Language Review* 43 (1948): 175–81.
[9] At the end of her story she asks the emperor, who is listening to her, "Ore, sire empereres ... fu cil bien guilez et par celui, en cui il se fioit et qui ses escuiers avoit este?" ("Now, sir emperor, was he not well cheated by he who he trusted most and who had been his squire?" [my translation]). The emperor assents, and then the empress points out to him that he himself has been cheated similarly ("encore estes vos mieus guilez ..."). Quoted from *Le Roman de Marques de Rome*, ed. Johann Alton (Tübingen: Bibliothek des Literarischen Vereins, 1889) 111. All quotations from the French romance come from the same edition, and all translations of the romance are mine.

stod upon knihthode" (2513) were not happy with Rome's peaceful time. One of those knights was the son's emperor, who

> ... most of alle of his manhode
> ...
> Began his fadre to beseche
> That he the werres mihte seche.   (2514, 2519–20)

Out of "manhode" the son wants to seek wars and become a knight. Genius has "knihthode" rhyme with "manhode," emphasizing the link between knighthood and masculine identity.

The Roman knight wants to realize his manhood through active participation in battles. Genius significantly observes in lines 2572–73 that when the knight fought "He wroghte such knihthode there, / That every man spak of him good." The verb "wroghte" in line 2572 indicates that knighthood is not something with which one is born, but an identity that the knight has to create and forge for himself through repeated participation in battles. Through the repeated enactment of his "knihthode," the knight forges his gender identity. We may recall here Butler's definition of gender as "the repeated stylization of the body, a set of repeated acts within a highly rigid regulatory frame that congeal over time to produce the appearance of substance, of a natural sort of being."[10] As a gender-defining activity, knighthood is based primarily on performance. In order to be a knight, one must primarily act like one. And through the repetition of these acts, knighthood creates the illusion of a natural trait, a trait that defines one's gender "naturally." (Notice Genius's remark that the "kniht" wants to fight wars "most of alle of his manhode.")

The Roman knight's need to act leads him to fight a war in the East that has nothing to do with him. It is significant that no reasons are given for the Roman knight's choice of sides; we do not know why he fights for the sultan of Persia instead of the caliph of Egypt. In fact, we suspect it does not matter. No higher purpose drives the Roman knight but fighting for fighting's sake, or rather, for masculinity's sake. In this sense, when Gower (or Genius) confuses Cairo with the capital of Persia – as Macaulay notes – one wonders if it is a mistake on Gower's part, or an indication that it does not really matter in the context of this tale.[11] What counts for the knight is that there is a war in which in order to participate he has to take one side.

---

[10] Butler, Gender Trouble 33.
[11] See English Works of John Gower, ed. Macaulay, EETS, e.s. 81, note to l. 2558. The Roman knight's fighting for fighting's sake reminds us of Chaucer's knight, who not only fought for Christianity but also for "heathens": "This ilke worthy knyght hadde been also / Somtyme with the lord of Palatye / Agayn another hethen in Turkye" ("General Prologue," Canterbury Tales 64–66). As in the case of the False Bachelor, we are not given any reason why Chaucer's knight decided to fight for a heathen against another heathen – beyond the fact that he fights because he is a knight.

A knight's identity is not only based on waging war. To become a part of his community, and a full man, the knight also needs to have a female beloved. As Aers has argued in his essay on Chaucer's *Troilus and Criseyde*, "the development of masculine identity in the knightly class demanded more than the cult of a public face of invulnerable mastery ... It involved ... 'love', with its courtly 'observaunces.' "[12] Writing about Troilus, Aers has noted that he " 'needs' a woman as marker of his own subjectivity and worth as an adult knight" (121). The woman, then, is just a marker, someone acted upon who responds passively to the man's desire. As in war, the man also has to act aggressively in love. Loving and fighting forge the knight's masculine identity and both are depicted by Genius as being driven by the same active impulse. Genius's description of the Roman knight's "desire" to go to war is significant in this respect: the emperor's son, who wanted to be a warrior, "As he that was chivalerous / Of worldes fame and desirous / Began his fader to beseche" (2517–19). The striking hyperbaton in line 2518 ("Of worldes fame and desirous," i.e., "and desirous of worldes fame") foregrounds the adjective "desirous" by leaving it hanging at the end of the line, thus making us wonder for a moment if "desirous" could also refer to something else, or, even, whether the desire itself is more important than the object of desire, which could be "fame" or a lady or anything else. In addition, the rhyme "chivalerous-desirous" emphasizes the intimate link between chivalry and desire.

The culturally-created chivalric need to have a lady is so internalized, as Aers has noted, that it appears to be a "product of nature" (122).[13] "Naturally," too, after forging his chivalric identity, Genius's Roman knight falls in love with the beautiful sultan's daughter, bowing

> ... unto that ilke lawe
> Fro which no lif mai be withdrawe,
> And that is love, whos nature
> Set lif and deth in aventure
> Of hem that knyhthode undertake.   (2581–85)

In this passage, as in his explanation of the incest taboo, which I discussed in the first chapter, Genius naturalizes love as that law that no "lif" can escape, especially those "that knyhthode undertake." Once the knight submits to the law, love becomes a spur for him. Thus, in the case of his Roman knight:

> This lusti peine hath overtake
> The herte of this Romein so sore,

---

12 Aers, "Masculine Identity and the Courtly Community" 121.
13 Dinshaw, "A Kiss Is Just a Kiss," notices that in *Sir Gawain and the Green Knight* the lady also makes a similar point:
> [She] explicat[es] to Gawain the nature of knighthood: its essence is deeds of love, 'þe lel layk of luf, þe lettrure of armes [the faithful practice of love, the doctrine of arms]' [1513]. Love of a lady is the rubric, the text of knights' works [1515], and it is only known through 'teuelyng' (striving) [1514]. (212)

> That to knihthode more and more
> Prouesce avanceth his corage. (2586–89)

Love is thus portrayed as a necessary part of a knight's (or a man's) identity, a part that contributes to his "knihthode," and thus to establishing his masculinity.

In his later discussion of chivalry in Book 4, depicting love once again as an originary desire, Genius notes that love constructs gender identity. It makes men bold:

> ... to the couard hardiesce
> It yifth, so that verrai prouesse
> Is caused upon loves reule
> To him that can manhode reule. (2301–04)

And it makes women "affait" their femininity, as they worry about their physical attractiveness: "And ek toward the wommanhiede ... / For thei the betre affaited be / In every thing, as men may se" (2305, 2307–08). Love thus makes men and women perform their assigned gender roles.[14] They repeat certain acts to create and affirm their gender identity. But love in the chivalric world, as Aers has argued, is not an originary desire that can be divorced from the construction of gender. It is a culturally-created need that is so internalized that it appears to be "a product of nature" (122).

That the identity of the self depends on the repetition of certain acts rather than on a "natural" self or identity, or, to put it differently, that the gender identity of a man or a woman depends on action, indicates that this identity is unstable; as Butler puts it, "[t]hat the gendered body is performative suggests that it has no ontological status apart from the various acts that constitute its reality."[15] The exclusive dependence of the emperor's son on performance to construct his identity makes him vulnerable to supplantation. His dependence on public action (war) and on public signs of identity, like the ring that the sultan gives him, rather than on some "ontological self," makes it easy for another person to claim those exterior signs as his. The fact that this supplantation can take place, though, is explained by the performative character of gender construction. Butler notes that, due to the performativity inherent to gender construction, the repetition of certain acts allows for the possibility of "the parodic proliferation and subversive play of gendered meanings" (33). Butler is referring here to the possibility of crossing genders. The "Tale of the False Bachelor" demonstrates a different point. If the gendered body is performative, if it has no ontological status, then men are interchangeable as long as they act in similar ways. Indeed, in Gower's tale there is no subversion of gender, a man supplants another man; but the

---

[14] It should be noted that the Old French version does not establish any connections between love and knighthood.

[15] Judith Butler, *Gender Trouble* 132

easiness with which the false bachelor replaces his master manifests the constructedness of the Roman knight's masculine identity. Since both men are mainly identified by their performance, it is not possible to distinguish between the two. One can parody the other (and vice versa).

In this respect, Gower introduces a significant change in relation to his source. Since in *Le Marques de Rome* the empress's purpose in telling the story is to show that even the most trusted servants can be false, the empress explicitly identifies the false bachelor as a servant of the knight (he is a "valre, qui ses escuiers estoit," 109). In Gower's tale, however, the false bachelor, like the emperor's son, is always identified as a "kniht"; thus the similarity between the two men is emphasized. As another "kniht," another man only identified by his fighting, the false bachelor is not significantly different from the son of the emperor of Rome. At the end of the tale, the identification between the two men also becomes evident when Genius notes about their return to Rome that, "The qwike body with the dede / With leve take forth thei lede" (2779–80). Joined in the same line and identified by the same noun, "body," it seems as if the two men are the same person. A few lines later, when Genius reflects on the sin, he tells Amans that he should "take hiede also / What Supplant doth in other halve" (2786–87). Does "halve" here mean the other half of one person? Does it then imply that the supplanter is part of another person?

While the "Tale of the False Bachelor" is ostensibly about a bachelor's supplantation of another bachelor, at another level it is also about a less obvious form of supplantation: that of a father by his son-in-law. When a father marries his daughter off to another man, the daughter's future husband supplants the father. This form of supplantation is not considered a sin. Quite to the contrary, it is actually sanctioned and enforced by society: the father has to agree to his own supplantation. Nevertheless, the father's enforced agreement, the fact that the exchange is demanded and sanctioned by society, is the only crucial factor that makes the replacement of the father by another man, his son-in-law, different from supplantation.[16] The "Tale of the False Bachelor" makes this especially evident. By dealing with these two forms of supplantation at the same time, Genius suggests that they are both informed by the same fundamental principle: the distinction between the masculine and the feminine gender. The fundamental importance of gender to define the identity of the subject makes any masculine subject replaceable

---

[16] Dinshaw, "Gower's Captive Women," John Gower Society Panel, 24th International Conference on Medieval Studies, Kalamazoo, 6 May 1989, also notices the structural similarity between supplantation and the exchange of women:
> [S]upplantation in love affairs has to do with men's taking one another's places and women. And when one man takes another man's woman, the woman is thus traded from one to another. Now, this is a socially and morally transgressive structure of exchange, in Genius's scheme of vices. But it is also strikingly similar to the way society itself is structured, as Lévi-Strauss analyzes it. (5)

(I thank Carolyn Dinshaw for generously providing me with a copy of her paper.)

by another masculine subject, both in the case of the wrongful supplantation of one young knight by another and in the replacement of a father by his son-in-law. Thus, there appears to be a basic sin of supplantation at the heart of the system of exchange.

That the woman's husband acts as a replacement of her father is suggested during the scene in which the sultan tells his daughter that if he dies in the next battle she should marry whomever brings back her ring. Their actions during this scene as well as the solemnity of the scene evoke a marriage ceremony, suggesting again the structural similarity between father-daughter and husband-wife relationships:

> The Soldan in gret privete
> A goldring of his dowhter tok,
> And made hire swere upon a bok
> And ek upon the goddes alle,
> That if fortune so befalle
> In the bataille that he deie,
> That sche schal thilke man obeie
> And take him to hire housebonde
> Which thilke same Ring to honde
> Hire scholde bringe after his deth.   (2606–15)

The imagery and vocabulary used in this scene suggest a secret marriage between daughter and father: the scene takes place "in gret privete"; the daughter has to swear upon a book and upon the gods; and he takes her ring.[17]

Furthermore, it is significant that the father does not want his daughter to marry, or even to know whom she shall marry, until he dies, and that the daughter agrees to obey her father without knowing who will be her husband and without having any say in the matter. Only the father's will is important. In psychoanalytic terms, Jane Gallop has argued that the power of the father's law is the standard of value and that it influences the father's relation with his daughter: "[t]he daughter submits to the father's rule, which prohibits the father's desire, the father's penis, out of the desire to seduce the father by doing his bidding and thus pleasing him" (70–71). In the "Tale of the False Bachelor" the daughter submits to her father's desire. After the sultan's death, Genius remarks that the Parliament convenes in the presence of the daughter. Upon being asked whom she wants to marry, the daughter responds that her only will is her father's:

> ... of Mariage
> Thei trete and axen of hir wille,
> Bot sche, which thoghte to fulfille
> Hire fader heste in this matiere,

---

[17] In Book 5, interestingly enough, Genius accuses sacrilegious lovers of trying to steal rings from their beloveds while they are in church: "Or elles thei take ate leste / Out of hir hand or ring or glove" (7046–47).

Seide openly, that men mai hiere,
The charge which hire fader bad. (2688–93)

It is interesting that the Parliament does give her a chance to express her "wille," since they do not know what the sultan had arranged. She, however, caught in the father's rule, wants only to please him. The daughter's "wille" is simply her "fader heste." Her desire is a mere mirror of her father's desire.[18]

The characters in the tale, I noted above, are defined by their role or function rather than by a specific identity. Accordingly, the sultan's daughter is just that, the "daughter." There is nothing else by which we could identify her. Indeed, we never know what the daughter thinks or desires as an individual, but only what she wants to do *as* the daughter of the sultan. There is one instance in which it might seem that we have a glimpse of her desires. In lines 2742–43, Genius points out that when the supplantation was discovered, the Roman knight died, "Wherof was sory manyon, / Bot non of alle so as sche". One might be tempted to interpret these lines as a revelation of the daughter's love for the Roman knight. But even at this point, since there have been no indications that the daughter felt anything for, or had even met, the knight, one could more plausibly see the daughter's sorrow as the consequence of realizing that she would not be able to fulfill her father's will, because the knight chosen by her father (not by herself) has died.

The sultan's daughter's function within the familial structure cannot be dissociated from her function in the political structure of Persia. Genius presents her first as most beautiful (2577), and, in the next line, he points to her political importance: "Sche scholde ben hir fader hair" (2578). The French version of the story also notes that the daughter is her father's heir, but does not make a point of her beauty, nor of the workings of the law of love. Neither does it present her as an object of men's desire. The narrator of the story, the wife of the Roman Emperor Diocletian, points out only that the emperor's son fell in love with her: "Ore ot li soudans une fille et n'ot plus d'oirs, si l'ama mout li damoiseaus par amors" (109).[19] Then she goes on to relate that, due to an imminent battle between the sultan and the caliph, the former decides to talk to his daughter and tell her whom she shall marry.

As the sultan's daughter and only heir in the "Tale of the False Bachelor," this woman, like the men in the tale, is performing a social and political function. Her function is to become the wife of the heir to her father's political

---

18 Dinshaw, "Gower's Captive Women," develops a similar observation:
[T]he daughter, symbolized by the ring, is passed between men . . . The necessarily mimetic nature of her own desire – she must desire him who has possession of her, and she must not have ideas of her own as to who she'd like to sleep with – is precisely rendered in her representation as a ring – as a blank, a zero, an "O" to be filled in by the man who gets her. (7)

19 "Now, the sultan had a daughter and could not have any more; thus the bachelor loves her greatly *paramours*" (my translation).

position and thus to make it possible for her father to control her offspring and his future heirs. As David Willbern puts it, interpreting Freud's theory of the unconscious response to the loss of a child: "The daughter . . . like the son, symbolizes the father's generative extension into the future and remains in reality and in fantasy his flesh."[20] In Gower's tale the daughter's role as the father's generative extension is even more important because he has no son. She is the only person who symbolizes his generative extension into the future.

The absolute importance of the daughter's generative role and the denial of her desire make the supplantation possible. As Aers has observed, the definition of masculine identity as active and predatory depends "on the simultaneous construction of 'feminine' identity as passive, powerless object" (120). The insistent definition of masculinity as active in this tale necessitates the definition of the sultan's daughter as a passive object who simply obeys her father's commands. The only proofs the daughter will have that the person she is supposed to marry is her father's choice are external: the ring and the masculine identity of that person. And, thus, as long as the person who claims to be the one chosen brings the ring and is a fully active and acting knight, he can be her husband. The sinful supplantation can easily take place because, as in the supplantation sanctioned by the laws of exchange, the daughter is rendered as a passive object to be traded between men.

In conclusion, the False Bachelor's supplantation of the Roman knight, the one Genius condemns as sinful, resembles in a troubling way the accepted structure of supplantation underlying the system of exchange, whereby the son-in-law replaces the father. This resemblance suggests that supplantation is at the core of the system of exchange. The only difference between the two forms of supplantation, the Bachelor's and the one sanctioned by the system of exchange, is that the former is not authorized by the father, while the latter is. To put it differently, in the system of exchange, the father agrees to be supplanted. The way the sultan relates to his daughter in the tale, moreover, suggests that there is very little difference between the father and the son-in-law, as there is very little difference between the Roman knight and the False Bachelor. The three men are primarily defined by their doing, by their knightly deeds, and in this sense, they are all fundamentally the same.

The "Tale of the False Bachelor" exposes the gaps and fissures created by gender's dependence on performativity through its examination of chivalry's dependence on external and aggressive action. The young knight's impulsiveness and desire to prove that he is "chivalerous" by making war contrasts with Rome's peace, which Genius insists upon at the beginning of the tale. The emperor, he notes, led Rome

> In pes, that he no werres hadde;
> Ther was nothing desobeissant

---

[20] David Wilbern, "*Filia Oedipi*: Father and Daughter in Freudian Theory," *Daughters and Fathers*, ed. Boose and Flowers, 93.

>   Which was to Rome appourtenant,
>   Bot al was torned into reste.   (2506–09)

Notice Genius's emphasis on Rome's peaceful period ("In pes," all "into reste," etc., "nothing [was] desobeissant"). The only one who challenged the peace, the only one who disobeyed, was the emperor's son. His uncontrollable desire to be "a werreiour" (2516) leads him to disobey his own father, who does not want him to go to war. The fatal consequences of disturbing the "pax Romana" and circumventing the father's authority are clear by the end of the tale. The chivalric ethos both in war and in love proves disruptive in the tale. Only the good governance of the peaceful Roman emperor can restore order at the end.[21]

In the next tale under consideration, the "Tale of Albinus and Rosemund," Gower's critique of chivalry's intrinsic need to perform, to do deeds of arms, and of its incompatibility with peace and good governance is developed more fully. The aggressive and performative definition of the knight in this tale proves to be incompatible with his role as king. Moreover, it renders the woman passive initially. Nevertheless, even when later on in the tale the woman takes on an active role, her initiative has tragic consequences, because she simply mirrors her husband's self-serving actions. As in the "Tale of the False Bachelor," Albinus's replacement of Rosemund's father not only suggests again the interchangeability of father and son-in-law, but, in fact, becomes ultimately the cause of Albinus's demise.

The Tale of Albinus and Rosemund

"Drink with thi fader, Dame," says Albinus to his wife Rosemund during the feast he has organized in her honor (1.2551). Or, as the Latin gloss to the tale, and Godfrey of Viterbo's *Pantheon*, Gower's probable source for the story, phrase it: "Bibe cum patre tuo."[22] What does Albinus mean by such a command? Who is the father with whom Rosemund is supposed to drink? Is he her biological father, Gurmond, whom Albinus had previously killed in battle and whose skull he has transformed into a wine cup? Or, could the father be Albinus himself?

Albinus's equivocal command to his wife, whether in Latin or in English, becomes crucial in the story, and Gower exploits its ambiguity, more than Godfrey does, for reasons that will be analyzed below. Albinus's command

---

[21] Notice the contrast between secrecy and openness in this respect. The secrecy of the arrangements made by the father (he meets "in gret privetee" [2606], with his daughter, and he gives the ring to the Roman knight about which "non it wiste," [2640], also in private) contrasts with the moment when the truth is finally discovered and told, as Genius puts it, "openly" (2746).
[22] Godfrey of Viterbo, *Pantheon*, *Monumenta Germaniae Historica*, ed. Georgius Heinricus Pertz, vol. 22 (Hannoverae: Impensis Bibliopolii Aulici Hahniani, 1872) 214. All other quotations from the *Pantheon* are taken from the same edition.

suggests that husband-wife and father-daughter relations share a similar dynamics of power. When a father chooses his daughter's husband, he is choosing his own replacement (or agreed "supplantor"), someone who will replace him as the authority figure over the woman. Although Gurmond does not choose Albinus as his daughter's husband (quite the opposite, since he is killed by Albinus), nevertheless, Albinus replaces Gurmond as the male authority figure over Rosemund. Furthermore, Albinus replaces Gurmond in yet a different way: he also becomes king of the Gepids. The simultaneity of Albinus's two forms of replacement of Gurmond – as king and as Rosemund's father-figure – allows Gower to explore the intricate connections between family and politics. As a consequence of his military victory over Gurmond and the Gepids, Albinus wins his lady and marries her at the same time as he acquires new political power; later on, because of his "avantance," his boasting, he loses everything: his wife, his political power, and his life. His proud behavior causes the ruin of his familial and private life, as well as of his public authority as king.

Gower's tale, though, does not simply show the connection between family and politics. Albinus's poor performance in both spheres originates in his chivalrous character. At the beginning of the tale he is characterized as a king and a knight:

> Of hem that we Lombars now calle
> Albinus was the ferste of alle
> Which bar corone of Lombardie
> And was of gret chivalerie.   (2459–62)

The combination of chivalry and kingship will be problematic for Albinus. The "Tale of Albinus and Rosemund," I will argue, critiques chivalric ideology and stresses its incompatibility with the notion of kingship that was crystallizing in the fourteenth century. As Richard W. Kaeuper has put it:

> [C]hivalry, by and large represented a countercurrent to the movement toward the Western form of state which was so evident across the twelfth and thirteenth centuries in France and especially in England. The movement of kingship and the state was toward public authority vested in a sovereign and exercised theoretically for the common good. Chivalry was rooted in the intensely personal and private world of ancient Germanic custom, modified by the whole host of changes seen in almost every aspect of life, which shaped the Europe of the High Middle Ages.[23]

This incompatibility, of course, did not lead kings to detach themselves from the chivalric ethos. Quite to the contrary, kings fashioned themselves as knights – Edward III, we should remember, created the Order of the Garter,

---

[23] Richard W. Kaeuper, *War, Justice, and Public Order: England and France in the Later Middle Ages* (Oxford: Clarendon Press, 1988) 195–96.

and Richard II participated at tournaments and promoted an image of himself as leading knight.[24] Nevertheless, this assumption of chivalric identity by fourteenth-century kings was, as Kaeuper puts it, "a marriage of convenience" (194). One can see in the kings' use of a chivalric image, I would add, an attempt to control their knights by appearing as the first among them. This attempt, though, caused some fundamental tensions due to the different ideologies that drove chivalry and kingship in the late Middle Ages. Patterson points to Richard II as a case in which the tensions "became internalized in the monarch himself, who was at once chivalric knight and Crown, at once an honorman in a dispersed field of autonomous competitors and, as the sovereign, the locus of authority" (188). In the following pages, I will first argue that the "Tale of Albinus and Rosemund" focuses on this contradiction, and that Albinus, much like Richard II at the beginning of his reign, embodies the impossible combination of chivalry and kingship in its fourteenth-century sense and suffers the tragic consequences of such an inadequate combination. The difficulty of combining the individualistic ethos of chivalry, an ethos that often led to great violence, with a public-oriented notion of kingship is evident in Gower's tale.[25]

The importance of the notion of honor for the knight reveals the extent to which the chivalric ethos is individualistic, that is, the extent to which it is invested in creating a self-sufficient and independent identity. Genius himself alludes to this self-sufficiency in the "Tale of Capaneus" (1.1977–2009). When he introduces the proud knight Capaneus, Gower's priest notes that,

> ... he thurgh his chivalerie
> Upon himself so mochel triste,
> That to the goddes him ne liste
> In no querele to beseche.   (1.1982–85)

Chivalry tries to be above any rules, even above divine rules; it has its own codes with which it solves "quereles" or any personal attacks against a knight's honor. This individualistic self-sufficiency posed problems to the regulation of public order by the king. For the chivalric ethos would not subordinate itself to the interests of public order and would typically make use

---

[24] In his chapter on Chaucer's "Knight's Tale" and what he calls the crisis of chivalric identity, Patterson, *Chaucer and the Subject of History*, notes that at the beginning of his reign, Richard II tried to fashion himself as a knight, "a deliberate response on Richard's part to his troubled relations with his barons" (187). The aim of Richard's assumption of a chivalric identity was to assert "his role as the feudal overlord of England, the personal seigneur of all those who followed him to war" (188).

[25] It is probably not coincidental that Gower chose the story of a Lombard king to examine notions of tyranny and violence, for, as Wallace, *Chaucerian Polity*, has observed "violence ... by Chaucer's time had become synonymous with 'Lumbardye' " (5). Wallace later quotes Queen Alceste's reference in Chaucer's *Legend of Good Women* to "tyraunts of Lumbardye, / That usen wilfulhed and tyrannie" (quoted in Wallace 213).

of violence to achieve its ends. The knightly classes, according to Kaeuper, had a "tendency to violent self-help [which] was often proudly proclaimed and recognized as a right rather than condemned as a crime" (185). Indeed, as Louise Fradenburg has noted, violence was not just a means but a fundamental constitutive element of the chivalric identity: "Violence is the medium through which the honorable self, in its struggle to extort its own glorious image from the face and look of the other, must constitute itself."[26]

Gower's critique of chivalry's self-centeredness, I will further show, is linked to his examination of the structural similarities between father-daughter and husband-wife relationships in this tale. The individualistic and self-sufficient side of chivalry bears an uncanny resemblance to the self-sufficiency implicit in the act of incest. By refusing to exchange his daughter, the incestuous father creates his own rules, asserting his independence from society and social rules. Joining one's close relatives lessens one's dependence on society, on outside social and political structures. Conversely, marriage, as a social contract, is a reminder of one's dependence on society. As Boehrer has put it, "[i]f marrying out solidifies one's social position, it also suggests that that very position is to a large degreee beyond one's own control – that other people and other things . . . supply it, and thus that other people may take it away."[27] In this sense, the self-sufficiency implicit in the incestuous hints in Albinus's equivocal command to Rosemund is congruent with the individualism inherent in his chivalric identity.

The "Tale of Albinus and Rosemund" is one of the tales in the *Confessio Amantis* that showcases Gower's deft adaptation of his sources to his own purposes.[28] On the basis of similarities of plot and even vocabulary, Macaulay argues that Gower's most likely source is Godfrey of Viterbo's *Pantheon* (XXII.5–6), which is based on the version in Paul the Deacon's *Historia Langobardorum* (II.28–29).[29] The purpose and focus of Gower's story differ significantly from those of Godfrey's and Paul's versions. The version in the *Historia* seems to be based on an epic story of Germanic origin that has been lost.[30] Accordingly, Paul puts more emphasis on the military side of the story than on the love between the king and Rosemund. Albinus is depicted as the victim of his wife's wiles – Paul starts his account by noting: "Qui rex

---

[26] Louise Olga Fradenburg, *City, Marriage, Tournament: Arts of Rule in Late Medieval Scotland* (Madison: U of Wisconsin P, 1991) 206. On honor and violence, see also Julian Pitt-Rivers, "Honour and Social Status," *Honour and Shame: The Values of Mediterranean Society*, ed. J. G. Peristiany (Chicago: U of Chicago P, 1966) 19–78.
[27] Boehrer, *Monarchy and Incest in Renaissance England* 145.
[28] For a close examination of Gower's transformation of Viterbo's account, see Yeager, *John Gower's Poetic* 145–52.
[29] *English Works of John Gower*, ed. Macaulay, EETS, e.s. 81, 476.
[30] On the strong possibility that the source for Paulus's version of the story of Albinus and Rosemund was a Langobard epic song now lost, see William Dudley Foulke's discussion in Paul the Deacon, *History of the Langoboards*, trans. William Dudley Foulke (Philadelphia: U of Pennsylvania P, 1907) 344–52.

[Albinus] postquam in Italia tres annos et sex menses regnavit, insidiis suae coniugis interemptus est."[31] Except for suggesting that he had drunk more than was appropriate during the feast ("in convivio ultra quam oportuerat aput Veronam laetus resederet," 104), Paul does not criticize the ruthlessness of Albinus's command to his wife to drink from her father's skull.[32] Throughout Paul's version, Albinus remains a valiant king who vanquished Gurmond and married his daughter Rosemund for no other reason than the death of his first wife. Love does not play any role in their relationship. Neither does it play a role in Rosemund's relationship with her two accomplices, Helmegis and Peredeo, who kill the king at her command.[33]

Godfrey of Viterbo's version is similarly concise about the relationship between Albinus and Rosemund. We are told that Albinus married Rosemund after he lost his own wife, but love plays no role either in this marriage or in the further development of the plot. Unlike Paul, though, Godfrey explicitly disapproves of Albinus's cruelty, which he calls "Crimen inauditum" ('outrageous crime') also calling Albinus "impius" ('evil'). To a certain extent, Godfrey's criticism of Albinus draws our sympathy towards Rosemund. Nevertheless, he does not approve of her "arte" ('stratagem'), as he calls it, and, at the end of his version, he calls her adulterous and remarks that her death (she drinks from the poisoned drink that she herself had prepared for Helmechis) was well deserved: "Fraus ibi fraude perit, moritur mors morsa decenter. / Sic gravis ira Dei digna rependit ei" (215, ll. 68–69).[34]

Without altering the plot significantly, Genius's "Tale of Albinus and Rosemund" introduces two fundamental changes. First, Genius radically changes the interest and purpose of the story by introducing a new element behind the characters' motivations: love. In the other two versions, either the characters act out of political reasons or their motivations are not clear at all. In contrast, Genius's story develops in a courtly and chivalric atmosphere absent in any of the earlier versions. In his account, love is the reason Albinus marries Rosemund, and love, as well as self-preservation, is the reason Helmegis kills the king. (We will see, though, that the development of the events questions the nature of Albinus's, as well as Helmegis's, love for Rosemund.) The second fundamental change Genius introduces is making Albinus ultimately responsible for his own tragic end: the reason for Rose-

---

[31] Quoted from Paulus Diaconus, *Historia Langobardorum*, ed. G. Waitz, Scriptores Rerum Germanicarum (Hannoverae: Impensis Bibliopolii Hahniani, 1878) 104. The passage can be translated as follows: "This king, who afterwards reigned in Italy for three years and six months, was killed through the treachery of his wife." (All translations of the *Pantheon* and the *Historia Langobardorum* are mine.)
[32] "During the banquet in Verona he, happy, celebrated more than was appropriate."
[33] In the case of Helmegis, no special reason is given except that she persuaded him. In the case of Peredeo, the man she sleeps with in Diaconus's version, he had to choose between cooperating with her or being killed by the king.
[34] "Deceit dies by deceit, the bitten death dies appropriately. Thus, God's stern wrath rewards her fittingly."

mund's revenge is Albinus's proud and offensive command. Thus, Albinus's pride is Genius's overt reason for telling his story. And the "Tale of Albinus and Rosemund" serves as an example of the sin of boastfulness or "Avantance," a branch of the capital sin of pride. Genius's introduction of these two elements – Albinus's pride and courtly love – raise important questions and contribute to Genius's complex generic transformation of Viterbo's historical and, in Yeager's words, "pragmatic" (147) account into a tragic courtly romance.

Prior to the tale, Genius teaches Amans about "Avantance," and his discussion, significantly, links the sin to the chivalric world. He personifies "Avantance" as someone who takes the role of heralds and boasts about his own deeds:

> The vice cleped Avantance
> With Pride hath hake his aqueintance,
> So that his oghne pris he lasseth,
> When he such mesure overpasseth
> That he his oghne Herald is. (2399–2403)

As Keen has observed, heralds played a fundamental role in the chivalric world.[35] In the later Middle Ages, one of their most important roles was that of "official registrars of deeds of prowess" (138). Indeed, Genius mentions the role of heralds in his discussion about chivalry in Book 4. It is a knight's job to fight valiantly, "So that these heraldz on him crie, / 'Vailant, vailant, lo, wher he goth!' " (4.1632–33). Hence, the knight who boasts of his own deeds in a sense usurps the role of the heralds. In praising himself, he achieves the opposite of what he intends:

> ... thurgh the blastes that he bloweth
> The mannes fame he overthroweth
> Of vertu, which scholde elles springe
> Into the worldes knowlechinge. (2411–14)

By referring to heraldry in his introduction to the sin of "Avantance," Genius puts this sin in a chivalric context and prepares the ground for his critique of chivalry in the "Tale of Albinus and Rosemund."

Albinus indeed acts like the boasting knight. He is not only a man "of gret chivalerie" (2462), but he is obsessed with acting like one – he displays his worth and prowess as a knight and shows throughout the tale that he wants to

---

[35] Keen, *Chivalry* 134–42, analyzes the development of the office of heralds in the Middle Ages and notes that, while one of their initial functions was related to the staging and ceremony of tournaments (135), their duties developed later in different directions, one of them being that of recorders of prowess (138). Interestingly enough, heralds were also related to literary creation: "Their early connection with the minstrels ensured that the heralds were literary men. Their later role as the general registrars of prowess, which called for celebration in fashionable literary mode, ensured that they remained so" (139).

be identified as such. Ordering the defeated Gurmond's skull to be turned into a cup is his way of ensuring that his feat will not be forgotten: "To kepe and drawe into memoire / Of his bataille the victoire" (2475-76). Moreover, the tournament he organizes in Rosemund's honor and which Genius describes in great detail (2508-26) becomes primarily an occasion for his chivalric display.[36] The tournament was designed to show his wife the extent of his power, so that "sche the lordes ate feste, / That were obeissant to his heste, / Mai knowe" (2501-03). It also becomes the occasion to show everybody else the extent and splendor of his chivalric power. Albinus orders "grete Stiedes" (2508) to be brought; he has "many a perled garnement" (2509) embroidered, and "lordes in here beste arrai / Be comen ate time set" (2512-13). As Peck puts it, the tournament is Albinus's "ultimate ego trip."[37]

Prowess is one of the essential elements in the construction of a knight's identity. Love, as I noted in my analysis of the "Tale of the False Bachelor," is also a constitutive part of it.[38] Writing about the beginnings of chivalric ideology, Keen notes that courtly love was one of its distinguishing features from its inception:

> [Chivalry] distinguished itself from the Germanic warrior ethic of earlier times partly by its new elitist pride in the art of fighting on horseback, partly by the new measure of secular cultural independence that we see reflected, in differing moods, in the twelfth-century vogue of genealogical histories among great families and in the troubadours' concept of courtly love as an ennobling force at the secular level. (42)

Love and the lady distinguish the knight from mere warriors and mercenaries.[39] Keen's point seems especially appropriate in the case of the "Tale of Albinus and Rosemund." As noted above, its sources seem to follow a Germanic epic song, and the absence of love as part of the motivation of the plot in the sources indicates that they repeat the Germanic warrior ethic, in which love plays no significant role.

In Book 4, Genius and Amans have a discussion on precisely this topic: the combination of love and arms. Book 4 is devoted to the theme of idleness

---

[36] On medieval tournaments as occasions for chivalric display, see Fradenburg *City, Marriage, Tournament*, chs. 9-13. In ch. 11, Fradenburg offers a summary and a critique of some of the major interpretations of the role of tournaments in the late Middle Ages. See also Kaeuper, *War, Justice, and Public Order*, 199-211, on tournaments in thirteenth- and fourteenth-century England. Kaeuper argues that with Edward III "tournaments became ... a function of the monarchy" (206-07).

[37] Peck, *Kingship and Common Profit* 53.

[38] Patterson's analysis of chivalry (*Chaucer and the Subject of History*, ch. 3) does not consider the significance of the role of love and the lady in the creation of the chivalric identity. Unlike Patterson, I argue in this chapter that love is an intrinsic part of a knight's identity.

[39] In Gower's tale, when the tournament is finished, the knights and ladies talk "of armes and of love" (2528).

in love, and Genius argues that, for a knight, being active in love should mean first and foremost being active in battle. Love is the prize for fighting:

> ... whilom men here loves boghte
> Thurgh gret travaill in strange londes,
> Where that thei wroghten with here hondes
> Of armes many a worthi dede.   (1610–13)

A knight should first gain fame, and then he will be succesful in love; for "wommen loven worthinesse / Of manhode and of gentilesse" (2197–98). For Genius, the situation prevalent in the past was the ideal one. A knight would fight "Somtime in Prus, somtime in Rodes, / And somtime in Tartarie" (1630–31); heralds would then proclaim his exploits, and these would reach his lady's ear so that "danger [she] pute out of hire mod" (1641).[40] Love is thus the necessary corollary of prowess.

The same link between love and battle is established from the beginning of the "Tale of Albinus and Rosemund": Albinus's victory in battle brings as a consequence his victory in love. When Albinus defeated King Gurmond, he overran and seized his land, where, as Genius puts it,

> ... he Gurmondes dowhter fond
> Which Maide Rosemounde hihte,
> ...
> His herte fell to hire anon,
> And such a love on hire he caste
> That he hire weddeth ate laste.   (2480–81, 2484–85)

Genius's depiction of this moment is significant. Rosemund is introduced as Gurmond's daughter, and thus she is just one more spoil from the war that Albinus wins against Gurmond. Gower's priest, moreover, describes the seizure of the land and of the lady as simultaneous events: "The lond anon was overronne / And sesed in his oghne hond, / Wher he Gurmondes dowhter fond" (2478–80). A similar identification can be seen in other tales in the *Confessio*, as for instance, in the "Tale of Galba and Vitellius" (6.537ff), mentioned in Chapter One. The rulers' abuse of their country in this tale parallels their abuse of its women. Galba and Vitellius, two powerful

---

[40] Two observations need to be made here. First, Genius's defense of chivalry's ethos and its intrinsic demand to perform deeds of arms as well as to impress the passive lady in Book 4 conflicts with his critique of chivalry in the "Tale of the False Bachelor" and in the "Tale of Albinus and Rosemund." This conflict, I would argue, stems from Genius's complexity as a character. While, on the one hand, he is an advocate of social, rational order and love, he still has traces of the traditional Genius, the representative of the "irrational" and "natural" impulses of sexual desire. Second, Amans shows total disagreement with Genius on this matter. The lover thinks that one should not have to fight foreign wars in order to win his lady's love. In fact, fighting wars may have the opposite effect: "What scholde I thanne go so ferr / In strange londes many a mile / To ryde, and lese at hom therwhile / Mi love?" (1706–09). Fighting may be the cause for losing, rather than winning, one's lady.

Spanish princes, are set as examples of "glotonie and drunkeschipe" (543). According to Genius, through their drunkenness, they "Oppressede al the nacion / Of Spaigne" (568–69). This oppression is manifested through the rape of the women: "Ther was no wif ne maiden there, . . . Whom thei ne token to defoule, / Wherof the lond was often wo" (572, 574–75). The rape of the women thus stands for the oppression of the land and vice versa. Similarly, Albinus's seizure of Gurmond's land stands for the seizure of Rosemund and vice versa.

Genius's development of the plot in the "Tale of Albinus and Rosemund" – success in battle brings success in love – is in accordance with his own view of a knight's ideal combination of love and battle as expressed in Book 4. We should note, however, that Albinus's particular situation differs from that of Genius's ideal knights: his lady is the daughter of his own victim.[41] In *John Gower's Poetic*, Yeager puts his finger on the problem:

> Alboin's feelings – and his circumstances – are more precarious than he knows. Indeed his wife *has* been the result of his prowess: By defeating his enemy, Alboin at once found love and enabled his marriage. The difficulty of course is that the king he defeated and killed was Rosamund's father – a detail irrelevant in the *Pantheon*'s loveless account but so obviously a problem for Alboin the lover that we wonder how he could have forgotten it. (147)

Indeed, Albinus has not forgotten that he had killed Rosemund's father. What is more, he even wants everybody to remember. And that is precisely what casts some doubts over the nature of his love for Rosemund. His desire to boast of his conquest reveals that his love for her is one more part of his chivalric self-fashioning, like the tournament.

In evoking his victory over Gurmond, Albinus tries to accomplish a further goal: he asserts his kingly authority as the replacement of Gurmond. He does so by suggesting that even in his relationship with Rosemund he "is" Gurmond. Let us return to the toasting scene. Godfrey of Viterbo gives two different versions of the toast: one in a prose summary that precedes the poetic version, the other in the poetic version itself. Both versions, though, quickly dispel the ambiguity of Albinus's command explaining that Albinus is referring, metonymically, to Rosemund's biological father. In the prose summary, as soon as she hears her husband's command, Rosemund knows that Albinus's "patre" refers to the cup she is holding. She knows that the cup was made out of her father's skull. Thus, as she drinks, Rosemund cries and thinks of her revenge: "Que dum facti sceleris ignara poculum bibitura tulisset, dicit ei rex Alboinus: *Bibe cum patre tuo*. Quo dicto, Rosimunda regina magis quam credi valeat contristata, ingenium et animum ad huius sceleris ultionem

---

[41] For this same reason, moreover, it is not surprising that she does not fall in love with his exploits. The reason they get married is that he falls in love with her. It is only after they are married that, according to Genius, she starts loving him too.

convertit" (214).[42] In the poem, Albinus himself makes it explicit that Rosemund's father is the primary referent of his command by telling her first that the cup is made out of her father's skull, and only subsequently commanding her to drink with her father, even calling her daughter: "Testa tui patris est; cum patre, nata, bibe" (215, l. 24).[43] In this way, Godfrey draws our attention to Albinus's cruelty, playing down the ambiguity with respect to his familial role. It should be remarked, though, that Godfrey's attempt to dispel this ambiguity does not succeed completely. After all, Rosemund does drink *with* Albinus, too.

Genius's version of the toasting scene, unlike Godfrey's, encourages us to dwell on the ambiguity for a moment. It is true that when Albinus issues his command to Rosemund the reader already knows that at least one of the fathers meant by Albinus's command is Rosemund's father. Genius notes first that Albinus saw the cup "Which mad was of Gurmoundes hed" (2535), then describes the cup, and, subsequently, Genius tells us that the king commanded his wife to drink from it. But, if we as readers know how the cup was made, Rosemund herself certainly does not know. Let me quote the passage in full:

> ... Upon his word
> This Skulle is fet and wyn therinne
> Wherof he bad his wif beginne:
> 'Drink with thi fader, Dame,' he seide.
> And sche to his biddinge obeide,
> And tok the Skulle, and what hire liste
> Sche drank, *as sche which nothing wiste*
> *What Cuppe it was*: and thanne al oute
> The kyng in audience aboute
> Hath told it was hire fader Skulle,
> So that the lordes knowe schulle
> Of his bataille a soth witnesse.   (2548–58 [my emphasis])

Genius makes a point of noting that Rosemund does not know what the cup is made of. That she does not know, then, raises these questions: Who does Rosemund think Albinus commanded her to drink with? Who does she interpret the "fader" to be? More to the point, who does Albinus want Rosemund to think of when he uses the word "fader"? Since Rosemund's father is dead, and since she does not know that the cup is made out of his skull, there is a strong hint that Albinus is referring to himself, that is, that she is commanded to drink with the one who is acting as her father: Albinus.

The tournament and the moment of the offer not only suggest, but also

---

[42] "When she, ignorant of the criminal deed, has taken the cup to drink, King Albinus says to her: 'Drink with your father.' This having been said, Queen Rosemund, more afflicted than can be believed, turns her thoughts and intentions toward avenging that crime."
[43] "This is your father's skull; drink with your father, daughter."

enact Albinus's assumption of the role of Rosemund's father. Tournaments were sometimes part of wedding celebrations. The tournament organized by Albinus evokes a wedding celebration and his offer of the cup to Rosemund alludes to the chalice, a prominent element in the mass during which the marriage takes place. It is during the wedding ceremony that the similarities between husband-wife and father-daughter relations become more explicit. Lévi-Strauss has analyzed the significance of the moment of marriage in the following terms:

> [M]arriage is an arbitration between two loves, parental and conjugal. Nevertheless, they are both forms of love, and the instant the marriage takes place, considered in isolation, the two meet and merge; 'love has filled the ocean.' Their meeting is doubtless merely a prelude to their substitution for one another, the performance of a sort of *chassé-croisé*. But to intercross they must at least momentarily be joined, and it is this which in all social thought makes marriage a sacred mystery. At this moment, all marriage verges on incest. More than that, it is incest, at least social incest, if it is true that incest, in the broadest sense of the word, consists in obtaining by oneself, and for oneself, instead of by another, and for another. (489)

In Albinus's and Rosemund's "wedding," there is no *chassé-croisé* between father and groom, since they are one and the same person. Albinus is both the father and the husband, both the one who gives the daughter away, and the one who receives her. Everything ultimately reverts to himself.

We could perhaps push the analogy between Albinus's feast and the wedding ceremony a bit further by taking into account another important figure in the ceremony: the higher Father. In "The Father's House and the Daughter in It," Lynda Boose has analyzed the church service of Western tradition in terms of "a performative script that visually narrates and spatially resolves the problems of retention and separation [of the father from his daughter]" (68). Although the ceremony dramatizes "the replacement dynamics" whereby the groom replaces the father, "the father-daughter-(other) son triangulation . . . is not allowed to control the drama at the altar" (68). There is another, more powerful, figure who presides over the ceremony, the Father, represented by the priest: "[A] rival father [is] spatially located on what is literally and figuratively a higher plane. By standing directly above the bride, the representative of the divine Father creates the dominant triangle that visually defeats the earthly one" (68). In the particular "wedding" ceremony in the "Tale of Albinus and Rosemund," there is no priest. But Albinus acts as one when he performs the priest-like function of offering the wine in the chalice. In this way, Albinus's feast tries to assert his omnipotent and self-sufficient power – as husband, father, and priest/Father.

Albinus, then, is exclusively focused on himself, on being absolutely self-sufficient. His focus on his own self is shown to be fundamentally narcissistic. Let us return again to Albinus's boast, to the most peculiar and salient moment of Albinus's chivalric display: the moment he offers the skull/cup to his wife. Albinus orders the skull of the defeated Gurmond to be turned into a cup, as noted above, to ensure that his feat will not be forgotten, or in Genius's words: "To kepe and drawe into memoire / Of his bataille the victoire" (2475–76). Memory plays a fundamental role in the construction of a knight's honor. Fradenburg has noted the complexity of the medieval concept of honor as a crucial part of a knight's identity:

> Even as the honorable self is constituted through violence, it is also constituted through nostalgia . . . The perpetual need to assert honor as an interior essence thus produces the *meaning* of a life . . . The identity and continuity of the honorable self with its exterior images find expression in the worship of death and the worship of the past: the life of a knight is always an imitation of a past model. (206)

Fradenburg is referring here mainly to hereditary honor and the knight's need to imitate his honorable ancestors. Her analysis, though, proves relevant in Albinus's case, too. While Albinus is not trying to preserve some inherited honor, he is interested in preserving the honor he won for himself on the battlefield. Drawing attention to Gurmond's skull and making his wife drink from it is his way, to use Fradenburg's own phrasing, of worshipping his own past. In doing so, he reasserts his honor as a knight of prowess. In a way, this reassertion actually performs and thus forges his honorable self.

Albinus is proud of *his* victory. (Notice how he is just thinking about "*his* bataille," not his people's battle and victory.) But his worship of his own past represented by the skull bears the seed of his own destruction. Gurmond's skull is a memento of Albinus's victory, but, as a skull, it is also a "memento mori" that finally causes his own death. As I noted at the beginning of this analysis, according to Fradenburg, the honorable self struggles to extort its own glorious image from the face and look of the other (206). The honorable Albinus looks at his own image in the skull of his enemy, and this self-contemplation is ultimately the cause of his death. It is certainly significant in this sense that Genius narrates the "Tale of Albinus and Rosemund" immediately after having narrated the "Tale of Narcissus." Like Narcissus, whose obsession with his own reflection brings about his own death, Albinus's excessive contemplation of his own honorable self in the skull brings about his own tragic end. The irony, though, is that as he looks at Gurmond's skull, he is looking at his own death. I noted before that Albinus's words as he offers the cup to Rosemund have incestuous connotations because he suggests that he *is* Gurmond. Albinus takes the place of Gurmond, indeed; like Gurmond, he is finally slain.

Albinus's narcissism is manifested in his excessive self-contemplation, in his exclusive focus on his own interest. This self-interest, an interest in his own private self, is incompatible with the public interest and renders him inadequate to perform his office as king. It is very fitting then that Albinus's end, his tragic death, is effected by someone from his own private world, his wife. And it is very fitting also that his wife does not act out of concern for the public interest, but out of personal spite.

That Rosemund was not offended by Albinus's incestuous allusion, nor by his assumption of her father's role, suggests that she also accepts the structure of replacement whereby her husband must take the place of her father. In fact, she does not only accept it, but she herself even repeats this pattern of replacement, albeit in a somewhat different manner. Rosemund's revenge follows the example set by Albinus's own behavior. First, she assumes someone else's identity – as Albinus assumed her father's identity. She replaces her maid Glodeside for a night in order to sleep with Glodeside's lover, Helmegis. Second, she uses her political power as well as love to achieve her own goal. After she sleeps with Helmegis, she reveals her "real" identity to him: she is the queen, and she tells him that he should prove his love by killing the king (2611–19).[44] Helmegis, who, Genius had remarked, "Glodeside he loveth hote" (2595), suddenly feels a "wylde loves rage" (2620) for the queen. However, although love seems to be Helmegis's primary motivation for killing the king, the suddenness of his change of love allegiance suggests that Rosemund's political power is in great part the cause of his love for her.[45] In this way, Rosemund uses her political power for her own individual needs.

Using political power to advance his own individual needs is indeed what Albinus has been doing all along. His newly acquired power over the land of the Gepids served him to gain Rosemund. Subsequently, he tried to use their love and marriage in order to reinforce his political power as Gurmond's replacement. But this focus on his own needs shows why chivalric ideology is inadequate for proper governing; as Patterson has pointed out in *Chaucer and the Subject of History*, "[b]y defining its values almost entirely in terms of personal worth, chivalry tended to privatize all historical action . . . [I]ts deepest ambition was to produce not a better world but a perfect knight" (175). Albinus's offer of the cup to Rosemund privatizes his historical defeat of the king of the Gepids. It draws attention to his own individual feat, turning our attention away from the larger historical significance of the victory for the Lombards. It is, therefore, not surprising that Albinus's "privatization" of his military action brings about a "private" tragic ending for himself. He is killed, not by political enemies, but by his own domestic enemies: his wife and her lover. And he is killed not for overt political reasons (neither the wife nor her lover are interested in obtaining the throne), but due to a domestic conflict. Rosemund is offended by the cruelty of Albinus's offer of her father's skull – Genius observes very graphically that she resented

---

[44] By contrast, in the *Pantheon*, love plays no role: Rosemund tells Helmegis to choose between killing the king or being killed by him.
[45] As Yeager, *John Gower's Poetic*, puts it, "Helmege's 'wylde loves rage' for the queen is thematically correlative in the *Confessio*, where Rosemund's use of sex to implement her revenge acquires an aptness missing from the *Pantheon*" (150).

how Albinus "Avanteth him that he hath slain / And piked out hire fader brain" (2567–68). Albinus's offer also offends her because it is a humiliating reminder that she is a prize won through the defeat of her father, and that she is a living memory of that defeat. She thinks it shows "despit / Of hire and of hire fader bothe" (2580–81). Like her husband, Rosemund focuses only on the private offense, on the insult to her and to her father, rather than on the defeat of her people, and thus her revenge, very appropriately, is private: she takes a lover and kills her husband. In this way, self-serving, "private," violence receives its payment back in kind, that is, through a private revenge.

It has to be an outsider, a ruler from another region, the duke of Ravenna, who can finally break the circle of violence. The duke, in fact, seems to be the only positive authority figure in the tale. In this respect, Genius's version differs significantly from those of Godfrey of Viterbo and Paul the Deacon. After Rosemund and Helmegis kill Albinus, they flee to Ravenna, where they hope to be helped by the duke. At first, the duke gives them a place to dwell, but when he learns about the murder they have committed, he decides to have them killed with poison, thus restoring order. In the Latin sources the duke falls in love with Rosemund and proposes marriage to her, provided she kills Helmegis. This plot fails because, upon noticing that he is being poisoned, Helmegis forces Rosemund to drink of the same cup so that both of them die. The duke's attempt to gain Rosemund in these versions shows that he too is as much driven by self-interest as the other characters in the tale. In Genius's account, by contrast, the duke does not enter into any kind of relationship with Rosemund, and he decides to have her and Helmegis killed when he learns about their story. Genius says that "whan he herde telle / Of the manere how thei have do" (2642–43), he decided to have them poisoned. Instead of looking for his own private satisfaction, Genius's duke decides to punish them for the murder of Albinus. The duke then provides the one example in the story of a supposedly good governor, someone who, unlike Albinus, is not simply driven by an impulse to satisfy his own ego and desires.

Nevertheless, the brevity of Genius's account of the duke's intervention and the laconic character of his own comment on the couple's ending ("al this made avant of pride," 2647) still questions the adequacy of the duke's use of power, and, more importantly, even that of Genius's interpretation. Throughout the tale, Genius's account of the events has given us a complex view of the different characters in it and of their motivations. For instance, it is difficult to condemn Rosemund too rashly; we feel some sympathy for her, because the reason for her revenge is Albinus's proud and offensive gesture towards her. Ignoring this complexity, the duke's command to have Rosemund and Helmegis killed seems too rash and simplistic – he does not give them a chance to defend themselves and explain the reason for their action.

The "Tale of Albinus and Rosemund," I have been arguing, criticizes chivalric ideology and its inadequacy for governing. It serves as a critique of narcissistic pride and the concomitant violence necessary for the construction of the chivalric self, a self-serving violence that proves to be incompatible with the notion of kingship that was crystallizing in the fourteenth century. Precisely because of this criticism, it is more striking that the one example of a good governor in the tale – a governor who is not depicted as a knight – is not ideal either. Genius's laconic moral, like the duke's sentence, also ignores the complexity of his own narration. While his narrative raises questions about the system of exchange, its structures of replacement and gender dynamics, as well as about the inadequacy of the chivalric ethos for proper governance, by trying to impose one single moral on the tale, he ignores these questions. His moral forgets that, while it is pride that leads Albinus to make his offensive boast, it is *not* pride, but other, more complex, motivations that lead Rosemund to take revenge. Genius's interpretations of the tales, his own authoritative role, will be examined more thoroughly in the next two chapters and in the context of tales that raise other issues about authority in father-daughter, king-subject, and author-text relationships. For now, let me just restate that the "Tale of Albinus and Rosemund" and the Tale of the False Bachelor" reveal the ambiguity at the heart of the system of exchange: the easy interchangeability of roles between men within the family. Due to this ambiguity, Genius's attempts to define the limits of authority within the family can only but fail.

CHAPTER FOUR

LIMITING AUTHORITY:
LEUCOTHOE, VIRGINIA, AND CANACE

Introduction

The tales of Leucothoe, Virginia, and Canace explore the limits of three different types of authority – familial, political, and textual. In each of these tales a daughter is killed, either directly or indirectly, by her father. In the "Tale of Canace and Machaire," Eolus commands his daughter to kill herself when he learns that she is pregnant by her brother. In the "Tale of Virginia," Virginius stabs his daughter when he realizes that he cannot prevent her from being taken by the king and his brother. And in the "Tale of Leucothoe," Orchamus kills his daughter by burying her alive, because Phebus has raped her. These three tales suggest that, by killing their daughters, the fathers overstep the limits of their authority and power over them. In two of these tales, moreover, it is not only the biological father who abuses his power over his daughter: there is a third figure who also abuses his power over her, and, consequently, in Genius's depiction, over the biological father as well. There is thus a conflict of authority between two male authority figures, the father and a second figure, a king in the "Tale of Virginia" and a god in the "Tale of Leucothoe." This second male figure exerts his authority in a tyrannical manner by violating the private property of the father, namely, the daughter. But the fathers' responses to the male figures' actions have a similarly tyrannical character as they violate their daughters' only private possession, their bodies. The "Tale of Canace and Machaire" presents a slightly different situation, as it does not focus on the conflict between the two male figures in the tale, the father and the son, even though this conflict is also an important element in it; rather, it centers its attention on the father's absolutist exertion of his authority over his daughter. In this tale the father abuses his power both as biological father and as king.

These three tales are also about the power of another type of authority: that of the author, in this case the narrator of the tales, Genius. While this theme is more fully explored in the tales analyzed in the next chapter, in which Genius's abuse of power is more explicit, an analysis of Genius's attitude towards the fathers in the tales of Leucothoe, Virginia, and Canace hints at the limiting character of his own authority. In the "Tale of Canace and

Machaire," Genius laments and blames the father for his cruelty towards his daughter (even though she has committed incest with her brother); Canace is portrayed with great sympathy as the victim of her father and is given a clear voice. Virginia and Leucothoe, by contrast, are passive victims without a voice whose deaths are treated with some indifference. Other concerns in the tales of Virginia and Leucothoe override the kind of sympathy that Canace generates. In the "Tale of Virginia," diverting our attention to public matters, Genius comments only obliquely on the father's cruelty, and in the "Tale of Leucothoe," in which nobody is blamed for the daughter's death, not even the rapist, Phebus, there is almost no comment on Orchamus's cruel action. Genius thus treats the three daughters differently and, like another father, tries to control or limit the meaning and significance of their sacrifices.

Any discussion about the relationship between family and politics as well as about issues of authority and power in Western culture, as I have mentioned in the first chapter, will raise questions about the private and public spheres.[1] Words like "privite," "prive," and "prively," on the one hand, and "open," "openli," on the other, recur with great frequency in the *Confessio Amantis*, as I have noted. In the three tales that concern us in this chapter, an emphasis is placed on these words as well as on images that evoke the public and private spheres. Gower uses this spatial imagery as a metaphor for exploring issues of power and authority in these two spheres. As Duby has observed, "the opposition between private life and public life is a matter not so much of place as of power."[2] This opposition is particularly significant in the context of the relationship between fathers and daughters, for in this case gender, which is always at least implicitly a defining element in the conceptualization of public and private, becomes an explicit and fundamental part of the opposition. (Although I am borrowing here the term "opposition" from Duby, I will show later that the relationship between the two spheres is more than a simple opposition.)

Through spatial images, Genius draws parallels and suggests the links between the daughter's body and the daughter's chamber as private spaces, on the one hand, and the outside world, the public spaces, such as the streets where the daughters are seen, on the other.[3] In the *Confessio*, the "chambre"

---

[1] I specify that this is a typical phenomenon in Western culture, because there is disagreement among scholars on whether notions of privacy are primarily Western or common to all cultures. See Helly and Reverby, *Gendered Domains* 6, for studies that suggest that it is not a concept common to all cultures, and Stanbury, "Women's Letters" 276, for studies that make the opposite argument. For the purposes of my study, it is enough to note that the private/public dichotomy is not "natural," but constructed. Even if one finds that it is a universal distinction common to all cultures, one will also find that there is no one way of constructing the dichotomy.

[2] Georges Duby, ed. *A History of Private Life: Revelations of the Medieval World*, trans. Arthur Goldhammer, vol. 2 (Cambridge: The Bellknap Press of Harvard UP, 1988) 7.

[3] For an analysis of a similar parallel between architectural and bodily space in Chaucer's *Troilus and Criseyde*, see Stanbury, "The Voyeur and the Private Life."

is a recurring symbol that represents private space. Thus Canace is always in her private "chambre" and her tale reveals the tragic consequences that stem from the attempt to isolate the private from public interaction. The "Tale of Virginia" exposes the "risks" a daughter's public interaction entails for her father (when his daughter is publicly exposed, when her beauty becomes known outside their house, he loses some control over her). The "Tale of Leucothoe" enacts a man's fantasy of breaking into a woman's "chambre," her most private bodily part, to rob her of her virginity, thus erasing the line between the public and the private. As Stanbury has argued, commenting on Duby's definition of privacy in terms of degrees of seclusion, "the zone of private authority proceeds outward from our physical body (*corpus*) to our intimate walled space, the bedchamber, outward along a radius to town, city, and nation, in which private power is dispersed, subsumed by the body politic, the *res publica*."[4] This notion of degrees of seclusion will help us to understand the parallels Gower draws between private and public authority; it will also explain why sometimes the public and the private seem to be indistinguishable, why the line between the two is erased. Even if the chamber and the body seem private spaces, the tales show that the private can easily become public, while that which is public in a certain context may be considered private in another context. This fluidity, in fact, suggests that even the most private of spaces is inevitably defined by the public. It is my contention that in the three tales discussed in this chapter Genius tries to fix and delimit those fluid boundaries, but he fails in his attempt, precisely because they are fluid.

Exploring the notions of public and private through stories about the invasion of the private sphere recognizes that privacy, as Stanbury has remarked, "is defined by violation."[5] The possibility of violation of the private sphere was a concern during Richard II's time. Richard was accused of violating his subjects' private property. As explained in Chapter One, he was accused of disposing arbitrarily of the property of his subjects, and of having said, according to Thomas Walsingham, that "[t]he lives, lands, properties, goods and chattels of my subjects are mine."[6] Such a statement points to some of the concerns in Gower's stories. It also suggests the link between privacy and notions of property, specifically, private property.[7] That Richard would have power over his subjects' goods suggests that he had power over their private spaces and what was kept in them. Daughters would be among the subjects' possessions, the fathers' private property. The "Tale of Leucothoe," a story about a rape that is defined as an act of stealing a daughter's virginity, is a

---

[4] Stanbury, "The Voyeur and the Private Life" 141.
[5] Stanbury, "Women's Letters" 285. Stanbury goes on to quote from Peter Brooks: "we know privacy by way of its invasion, just as we know innocence by way of its loss, and indeed could not know it otherwise" (285).
[6] Quoted from Hutchinson, *The Hollow Crown* 199.
[7] For studies about the link between privacy, property, and gender, see Chapter One.

telling example of the link between privacy and property. Gower thus used the tales of threatened daughters as a powerful metaphor to express the subjects' fear concerning their private rights and property.[8]

But we should also notice a reference to the subjects' lives in the quotation from Walsingham. The king also claimed (according to Walsingham) that he had power over his subjects' lives. This claim raises the following questions: if Richard's subjects did not agree that the king should have power over their lives, their private bodies, should the fathers' power over their daughters' lives also be limited? Do the daughters themselves have a right to privacy, a right to their own bodies? Stanbury has argued that, obviously without using a modern sense of private rights, Chaucer's women "could indeed claim privacy as a territory of the person."[9] In raising the question of private property and using the daughter as a metaphor, Gower is also raising the question of whether daughters also have private selves, whether they are individuals and whether their bodies constitute their own private territory. In the "Tale of Canace and Machaire," he recognizes the daughter's right to have her private possession, her own body, as regulated by "kinde," not by her father. One wonders, though, why he does not unambiguously recognize the same right in the cases of Virginia and Leucothoe. Genius's silence about the cruelty of Viriginia's and Leucothoe's fathers suggests that he fails to limit the fathers' authority over their daughters' private selves.

In those two tales it is something else, I will show, that concerns Genius, namely, establishing the inevitability of authority in the "Tale of Leucothoe," and establishing the importance of the political good of the community as well as the need for the king to respect individual rights in the "Tale of Virginia." But in turning our attention away from the daughters' deaths in order to subordinate them to other meanings, Genius acts like the fathers by diverting our attention from the issue of the privacy of the daughters' bodies to other public concerns. It is only in the "Tale of Canace and Machaire" that he explicitly acknowledges a daughter's independence from her father, her "right" to her body. But even in this tale such an independence is limited by Genius himself. These three tales, I will argue, point to Genius as a fatherly authority and suggest that, as a father of sorts, Gower's narrator is himself implicated in the model of authority that his own tales atttempt to explore and define.

---

[8] We should remember that, as I noted in Chapter One, according to Kelley, *The Human Measure*, English common law seems to have what he calls a "property fetish" (171). Kelley argues that "[w]hat distinguished English from French society (at least before the French Revolution) was above all the respect for property, expressed, for instance, in the prohibition of the billeting of troops and of arbitrary taxation without consent ... Property, indeed, was the subject of the greatest legal treatise of that age – 'Littleton on Tenures' " (170). Gower's *Confessio* can thus be seen as an exploration of such a property fetish and its various ramifications.
[9] Stanbury, "Women's Letters" 279.

The Tale of Leucothoe

In the "Tale of Leucothoe" (5.6713–83) a father, Orchamus, kills his daughter, Leucothoe, because she has been raped. This father, though, remains blameless in the end – unlike Eolus in the "Tale of Canace and Machaire," who is clearly blamed for his cruel action, or Virginius in the "Tale of Virginia," whose guilt is at least hinted at indirectly. Genius's depiction of Orchamus almost ignores the horror of his action – he buries his daughter alive. The only suggestion that there might be something wrong with what he does is that, like Eolus and Virginius, he shows "no pite" (6773) in killing his daughter.[10] Leucothoe does not have a chance to defend herself from the attacks of either the rapist (the god Phebus) or her father. While in Gower's source, Ovid's *Metamorphoses* (4.190–255), Leucothoe is at least given a voice to plead her innocence in front of her father, in the *Confessio Amantis* she is completely silent. In this sense, she is like Philomela, whose tale Genius related about a thousand lines before and also in the section about stealing; after her rape, Leucothoe has neither her virginity nor a voice.[11] Language and sexuality are again intertwined. Leucothoe is no Thaise; she does not (cannot) use language to displace the god's sexual desire for her, and once the god fulfills his sexual desire for her, she is silent.

That Leucothoe does not have a voice is one of the indications that her tragic fate does not concern either of the two male figures in the story, Phebus and Orchamus, or even its male narrator, Genius. In addition to failing to blame Orchamus, Genius does not punish the god, the one who committed the crime that his tale illustrates. His final moral verdict is in fact difficult to assess. Olsson has remarked that, although the story is tragic, Gower's priest trivializes it by introducing some changes that are difficult to account for and leaving out certain significant details present in Ovid.[12] For instance, in the *Metamorphoses* Phoebus shows signs of suffering for Leucothoe's death, and, to that extent at least, he has his punishment: "nil illo fertur volucrum moderator equorum / post Phaethonteos vidisse dolentius ignes" (245–46).[13]

---

[10] In Book 7.3103ff. Genius explains that "pite" is one of the five points of policy that a king should have. Although Orchamus is not a king, as Gower develops a parallel between kings and fathers, the following lines suggest that pointing to Orchamus's lack of "pite" may be meant as a criticism of his action:
> It sit a king to be pitous
> Toward his poeple and gracious
> Upon the reule of governance,
> So that he worche no vengance,
> Which mai be cleped crualte. (3125–29)

[11] Genius makes a parallel between speech and virginity on two occasions in the "Tale of Tereus." In lines 5.5748–49 Philomela says she wishes she had not been born, "For thanne I hadde noght forlore / Mi speche and mi virginite." Later, Genius notes that Progne "most of sorwe made" when she saw her sister "specheles and deshonoured" (5809–11).

[12] Olsson, *John Gower and the Structures of Conversion* 157–58.

[13] "They say that never, since the thunderbolt slew Phaethon, had the god . . . seen

In Genius's account, however, as Olsson puts it, "Phoebus act[s] tardily, and mostly out of self-regard: 'for the reverence / Of that sche hadde be his love' (6676–77), he causes her to spring 'up out of the molde / Into a flour' (6679–80)" (158). The god is not particularly affected by Leucothoe's death; neither is he punished in any other way. All these anomalies not only suggest that Genius's interest lies elsewhere, but they also expose Genius's own (ab)use of his authority.

The "Tale of Leucothoe" suggests that there is a fundamental connection between privacy and property. The daughter in the tale becomes a mere site for the examination of this connection. The story is found in Book 5, a book devoted to the sin of avarice, and the particular sin it illustrates is "stelthe" or stealing. Stealing is a branch of avarice, and, depending on the method, Genius distinguishes between different types of stealing. Significantly, he illustrates three of the main types, namely, "stelthe," "robbery," and "ravine" by means of stories about rapes of virgins.[14] In this way, Genius presents virginity as a private piece of property, pointing to the etymological connection between rape and "ravine."[15] In the "Tale of Leucothoe," the god covets Leucothoe's virginity, not Leucothoe herself. And it is only as a virgin that her father has an interest in her. Once her virginity is lost, once the property has been stolen, Leucothoe loses her value as an object of exchange; she cannot be part of what Lévi-Strauss calls the "great communication function" of the process of exchange.[16]

Even though Genius tells the tale in order to illustrate the sin of "stelthe," the act of stealing in and of itself is not the major focus of the tale. Stealing is important insofar as it raises questions regarding two major issues, both of which relate to notions of privacy: sexual desire and political power. These two issues are presented as part of the natural order. Genius presents sexual desire as inevitable, as part of a larger order controlled by Venus:

---

anything which caused him more bitter grief." (Translation taken from Ovid, *Metamorphoses*, trans. Mary M. Innes [Oxford: Penguin, 1955] 100. All further translations from the *Metamorphoses* are taken from the same edition.)

[14] While "stelthe" acts furtively and under cover ("[stelthe] takth his preie so covert / That noman wot it in apert," 6499–6500), "robbery" acts more openly (it robs "In wodes and in feldes," 6099), and "ravine" uses violence to obtain its prey ("Ravine makth no other skile, / Bot takth be strengthe what he wile," 5521–22). The "Tale of Leucothoe" illustrates the sin of "stelthe." The "Tale of Neptune and Cornix," an account of a frustrated attempt at rape, and the "Tale of Calistona," in which Jupiter rapes the maiden Calistona, serve as examples of robbery. The "Tale of Tereus," finally, illustrates the sin of "ravine."

[15] See Kathryn Gravdal, *Ravishing Maidens: Writing Rape in Medieval French Literature and Law* (Philadelphia: U of Pennsylvania P, 1991). As Gravdal has pointed out,

[s]ome of the more common meanings of [the classical Latin] *rapere* are to carry off or seize; to snatch, pluck, or drag off; to hurry, impel, hasten; to rob, plunder; and, finally, to abduct a virgin . . . From *rapere* is derived the popular Latin **rapire*, which gives the Old French *ravir*. (4)

The Middle English noun *ravine* derives from the Old French *ravine*.

[16] Lévi-Strauss, *Elementary Structures of Kinship* 494.

> Venus... hath this lawe in honde
> Of thing which mai noght be withstonde
> As sche which the tresor to warde
> Of love hath withinne hir warde.   (6715–18)

Drawing on Howard Bloch's explanation of the poetics of virginity in connection with Chaucer's "Physician's Tale," I suggest that in Genius's tale there is a sense that the mere fact that Leucothoe is a virgin provokes male desire and, consequently, already entails, or at least anticipates, the loss of her virginity.[17] Due to the nature of sexual desire, virginity is an impossibility that not even the walls in Leucothoe's "chambre" can protect, unless, that is, the one who desires exercises self-restraint. For despite Genius's depiction of the desire as inevitable, he also implies that it can and needs to be controlled.

The theme of sexual desire converges with the theme of power in the tale. At the same time that Genius suggests the inevitability of sexual desire as part of a larger order, I will argue, he is also suggesting the inevitability of power and authority. Genius's framework also suggests that authority, like sexual desire, is a given; it is a "natural" part of the social order. Like sexual desire, though, it can, and should, also be controlled. Furthermore, in the same way that uncontrolled sexual desire breaks down the distinction between private and public, so an uncontrolled use of power also breaks down the distinction between the two spheres. Phebus abuses his power by entering Leucothoe's room and thus invading the father's private property. The father at the same time abuses his power by violating the daughter's privacy (her body). Finally, the allusions to King Richard that, I will argue, can be found in the tale further suggest that unrestrained kingly power also breaks down the distinction between the public and private spheres.

The victim of the conflict, the daughter, counts only as the site on which the conflict is played out. But even if the tale does not explicitly show sympathy for the daughter, we can still raise the following question: what do these two overlapping frameworks, erotic desire and political authority, suggest about the daughter? By posing sexual desire as inevitable, Genius poses the woman's subjection to male control as inevitable as well; correspondingly, the king's authority and his subjects' subordination to him are also inevitable. They are part of the natural order. Nevertheless, although the tale does not question authority per se, Genius suggests that authority, like sexual desire, should be controlled by rules of restraint. It should be governed by self-control. Even though sexual desire is inevitable and even though virginity as a pure state may be impossible to maintain indefinitely, both Genius and Venus in the tale emphasize that sexual desire must be controlled. Even though women are subject to men, there are limits to men's power over them. While creating a framework within which sexual desire is a given,

---

[17] Bloch, "Chaucer's Maiden's Head: 'The Physician's Tale' and the Poetics of Virginity," *Representations* 28 (1989): 113–34.

Genius also indicates the need for controlling desire. This story about abuse of power, about the violation of privacy, is thus a tale about limiting authority.

The notion of virginity as a piece of property is introduced in the discussion on the sin of "stelthe" which precedes the "Tale of Leucothoe." Amans has a long speech in which he admits that, even though he has not committed the sin of "stelthe," he has fantasies about it. Amans first depicts virginity as a precious treasure (a "Tresor") that he desires to "pyke and stele." The treasure, however, is well guarded by Danger. This figure, Amans says,

> ... under lock and under keie,
> That noman mai it stele aweie,
> Hath al the Tresor underfonge
> That unto love mai belonge.   (6621–24)

In this passage Amans presents virginity as an impersonal and highly valuable object to be stolen, but also as an impossible object of "stelthe" – "that noman mai it stele aweie."

Amans then proceeds to describe his fantasy: at night he looks out of his window at the other buildings, "So that I mai the chambre knowe / In which mi ladi, as I trowe, / Lyth in hir bed and slepeth softe" (6663–65). Amans imagines himself entering his lady's chamber, as Phebus does in the "Tale of Leucothoe." He wishes he were Nectanabus or Proteus (6671–72), so that he could transform himself and fly,

> Into the chambre forto se
> If eny grace wolde falle
> So that I mihte under the palle
> Som thyng of love pyke and stele.   (6678–81)

The allusion to Nectanabus is very appropriate. Nectanabus, whose tale Genius narrates in Book 6.1789–2366, had told queen Olympias that a god wanted to conceive a child with her. Then, he changed his shape, and, with the appearance of a god, went into her chamber, and lay with her. This story clearly plays on the Annunciation motif that is so important in other father-daughter stories in the *Confessio Amantis*, and it is thus no coincidence that Leucothoe's depiction, as I will argue later, reminds us of the Virgin Mary.[18] What I would like to emphasize now, though, is that Nectanabus acts out Amans's fantasy; he uses his power to transform his shape and to obtain the same prize that Amans desires. Similarly, we will see, the "Tale of Leucothoe" is in some ways an acting out of Amans's fantasy through Phebus. But the tale's fascination with Phebus's power suggests that Amans's desire to steal into his beloved's chamber is actually both a desire for the woman's virginity

---

[18] See Gallacher, *Love, the Word, and Mercury* 40–43, on the Annunciation pattern in the "Tale of Nectanabus."

per se and a desire to enjoy the absolute power implicit in doing so. These two desires are portrayed as desires to violate private spaces.

The "Tale of Leucothoe," as already mentioned, echoes the themes in Amans's speech, also initially presenting virginity as a treasure, a piece of private property – Venus, Genius says, guards the "tresor" of love (6715–17), and to Phebus, Leucothoe's maidenhood is "al his worldes welthe" (6745). Because the focus is on the act of stealing something valuable, virginity is reified to the point that the virgin herself does not have much to do with it. She is just the person who happens to carry it. In Ovid's version of the story, we are told how Leucothoe reacts when Phoebus enters her chamber. Ovid hints that Leucothoe might share some guilt: "at virgo quamvis inopino territa visu / victa nitore dei posita vim passa querella est" (232–33).[19] In Genius's account, Olsson has pointed out, "[w]hatever hint there may be in Ovid of Leucothoe's guilt ... is dropped" (157–58). Indeed, not only is any hint of her guilt dropped, but Leucothoe herself is "dropped" from the scene. The account of the actual rape takes only three lines, and Leucothoe is not even mentioned: "he thurghout hir chambre wal / Cam in al sodeinliche, and stall / That thing which was to him so lief" (6749–51). The rape is reduced to the stealing of a "thing," while Leucothoe is completely ignored. Since virginity is an object owned by a man, the effect of its "robbery" on the woman is not an object of concern; once her virginity is lost, the woman loses her value. In a sense, what counts is the private object, not the private self.

Genius's tale carries a sense of fatality, of inevitability, suggesting that Leucothoe is bound to lose her virginity.[20] The inevitability of erotic desire in the "Tale of Leucothoe" is emphasized from the very beginning of the narration and predisposes us to expect the daughter's tragic fate. The tale starts by commenting on the unlimited power of Venus – "Venus ... hath this lawe in honde / Of thing which mai noght be withstonde" (6715–16). Through her power, she makes Phebus fall in love with a "Maiden" (6722). It is significant,

---

[19] "Leucothoe, though frightened by the unexpected sight, was overcome by his magnificence, and accepted the god's embraces without a murmur" (100). Of course, the questions of how much Leucothoe did or did not resist and the extent to which she did or did not consent are very problematic ones, as any modern discussion of rape would show. Leo C. Curran, "Rape and Rape Victims in the *Metamorphoses*," *Arethusa* 11 (1978): 213–41, has argued in this respect that in Ovid's version,

> [n]o force or threat of force is present, but the effect is the same. [Leucothoe] recognizes that resistance or demurrer would be futile. To many jurors in a trial today this would not constitute rape at all. Ovid knows better; and so does the woman, if one were to imagine a modern parallel to Leucothoe's situation, who is alone in her house when a powerfully built man of supreme self-confidence enters her bedroom and announces to her that he wants her. (221)

For our purposes here, it is important to note that Genius does not even raise this question.
[20] In his analysis of Chaucer's "Physician's Tale," Bloch has noticed a similar sense of fatality hanging over Chaucer's version, although he relates this to medieval notions of viriginity as they relate to what he calls "a poetics of praise" (115).
[21] Cf. the Middle English lyric "In Praise of Mary" in which Mary is "Moder unwemmed

we should note, that Leucothoe is not introduced by her name but as a virgin; Phebus does not fall in love with Leucothoe but with a "Maiden." The power of Venus and Phebus's total and inevitable subjection to that power – "he withoute reste is peined / With al his herte to coveite / A Maiden" (6720–22) – suggest from the very beginning that Leucothoe will not have a chance to preserve her virginity.

The parallels between Leucothoe and the Virgin Mary in Genius's description of the maiden underscore the sense of inevitability, of the inevitable fate of a virgin who is destined to open her "chambre" to a god. As in the "Tale of the Three Questions" and the "Tale of Constance," the story of God's conception of his son through his own daughter, the Virgin Mary, serves as matrix for the articulation of the story of Leucothoe. The description of Leucothoe echoes traditional descriptions of the Virgin Mary. She is introduced as,

> A clene Maide and a Virgine,
> Upon the whos nativite
> Of comelihiede and of beaute
> Nature hath set al that sche may,
> That lich unto the fresshe Maii,
> Which othre monthes of the yeer
> Surmonteth, so withoute pier
> Was of this Maiden the feture.   (6732–39)

Like the Virgin Mary, she is a clean maiden, and she is without peer.[21] She is also like May, the month of the Virgin.

The equation between Leucothoe's chamber and body also relates her to the Virgin and more generally to other virgins. Mary is often described as a chamber or a palace. A fourteenth-century lyric attributed to William of Shoreham calls her a "Chambre of the Trinite" (2), and a fifteenth-century lyric titled "The Nativity" describes Mary's conception as follows: "Mekely on thee the Holy Ghoste / Palacium intrans uteri" (15–16), that is, the Holy Ghost descended upon Mary entering the palace of her womb.[22] The equation body-"chambre" was also common in religious treatises about virginity. Karma Lochrie has shown that in medieval discussions of virginity, the body is often seen in spatial terms as a place that has to remain sealed, closed to interaction with the outside, *but* open to interaction with God.[23] Virgins

---

[without spot] and maiden clene" (l.3). Quoted from R. T. Davies, ed. *Medieval English Lyrics: A Critical Anthology* (Chicago: Northwestern UP, 1964) 64. And in the fourteenth-century poem *Pearl* the Virgin is "Makele" (435), that is, without peer. Quoted from E. V. Gordon, ed., *Pearl* (Oxford: Clarendon Press, 1953).
22 *Medieval English Lyrics* 103 and 218.
23 Karma Lochrie, *Margery Kempe and Translations of the Flesh* (Philadelphia: U of Pennsylvania P, 1991). Lochrie argues that:
> When virgins are then instructed not to break that which seals them together *with* God and with themselves, they are being called to enclosure at many levels.

should keep their virginity for themselves and for God. A passage in Jerome's *Epistola* 22, devoted to virginity, makes precisely the case that virgins should be open to God. The passage is worth quoting in full, as it relates a scene that is similar to the rape scene in the "Tale of Leucothoe." Jerome tells his addressee, a woman named Eustochium:

> Let the secret retreat of your bedchamber ever guard you. Ever let the Bridegroom hold converse with you within. When you pray, you are speaking with your Spouse. When you read, he is talking to you, and when sleep comes upon you, He will come behind the wall and He will put His hand through the opening and will touch your body. You will arise trembling, and will say: *I languish with love.*[24]

The sexual implications of this passage have been made clear by Jerome himself. Some paragraphs before, Jerome interprets a passage in Daniel 2:34 ("As you looked, a stone was cut out by no human hand"), as a prophecy that Christ was going to be born without sexual intercourse. To explain the passage in Daniel, Jerome interprets the meaning of the hand as follows: " 'Hands' is, of course, to be understood of the marital act, as in the verse: *His left hand is under my head, and his right hand shall embrace me*" (151). The verse he quotes here comes from Song of Songs 2:6. The verse he quotes in the passage above ("He 'will put His hand through the opening and will touch your body' ") comes from Song of Songs 5:4. In the passage, the image of God entering through the wall and touching the woman's body, especially in the light of Jerome's interpretation of the hand, resembles the scene in the "Tale of Leucothoe." When Phebus suddenly enters Leucothoe's room, while the maiden is alone in her chamber, medieval readers would have recognized the references to the Annunciation.[25] Phebus's action responds to a familiar pattern.

In the light of these references, the persistence in emphasizing the boundaries that enclose Leucothoe in both the Latin gloss to the tale and in Genius's own account almost acquire an ironic tone. They are useless barriers against the inevitable. Genius introduces Leucothoe as follows:

> A Maiden, which was warded streyte
> Withinne chambre and kept so clos,

> The unbroken flesh ultimately means bodily closure and silence. (25 [my emphasis])

The same sense of the body as a physical boundary between the inner and the outer is manifest in the Middle English rule for anchoresses, the *Ancrene Wisse*. See Elizabeth Robertson, *Early English Devotional Prose and the Female Audience* (Knoxville: U of Tennessee P, 1990).
[24] Quoted from *The Letters of St. Jerome*, trans. Charles Christopher Mierow (Westminster, MD: The Newman Press, 1963) 158.
[25] Genius further emphasizes the privacy of the "chambre" by slightly changing Ovid's account of the rape scene. In Ovid's version twelve servant maids keep Leucothoe company, when Phebus enters disguised as her mother. He dismisses the servants and changes his shape before raping her (100).

> That selden was whan sche desclos
> Goth with hir moder forto pleie. (6722–25)

Like Amans's lady, Leucothoe is well kept in a "chambre" and she also has her own Danger (her mother) to guard her well. The Latin gloss goes even further in emphasizing the confinement, as it does not even "allow" Leucothoe to go outside "forto pleie": "Leuchotoe Orchami filia in cameris sub arta matris custodia virgo preseruabatur."[26]

The image of the "chambre" conveys the idea of inviolable space with clearly defined boundaries (the walls) that separate private life from public life, the inside from the outside. It is the private space where Leucothoe is hidden from the public eye, a symbol of her isolation from society. In the passage quoted above "clos" and "desclos" emphasize this neatly-defined separation. Leucothoe is kept "clos" in her "chambre." "Clos" is glossed in the *Middle English Dictionary* as "tightly, firmly, securely (fastened, closed, held, surrounded)," thus conveying the idea of physical closure. The verb "closen" carries the same connotations: "to obstruct a passageway," "to close an opening or gap," "to fortify (a city, castle, etc.) by surrounding it with a wall and/or a moat," etc. By contrast with Leucothoe's enclosure in her "chambre," the few moments she goes outside, she goes "desclos" (6725). "Desclos" as the opposite of "clos" points again to physical boundaries. The verb "desclosen" can mean "to open up (sth.)."

More significantly, Genius exploits the inherent metaphorical correspondence between the "chambre" in the house where Leucothoe lives and her own bodily "chambre." Thus, the moment when Phebus enters the "chambre" in the house coincides with the moment when he enters Leucothoe's bodily "chambre": "he thurghout hir chambre wall / Cam in al sodeinliche, and stall / That thing which was to him so lief" (6749–51). The moment of rape and the moment of breaking in (of stealing) are fused into one single moment. Leucothoe is just a private space to be transgressed.

The father's reaction to the rape and his justification of his sacrifice of his daughter are ludicrous in this context. When Clymene tells Orchamus about the rape, Genius points out that he is "for sorwe welnyh wod" (6762), and then gives the father a speech in which he reveals his decision to kill Leucothoe, among other reasons, so that other women may learn from her example.[27] Orchamus's justification of the sacrifice of his daughter (not mentioned in Ovid) is ludicrous for at least two reasons. First, it is ludicrous because in this tale virginity seems an impossible state to preserve. Leucothoe has absolutely no chance not only to counter Phebus's actual attack, but even

---

[26] "Leucothoe, Orchamus's daughter, is preserved a virgin in the chambers under the close custody of her mother" (my translation).

[27] That this father is "welnyh wod" reminds us of Canace's father's own wrath, a wrath that Genius condemns very explicitly. He does not do so in the case of Orchamus, partly, as I argue, because the father is confronting a divine power.

simply to hide from his gaze. Hence there is little other women can learn to do or avoid doing on the basis of the example. What Olsson calls Genius's "trivialization" of the story is not so much a trivialization as it is a ludicrous reading of the events that, in turn, emphasizes the ludicrous character of Orchamus's "exemplary" punishment of his daughter.

For indeed the tale shows that it is not the virgin herself but the one who desires who needs to exercise self-control. Venus herself advocates self-control. Although she makes people fall in love and lose some control over themselves ("Venus . . . hath this lawe in honde, / Of thing which mai noght be withstonde"), she also believes that lovers should control their sexual drives. Hence, she is the one who denounces the rape to Clymene, and she does so because she is the "enemie / Of thilke loves micherie" (6753–54). Erotic desire is a given, and is controlled by her, but it still has its own rules. The "Tale of Leucothoe" thus allows Genius to pose sexuality as a force controlled by Venus; Genius creates a framework in which erotic desire is represented as a desire (a natural force) for which humans are not responsible, but which, nevertheless, both Venus and Genius insist must be controlled.

The second reason Orchamus's revenge seems ludicrous is that it misses the point. What is at stake is not his daughter's wrongdoing but the fact that his own authority has been circumvented by a figure who has used his greater power in an abusive manner. In this sense, the walls emphasize the abuse of power and suggest an abuse of privacy. Phebus violates the zealously-guarded privacy of the father and the daughter. In doing so, Phebus manifests a lack of self-control. Self-control, a critical issue in the "Tale of Canace and Machaire," is for Gower one of the main virtues of a good ruler, as critics have pointed out.[28] The political implications of the notion of self-control is one of the indications that leads us to a political reading of the "Tale of Leucothoe" as an allegory about unrestrained kingly power. Such a political reading is also apt for two other reasons. First, the "Tale of Leucothoe" is immediately preceded by the tale titled the "Chastity of Valentinian." And, second, Gower associates Richard II with Phebus in the *Confessio Amantis* and in the *Cronica Tripertita*.

In the "Chastity of Valentinian" (5.6395–6417) Genius, rather uncharacteristically, praises Valentinian's preservation of his virginity. The Roman emperor never married, and, according to Genius, even though he was "a worthi kniht / Bothe of his lawe and of his myht" (6403–04), he did not want to be praised for his knightly deeds. Instead, he wanted to be praised for winning another kind of battle, the battle against his own flesh: for "he his fleissh hath overcome: / He was a virgine, as he seide; / On that bataille his

---

[28] Scanlon, *Narrative, Authority, and Power*, for instance, remarks that in Book 7, "Gower continually presents monarchy as a form of exemplary self-restraint whose overriding purpose is maintaining first its own privilege and then the privilege of those who share his power" (286).

pris he leide" (6414–16). When Amans reminds Genius that the example of Valentinian should not be imitated by everybody, lest humanity should die off, Genius's reply ignores this problem and insists on the notion of order and self-restraint implicit in Valentinian's chastity: "If maidenhod be take aweie / Withoute lawes ordinance, / It mai noght failen of vengance" (6430–32). The "lawes ordinance" should govern sexual desire. Otherwise, revenge will ensue. The "Tale of Leucothoe," narrated after these remarks and after Genius's discussion about "Stealth," demonstrates this point. Phebus ignores any "lawes ordinance" when he rapes Leucothoe, and the consequence of his lack of restraint is the father's revenge, a revenge, though, that is taken on the victim rather than on the culprit.

Genius also suggests a political reading of the tale by understating Phebus's divine character. He never mentions in the tale that Phebus is a god, and, except for the fact that Phebus enters Leucothoe's chamber through the wall, there is no emphasis on his divine power. He is more like a human being when, instead of using his divine power to rape Leucothoe whenever he likes, he has to wait "lurkende" until he finds a good moment to enter her room. Moreover, unlike Ovid's Phoebus, who adopts the appearance of Leucothoe's mother, Genius's Phebus does not transform himself at any point.

The depiction of Phebus as a human character and Gower's comparisons between Phebus and Richard II in the first recension of Book 8 of the *Confessio* and in the *Cronica Tripertita* point to a possible allusion to the English king. In Book 8 of the *Confessio* (3001*ff), in a section later dropped in the version dedicated to Henry of Lancaster, Gower compares Richard to the sun: he is "Lich to the Sonne in his degree, / Which with the clowdes up alofte, / Is derked and bischadewed ofte" (3006–08*) and this sun is "evere briht and feir" (3010*). In the *Cronica Tripertita* the comparison between the sun and Richard is no longer an occasion for praising Richard. Gower notes that Richard has a badge that is the sun and then writes: "Qui solem gessit tenebrosus lumina nescit, / In Troie metas dum vendicat ipse dietas" (I.57–58).[29] And, some lines later,

> Obsistunt turbe Phebo, ne scandat in vrbe,
> Dumque suis alis Cignus fuit imperialis,
>   Fraus tamen obliquas nubes commouit iniquas,
> Extera dum rebus temptauit lumina Phebus.   (61–64)[30]

In these lines, Phebus/Richard appears as a danger to public order and is accused of trickery ("fraus"). A similar fraudulent use of his power is exercised

---

[29] "The shadowy one who bore the sun did not see the light, for during Troy's extremities he took vengeance upon the assembled peoples" (*Major Latin Works*, trans. Stockton, 292).

[30] "The crowds resisted Phoebus, and he did not ascend the wall, for the Swan held sway with his wings. Phoebus's trickery moreover stirred the wicked crowds into disorder, as he exerted his efforts against the luminaries on the outside" (*Major Latin Works*, trans. Stockton, 292).

by Phebus in the "Tale of Leucothoe." The political allusions in the tale suggest that the tale's focus also falls, then, on Phebus's abuse of power. It is significant that what Phebus lusts after is referred to as no more than a "thing" in Genius's words: "he thurghout hir chambre wall / Cam in al sodeinliche, and stall / That thing which was to him so lief" (6749–51). By calling it a thing, Genius diverts our attention from virginity to the act of stealing itself and to Phebus's abuse of power. In order to fulfill his desire, Phebus creates disorder that has tragic consequences within Orchamus's family.

Orchamus's reaction to the rape also represents an abuse of power. The father admits that he decides to kill Leucothoe, because he does not dare confront Phebus: "To Phebus dar I nothing speke, / Bot upon hire I schal be wreke" (6765–66). Hence, Orchamus's revenge on his daughter rather than on Phebus actually exemplifies his impotence in the face of a tyrannical power. His revenge, moreover, is significant in another sense. Orchamus's abuse of his power over his daughter actually mirrors Phebus's absolutist use of his power against him. If Phebus takes Orchamus's private property, his daughter's virginity, Orchamus takes what belongs to his daughter, her body. Notice how he is "welnyh wod" (6762) – like Canace's and Virginia's fathers – when he decides to sacrifice his daughter. Like Phebus, he is far from exemplifying self-restraint. Furthermore, the method Orchamus uses to kill her – putting her in a pit and burying her alive – echoes his previous stifling confinement of his daughter within walls and his attempt to exert an absolute control over her body. The fact that Genius's Leucothoe, unlike Ovid's, does not utter a single word either during the rape scene, or when the father decides to kill her, indicates that Leucothoe is the victim of two authorities who abuse their power over her, Phebus, and her father.

But we should return to the question posed at the beginning: what does this mean for the daughter? It is significant that Genius insists on Leucothoe's virginity and, especially, as I have argued, that he creates the sense that Leucothoe's loss of her virginity is inevitable. Presenting virginity as inherently violable suggests that women and their virginity are subject to male authority. Genius thus suggests the opposite of what medieval treatises on virginity for women sometimes emphasized. The preservation of virginity, as various critics have shown, was presented sometimes in those treatises as women's opportunity to maintain some independence from patriarchal power. In order to encourage women to become nuns and preserve their virginity, these treatises can paint a dismal picture of marriage and the woman's concomitant subjection to a man. Barbara Newman has called this the "misandronist motif" and she gives various examples in which, as she puts it, the writer tries to "persuade the virgin to avoid the tyranny of husbands."[31] Jocelyn Wogan-Browne also gives an example – from the *Letter on Virginity for the*

---

[31] Barbara Newman, *From Virile Woman to WomanChrist: Studies in Medieval Religion and Literature* (Philadelphia: U of Pennsylvania P, 1995) 32–33.

Encouragement of Virgins in the Katherine group – about which she remarks: "The socio-economics of marriage are unmasked along with its tribulations: if in marriage, the *Letter* asks, even the wealthiest queens and countesses are 'licking honey off thorns' (6/32), what is it like for poor women – 'like almost all gentlewomen living at present who . . . give themselves up to the service of a man of lower rank' (8/2–5)?"[32] Wogan-Browne further observes that these comments "expose aspects of socio-economic destiny usually kept well veiled from the medieval romance heroine" (170). In the "Tale of Leucothoe," by establishing the inevitability of sexual desire, Genius is in a way veiling from Leucothoe, from daughters in general, the possibility of another destiny – a destiny that does not entail subjection to men. Similarly, at the same time as he opens up the possibility of questioning tyrannical political authority by marking the limits between private and public, he is also veiling from the subjects the possibility of a political system that is not based on royal authority.[33]

In the next tale we will analyze, the "Tale of Virginia," there is a similar conflict of power between men. In this case, the action of the human authority, a king who tries to use his power in a tyrannical manner, is very explicitly condemned by Genius. However, the father's own abuse of his daughter is still only indirectly questioned. We will have to wait until the "Tale of Canace and Machaire" to see an explicit condemnation of the sacrifice of a daughter by Gower's narrator.

The Tale of Virginia

In the "Tale of Virginia" (7.5131–5306), the father-daughter relationship is used to explore the relation between public and domestic affairs within an explicitly political context. The two authorities who come into conflict are this time human, and the conflict centers once again on a daughter. The moment the daughter crosses into the public space (when her beauty becomes well known and the king, Apius Claudius, hears about it), a conflict arises between public and private powers – between Virginia's father's prerogative over his family, and Apius's political power as king, a power he tries to use to obtain Virginia. Apius, as Virginius sees it, goes beyond the limits of his authority over his subject. But Virginius himself also goes beyond

---

[32] Jocelyn Wogan-Browne, "The Virgin's Tale," *Feminist Readings in Middle English Literature: The Wife of Bath and All Her Sect*, ed. Ruth Evans and Lesley Johnson (London: Routledge, 1994) 171. Wogan-Browne is quoting from Bella Millett and Jocelyn Wogan-Browne, eds. and trans. *Medieval English Prose for Women: The Katherine Group and Ancrene Wisse* (Oxford: Oxford UP, 1990).

[33] Genius's support of royal ideology is not surprising. Ferster has made a point about Gower concerning this issue that can also apply to Genius: To say that Gower was not a republican "is not to say very much. There were no viable alternatives to monarchy during the English Middle Ages" (*Fictions of Advice* 120). Nevertheless, I would argue, we can still analyze the ways in which the text reveals the constructedness of medieval royal ideology.

the limits of his authority over his daughter. As in the "Tale of Leucothoe," virginity in this tale, I will argue, becomes a site for the exploration of the boundaries between the private and the public and of the limits of authority over these realms. It also points, more clearly than the "Tale of Leucothoe," to the fluidity of those realms and thus to the difficulty of marking the limits of authority.

This political aspect is indeed more evident in the "Tale of Virginia" than it is in either the "Tale of Leucothoe" or in the "Tale of Canace and Machaire." Based on Livy's account in his *History of Rome* (Book 3), the story of Virginia, according to C. David Benson, was traditionally used as a moral example about politics and was popular in medieval literature, especially as an *exemplum* of evil government.[34] Livy himself was mostly interested in the story as one of the historical incidents that proved the failure of the *decemvir* system of governance in Rome. Hence, the Roman historian expands greatly on the fate of the *decemvir* Apius Claudius after the sacrifice of Virginia – he is overthrown and commits suicide – and depicts his ending as a consequence of his tyranny and lust.

Two medieval analogues, and possible sources for Gower, the versions in *Le Roman de la Rose* (5589–5663), and in Chaucer's "Physician's Tale" play down the political aspects. In the French poem Jean de Meun uses the story to criticize the corruption of judges, while Chaucer's Physician blurs the political moral of the tale, extracting a general moral about the need to forsake sin, because "synne hath his merite" (277). Unlike Chaucer and Jean de Meun, Genius points to the more traditional moral, echoing Livy's political lesson. At the end of the tale he remarks: "And thus thunchaste was chastised / Wherof thei myhte ben avised / That scholden afterward governe" (5301–03). Those who govern should learn from the tale "Hou it is good a king eschuie / The lust of vice and vertu suie" (5305–06).[35] He also emphasizes the political, as Ferster has observed, by calling Apius not a *decemvir* but a king, and by using the verb "deposed" (5295) to refer to his removal from office; "deposed," Ferster argues, would have resonated in the fourteenth century "with the deposition of Edward II and the threats of deposition against Edward III and, most immediately, Richard II."[36]

The particular placement of the "Tale of Virginia" within the *Confessio*

---

[34] See C. David Benson's explanatory notes on Chaucer's version of the story of Virginia, "The Physician's Tale," in L. D. Benson, ed. *The Riverside Chaucer* 902.
[35] In his *Fall of Princes*, where we can also find a version of the story of Virginia, John Lydgate, like Gower, stresses the political lesson:
> Wherfore, ye Pryncis, yiff ye list longe endure,
> Beth riht weel war, be ye neuer so strong,
> In your lordshepis nat to moche assure
> Off surquedie the poraile to do wrong.   (II.1422–25)

Quoted from John Lydgate, *The Fall of Princes*, ed. Henry Bergen, EETS e.s. 122 (Oxford: Oxford UP, 1925).
[36] Ferster, *Fictions of Advice* 121.

Amantis also stresses its political aspect. The tale comes towards the end of Book 7, the only book in the *Confessio* which does not deal with one of the deadly sins, and a book which critics have often characterized as a kind of "de regimine principum," a political treatise about the education of a king.[37] "The Tale of Virginia" also follows another tale about lust and political tyranny – the story of the "Rape of Lucrece." In the "Rape of Lucrece," as well as in the "Tale of Virginia," a political tyrant causes his own overthrow. Livy himself establishes an explicit connection between the stories of Lucrece and Virginia, although he tells each story in a different book. He introduces the story of Virginia by calling it a "crime," and he continues: "Its origin was lust and in its consequences it was no less dreadful than the rape and suicide of Lucretia which led to the expulsion of the Tarquins. The *decemvirs*, in fact, met the same end as the kings and lost their power for the same reason."[38] Genius states an explicit connection between the two stories by extracting a similar moral. At the end of the "Rape of Lucrece," he introduces the "Tale of Virginia" by saying that the latter is:

> . . . an other remembrance
> That rihtwisnesse and lecherie
> Acorden noght in compaignie
> With him that hath the lawe on honde.   (5124–27)

Moreover, the "Tale of Virginia" immediately precedes the "Tale of Apollonius," which is also, among other things, about the relationship between political tyranny and lust.[39] As Peck has noted, Genius's moral to the tale, "thus thunchaste was chastised" (5301), is a pun that "pertains significantly to Gower's emphasis in Book VIII on incest (incastus) as the epitome of all sin" (157).

While the traditional moral to the story of Virginia focuses on its political aspect, on the strife between Virginius and Apius over Virginia, it glosses over the implications of the sacrifice for the daughter herself, as Genius's moral also does in the "Tale of Leucothoe." Linda Lomperis has noted a similar silence concerning the daughter in Chaucer's "Physician's Tale."[40] Both Virginius and even the critics of the tale, she argues, tend to "privileg[e] the

---

[37] See A. Minnis, "John Gower: *Sapiens* in Ethics and Politics," *Medium Aevum* 49 (1980): 216. For more recent analyses of Book 7 as a kind of "de regimine principum," see Scanlon, *Narrative, Authority, and Power* 282–97, and Ferster, *Fictions of Advice*, ch. 7.
[38] Livy, *The Early History of Rome*, trans. Aubrey de Sélincourt (Edinburgh: Penguin, 1960) 215. All other quotations from Livy come from the same edition.
[39] As Minnis and Peck have observed, the "Tale of Virginia" thus provides an appropriate transition to the "Tale of Apollonius." See Minnis, " 'Moral Gower' and Medieval Literary Theory" *Gower's* Confessio Amantis, ed. Minnis, 75–76; Peck, *Kingship and Common Profit* 165.
[40] Linda Lomperis, "Unruly Bodies and Ruling Practices: Chaucer's *Physician's Tale* as a Socially Symbolic Act," *Feminist Approaches to the Body in Medieval Literature*, ed. Linda Lomperis and Sarah Stanbury (Philadelphia: U of Pennsylvania P, 1993) 21–22.

metaphysical at the expense of the physical" (21), thus ignoring the death of the daughter. In this way, to Lomperis, the critics, like Virginius, "respond to the tale's representation of bodily considerations by effectively cutting them off" (21). In Genius's case, the body of Virginia is not cut off, but it disappears towards the end of the tale. Her plight, moreover, is presented not so much as it affects Virginia, but in Virginius's terms, as it affects him (and later by extension as it affects the other subjects). The father's main worry concerning Virginia's plight is that she, and, more importantly, he, will be shamed:

> For me is levere upon this thing
> To be the fader of a Maide,
> Thogh sche be ded, than if men saide
> That in hir lif sche were schamed
> And I therof were evele named. (5248–52)

Of course, even if Chaucer's and Gower's narrators focus their attention on the father, on the "comune," or on metaphysical implications, while ignoring Virginia's role, critics do not need to follow their lead. We can still look at the tale from the daughter's point of view and analyze the implications of their neglect of Virginia.

In the following pages, I will analyze Genius's treatment of those other implications that the explicit moral of the story tries to gloss over. I will argue that the "Tale of Virginia" is not only about the political consequences of tyranny and lust, but also about the conflicts arising from the construction of two separate spheres of power, the public and the private spheres, over which different figures of authority dominate. More specifically, the tale is about a king's abuse of power over one of his citizens and about his infringement of the laws that he himself is expected to respect. Thus, it explores the limitations of kingly authority. But I will go further and suggest that it is also about the limits of a father's authority over his daughter. The political context of the tale, its theme of kingly tyranny, puts the father's sacrifice of his daughter in a significant light. It suggests that the king's violation of his father's property, his daughter, is comparable to the father's violation of his daughter's body. As Apius's invasion of Virginius's privacy blurs the lines between the private and the public, Virginius's sacrifice of his daughter is a refusal to recognize a line separating Virginia from Virginius, a refusal to allow Virginia to be a different being, to own her private body. Finally, Genius's version of the end of the story, in which he forgets about Virginia, also questions his use of his own authority as narrator. In his narrative, her private body is transformed into a public conflict; even as he advocates the need for the head of state to respect the line between the private and the public lives of his citizens, Genius also blurs the line that he himself is trying to draw.

The opening of the tale sets it in its political context:

> At Rome whan that Apius,
> Whos other name is Claudius,
> Was governour of the cite,

> Ther fell a wonder thing to se
> Touchende a gentil Maide, as thus,
> Whom Livius [sic] Virginius
> Begeten hadde upon his wif. (5131–37)

The political situation of Rome at the time is mentioned first, enveloping the private life of Virginius and his daughter. Genius then notes that Virginia is beautiful and that her beauty cannot be kept in private; "Men" (5138) talk about it, and so "This fame . . . goth up and doun" (5140). Writing about certain Renaissance women writers, Helen Wilcox has noted that for these women, "[t]o be seen, to be known beyond the confines of their own homes, was to begin to breach the boundary between private and public worlds."[41] Unlike Leucothoe, whose father seems to have managed to keep her almost completely away from the public eye (he hardly allowed her to go out), Virginia becomes an object of public admiration, thus crossing the boundary between private and public. It is through the public comments on her beauty that Apius's desire is kindled. In Gower's version, then, the moment Virginia's beauty becomes public knowledge, her father loses control over her. He cannot prevent others from desiring her and he cannot prevent her virginity from becoming a desired commodity, a prize that men fight over. As Genius puts it, when Apius hears about Virginia's beauty and virginity, he "began the flour desire / Which longeth unto maydenhede" (5144–45). The moment she crosses the threshold of her house, she becomes a public object of desire.

The adjectives and images Genius uses to describe Apius's behavior reveal clearly that he disapproves of this king's abuse of political power. Genius depicts his desire as unbridled and blind from the beginning (for example, he mentions "the blinde lustes of his wille" [5147], which reminds us of Antiochus's blindness). It is a desire, moreover, that shows a mixture of lust and wrath. Apius is described as a man of "riote" (5168). And when the father arrives and he realizes that his plan may fail, acting "half in wraththe as thogh it were" (5221), Apius manipulates the law "out of kinde" (5220), like Canace's father, King Eolus, and like Leucothoe's father. He is also "Deceived of concupiscence" (5223). This negative portrayal makes clear what Genius thinks about him.

What is less clear is what he thinks about Virginius's actions. Things are more complicated with him. A significant detail distinguishes Genius's story from his Roman source, a detail that contributes to Virginius's characterization as a father. In Livy's *History* Lucius Icilius, Virginia's fiancé, plays an important role. When Livy introduces him, he hints at a possible source of political enmity or disagreement between Icilius and Apius Claudius:

---

[41] Helen Wilcox, "Private Writing and Public Function: Autobiographical Texts by Renaissance Englishwomen," *Gloriana's Face: Women, Public and Private in the English Renaissance*, eds. S. P. Cesarano and Marion Wynne-Davies (Hertfordshire: Harvester Wheatsheaf, 1992) 54.

Virginia's fiancé is "a keen and proven champion of the popular cause" (215), which will later help him gather the support of the people against Apius. Icilius is very outspoken in defending his rights as Virginia's fiancé. Interestingly enough, as he defends those rights he also attacks Apius's political leadership:

> I am to marry this girl, and I mean to have a virgin for my bride . . . I refuse to let my promised wife pass the night away from her father's house. You have made slaves of us all – you have robbed the people of their right to appeal and of the protection of their tribunes; but that does not mean you have the lordship of your lusts over our wives and children. (217)

In this speech Icilius demands that Apius separate his political power as judge from his lustful desires, but by asking him to separate the two, he is already establishing a link between his personal case and Apius's political performance. After Virginius arrives, Icilius plays a secondary role, since Virginius is the one who has legal rights over Virginia, but he remains active gathering the people's support. Once Virginia is killed and her father escapes, Icilius gets the people to mutiny, organizing them to go to Rome and help to overthrow Apius (223).

In contrast, Genius agrees with the *Roman de la Rose* and Chaucer's "Physician's Tale" in playing down Icilius's role and concentrating on the triangle father-daughter-authority figure (a king in Gower, a judge in Jean de Meun and Chaucer). It is remarkable that, while each of these three medieval versions has a different purpose, all three authors show little or no interest in the future son-in-law. Virginia's fiancé is not even mentioned in Chaucer's and Jean de Meun's versions, while in Gower's version Ilicius (as Gower spells his name) is just a passive figure in the background. He is mentioned only twice, and both times by Genius. First, when the priest mentions him as Virginia's fiancé, and characterizes him as "a worthi kniht of gret lignage" (5150); and later on when he notes that Virginius reacted like a lion because his daughter was going to be deceived and Ilicius was going to be "weyved / Untrewly fro the Mariage" (5238–39).

That Ilicius does not play an active role in the tale points to the identification between father-in-law and son-in-law that I analyzed in Chapter Three. Ilicius is just a replacement for Virginius, the man Virginius has chosen to replace him as the owner of his daughter's virginity. It is also indicative of the identification between the two men that the only description Genius gives us of Ilicius ("a worthi kniht of gret lignage") echoes other descriptions of Virginius by Gower's priest. The adjective "worthi" is used repeatedly to refer to Virginia's father, sometimes modifying the same noun, "kniht" (as in "this noble worthi knyht," 5189, and "This worthi kniht," 5259), or modifying another noun (as in "this worthi capitein," 5210). As Virginius's replacement, Ilicius does not have a separate identity or an independent role, and it is Virginius in whom Genius is interested.

The tale concentrates on Virginius as the protagonist, the one who has absolute power over Virginia. The extent of his power over her goes beyond moral considerations. In an article on Chaucer's version of the tale, Emerson Brown has remarked that, "[t]he story seems to have bothered Gower . . . for he mitigates Virginius' responsibility for his daughter's death on the grounds of something much like temporary insanity."[42] Indeed, although I would substitute Genius for Gower, I agree with Brown that he (Genius) not only mitigates Virginius' responsibility, but also avoids bringing in a moral framework that would explain and justify Virginia's death – Virginius himself offers no moral explanation for his action. I would add, though, that Virginius's action cannot be explained as "temporary insanity." If he is insane, his insanity is not really temporary, since, after killing Virginia, he does not seem to recover his sanity for some time – he rides with his sword dripping with her blood, and showing no sign of repentance, to plead for his case. What is more, Genius does not suggest that he is insane – he calls him "This worthi kniht" (5259) when he is riding with his sword to Rome.

Genius's reluctance to judge Virginius's action becomes evident again when we notice the discrepancy between Genius's and Virginius's explanations of the latter's motive for killing Virginia. Gower's priest gives the following reasons:

> That for the lust of Lecherie
> His douhter scholde be deceived,
> And that Ilicius was weyved
> Untrewly fro the Mariage. (5236–39)

These two reasons give the impression that Virginius is concerned for his daughter and her fiancé as independent beings; they suggest that Virginius is thinking beyond himself. Virginius's own words, though, contradict this impression:

> For me is levere upon this thing
> To be the fader of a Maide,
> Thogh sche be ded, than if men saide
> That in hir lif sche were schamed
> And I therof were evele named. (5248–52)

In this speech Virginius does not distinguish between himself and his own daughter. (This lack of distinction is emphasized by the fact that, like Constance and Constantine, she bears the same name as her father, only in its feminine version.) Not only his daughter's shame – which would stigmatize socially both Virginia and himself – but especially the effect that her shame would have upon himself – what men might say – is his main worry.[43]

---

42 Emerson Brown, Jr., "What Is Chaucer Doing with the Physician and His Tale?," *Philological Quarterly* 60 (1981): 138.
43 I will note in my analysis of the "Tale of Canace and Machaire" that Virginius's notion of

Virginius is acutely aware of the implications that his daughter's loss of virginity would have for his public life and status. The discrepancy between Genius's and Virginius's explanations is especially significant when compared to Livy's version. In one single speech Livy's Virginius uses all those arguments (both the ones Genius uses and the ones Virginius himself uses in Gower's version) to justify his action. By dividing them up between Genius and Virginius, Gower puts the knight's "real" reasons in question. At the same time, the discrepancy between Genius and Virginius makes us wonder to what extent we can rely on Genius's perceptions. Is Virginius the disinterested father that Genius depicts? Or, is he the more self-centered father that his words seem to suggest?

As a self-centered father Virginius replicates Apius's self-centered actions. Interestingly enough, though, as a subject to Apius, Virginius takes on a daughter-like role. He becomes a reflection, or microcosm, of Roman subjects. Rome's domestic problems both cause and mirror Virginius's own domestic problems. Virginius himself offers his case as a mirror in which Rome should look at itself. When he rides to Rome to manifest his complaint, he presents his plight as a lesson for the Roman authorities: they should "liere / Upon the wrong of his matiere" (5267–68). Like his own daughter, Virginius also becomes a symbol that stands for the Roman people and their subjection to the tyrannical Apius.

Apius had a chance to obtain Virginia because her father had to attend to Rome's wars and leave his family, losing direct control over his private affairs. Gower calls attention to Virginius's conflict between his public and private affairs by making two significant comments, which have no parallel either in his source, Livy, or in his closest analogues (Chaucer's "Physician's Tale" and *Le Roman de la Rose*). Virginius's loss of control over his private life is manifested when Genius remarks that Virginia and Ilicius could not get married right after their betrothal, because the father, leading the Roman "chivalerie" (5154–60), had to go to war. For this reason, "So was the mariage left, / And stod upon acord til eft" (5161–62). On the other hand, when he learns that he might lose his daughter, he has to return home to remove the threat from his private life, thus losing control over his public duties. As Genius remarks, "[Virginius] lefte upon the field liggende / His host, til that he come ayein" (5208–09). His host suddenly has to be left without its leader, because he has to return to attend to his private affairs.

But are these private affairs really private? Virginius has to deal with a conflict in his private life that is intricately connected to his own public life. His difficulty stems ultimately from Rome's policy of attending to foreign affairs to the detriment of its own domestic problems. One of Virginius's main arguments when, after killing his daughter, he asks for help from the political authorities in Rome is that,

shame, as opposed to its absence in the case of Canace, emphasizes the theme of the private versus the public.

> ... betre it were to redresce
> At hom the grete unrihtwisnesse,
> Than forto werre in strange place
> And lese at hom here oghne grace. (5269–72)

Since Rome was paying more attention to foreign wars than to its domestic conflicts, the political situation in the country was degenerating. Rome's neglect of its domestic affairs, as Virginius points out, affects the private lives of Roman citizens:

> ... thus stant every mannes lif
> In jeupartie for his wif
> Or for his dowhter, if thei be
> Passende an other of beaute. (5273–76)[44]

The degrees of seclusion inherent in the notion of privacy and mentioned by Duby and Stanbury become evident in these lines. Public concerns, like a king's abuse of his authority, become domestic or private concerns (notice that "at hom" in line 5270 means "in Rome"), when they are opposed to concerns about foreign wars. But the concerns about a king's abuse of his authority are public when the issue is presented as an invasion of someone's family. Public and private are always defined in relation to each other. If this is so, if the two terms constantly define each other, is there a private/public distinction within the family? The tale suggests that in the domestic realm there is also a kind of public-private distinction, for, like the king's power over his subjects, the father's power over his daughter's body, over her private self, also needs to be limited. I will return to this point below.

Towards the end, after he arrives in Rome, Virginius recedes into the background, and it is the people, all the men who were under Apius's rule, who depose the king. Neither Virginius nor any of the political leaders who in Livy's version guide the people in their revolt against Apius play a significant role at this point in Genius's version. Indeed, Virginius is not mentioned again after his trip to Rome. And it is the people without a leader (Genius refers to them as "every man" or "thei") who handle the situation properly. Such a change of focus suggests that in this story Genius is more interested in showing the power of the common will against the tyranny of kings than in Virginius's plight. He is interested in the public nature of Virginius's plight.

Anne Middleton has argued that Gower's *Confessio Amantis* aspires to become a public expression of the common voice, stressing the importance of the "commune."[45] Middleton points out that in Gower, and, in general, in fourteenth-century public poetry,

---

[44] Virginius's words remind us of Amans's own view of his relationship with his lady, his private life, as being more important than fighting foreign wars (4.1706–09).
[45] Anne Middleton, "The Idea of Public Poetry in the Reign of Richard II," *Speculum* 53 (1978): 94–114.

> [t]he 'commune', like the 'public' for Cicero, is not a theoretical or logical construct, derived from postulates about human nature; it is an association neither ideal nor fully voluntary, but evolved, historical, and customary, a creature of time, place, event, and language. It is society regarded experientially, an immanent rather than a transcendent notion. (100)

In the "Tale of Virginia" the reaction of the people as a unity shows Gower's ideal of the 'commune' in action, working with concrete worldly circumstances. Indeed, Gower's choice of vocabulary in the tale, as Ferster has demonstrated, shows that he saw the reaction of the people as the ideal reaction against a tyrannical king and as a reaction that could be translated to his own contemporary times. Ferster, for instance, notes that the phrase "comun conseil" (5294), which appears in the following lines "er that it worse falle, / Thurgh comun conseil of hem alle / Thei have here wrongful king deposed" (5293–95), describes the consultation of those who depose Apius, and "is an important idiom in late fourteenth-century England, used in chronicles and parliamentary records, in Magna Carta and the notices of Edward II's deposition."[46] We should also note that the adjective "comun" appears other times – e.g., when Apius Claudius tries to give Virginia to his brother before her father can claim his rights, the people try to stop him by invoking the "comun lawe" (5188) and her father's "comun riht" (5190); later, he mentions that the people have "comun feere" (5290). At the end of the tale, then, it is the people who solve the problems created by individual leaders.

Middleton has argued that the common voice has certain values: "It assigns new importance to secular life, the civic virtues, and communal service" (95).[47] Such values

> exemplify an ideal of communal responsibility founded not primarily in an estates conception of one's duties, but in an altruistic and outward turning form of love that might be called 'common love' to emphasize its symmetry and contrast with that singular passion which expresses itself in literature in the inward self-cultivation sometimes called 'courtly love.' (96)

In the "Tale of Virginia," Apius Claudius is dominated by a singular passion: the desire to satisfy his own individual lust at all costs.[48] But Virginius does not show a much more altruistic sense of love than Claudius. His reasons for killing his daughter stem mainly from his desire to preserve his own name and

---

[46] Ferster, *Fictions of Advice* 121.
[47] She also characterizes this voice as "vernacular, practical, worldly, plain, public-spirited, and peace-loving – in a word 'common', rather than courtly or clerical" (96).
[48] As Scanlon, *Narrative, Authority, and Power*, puts it, "Appius fails to maintain the moral obligations that accrue to him personally as part of his unconstrained royal prerogatives ... he fails to make the exchange Lycurgus makes – self-restraint for power" (295).

status – which is manifested in his rights of ownership over his daughter's virginity – rather than from a moral or loving concern for her. As I argue in this book, the *Confessio Amantis* explores the ways in which state and family resemble each other. That Apius and Virginius act similarly suggests the resemblance. Virginia's end, in fact, demonstrates this point with particular poignancy.

As a daughter at a marriageable age, Virginia is an ideal site for the exploration of the interaction between private and public authority and for the definition of the limits of both types of authority. Even though Virginius tries to keep his daughter under his control, as part of his private sphere, the moment her beauty is known publicly he cannot stop others from desiring her. Virginia's most important aspect, as Genius's depiction of her death makes clear, is her sexuality. Genius's depiction is significantly original with him. In Livy's, Chaucer's, and Jean de Meun's versions the father cuts her head off and presents it to Apius. Although the beheading can also be seen in sexual terms, in Genius's version, Virginius kills his daughter in a way that hints more explicitly at the sexual symbolism of the act.[49] The father does not cut her head off but thrusts his sword through her side. Then he jumps on a horse and rides away "with his swerd droppende of blod / The which withinne his douhter stod" (5263–64). The sexual symbolism of the act suggests that what Virginius worries about is not whether Virginia should remain a virgin or not, but to whom her virginity, or her virginal blood, will belong. Since it will not belong to Ilicius, the man he had designated as his replacement, he symbolically takes it himself.

In this respect, Virginius reminds us of both Canace's and Leucothoe's fathers, and Virginia's death reminds us especially of Canace's death. As in the "Tale of Leucothoe," in the "Tale of Canace and Machaire," we will see, the father, Eolus, is full of wrath when he hears about his daughter's pregnancy (Genius says that he was "Betwen the wawe of wod and wroth," 3.217). Virginius's reaction is similar. He, like Orchamus and Eolus, is full of "rage" (5240) when he kills his daughter. Like Eolus too, whose cruelty "Ther mihte attempre no pite" (3.236), and like Orchamus, who had "no pite" (6773) either, Virginius shows no pity (he acts like a lion who "not what pite scholde amounte," 5242). Rather than losing their daughters to men they did not choose, the fathers prefer to kill them, thus asserting their ownership and incestuous possession of their daughter's bodies.

The parallels between Apius's and Virginius's actions, between Apius's tyrannical attempt to invade Virginius's privacy and Virginius's actual invasion of his daughter's "privacy," indicate that Virginius's action is certainly problematic. As I argue in this book, in Gower's *Confessio Amantis*, the public and the private, state and family, resemble each other *because*, driven by the same ideology, they support and define each other. In the "Tale of Virginia,"

---

[49] For other connotations, sexual and otherwise, of the scene in Chaucer's tale, see Lomperis, "Unruly Bodies and Ruling Practices" 32.

the head and authority of the state and the head and authority of the family act similarly: they infringe upon the private rights of someone else (Apius infringes on the private right of Virginius, ignoring the laws of the realm, and Virginius also ignores any laws by killing his daughter). I have used before the metaphor of the mirror to explain how Virginius sees himself in relation to Rome. The metaphor of the mirror applies also to his own relationship with his daughter. If Rome expects its subjects passively to mirror its own interests (for instance, going to war when it needs them to), Virginius also expects his own daughter to mirror his own private interest in the preservation of his good name (i.e., he expects her to marry and surrender her virginity to whomever *he* chooses). Moreover, by creating these correspondences, Genius opens up the possibility that the daughter may also have her own private self, and thus that the father's authority over his daughter is similarly limited – if the father has a private right over his daughter, the daughter has a private right over her life.

It is remarkable, though, that, despite these correspondences, Genius shows little concern for the daughter as an individual, especially at the end. In his tale, Virginia is little more than a site for the playing out of the conflict. In Livy's account she reappears as a ghost after her death and does not rest until Apius and Marcus Claudius receive their punishment: "Thus not a single man who had any share in Virginia's death remained, and her ghost, which so long had wandered from house to house in search of satisfaction, found rest at last" (233). When Genius's Virginius kills his daughter, both the father and Gower's priest completely forget about her. There is no lament for, or reflection on, her death, and her body (and ghost) disappear from the tale, while the political concerns of the "comune" take over. The final moral to the tale is just a general comment on how those who govern should be chaste: those who are unchaste "receiven the penance / That longeth to such governance" (5299–5300).

Virginia's disappearance at the end indicates that what happened to her does not matter to Genius as much as the social and political interest of the "comune." But Genius's exploration of the private and the public exposes this disappearance as a contradiction that undermines his own moral. It seems that, even as he tries to draw a line between the private and the public spheres, his own tale blurs such a line and suggests that the private is, to borrow Lomperis's and Stanbury's remarks about the body, "a politically charged discursive construct, a representational space traversed in various ways by socially based power relations."[50] It should be noted that the adjective "comune" is interesting in another sense than the political one noted by Ferster. It bears the connotations of public, in the sense of that which everybody has in common; it is thus significant that in the end the public interest overrides any individual or private interest. The private sphere in the end appears to be fundamentally defined by and dependent on the public sphere.

[50] Lomperis and Stanbury, Introduction, *Feminist Approaches to the Body* ix.

Thus Genius's final focus on the public interest is paradoxical given the theme of the tale. If Rome, and Virginius as its mirror, fail to address their domestic and private affairs by attending to public affairs, so does Genius. By forgetting about Virginia and diverting our attention to the political claims of the "comune," instead of reflecting on her death and her father's responsibility, he subordinates the private interest to the public interest; he subordinates the individual to the community. He acts like Rome.

One could consider Virginia's tragic end as the reason Virginius recedes into the background. His cruel action towards his daughter is too uncomfortable for Genius. While he could approve of his action because it led to the actions of the "comune," he had problems with an action that replicated Apius's own action. However, I would argue that the fact that Genius forgets about the daughter suggests that the narrator himself is also participating in similar power structures that subordinate an individual's interest to someone else's (in this case the narrator's) interest. Genius's own immediate interest in the "Tale of Virginia" is the critique of a king's abuse of his authority, rather than the cruel end and waste of a daughter. But all along he has used daughters as metaphors for the subjects. Hence, by downplaying the daughter's role, he neglects the private, the daughter's private body, and thus undermines his own moral.

The "Tale of Virginia" shows the fluidity of the notions of private and public and the gendered character of these notions. The private can easily become public and vice versa, because both notions depend on complex circumstances and are in a continual process of mutual definition. Virginia's beauty becomes a public issue when she goes outside. Similarly, the private plight of her father is easily turned into a public issue when it becomes the grounds for Apius's deposition. Conversely, a public matter can be turned into a private issue, e.g., when Virginius complains that going out to war will be detrimental to his private life. Genius himself turns the private plight of the daughter into a public problem. The fluidity and even overlap of the public and the private suggests that the private is always already traversed by socially, and hence publicly, based power relations. The private is always implicated in the public.

I have noted the role Genius plays in the portrayal of daughters, his attempt to make the tales mirror his own interest. This theme is particularly examined in "Pygmaleon and the Statue" and is the focus of the final chapter. But before turning to this reflection on the nature of authorship, we need to analyze a tale that explores the power of narration and that, among other things, indicates, through the way Genius portrays another daughter, Canace, that he sees himself as a narrator and that such a role shapes his moral teachings. In the "Tale of Canace and Machaire," unlike in the two tales just analyzed, Genius does foreground the tragic end of the daughter and does condemn the father's sacrifice of her. This time he shows sympathy for the daughter because his interest lies in how her death represents both a waste of "kinde" and *also*, more significantly, the interruption of a narrative.

The Tale of Canace and Machaire[51]

A conflict between public and private authority, between a king and a father, is central to the "Tale of Virginia." The conflict centers on a third individual, the daughter, and is played out on her body. In the "Tale of Canace and Machaire" (3.143–336), the conflict of authority is also played out on the daughter's body, but the one who challenges the father's authority is not so much the male suitor but the daughter herself. Canace takes her own lover without her father's consent and becomes pregnant. Although the fact that her lover is her own brother seems problematic, neither Genius nor the father are specifically concerned about this; the father does not react to the incestuous act in and of itself. What is especially troubling for the father is that the daughter ignores his authority in the private sphere, showing her independence from him. Even though in this tale the conflict seems to be contained within the domestic sphere, it also has large implications in a political sense – it is no coincidence that the father, Eolus, is also a king. The father's abuse of his authority over his daughter, an act that denies the independence of the daughter as a different being, serves as metaphor for the abuse of authority in the public sphere, when the tyrannical king denies the independence of his subjects by infringing on their private rights.

The "Tale of Canace and Machaire" is based on Ovid's *Heroides* 11, Canace's farewell letter to her brother Macareus. As the writer of the letter, Canace is the only narrator of Ovid's version of the story. In the letter she provides a flashback to the incidents, and, admitting her love for her brother, she laments her father's cruelty – he has ordered her to kill herself and has had her child taken to the woods to be killed. Being the only narrator, Ovid's Canace tries to draw our sympathy towards herself and her child and against her father.[52]

Even though the letter is only one part of Genius's narrative, his version is even more sympathetic towards the two lovers, especially towards Canace. Traditionally, scholars have been puzzled by this sympathetic portrayal of the two siblings, since it leads him to condone their sin of incest, while he condemns the father's wrath and melancholy.[53] Genius's treatment of the tale has seemed puzzling to critics because they have generally focused on the

---

[51] The following analysis has been adapted from my article "Confining the Daughter: Gower's 'Tale of Canace' and the Politics of the Body," *Essays in Medieval Studies* 11 (1994) 24 June 1999 <http://www.luc.edu/publications/medieval/vol11/bullon.html>. Used by permission of the Illinois Medieval Association.

[52] Critics of the Ovidian story differ on whether or not Canace succeeds in drawing our sympathy. A summary of recent studies on the *Heroides* can be found in Joan DeJean, *Fictions of Sappho, 1546–1937* (Chicago: U of Chicago P, 1989) 60–71. Florence Verducci, *Ovid's Toyshop of the Heart* (Princeton: Princeton UP, 1985), for instance, argues that she does not. To Verducci, there is a "comic banality" in Canace's laments (230). Unlike the other letters in the *Heroides*, Canace's letter, according to Verducci, does not convey "the 'serious' expression of 'grief or passion' but just the reverse" (234).

[53] For instance, C. D. Benson, "Incest and Moral Poetry in Gower's *Confessio Amantis*,"

siblings' incest and on Eolus's sin of wrath and its branch melancholy, which the tale serves to illustrate (Eolus's wrathful reaction when he discovers Canace's pregnancy serves as an example of the sin). If, as has been the case with recent studies, we turn our critical interest to the possibility that Genius hints at the incestuous character of the father's ownership of his daughter, Genius's attitude acquires a different significance.[54] I will develop here that possibility and argue that this tale is about the father-daughter relationship, and hence about the uses and abuses of authority, more than it is about sibling incest; or, to put it more accurately, this tale manifests the incestuous aspect of fathers' control over their daughters' bodies in patriarchal families. Much like Orchamus's and Virginius's sacrifices of their daughters, Eolus's command to Canace to kill herself represents a father's abuse of his authority over his daughter.

The private plight of this daughter also has political implications in Gower's tale. I have noted throughout this book that the English author sees a correspondence among political rule within the state and familial rule within the household. As Yeager, for instance, has put it, "[f]or Gower and his audience, succesful 'kingship' began most intimately at home."[55] Gower's notion of this correspondence, interestingly enough, concurs with recent feminist theories about the politics of the private, and more specifically about the politics of the private body. Even the body, that most private possession, is, to quote Lomperis and Stanbury again, "a politically charged discursive construct, a representational space traversed in various ways by socially based power relations."[56] In the "Tale of Canace and Machaire," Canace's body is thus a site for the enactment of tensions that have political resonances. It is, indeed, no coincidence that, whereas in the *Heroides* Æolus is the mythological god of the winds, in Gower's tale this pagan god is turned into a king. Thus, Gower's tale is not only about the confinement of the daughter within the family, but also about the confinement of the body politic by the absolutist king. This parallel thus develops a notion that we have seen in other tales in the *Confessio Amantis*.

Chaucer Review 19 (1984): 100–109, has lamented "Genius's failure to condemn Canacee" (102).

[54] See Wetherbee, "Constance and the World in Chaucer and Gower," Donavin, *Incest Narratives*, 112, and A. C. Spearing, "Canace and Machaire," *Mediaevalia* 16 (1993 [for 1990]): 211–21. Wetherbee, for example, has remarked that "the violence with which Aeolus responds to the discovery of his daughter's incest by compelling her to suicide has strong incestuous overtones of its own" (86). Allen, "Chaucer Answers Gower," has also examined the incestuous implications of Eolus's rage, noting too the tyrannical overtones of the story (633ff).

[55] Yeager, *John Gower's Poetic* 208.

[56] Lomperis and Stanbury, Introduction, *Feminist Approaches to the Body* ix. Elaborating on the same notion, Lomperis and Stanbury also note that the essays they edit consider, as I also do, "the signifiers 'gender' and 'body' . . . not simply as object designations, but rather as socially based categories that are eminently and inextricably connected with questions of power" (ix).

The "Tale of Canace and Machaire," though, goes one step further by suggesting another parallel: Canace is also confined by her literary father, Genius, and ultimately by male discourse. Gower draws a parallel between the daughter's body and her narrative, associating the act of procreation with the act of literary creation. It is significant in this sense that, while the moral to the tale focuses on Eolus and his sin of wrath, the narrative itself centers its attention upon Canace. Eolus's daughter is the protagonist of the tale and the creative impulse behind the narrative. By joining Machaire, she separates from her father and to a certain extent creates her own story and her own child. By writing the letter, she also attempts, though in a limited way, to author her own story. From this perspective, Eolus's command to Canace to kill herself, while restating his ownership of her body, also represents an attempt to stop his daughter's narrative. It is primarily because Canace exemplifies literary creativity, I will argue, that Genius portrays her sympathetically.

Let us turn first to Eolus's incestuous abuse of his authority over Canace. In a society in which the father has rights of ownership over his daughter, the exchange of his daughter entails a loss for him. As Boose argues, "the daughter's movement to cross [the] threshold and move out of the father's house, whether into the house of another man or into the world of paternal institution, threatens the father, familial or cultural, with loss."[56a] The loss is compensated by the father's power to determine his daughter's husband. But when a daughter takes a husband or a lover without her father's consent, she circumvents his authority and power to determine his own replacement. The father's loss is then greater, as in the case of Eolus. Eolus's reaction to Canace's pregnancy is thus an act of despair provoked by his loss of control over his daughter's body. Gower, in fact, emphasizes Eolus's sense of loss, suggesting incestuous connotations, by making the father a personification of the typical lovers' sickness, melancholy, and hinting at the similarities between Eolus and Amans with respect to the sickness. Melancholy, we will see, also brings Eolus close to Antiochus, the one father in the *Confessio Amantis* who – apart from Lot, whose incestous relationship with his daughters Genius tells briefly (8.222–270) – does commit literal incest with his daughter.

In Chapter Two, I alluded to the link between melancholy and lovesickness in connection with Antiochus. Such a link is also crucial in this tale. Medical and literary texts from antiquity and the early Middle Ages, as Mary Wack has shown, have depicted melancholy mainly as a form of lovesickness.[57] In modern time, Freud has also shown the correlation between melancholy and love: "Melancholia may be the reaction to the loss of a loved object . . . The object has not perhaps actually died, but has been lost as an

---

56a Boose, "The Father's House and the Daughter in It" 47.
57 Wack, *Lovesickness in the Middle Ages* 162. The *Middle English Dictionary* gives two definitions of "malencolie" in its emotional manifestations: "A mental disorder or emotional disease due to unnatural melancholy . . .; – may be brought on by love, disappointment, etc."; and "Anger, rage, hatred."

object of love."⁵⁸ The melancholic's response to the loss, according to Freud, is "an extraordinary diminution in his self-regard, an impoverishment of his ego on a grand scale" (246). Once the object is lost "the free libido [is] not displaced on to another object; it is withdrawn into the ego" (249). The melancholic's typical reaction to the loss highlights the link between melancholy and anger; according to Wack, "the depression and self-abasement characteristic of melancholy – or lovesickness – is nothing other than hostility toward the object redirected to the self" (162).

In the "Tale of Canace and Machaire," Eolus turns melancholic when he realizes that his daughter is pregnant and thus that he has lost her. It might be objected that Eolus's reaction seems unlike that of the typical melancholic, because he does not direct his hatred towards himself, but towards his love object: Canace. But that Eolus directs his hatred towards the love object actually points to his problem: he does not see his daughter as an independent being, but rather as the flesh of his flesh and bone of his bone, as part of himself. In this sense, he acts like a melancholic lover: when he orders Canace to kill herself, he is destroying part of himself. By making the father, Eolus, an example of melancholy, Gower suggests that the father's reaction stems from his emotional disappointment at the loss of his daughter, rather than from a moral impulse to punish her for her incestuous act with her brother. The way Eolus sacrifices Canace – she has to kill herself – is also significant in this respect. As Spearing has noted, it is "as though [he] is proposing incest at a double remove, substituting the knight for himself and the sword for the phallus" (217).

Genius further emphasizes the link between love and anger by suggesting parallels between Amans and Eolus.⁵⁹ Before starting the tale in Book 3, the priest engages in a discussion about the sin of melancholy with his penitent in which the latter admits he becomes melancholic and wrathful when he thinks he "mai noght spede" in love (40). His unfulfilled erotic desire, he continues, provokes his wrath, making him, "distempred and esmaied" (58), as a result of which, he says, "Thus be my wittes as forlore" (62), and "I wode as doth the wylde Se" (86). At one point, Amans remarks that "Malencolie . . . groweth of the fantasie / Of love" (125–27). Some lines later, in the tale itself, Eolus's melancholy reminds us of Amans's condition. Like the lover, Eolus falls "into Malencolie, / As thogh it were a frenesie" (209–10), when he learns that his daughter has given birth to a child.⁶⁰ And using the same sea

---

⁵⁸ Freud, "Mourning and Melancholia" 245.
⁵⁹ Allen, "Chaucer Answers Gower," has made an interesting point in this respect. Although the text draws such parallels, she argues, Amans refuses to see them: "Amans insists on limiting his vision to his own love affair, and further, on viewing his response as a state of embattled weakness rather than tyranny" (635). He prefers to see himself as a victim, like Canace. Amans thus becomes an example of misreading. I would add that his misreading reveals a self-absorption that itself accords with the theme of the self-centeredness that is considered to be characteristic of wrath.
⁶⁰ Benson, "Incest and Moral Poetry in Gower's *Confessio Amantis*," has compared Eolus's

metaphor that Amans had used previously, Genius says that, when Eolus enters his daughter's room, he is "Betwen the wawe of wod and wroth" (217).[61] The parallel between Amans and Eolus suggests that the father's wrathful reaction, like Amans's, stems from a sense of impotence, given his inability to fully possess what he loves.[62]

Like the tales of Leucothoe and Virginia, the incestuous dimension of the father-daughter relationship in the "Tale of Canace and Machaire" has crucial political implications. These implications do not deny the relevance of the daughter's situation. Quite to the contrary, they demonstrate again the ways in which, particularly in Gower's *Confessio Amantis*, the private is inevitably traversed by the political, even as this tale shows Eolus's attempt to isolate the private from the public. In this chapter I argue that one of Gower's concerns in his poem is to mark the limits of authority. Gower's view of governance is hierarchical – in the Prologue to the *Confessio*, writing about the king and the state, he remarks that "unto him which the heved is / The membres buxom scholden bowe" (152–53). The people are subject to the king. Nevertheless, the king's power over his people is limited by the people themselves. In this way, Gower agrees with contemporary political thought, which was primarily influenced by the Aristotelian/Thomistic view of the natural state.[63] This view, as Strohm has shown, sees the state as an organic whole composed of interdependent parts, and more specifically, as a body whose members (the people) are subject to the head (the king) (146).[64] The head guides the diversity of interests of the different members of the body towards the common good. Even though this system is strongly hierarchical, with the king as the head, Strohm remarks that the king's rule "is not . . . ordained by God but based on the consent of the people," and thus there are some limits to the king's power over the body. According to Aquinas, when the king acts only in regard to his own well-being rather than that of the commonwealth, he becomes a tyrant; his people then have the right to remove him from power (Strohm 147).

"frenesie" to Canace's and Machaire's frenzy of love: "there are suggestions that [Eolus's] 'frenesie' (210) of anger is not only the result but also the equivalent of his children's frenzy of love" (104–05). Benson, though, does not elaborate on the similarities between anger and love.

[61] We should note that Canace's own description of her experience of love also evokes the water imagery: "That I misdede yowthe it made, / And in the flodes bad me wade" (227–28). However, Canace, unlike her father, or Amans, describes her situation with a certain detachment. It was "yowthe" that made her "wade."

[62] For further discussion of the parallel between the concupiscible and the irascible passions according to fourteenth-century theories, see Thomas Hatton, "John Gower's Use of Ovid in Book III of the *Confessio Amantis*," *Mediaevalia* 13 (1987): 257–74. Hatton notes, for instance, that it was a commonplace in the fourteenth century "[t]hat unreasonable love may quickly lead to unreasonable anger. These two passions, concupiscence and irascibility, were thought to make up the sensate part of the human personality" (262).

[63] See Strohm, *Social Chaucer* (Cambridge: Harvard UP, 1989) 147.

[64] See also Kantorowicz, *The King's Two Bodies*, esp. 207–32.

It was a king, Richard II, who commissioned Gower to write the *Confessio Amantis*, according to the first recension of the poem.[65] Richard II, as I argued in Chapter One, had the reputation of being a tyrant. In Richard Jones's words, "[t]he most widely publicized contemporary tradition of Richard [II] is that of the tyrant, a tradition, substantially documented by the charges of the parliament roll."[66] According to this tradition, which contributed to his deposition, Richard saw himself as the absolute owner of his country. In his *Annales Ricardi II et Henrici IV*, Thomas Walsingham, for instance, attributes the following line to Richard: "The lives, lands, properties, goods and chattels of my subjects are mine."[67] Walsingham also reports him to have said that he was the origin of the law: "laws were within his own breast and . . . he alone could change and make the laws of his realm."[68] Of course, Walsingham's *Annales* are unambiguously anti-Ricardian. Nevertheless, whether these accusations of tyranny were true or not is irrelevant for my argument that Richard was seen as a tyrant. What is relevant is that those accusations of tyranny did circulate, that tyranny was seen in terms of selfishness, and that a king's alleged tyranny was seen as a valid reason for his deposition.

Significantly, Richard II was also renowned for his anger, Eolus's sin.[69] Anger was often represented in medieval books of vices and virtues as a self-destructive force. In the *Psychomachia*, Prudentius allegorizes Wrath as a feminine figure who, unable to defeat Patience, kills herself.[70] In *The Book of Vices and Virtues*, a fourteenth-century translation of *Somme le Roi*, and a kind of penitential treatise on which Gower's *Confessio* heavily depended, the angry man is said to make four wars, the first one being a war with himself:

Þe first is þat he haþ werre wiþ hymself, for whan wraþþe is ful in a man, he turmenteþ his soule and his body so þat he may haue no sleep ne reste; and oþerwhile it . . . makeþ hym falle . . . in-to suche a sorwe þat he takeþ his deþ.[71]

---

[65] In the "Prologue" to the first version of the *Confessio*, Gower writes that Richard II commissioned him to write "Som newe thing . . . / That he himself it mihte loke / After the forme of my writynge" (*51–53).

[66] Jones, *The Royal Policy of Richard II* 167. See also my discussion in Chapter One above.

[67] Quoted from Hutchinson, *Hollow Crown* 199. On Walsingham and his writings, see also Chris Given-Wilson, ed. and trans. *Chronicles of the Revolution: 1397–1400* (Manchester: Manchester UP, 1993).

[68] Hutchinson, *Hollow Crown* 199. Wallace, *Chaucerian Polity*, has commented on this quote and remarked that with it "Richard arbitrarily claims that his own body and the body politic are one and the same" (297).

[69] Hutchinson, *Hollow Crown*, for instance, has commented that "[w]e are told by most of the chroniclers of Richard's violent outbursts of temper, and there is no need to doubt them" (199).

[70] See Prudentius, *Psychomachia, Aurelii Prudentii Clementis Carmina*, ed. Johan Bergman, Corpus Scriptorum Ecclesiasticorum Latinorum 61 (Vindobonae: Hoelder-Pichler-Tempsky, 1926) 175–78, ll.109–77.

[71] *The Book of Vices and Virtues: A Fourteenth-Century Translation of the Somme Le Roi of Lorens d'Orléans*, ed. W. Nelson Francis, EETS o.s. 217 (London: Oxford UP, 1942) 25.

The result of this first war is his own death. He kills his own body. Following this allegorical interpretation, if the state is represented as an organic whole with a head and a body, a wrathful king, as head of the state, is especially dangerous to his own body, that is, to his own country.

Hence, it is no coincidence that in the "Tale of Canace and Machaire" Eolus is a king, rather than a pagan god. I must state, though, that I am not trying to prove that Eolus is some kind of allegorical representation of King Richard II, even though it is likely that Richard's reputation as an angry king led Gower to examine the sin of anger and its impact on a relationship of authority. Rather, I want to point to the intersection of familial and political power relationships as it is manifested in Gower's tale. Fathers in patriarchal society have rights of ownership over their daughters. Society, however, limits the extent of their rights by compelling them to exchange their daughters. A medieval monarch was considered, in Hutchinson's terms, "the father of his subjects and the fountain of law and justice" (200). But, like the father, a king ought not to have absolute power over his subjects and the law. Society and the Parliament as its representative have the right to put certain limits on that power. The tyrant who looks after only his own well-being and who uses his subjects as if they were his property, a simple extension of his self, resembles the father whose selfish sense of ownership over his daughter leads him to exert absolute power over her by keeping his daughter to himself and, in the worst case, by taking possession of her body and committing incest. Gower made such a point probably prompted by Richard's behavior, but this was applicable to any other tyrannical king or tyrannical authority figure.

In the light of this political reading, Genius's condemnation of the father and his sympathy towards the two incestuous siblings, especially towards Canace appears to be more understandable. Jones has noted that, "[t]he self-sufficient monarchy to which [Richard II] was committed could only become a reality through the suppression of inherent particular rights" (175). Eolus's melancholy suggests that his violent reaction does not stem from a sense that Canace's incest with her brother is immoral, but rather from his realization that he has lost absolute control over his daughter's body. In this way, Gower also denounces the dangers of an absolutist king for his country. Canace's tragic death highlights the self-destructiveness of any type of absolute patriarchal power that, at the familial and, at the same time, at the state level, ignores any laws that limit the power of the authority figure over the subordinate body. In confining his daughter to his private family space and exerting an absolute control over her body, Eolus, like an absolute monarch, suppresses her rights as a being independent from himself.

While Genius's critique of Eolus does not stem from a modern sense of the rights of the daughter as an individual with a private self, it does point to what Stanbury has observed in Chaucer's women, that is, that "[they] could indeed claim privacy as a territory of the person."[72] In her analysis of

---

[72] Stanbury, "Women's Letters" 279. See also my discussion in Chapter One above.

women's letters in Chaucer, Stanbury has argued that "[e]manating from a zone of female 'pryvetee' that prefigures modern territorial private rights, letters of women seem to mark a protected base of autonomy and power in which the individual self can act alone" (280). Writing the letter can thus be seen as Canace's attempt to create a private space for herself. I would even argue, in this respect, that perhaps both Chaucer and Gower explored and developed a sense of the privacy of the self in their work partly as a response to Richard's pretense that he owned both everybody's goods and their lives. Both writers may have seen a need to explore and define the private realm urged by Richard's attempt to erase the line between the private and the public.

Indeed, the notion of privacy and the threat to privacy posed by an unrestrained ruler constitute major issues in the tale. The self-destructiveness and circularity of Eolus's melancholic passion is emphasized in the tale by the atmosphere of confinement and privacy. Genius stresses the children's isolation from the rest of society, more so than Ovid. Canace and Machaire are confined to the private family space. They have been brought up in the same chamber, and they have no contact with the outside world: "Be daie bothe, and ek be nyhte, / Whil thei be yonge, of comun wone / In chambre thei togedre wone" (148–50). They also kiss for the first time, Genius says, "Whan thei were in a prive place" (168). By contrast, we are reminded of Eolus's public side and his contact with the outside world in several instances. In lines 321–23 Genius reveals Eolus's capacity to exert justice: "Bot al that mihte him noght suffise, / That he ne bad to do juise / Upon the child, and bere him oute." He has the child taken out to a forest. Later on, he shows again his capacity to give commands ("Al that he bad was don in dede," 329). Eolus lives in a world of realities ("dedes") over which he can have control – he has servants (he orders a knight to bring a knife to Canace), and political power outside the world of his family. The siblings, however, interact only with each other and with their father.

The sense of confinement and isolation is even more acute in the case of Canace than in the case of her brother. Her life is limited to the private sphere and she is prevented from interacting with the public sphere. Ovid's Canace had a nurse to whom she could talk and whom she could trust.[73] In Gower's story Canace does not relate to anybody else apart from the male members of her family (and apart from the knight who brings her father's sword to her and with whom she has a brief exchange). Throughout the tale, moreover, Canace remains and finally dies within her "chambre." At the beginning, as noted above, we are told that Canace shares a "chambre" with Machaire, and that they kissed for the first time in "a prive place." When she becomes pregnant, Canace stays inside, and the tale keeps its focus on the

---

[73] Her nurse was the first one to know that she was in love, and, when she knew Canace was pregnant, she tried to help her have an abortion. See 33ff. In Genius's version there is no allusion to the attempt at an abortion.

private space: Canace is in "hire chambre clos" (191) when she gives birth to her child. She is also in her "chambre" (218) when her father looks for her after he learns about her pregnancy, and it is in her "chambre" that she has to kill herself. The "chambre" represents the private family space separated from the outside, from public interaction, which Canace can never leave. Like an incestuous father who keeps his daughter inside his house for himself (like Antiochus, in fact), Eolus also keeps his daughter within a "chambre."

One significant detail emphasizes again Canace's isolation within the private sphere and her lack of interaction with the public world, with society and its morals. In the *Heroides* Canace is aware of the shame (the "pudorem") of her action. She remarks that her father made her shame known to all: "inruit et nostrum vulgat clamore pudorem" (79). The experience of shame, as Jean Elshtain has pointed out, indicates a person's awareness of the existence of two spheres (the public and the private), each one with different rules of behavior:

> Shame or its felt experience as it surrounds our body, its functions, passions, and desires requires appearances and symbolic forms, veils of civility that conceal some activities and aspects of ourselves even as we boldly or routinely display and reveal other sides of ourselves as we take part in public activities in the light of day for all to see.[74]

The notion of shame reveals a fundamental difference between Ovid's and Gower's Canace. The Ovidian Canace is aware of the public consequences of her action. Gower's Canace, always confined to the private sphere, her life limited to the interaction with her brother and her father, does not feel shame; she does not show an awareness of "civility" nor of the public consequences of her behavior. The significance of Genius's Canace's lack of "shame" is especially apparent when compared with the "Tale of Virginia" in which shame is a sign of "civility." Virginia never speaks in the tale, but one of her father's worries is, as I have noted, that if she becomes the dependant of the king's brother she will be "schamed" (5251) and his own name will be "evele named" (5252). The emphasis on the sense of shame in this tale indicates that Gower is here interested in the interaction between the public and the private spheres, or, rather, in the lack of interaction between the public and the private as well as in the consequences that arise from this lack of interaction. In the "Tale of Canace and Machaire," Canace does not feel any shame because she is not aware of the public sphere.

The facts that Canace shares her room with Eolus's son and that it is he who becomes her lover emphasize Canace's confinement even further. Boose has pointed out that in spatial terms, "the daughter – the liminal or 'threshold' person in family space – symbolically stands at the boundary/door, blocked from departure by the figure of the father (and/or the son or other

---

[74] Jean B. Elshtain, *Public Man, Private Woman* 9.

male heir to the father's position)" (33). Canace never comes out of her father's house literally, and even though she separates from her father by joining another person, the fact that this person is her own brother – that is, the heir to her father – suggests that even this act does not entail a complete separation. In a sense, Canace is blocked and confined not only by her father, but also by her brother. Thus, her attempt to separate from her father is very limited, since it is determined by the other male figure in her family, the son. And the son, as Boose has noted, can be seen ultimately as a replacement of the father, because "in patrilineal families [and] in [Christian] theology, the son is synonymous with the father" (33).

But even though Canace's gesture of independence is limited by her brother, it is still important to recognize that the moment she joins her brother without her father's knowledge signifies her father's loss of control over her body, or at least it is perceived by her father as such. This loss of control is perhaps more poignant for him, because the person who has taken his place is his own son, that is, the person who is going to replace him, but who is not supposed to do so yet.

As Canace's choice of a lover represents a limited gesture of independence, so does her letter represent an analogously brief and limited assertion of independence. I will turn now to the third type of confinement mentioned above – Canace's discursive confinement by her literary father, Genius. In the letter, addressed to her brother, Canace evokes an image, taken from Ovid, which epitomizes her position – encircled in between men: "In my riht hond my Penne I holde, / And in my left the swerd I kepe" (300–301). Pen and sword represent each of the male figures in Canace's life: the pen evokes her brother, for whom she is writing the letter, and the sword represents her father, who has ordered her to kill herself. This encircling of Canace evokes again her confinement.

In this context, the letter seems significant as a moment in which, figuratively, the daughter breaks out of her father's confinement and tries to define her life in her own terms. However, there is something striking about the letter. It is not a simple, informative piece of writing, but a very contrived poem that calls attention to its rhetorical status, as the first eight lines clearly indicate:

> O thou my sorwe and my gladnesse,
> O thou myn hele and my siknesse,
> O my wanhope and al my trust,
> O my desese and al my lust,
> O thou my wele, o thou my wo,
> O thou my frend, o thou my fo,
> O thou my love, o thou myn hate,
> For thee mot I be ded algate. (279–86)

The use of oxymorons places these lines in the tradition of courtly love poetry. Several critics have commented on the literariness of the piece.

Macaulay sees it as an example of "the finished style of some of [the poem's] more formal passages," Benson points to what he calls its "cliché oxymorons," Dean S. Fansler cites it as an example of anaphora in Middle English literature, and Masayoshi Ito notes the antithesis and the "traductio" in the piece.[75] This rhetoricity becomes even more remarkable when we arrive at line 286, "For thee mot I be ded algate"; we are struck by the realization that this last line is rhetorical but is also, at the same time, a statement of a fact. Canace "mot be ded" literally.

The finished style in Canace's letter asserts its status as a literary creation authored, it seems, by Canace. Quoting Edward Said, Sandra Gilbert and Susan Gubar note that, among other meanings, the word *author* conveys the notion of power over what one has created: "[T]he individual wielding this power controls its issue and what is derived therefrom."[76] The author also owns the characters in the story:

> For if the author/father is owner of his text and of his reader's attention, he is also, of course, owner/possessor of the subjects of his text, that is to say of those figures, scenes, and events . . . he has both incarnated in black and white and 'bound' in cloth or leather. (7)

While the creator of her letter is Genius and, ultimately, Gower, let me entertain for a moment, as the tale initially asks us to do, the notion that Canace is the author of the letter. Just as Gilbert and Gubar argue that the male author's literary creation represents a form of ownership and possession, I would suggest that, to an extent, as the author of her letter, Canace, though a woman, owns her text and her reader's attention, and she also owns and possesses the subjects of her text: herself, her brother, and their child. Her act of writing the letter represents an attempt to gain some authorial control over her life and over the characters in it, independently from her father. Nevertheless, I will note later, this ownership is limited. She is after all the creation of another father, Genius, and ultimately Gower. Moreover, the highly rhetorical style of her letter reminds us that she defines herself through the established discourse.

The parallel the tale draws between the child and writing emphasizes the

---

[75] G. C. Macaulay, "John Gower," *The Cambridge History of English Literature*, vol. 2 (1908; reprint, Cambridge: Cambridge UP, 1949) 152; Benson, "Incest and Moral Poetry" 105–06, Dean S. Fansler, *Chaucer and the Roman de la Rose* (New York: Columbia UP, 1914) 102n. Masayoshi Ito, *John Gower, the Medieval Poet* (Tokyo: Shinozaki Shorin, 1976): 240. The rhetoricity of the letter, moreover, also reminds us of the rhetoricity of Gower's source, Canace's letter in the *Heroides*. Verducci sees the letter in Gower's source as "a comic revision of literary and psychological expectations," which is achieved "by means of excessive but revealing conceits, by extravagant rhetorical display, innuendo or inopportune verbal point" (233). Although I would not see Genius's version in such comic terms, I do think that there is also a certain artificiality and a sense of creativity in Canace's letter.

[76] Sandra Gilbert and Susan Gubar, *The Madwoman in the Attic: The Woman Writer and the Nineteenth-Century Literary Imagination* (New Haven: Yale UP, 1979) 4.

notion of creation. In this respect, Gower modifies slightly but significantly Ovid's account. In the *Heroides*, as she writes to her brother, Canace has the roll of paper on her lap ("dextra tenet calamum, strictum tenet altera ferrum, / et iacet in gremio charta soluta meo," 3–4). In Gower's version, however, she has her son in her lap: "And in my barm ther lith to wepe / Thi child and myn, which sobbeth faste" (302–03). While this may seem a melodramatic touch (notice that the child's sobs parallel the sobbing "O" 's in the letter), the image also serves to link Canace's act of procreating the child through her body with her act of creating the letter with her pen. Canace creates with her body and with her pen. The link between body and pen is further emphasized by the fluids that come out of her body and out of her pen as she writes: "Now at this time, as thou schalt wite, / With teres and with enke write / This lettre I have in cares colde" (297–99). As if writing through her body, she spills tears from her eyes, as she spills ink from her pen.

Canace's two creative acts are set in sharp contrast with the father's sword, which she holds in her left hand. Eolus had sent her the sword with the command to kill herself. Unlike the pen, a symbol of creativity, the sword stands for destruction. Pen and sword are traditionally seen as opposites in their respective powers to create and destroy. Nevertheless, there is a sense in which the pen also kills. When an author creates characters, as Gilbert and Gubar have argued, "he silences them by depriving them of autonomy . . . even as he gives them life. . . . [H]e stills them, or – embedding them in the marble of his art – kills them" (14). When creating a character, the author gives it literary life, and, at the same time, freezes it on the page. In this sense, Canace's letter seems an attempt at freezing her story. The verbs she uses in the final image in which she describes herself holding the pen, the sword, and the child are all stative verbs ("holde," "kepe," "lith") that seem to freeze this final moment, as in a painting, as in a work of art.

The scene of her death, the final deadly moment, is thus Canace's final sublime moment of creation. This scene has provoked some uneasiness among critics – Spearing calls it "the tale's moment of supreme horror" (218). When she finishes writing, Canace stabs herself and creates a pool of blood in which her child, Genius notes, innocently bathes:

> Sche fell doun ded fro ther sche stod.
> The child lay bathende in hire blod
> Out rolled fro the moder barm,
> And for the blod was hot and warm,
> He basketh him aboute thrinne.   (311–15)

Spearing has pointed out that in this moment, "the identification of the unnatural with the natural is fixed in an unforgettable image that has no equivalent in Ovid: the child innocently and pleasurably bathing in his mother's warm blood" (218). But I would observe another, more significant, paradox. The blood once again is a fluid coming out of Canace's body, and this fluid expresses a different kind of paradox. The baby's bathing in his mother's blood reminds us of the moment of parturition, of giving life; at the same time, the unstoppable flow of Canace's blood is a sign of death. This moment then stresses the paradox of life and death implicit in the act of writing, a paradox which echoes the rhetorical paradoxes in Canace's letter.[77]

The "Tale of Canace and Machaire" exemplifies the daughter's struggle to separate from her father both literally, by affirming her own independent desire, and literarily, by creating her own narrative. Boose has established an analogy between the movement of a narrative and the movement of a daughter when she leaves her family: "For the narrative to progress – for the daughter to leave the father's enclosure – the outside rival male must arrive and create a magnetic pull on the daughter, who otherwise remains within, in psychological bondage to her filial bonds" (33). By joining another man, the daughter is supposed to help the narrative progress. In this sense, the significance of the parallels between Canace's act of writing and her body, and between her letter and her child, become apparent. These parallels suggest that Canace's death represents not only Eolus's assertion of his control over Canace's body, but also his desire to terminate a narrative (the story of Canace) over which he himself has lost authorial control.

Let us return now to the character who is ultimately in charge of the narrative, to Canace's literary father, Genius. As representative of nature and reproduction, Genius is also interested in the reproductive function of the daughter. It is this function, as well as nature's authority and power over death and life, that Eolus cuts radically when he orders Canace to kill herself. But Genius is also the narrator, the artistic creator of the tales. Wetherbee has noticed that in Alain de Lille Genius is associated among other things with the poetic principle.[78] Gower's Genius develops this side of Genius to a greater extent. As Simpson has argued, Genius performs the role of the artist in telling his stories.[79] Given such a role, Genius can only but condemn the actions of a father who cuts off the narrative.

In the moral to the tale, a single verb gathers some of the themes which we have analyzed and which run through Gower's version. Genius tells Amans:

---

[77] The link between writing and dying, between the pen and the sword, may also provide an explanation for a controversial passage in another tale in the *Confessio*: "Aeneas and Dido." Genius reports that in her letter to Aeneas, Dido compares herself to the swan which "For sorwe a fethere into hire brain / Sche schof and hath hirselve slain" (4.107–08). Macaulay ascribed this strange image to Gower's misunderstanding of the first two lines in Ovid's *Heroides*, 7, where Dido compares herself to a swan singing on the grass. However, Götz Schmitz, "Gower, Chaucer, and the Classics," *John Gower: Recent Readings*, ed. Yeager, has shown that this was not a misunderstanding, for the image can be found in several texts that Gower must have known (101–03). I would add that, in using this surprising image, Gower is hinting at the connection between writing and dying. The feather becomes a two-sided symbol: it can both create and destroy.

[78] Wetherbee, "The Theme of Imagination in Medieval Poetry and the Allegorical Figure 'Genius' " 58.

[79] James Simpson, *Sciences and the Self in Medieval Poetry: Alain of Lille's* Anticlaudianus *and John Gower's* Confessio Amantis (Cambridge: Cambridge UP, 1995) 3.

> . . . if thou evere in cause of love
> Schalt deme, and thou be so above
> That thou miht lede it at thi wille,
> Let nevere thurgh thi Wraththe spille
> Which every kinde scholde save. (339–43)

The verb "spille" carries significant connotations in the context of the tale. The *Middle English Dictionary* gives nine different definitions for it. The first meaning is "to kill." This is the most obvious sense of the verb in the tale, since Eolus is responsible for the death of his daughter and her child. Canace herself uses "spillen" in a similar sense too. When the knight gives her the sword and her father's message "That sche hireselven scholde slee" (261), she says, "Now . . . I wot my fadres wille, / That I schal in this wise spille" (263–64). "Spillen" also means "to flow out from a container onto the ground; to cause (a liquid) to overflow a container." The *Middle English Dictionary* points out specifically that it is also said of the flow "of tears [and] blood." This meaning refers back to the liquid imagery related to Canace. In her letter she writes: "Now at this time, as thou schalt wite, / With teres and with enke write / This lettre I have in cares colde" (297–99). As if writing through her body, she spills tears from it and ink from her pen. And when she stabs herself, she spills blood.

But "spillen" can also convey the idea of waste as in "to bring (sb.) to financial or social ruin," or "to waste," "to expend (speech, time, effort, etc.) in vain." Genius's moral points directly to this meaning, as evidenced by two other crucial words in the passage: "save" and "kinde." Eolus's spilling of what "kinde" should save represents a fruitless and wasteful action. When Canace says that she shall "spille" in line 264, her death acquires the connotation of "waste," and specifically waste of "kinde," of her natural reproductive function. "Spillen," thus, conveys the ideas of waste, death, and sterility that mark the tragic end of the tale. But, returning to the parallel between procreation and literary creation, I will argue that "spillen" can also be seen as a reference to Eolus's attempt to cut off Canace's narrative. His wrath and incestuous ownership of his daughter cause the total destruction and waste of the daughter, the narrative (the literary creation), and the child (or procreation). That Genius shows so much sympathy for Canace is explained in this light. For Eolus destroys two fundamental functions, human procreation and literary creation, that Genius himself represents as promoter of reproduction and as narrator.

Genius manifests a clear critique of the sacrifice of the daughter only in the "Tale of Canace and Machaire." Fathers like Virginius in the "Tale of Virginia," or Orchamus in the "Tale of Leucothoe," also act like Eolus. Even though they do not actually commit incest with their daughters, these fathers react violently and kill their daughters when they lose control over their sexuality. In these tales, as in the "Tale of Canace and Machaire," the daughters become the victims of their fathers' sense of absolute ownership over their bodies. In killing their daughters, they commit a kind of incest by taking possession of their bodies and assuming authority even over their lives. Nevertheless, these two daughters are ignored by Genius, unlike Canace. Eolus's daughter is not ignored because she represents the sexual/textual creativity that Genius also stands for in his traditional role as promoter of reproduction and in his role as narrator and creator of the tales.

Genius's sympathy leads him to imagine this daughter as a private self. However, we should note that the extent of Canace's privacy and independence is very limited. I noted above that she is limited by the fact that her lover is her brother. There is an additional limitation: courtly love discourse and Genius as producer of such discourse. Even though Canace manifests her creativity by authoring her letter, her use of a very contrived courtly love rhetoric raises the question of the extent to which she is also confined by male discourse and the extent to which she is confined by the ultimate fictional author of her discourse, that is, Genius himself. Canace's creative moment could be seen as an anticipation of Hélène Cixous's call to women in her famous essay "The Laugh of the Medusa": "Women must write through their bodies."[80] However, as Cixous also notes, in order to write through their bodies, women must break away from male discourse: "If woman has always functioned 'within' the discourse of man, a signifier that has always referred back to the opposite signifier which annihilates its specific energy and diminishes or stifles its very sounds, it is time for her to dislocate this 'within,' to explode it, turn it around, and seize it" (887). In Genius's tale Canace is still functioning within "the discourse of man." She defines her experience through traditional courtly love discourse and this discourse is controlled by another kind of father, by Genius. She is, after all, his creation. Her potential to dislocate the discourse, therefore, cannot be realized. Genius's (and ultimately Gower's) paternal relationship to his own tales is the subject of the next and last chapter of this book.

[80] Hélène Cixous, "The Laugh of the Medusa," *Signs* 1 (1976): 886.

CHAPTER FIVE

TEXTUAL FATHERS AND TEXTUAL DAUGHTERS:
THE "TALE OF ROSIPHELEE,"
THE "TALE OF JEPHTHAH'S DAUGHTER,"
AND "PYGMALEON AND THE STATUE"

Introduction

So far, this book has focused primarily on the fathers and daughters who are characters within the tales narrated in the *Confessio Amantis*. I will turn now to another fundamental father whose presence is evident throughout Gower's poem, a father who is not a character in any of the tales but who shapes those tales. I am referring to Genius. Genius is a father not only in his Christian role as father confessor, but also as the creator of the tales that he narrates to aid Amans in his confession. The three tales I analyze in this chapter, the tales of Rosiphelee, Jephthah's daughter, and Pygmalion, urge us in different ways to examine Genius's own role in relation to the daughters in his tales, and, more importantly, in relation to the tales themselves as "daughters." This examination will finally lead us to the textual father of the *Confessio* as a whole, to Gower.

The metaphor of the text as the female body, I noted in Chapter One, was common in the Middle Ages.[1] This metaphor also operates in the *Confessio*, but in Gower's poem it also intersects crucially with another metaphor, that of the author as father of his text. Gower uses the father-daughter metaphor to examine his own relationship with the text, suggesting that the relationship between a text and its author participates in the same dynamics of hierarchical authority as the relationship between king and subjects and father

---

[1] See Dinshaw, *Chaucer's Sexual Poetics*, Introduction and ch. 4. On other aspects of this metaphor, see the essays in Dolores Warwick Frese and Katherine O'Brien O'Keefe, eds. *The Book and the Body* (Notre Dame, IN: U of Notre Dame P, 1997), esp. Michael Camille, "The Book as Flesh and Fetish in Richard de Bury's *Philobiblon*" (34–77), which examines the use of the metaphor in a more physical sense – the manuscript itself, the skin of an animal, could also be perceived as a body and, specifically, as a female body; and Mary Carruthers, "Reading with Attitude, Remembering the Book" (1–33), which analyzes the use of the reverse metaphor, that is, the metaphor of the body as a book.

and daughter. This final chapter will examine the implications of these correspondences, focusing primarily on one of Gower's major questions in the *Confessio Amantis*, that is, to what extent is the author's desire to write, to (re)produce a text, and then to try to control its meaning, subjecting it to its author's will, an incest-like desire, with all the troubling implications that such a desire carries?

My analysis starts with the "Tale of Rosiphelee" and the "Tale of Jephthah's Daughter," tales which expose Genius's relationship to his stories and, more specifically, to the daughters in them. Both Rosiphelee and Jephthah's daughter represent potentially disruptive elements.[2] Boose has observed that "retaining the daughter involves figuratively if not literally incestuous choice . . . [T]he enclosure of the daughter resexualizes the space inside the family and compels the necessity for a detailed taboo to define illicit congress within it."[3] In the "Tale of Rosiphelee" the daughter is at a marriageable age, but she is not interested in leaving her father's house, thus refusing to enact the dynamic of separation that is imposed by the principle of exogamy and posing a threat to this principle. In the "Tale of Jephthah's Daughter," the daughter has not separated soon enough. Throughout this study, I have pointed to moments in which we can see Genius trying to fit his moral to the tale in ways that seem forced and incongruous. I have also noted that, despite his attempts at controlling the tales, they yield other meanings. In the tales of Rosiphelee and Jephthah, Genius tries to exert complete control over the meaning of his tales, and, in the case of Jephthah's daughter, even explicitly chastises a daughter for not responding to his teachings. Genius's treatment of Rosiphelee and Jephthah's daughter is commented upon by Amans, who notes his cruelty towards them, hence implicitly calling attention to Genius's use of authority.

It is significant that, as Genius enacts his authority in these tales, the role of the fathers, in contrast with most other father-daughter tales, is understated. Rather than presenting the crises in the tales as tensions between the daughters and their fathers, Genius presents them as tensions between the daughters and a higher order. Genius himself, moreover, becomes the voice of authority for this order – he takes charge and neutralizes the disruptive possi-

---

[2] Interestingly enough, both the "Tale of Rosiphelee" and the "Tale of Jephthah's Daughter" use women to prove their moral about sloth. This prompts Amans's complaint to Genius – he understands how and why slothful women are punished, but, since he is a man, he needs to hear about slothful men in order to understand the lesson better:

> Bot yit it falleth in my minde,
> Toward the men hou that ye spieke
> Of hem that wole no travail sieke
> In cause of love to decerte:
> To speke in wordes so coverte,
> I not what travaill that ye mente.   (4.1602–07)

Genius's focus on daughters suggests that he is here more interested in conveying a certain moral doctrine affecting women than he is interested in Amans himself.

[3] Boose, "The Father's House and the Daughter in It" 64.

bility introduced by these daughters. While he presents their fates as part of some kind of greater cosmological order, he does not hide his own role as the representative authority of this order. But, ultimately, even though he presents it as natural, the order appears to be discursively constructed, responding to the needs of the patriarchal system. Robins has argued that the *Confessio Amantis* urges "a recognition of the genres available for making sense of needs and desires. Indeed, in the Prologue Gower suggests that the reader's relation to society is conditioned by the possibilities of narrative."[4] The tales of Rosiphelee and Jephthah's daughter develop such a suggestion. In these tales, the fathers do not impose their authority over their daughters directly; discourse regulates female behavior and sexuality. In fact, Rosiphelee is not merely conditioned by the narrative, but, rather, she is coerced into loving by a vision that has a long tradition in courtly literature; the vision performs the father's role of ensuring that the daughter will be exchanged in marriage. In the case of Jephthah's daughter, Genius's incongruous moral, the incongruous way in which he blames the victim, reveals that the story functions as a discursive tool that enacts and promotes the daughter's submission to Genius's reproductive ideology, an ideology that depends on patriarchal control of the woman's body. This time the character is not persuaded by discourse within the tale, but she is used to "persuade" female readers of the need to reproduce, thereby conditioning the possibilities of their narratives.

Gower's narrator, then, becomes the authoritative voice of institutional patriarchal discourse. Critics have generally pointed out that the moral to these two tales is perfectly consistent with Genius's traditional role as promoter of fertility and procreation. But Gower's Genius is different from previous Geniuses. In his doctrine, the promotion of procreation usually goes hand in hand with the promotion of marriage. For this Genius, procreation should be contained within the bonds and boundaries of marriage. In adopting this stance, Genius is acquiescing in the interests of lineage, in its need to control the offspring. He is also acquiescing in the general principle of exogamy whereby the father has to exchange his daughter. Genius speaks as the voice or agent of patriarchal discourse, not of some "natural" Nature, as it were.

The fact that he is a priest, moreover, reinforces his position of authority – he is the priestly father who has moral and religious authority over the penitent Amans *and* over the tales. We may recall here Foucault's observation about confession as a ritual of discourse "that unfolds within a power relationship, for one does not confess without the presence (or virtual presence) of a partner who is not simply the interlocutor but the authority who requires the confession, prescribes and appreciates it, and intervenes in order to judge, punish, forgive, console, and reconcile."[5] Genius is the voice of authority, and he enacts his authority discursively not only in his relationship with

---

4 Robins, "Romance, Exemplum, and the Subject of the *Confessio Amantis*" 176.
5 Foucault, *History of Sexuality*, vol. 1, 61–62.

Amans, but, more significantly, in his relationship with the daughters in the tales.

Genius's literary role, moroever, is defined in paternal terms. His fatherhood is most evident in his version of the myth of Pygmalion, in which Genius explores the dynamics of authority in his own relationship with his tales as the creator, the *auctor*, of the narratives. Analyzing Gower's use of the word "enformacioun" in the *Confessio*, Simpson has explained that the poem presents God, Gower, and Genius as figures who perform similar functions as authors and creators.[6] As narrator and creator of the tales, Genius, and, ultimately, Gower, is also a kind of father to his text. This parallel, though, is problematic, due to the incestuous connotations of Pygmalion's love for the statue, and hence, due to the incestuous connotations of the relationship between the artist and his work of art, and between an author and his text – the artist authors/fathers his work. A comparison between Genius's awareness of these issues in other tales and his obliviousness of the same issues in "Pygmaleon and the Statue" raises larger questions about Genius's own relationship to his tales as the authority who imposes simple morals on tales that raise complex implications. Genius's identification with Pygmalion blinds him to the implications of these issues.

In arguing that Genius has an authoritative voice in these tales, I am not suggesting that he is the voice of a monolithic and central authority. In fact, the project of decentering authority is at the heart of the *Confessio*, as critics like Siân Echard and Theresa Tinkle have shown.[7] I mentioned in the first chapter that Genius is an authority with two different allegiances, as representative of Venus and as Christian priest; through him, Tinkle argues, Gower "coupl[es] erotic fiction and moralizing commentary" (181). Tinkle further observes that he does this, in order to "foreground[ ] the disjunctions" between the two discourses (181). Moreover, to Tinkle the disjunction between discourses in the poem, along with Amans's own speeches and reactions, the Latin glosses, and the Latin verses, contribute to the "multiplication of authorities and voices, with all their differences from one another, forcefully argu[ing] against the possibility of any single, unquestionably authoritative model of interpretation" (182). Genius's reworking of the myth of Pygmalion plays a crucial role in Gower's critical exploration of his own authority as writer in the *Confessio Amantis*. In fact, Gower's version of Pygmalion hints at the reason for the multiplication of voices in the poem. Gower imagines the relationship between an author and his work as a father-daughter relationship and recognizes the author's temptation to "commit incest" with the text, to exert an absolute control over its meaning. The ways in which authority in the *Confessio Amantis* variously shifts from the Latin glosses to the Latin poems to the vernacular, as Echard and Tinkle have shown, represents an attempt to question this notion of a stable textual

---

[6] Simpson, *Sciences and the Self* 1–10.
[7] Echard, "With Carmen's Help" and Tinkle, *Medieval Venuses and Cupids*, esp. 181–85.

authority. But, more significantly, I argue that by creating multiple authoritative voices and thus preventing his readers from locating his voice, Gower problematizes the illusion of total control over the body of his female text, revealing an authorial masculine anxiety about the incestuous connotations of such an illusion.

The Tale of Rosiphelee

Like "Pygmaleon and the Statue" and the "Tale of Jephthah's Daughter," the "Tale of Rosiphelee" is in Book 4, the book about the sin of sloth. It illustrates specifically the sin of idleness, a branch of sloth. Rosiphelee, the king of Armenia's only daughter and heir to the kingdom, is guilty of idleness: she has many suitors, but she refuses to love. Not content with the situation, Cupid and Venus decide to act. One day during the month of May the princess goes to the forest with her maidens. While she is sitting alone under a tree, she sees the animals mating, which leads to "a querele / Betwen love and hir oghne herte" (1302–03). Then, she suddenly has a vision; she sees a group of damsels richly clothed and riding beautiful horses. Rosiphelee notices another lady following the damsels, riding on a limping horse and wearing ragged clothes. Asked by Rosiphelee, the unhappy woman explains to the princess that she is seeing the army of the dead and that the richly-clothed ladies are those who accepted love and were truthful to the man they loved while they lived. She herself refused to love for most of her life and is therefore condemned now to wear ragged clothes and to be a servant of the ladies. But because she did love a knight for two weeks before she died, she also wears a jewelled bridle. The vision has an immediate effect on Rosiphelee: she decides that she will not be punished like the lady.

Pointing to the discursive character of the concept of courtly love, Genius portrays Rosiphelee's lack of interest in love in terms of learning. At the beginning of his tale, Genius notes that the princess is a bad student who learns too slowly about love: "That scole wolde sche noght knowe. / And thus sche was on of the slowe / As of such hertes besinesse" (1259–61). (Notice the wordplay on "slowe," an adjective that in this context can mean that she is slow in learning in the school of love and also that she is slothful, commiting the sin of which the tale exemplifies a branch.) Using again the same metaphor, Genius tells us that Venus will bring her "into betre reule" (1264) with the help of Cupid, who will act as the teacher and use a rod on the bad student (1275–77). Rosiphelee's slowness in love is later corrected by the vision, which finally does the job of educating her. By framing the experience of love within the world of schooling, Gower points to the social and linguistic origin of the concept of love. The proper rules of love, like the proper rules of language, are learned in "school." The need to learn formally how to love reveals the constructedness of the notion of love, a notion defined by society. Love does not arise spontaneously in certain individuals; neither is it provoked by a second person; rather, it becomes part of the process of socialization of the individual within the courtly community. In the "Tale of Rosiphelee," the princess has not assimilated courtly love discourse initially and is resistant to love. Nevertheless, courtly love discourse does not give up on Rosiphelee and finally effects the needed change in her. The "Tale of Rosiphelee" explores the extent to which the articulation of the loving subject, the ways in which a person thinks of himself or herself as a lover and acts as such, is itself conditioned by the genre of courtly love. It explores the ways in which courtly language and culture, understood in broad senses, "educate" the individual to love and even create the lover.

Genius's characterization of love as an "occupacion," and even a job (or "besinesse") which is taught in school acquires a special significance in the light of Howard Bloch's analysis of the close relationship between genealogy, language, and love in French literature from the twelfth to the fourteenth centuries.[8] Bloch has shown how grammar, lineage, and sexuality were part of the same ideological system and thus shared the same discourse in medieval France. The terminology used mainly during those centuries for grammar and rhetoric reveals that "a grammatical model was dominated by a familial one [and] the patterns of late medieval kinship were, in turn, molded by those of grammar" (65).[9] The discourse of early medieval grammar, what Bloch calls "the formal discourse on discourse" (90), and the discourse on the family shared similar forms of linear expression, and these forms articulated the paradigmatic laws of kinship (90–91). Moreover, the literature of courtly love itself often established a crucial link between grammar and lineage. Alain de Lille's *De planctu naturae* uses this link to show and denounce the close relation between adultery, false genealogy, and rhetoric. The figure "Nature" in Alain's work, Bloch notes, gives her handmaiden "two instruments of rectitude – orthography, or straight writing, and orthodox coition, or straight sexuality" (133). In the same vein, Alain equates the too-strained metaphor with verbal and moral vice (135). Grammar and rhetoric are thus tinged with sexual and genealogical connotations.[10]

---

[8] R. Howard Bloch, *Etymologies and Genealogies: A Literary Anthropology of the French Middle Ages* (Chicago: U of Chicago P, 1983).

[9] Bloch situates his discussion of genealogy within a more general epistemological context:

> Genealogy conceived along linguistic lines and language conceived along family lines represent two facets of a more general problematics of the sign prevalent in the thought of many of the most powerful intellectual figures from Augustine to the Renaissance. (35)

[10] For a monographic study of this same question in Alain's work, see Jan Ziolkowski, *Alan of Lille's Grammar of Sex: The Meaning of Grammar to a Twelfth-Century Intellectual* (Cambridge: The Medieval Academy of America, 1985). Ziolkowski also expands on a subject which is particularly relevant for the *Confessio* and Gower's interest in ethics. He shows the connection between grammar and ethics in the Middle Ages. In this respect, he cites a highly significant statement written by William Wykeham in the foundation deed of Winchester College in 1382: "... by the knowledge of grammar justice is cultivated and the prosperity of the estate of humanity is increased" (quoted in Ziolkowski 90).

Bloch distinguishes between different literary genres on the basis of their treatment of lineage concerns. From the twelfth century on, a new genre gained popularity – the courtly novel. This genre found a place in between the epic concern with lineage and the stability of the family, on the one hand, and on the other the troubadour lyric disruption of familial interests through the assertion of the desire of the individual. As Bloch characterizes it, "[t]he courtly novel is essentially *about* marriage and seems always to involve a conflict between a consensual attachment and a contractual bond, to problematize succession, and to combine structurally elements both of narrative progression and of lyric closure" (182). In the novel, moreover,

> the question of marriage is, ultimately, indissociable from that of land, of inheritance, and, in particular, of cognatic succession. Here the status of fiefs accruing to women is crucial, for if this group of romances is filled with those anxious for others to marry, those *others* are almost always heiresses (or heirs who have inherited from their mother) who, in some instances, succeed to entire realms. (194)

A similar anxiety concerning the marriage of heiresses, we will see, is fundamental in the "Tale of Rosiphelee," which shares some important features with the courtly novel. Rosiphelee stands for the continuity of the royal family line because she is the only heir to her father, the king of Armenia. Other daughters in the *Confessio*, such as Rosemund in the "Tale of Albinus and Rosemund" and the sultan's daughter in the "Tale of the False Bachelor," are also their fathers' only heirs, but Genius is more concerned about this problem in the "Tale of Rosiphelee" – in line 1252, he notes that she "scholde ben hire fader hair." Moreover, unlike those other two daughters, who submit to being united to men without showing much resistance, Rosiphelee shows no desire to submit to love and thus to leave her father's house. Hence, the princess's attitude poses two threats to her family and to her country: first, it threatens the continuity of the royal family line, since Rosiphelee is the only heir to the king; second, it threatens the principle of exogamy whereby the daughter has to separate from her father.

Before continuing the discussion about Gower's tale, let us turn briefly to another Middle English work contemporary with Gower's that also addresses this problem: Chaucer's *Parlement of Fowles*. Some critics have argued that Chaucer's *Parlement of Fowles* alludes to negotiations undertaken to facilitate King Richard II's marriage to Anne of Bohemia.[11] Whether Chaucer had this particular match in mind or not, marriage negotiations of this kind were certainly not an exception. This particular historical occurrence exemplifies

---

11 See, for instance, Larry D. Benson, "The Occasion of the *Parliament of Fowls*," *The Wisdom of Poetry: Essays in Early English Literature in Honor of Morton W. Bloomfield*, eds. Larry D. Benson and Siegfried Wenzel (Kalamazoo, MI: Institute for Medieval Studies, 1982) 123–44.

the type of situation that raises the marriage concerns explored in these fourteenth-century works.

Chaucer's poem resembles the story of Rosiphelee in significant ways. On Saint Valentine's day, the dreamer-narrator witnesses a meeting of birds, which is presided over by Dame Nature and during which birds choose their mates. All the birds who choose are male, while the ones chosen are female. The major controversy that arises during the gathering centers on a noble female bird, a tercel, who is courted by three different noble male birds. Unlike Rosiphelee, the formel in Chaucer's poem is eventually allowed to defer one more year a decision concerning her marriage. Dame Nature, the authority figure in the poem whom all the birds obey (see, for instance, ll. 306–08), allows her this postponement, justifying her decision on the grounds that she is not Reason: "But as for counseyl for to chese a make, / If I were Resoun, thanne wolde I / Conseyle yow the royal tercel take" (631–33). Since she is not Reason, she will let the formel decide for herself. The question of the formel's marriage is thus left unresolved.

Dame Nature's limited role in the *Parlement of Fowles* as representative of the natural contrasts with the role of the authority figure in the *Confessio Amantis*, Genius. Even though traditionally the figure of Genius functions as the representative of the sexual instinct, in Gower's poem Genius also assumes the role of Reason. Thus in the "Tale of Rosiphelee" not only is the female heiress not allowed to defer her decision (even though, as I will note later, what she decides is left somewhat unclear), but Genius also imparts a sense of urgency to her marriage on "reasonable" grounds – he uses two highly literary courtly motifs, the *carpe diem* motif and a vision of the court of love to "prove" the importance of not delaying marriage. In Genius's tale, there is a sense of urgency because the immediate political significance of Rosiphelee's situation is made much more explicit than that of the formel's marriage in Chaucer's poem. We know that Rosiphelee is the heir to the king of Armenia and that it is in her hands to ensure the continuity of the Armenian royal family line. Hence, her unwillingness to marry conflicts with the political interests of her country and of her family.

The tension between individual desire and the interests of the family and the state, then, is finally resolved in the tale in a manner quite different from the way it is resolved in the *Parlement of Fowles*; unlike Chaucer's poem, the "Tale of Rosiphelee" resolves it at the expense of the individual, who has to submit to the larger familial and political interests. Genius solves this tension in such a graceful manner that it is easy to forget the cost of the solution to the individual. In his influential essay, "Gower's 'Honeste Love,' " Bennett has remarked that "the sheer beauty of the tale of Rosiphilee, in which this doctrine [the defense of love within marriage] is most firmly embodied, has diverted attention from its sentence."[12] That the aesthetic pleasure of the

---

[12] Bennett, "Gower's 'Honeste Love' " 114–15.

tale seems to have diverted critics' attention from the implicit marriage ideology promoted by Genius is significant in and of itself. It points to the effective manner in which discourse can hide relations of power.

The "Tale of Rosiphelee" starts by introducing its main characters:

> Of Armenye, I rede thus,
> Ther was a king, which Herupus
> Was hote, and he a lusti Maide
> To dowhter hadde, and as men saide
> Hire name was Rosiphelee.   (1245-49)

The social and political context of the tale is given special prominence. Genius mentions first the kingdom of Armenia, then turns to the royal family, focusing only on the father and the daughter – he does not mention the king's wife. Rosiphelee's father is first and foremost identified as king. After he is introduced, we learn about Rosiphelee, who is first identified by her sexual status: she is a "Maide," that is, a woman who is not married and who is at the appropriate age for matrimony and thus for reproducing. Only after this reference to her sexual identity are we introduced to the daughter as an individual – Genius notes her name: "Hire name was Rosiphelee." Even here, though, the individualization is qualified by the phrase "as men saide." This phrase could mean 'people said,' but, since Gower could have used other phrases, such as "it was saide" without altering the meter, "as men saide" seems to highlight the role of men in the definition of Rosiphelee. (Gower uses the phrase "it is saide" several times in his poem, e.g., Prologue, 335.)

When three lines later Genius observes that Rosiphelee "scholde ben hire fader hair" (1252), we realize the social and political relevance of the princess; she is the only guarantee that the royal line will continue. Thus, that Rosiphelee "hadde o defalte of Slowthe / Towardes love," as Genius observes in lines 1253-54, not only points to a personal "problem" of Rosiphelee's, but it also reveals that the princess presents her lineage with a political problem as well. As Arno Esch has observed, "[r]ight at the beginnning, the erotic is closely bound with political significance: in a king's daughter, a failure in the *schola amoris* has consequences which go beyond the private domain and can result in a far-ranging blow to stability and order."[13] Her "Slowthe" is not only a lack of interest in sexual activity, but, due to her political role, it manifests also a lack of interest in the political future of her country.

More significantly, for Genius Rosiphelee's idleness in love presents him with an important challenge: she is a non-desiring subject – she "Desireth nother Mariage / Ne yit the love of paramours" (1268-69). Even when she is in the forest and she notices the animals mating, it is not clear that her sexual desire is aroused. Genius notes that when she sees the animals, she starts feeling something that he leaves undefined: "a querele / Betwen love and hir

---

[13] Esch, "John Gower's Narrative Art" 83.

oghne herte" (1302–03). "Querele" is a significant word in the *Confessio Amantis*. Macaulay glosses it as 'cause,' 'quarrel,' 'enterprise,' but we should note that it is often associated with love.[14] Rosiphelee's "querele" is also directly associated with love, one of the quarreling forces. But what the other quarreling force, "hire oghne herte," stands for seems initially unclear. In the context of the tale, "love" is an already culturally-charged term. It can mean love within marriage, or love of "paramours." Some lines before noticing Rosiphelee's struggle, Genius has already suggested that Cupid, the god of love, is going to play a prominent role in Rosiphelee's "education": "Cupide, which of love is godd, / In chastisinge hath mad a rodd / To dryve awei hir wantounesse" (1275–77). In the context of the tale, when we arrive at line 1302, "love" is not so much an individual, "natural" desire as it is a notion closely associated with Cupid and thus with a long literary tradition.

Some lines later Genius defines "love" differently, but its discursive definition is even more evident. For Genius, proper love does not equal sexual desire; unlike the latter, love is a social activity in which the noble class engages:

> Among the gentil nacion
> Love is an occupacion,
> Which forto kepe hise lustes save
> Scholde every gentil herte have.   (1451–54)

Love is an activity for the "gentil nacion," those in the higher classes, which serves to "tame" their sexual drives. Love in this courtly sense is inextricably bound with class consciousness and lineage, as Bloch has amply demonstrated. A similar point is made by Aers in an essay on *Troilus and Criseyde* and the courtly community in fourteenth-century England:

> 'Love' is certainly a powerful way of binding the individual into the class. It offers a system through which the cultural standards and ideals of the class are internalized. They are assimilated both to the individual's self-image and to basic sexual drives which may now only be legitimately acted out within the terms of this system.[15]

By presenting love as a social activity, Genius's version reveals courtly ideology at work as a means of socializing the individual. Nevertheless, Rosiphelee poses an interesting challenge to Genius because she does not seem to have even those "basic sexual drives" to which Aers refers. What Rosiphelee's "oghne herte" refers to seems clearer now. It refers to a lack of desire to love either within marriage or "paramours."

Dealing with a non-desiring subject is unusual, although not unique (e.g.,

---

[14] In Book 1, for instance, Amans asks Venus: "Behold my cause and my querele" (134). See a more detailed discussion of the significance of this word in my analysis of the "Tale of Constance" in Chapter Two.
[15] Aers, "Masculine Identity in the Courtly Community" 124.

the "Tale of Narcissus," 1.2275–2366) for Genius. Indeed, throughout the *Confessio Amantis*, as I have argued, Gower's narrator tries to present desire as a given, as a natural drive that precedes the law. In challenging this framework, Rosiphelee thus forces Genius to impose his reproductive ideology in a more discursively explicit manner, and thus to reveal the relations of power that discourse tries to hide. Since Rosiphelee does not even seem to desire, her vision of the court of love while she is in the forest represents an explicit use of a cultural and discursive tool whose purpose is to channel her sexual drive, but, first and more fundamentally, to create such a drive, so that she will finally "love" in the socially and politically acceptable way.

The court of love is one of the most elaborate traditions arising from the literature of courtly love.[16] The sudden apparition of the court to a human being in a vision is a very popular motif in medieval literature. Perhaps one of the most significant analogues is the vision a knight tells a lady in the fifth dialogue of Andreas Capellanus's *De arte honeste amandi*. There were many other versions, though, that seem to have been popular at the time: among others, the Old French *Lay du Trot* from around the thirteenth century, which seems the closest one to Gower's version, Richard de Fournival's *Conseils d'Amour* from the middle of the thirteenth century, and the medieval Catalan *Salut d'Amor*.[17] Boccaccio's story of Nastagio in the *Decameron* (5.8) resembles these stories as well; although in this story there is no explicit mention of the court of love, the punishment of a woman who rejects her wooer is presented as "the judgement of God."[18] None of these versions can be definitely established as *the* source of the "Tale of Rosiphelee," but any one of them could have inspired Gower.[19]

Whichever one is Gower's source, we should note some common features they share. It is always a man who has the vision, and in most cases the man has a personal reason for telling the story to a certain lady: he is trying to win her. Only in *Salut d'Amor* is the lady also present during the vision, when the vision appears for the first time, but the one who is in love is the man and he has a vested interest in the vision. In Boccaccio's story, the lover, Nastagio, first has the vision when he is in the forest by himself, then he takes the lady to the spot where he saw the vision, and the vision is re-enacted in front of the lady. In Andreas's work, a knight tells the story to a lady who refuses to love him or anybody else, because she thinks that loving is a form of slavery.

---

16 For a detailed study of this tradition, see William Allan Neilson, *The Origins and Sources of the* Court of Love, Harvard Studies and Notes in Philology and Literature 6 (Boston: Ginn & Company, 1899).
17 See Margaret Grimes, "*Le Lay du Trot*," *The Romanic Review* 26 (1935): 313–21; and William Allan Neilson, "The Purgatory of Cruel Beauties," *Romania* 29 (1900): 85–93.
18 Boccaccio, *Decameron*, trans. G. H. McWilliam (Harmondsworth: Penguin, 1984): 460.
19 In *English Works*, ed. Macaulay, vol. 1, Macaulay has noticed some similarities in vocabulary between the dialogue in *De arte honeste amandi* and the tale, but, as he also points out, there are too many differences as well (505). Thus, we cannot state with any certainty that Gower was using Andreas's dialogue as his immediate source.

The knight, then, relates his vision in order to convince her that she should love. His account relates, with great detail, the punishments that the ladies who refused to love in their earthly life, as well as those who loved indiscriminately, receive following their death. After hearing the account, the lady in the dialogue submits to love, but does not grant her love to the knight. In *Salut d'Amor*, a knight who is in love with a countess has the vision while he is riding with her in a forest. The vision again is very timely for the man, since he also has a vested interest in it (to win his beloved). Indeed, it convinces the lady to love the knight. In the other two versions under consideration, *Le Lay du Trot* and Fournival's *Conseils d'Amour*, again two men claim to have had the vision, although in these two cases they do not seem to have a personal interest in winning a certain lady's love, but seem just the voice of social interest. As all these visions offer threatening prospects to women who are not interested in responding to men's desires or social concerns, they amount to a form of verbal coercion. Or, as Wallace, commenting on Nastagio's initial vision of a punished lady while he was by himself, has put it, "[t]he knowledge of this text, gained in private, may then be exploited to influence behavior within the public domain. Control of the text, figured as a woman, facilitates control of woman in society."[20] In other words, the point is not only that male control of the text reflects male control of women, but that the text itself is used by men to effectively exercise control over women.[21]

The "Tale of Rosiphelee" functions in the same manner, but, by departing from the tradition in one significant respect, it reveals, more clearly than the other versions, the textual control of women, that is, the role of stories as discursive constructs that condition, even produce, female desire. Unlike traditional visions, Rosiphelee's is not linked to any particular man's love for her; no man is present during the vision; neither is any man part of the vision. Only one male figure is involved, the narrator of the story, Genius, but Genius is situated outside the story, and Rosiphelee herself, the woman who does not love, sees the vision directly, without any explicit male involvement. This difference is significant. By making Rosiphelee witness the vision directly, Genius cloaks her experience with an appearance of truth: in her case the vision is not the immediate product of a particular man's desire for her. Obviously, Genius has no personal desire to win Rosiphelee's love for himself, but his desire to see her submit to love, hence to his doctrine, resembles the desire of a male suitor. The tale thus enacts male control over the

---

[20] Wallace, *Chaucerian Polity* 277.
[21] In Andreas's version in *De amore*, the vision also points to the importance of discourse as the basis of courtly love. Commenting on this version of the vision, Toril Moi, "Desire in Language: Andreas Capellanus and the Controversy of Courtly Love," *Medieval Literature: Criticism, Ideology, and History*, ed. David Aers (New York: St. Martin's Press, 1986), has observed:

> The courtly lover's strategy is thus one of intimidation and verbal sadism: his language enacts his aggression (which becomes all the more menacing precisely because of its dependence on an abject surrender to the rules of discourse). (25)

female body, but hides this discursive male control under the guise of a natural, cosmic order governed by Cupid.

The moral of the tale, nevertheless, reveals Genius's motivations. At the end of it, Genius says that women should get married at an early age so that they can bear many children (1480–1501). Maidens should learn from Rosiphelee's example (1488–92); her idleness in love led her to lose some precious years:

> For thus a yer or tuo or thre
> Sche lest, er that sche wedded be,
> Whyl sche the charge myhte bere
> Of children, whiche the world forbere
> Ne mai, bot if it scholde faile. (1493–97)

This pro-marriage Genius is not the Genius who characteristically speaks for pleasure and sexuality in Alain's *De planctu naturae*, or in Jean de Meun's *Roman de la Rose*. This Genius links the *topos* of *carpe diem*, which traditionally emphasizes individual pleasure, with the social interest in marriage and procreation:

> Bot what Maiden hire esposaile
> Wol tarie, whan sche take mai,
> Sche schal per chance an other dai
> Be let, whan that hire lievest were. (1498–1501)

Unlike other Geniuses, Gower's Genius is an outspoken advocate for marriage, or "honeste love" as opposed to love of "paramours."[22] Despite his allegiance to Venus as one of her priests, Genius even explicitly condemns the disruptive love of "paramours." As part of his moral, he says that if women want to deserve Venus's thanks they can follow love of "paramours" (1467–71). But this type of love, he warns, is dangerous:

> Men sen such love sielde in pes,
> That it nys evere upon aspie
> Of janglinge and of false Envie,
> Fulofte medlid with disese. (1472–75)

Of course, this type of love also goes against the interests of lineage; as Bloch has noted in *Etymologies and Genealogies*, for the poets and theorists of courtly love, "the socially disruptive effects of sexual desire are directly linked to the destruction of genealogy" (129). By contrast, love within marriage is safe – as Genius himself remarks: "thilke love is wel at ese, / Which set is upon mariage" (1476–77). Marriage tries to control the disruptive effect of sexual

---

[22] Several critics have remarked on the significance of marriage and "honeste love" in the *Confessio*, most famously Bennett, "Gower's 'Honeste Love.'" See also Olsson, "Natural Law and John Gower's *Confessio Amantis*" 200–201; Schmitz, *'the middel weie'* 91–92; Esch, "John Gower's Narrative Art" 84.

desire, making that desire work for genealogy in helping to regulate women's (and men's) sexuality to guarantee the paternity of the offspring. Social interest becomes more important than individual pleasure.

By contrast, Chaucer's Dame Nature in the *Parlement of Fowles* performs a clearly different function. Nature lets the formel postpone her decision because she is less worried about the social need to have her married. As noted above, Nature herself mentions that if she were Reason she would have advised the formel otherwise (631–33). While in Chaucer's *Parlement* Nature defines herself as opposed to Reason, in the "Tale of Rosiphelee," Genius, traditionally the representative of an aspect of Nature, that is, of sexuality, combines both Nature and Reason. What is "reasonable," moreover, is defined as that which serves to promote marriage and the continuation of lineage.

That Genius is particularly interested in marriage as a social institution, not an individual choice, for the higher classes is evident throughout the vision. The ladies Rosiphelee sees constitute a group in which there are no individual distinctions and they are all richly clothed: "In kertles and in Copes riche / Thei weren clothed, alle liche, / Departed evene of whyt and blew" (1315–17). They are all dressed in the same way, thus representing a uniform society. The only one who shows a certain individuality, deviating from the norm, is the damsel, who, by showing no interest in love, acted differently than the other ladies while she was alive. Significantly, the result of her choice is the loss of social status: she is condemned to wear ragged clothes ("Hire cote was somdiel totore," 1355) and serve the other ladies. Rosiphelee realizes that the damsel, who was also a king's daughter, is a mirror image of herself – the princess exclaims after the vision: " 'Helas! / I am riht in the same cas' " (1439–40). This realization, along with the realization that a harsh punishment in the form of servitude awaits her if she does not change her attitude towards love, teaches her to follow society's norms, the norms represented by the ladies. By threatening Rosiphelee with a loss of social status, Genius emphasizes that love is a social activity that has primarily social implications.

Rosiphelee learns her lesson well, although what she decides as a result of the lesson is somewhat ambiguous:

> 'Bot if I live after this day,
> I schal amende it, if I may.'
> And thus homward this lady wente,
> And changede al hire ferste entente,
> Withinne hire herte . . .   (1441–45)

Persuaded, or, rather, threatened, by the vision, the princess changes "hire ferste entente." According to the *Middle English Dictionary*, "entente" carries the connotation of conscious, reasoned decision.[23] Hence, the phrase in the

---

[23] *MED* gives three definitions: 1. Purpose or intention; aim or object; reason (for doing something); 2. A plan or design; 3. Will, wish, desire. Only the translation "desire," a

tale suggests that Rosiphelee's previous aversion to love was conscious. But we should also note an interesting ambiguity in this phrase. What exactly is it that she has decided to do from now on? The lady in the vision does not urge Rosiphelee and other women to get married, but simply to love: "warneth alle for mi sake, / Of love that thei ben noght ydel, / And bidd hem thenke upon mi brydel" (1432–34). This warning could have led Rosiphelee to love "paramours," rather than to marry, as Genius would have it. Such an ambiguity suggests that Rosiphelee escapes Genius's control to an extent. This loss of control seems to constitute what Wetherbee would call one of "[Genius's] calculated ineptitudes."[24]

Nevertheless, even if he loses some control over her, Genius thinks of himself as the fatherly authority who controls Rosiphelee. He is the author of the vision; indeed, he is Roshiphelee's creator. Interestingly enough, in this tale we find one of the few Latin glosses in which Gower announces that he is detaching himself from Genius's teachings. Next to Genius's discussion about love as a social activity for the nobility, the gloss reads: "Non quia sic se habet veritas, set opinio Amantum" ['Not because this is true in itself, but because it is the opinion of lovers'].[25] Pearsall has interpreted this moment as a "caustic" moment that proves Gower's moralism in the *Confessio Amantis* (182). This gloss, though, is one of many authoritative voices in the poem and I do not see enough evidence that the glosses are to be taken as Gower's true perspective on the poem. The role of this particular gloss is not to reinscribe Gower's moral view as opposed to Genius's, but to provide another authoritative voice in order to call attention to Genius's use of his own authority.

The vision, we have noted, has an established tradition in the literature of courtly love, where it is presented by the different narrators and lovers as "truth." The reward or punishment of individuals according to their willingness to love or not to love is presented as a reality that governs human life and to which men and women have to submit. But, in fact, there is nothing but a "textual order" behind the "Tale of Rosiphelee" and Genius is its immediate author, while Gower remains in the background. At the end of the tale, Genius evokes the status of the story as reality to issue the following warning to Amans:

> For as the ladi was chastised
> Riht so the knyht mai ben avised,
> Which ydel is and wol noght serve

---

subdefinition of the third definition could indicate that Rosiphelee's "entente" was an unconscious desire. MED suggests that conscious decision rather than instinctive desire is the major connotation of the word.
[24] Winthrop Wetherbee, "Genius and Interpretation in the *Confessio Amantis*," *Magister Regis: Studies in Honor of R. E. Kaske*, ed. Arthur Groos (New York: Fordham UP, 1986) 244.
[25] Translation taken from Derek Pearsall, "The Gower Tradition," *Gower's Confessio Amantis*, ed. Minnis, 182.

>   To love, he mai per cas deserve
>   A grettere peine than sche hadde.   (1455–59)

Notice the construction of the sentence "he mai per cas deserve / A grettere peine." The agent who, on the basis of his authority, decides whether to inflict a "grettere peine" on the idle person is concealed, but it is the narrator who has the power to inflict the "peine." Since, within the fictional world of the *Confessio*, Genius "authors" the tales, he also exerts authorial control over his characters – they act in certain ways and are then rewarded or punished according to the moral he is interested in conveying.

Genius even displays an awareness of his authority and control over his own material at the end of the tale. Notice how, a few lines after setting his moral as part of a higher order, he addresses "maidens" in different terms:

>   Bot forto loke aboven alle,
>   These Maidens, hou so that it falle,
>   Thei scholden take ensample of this
>   Which *I* have told, for soth it is.   (1463–66 [my emphasis])

The "I" of the author appears with special force here. In these lines, Genius insists that the tale which he ("I") has told is true ("soth it is"). He also implies that the "ensample" to be drawn from it is equally true. In noting Genius's assertion of authority, I should reiterate, I am not implying that he does have complete control over his material. What I wish to emphasize is that Genius sees himself as a literary *auctor*, or, rather, that Gower depicts Genius as a narrator who sees himself as an *auctor*, and a father, who has control over the tale.

Genius creates an unruly daughter in order to enact his own fatherly power over her. The fundamental factor that compels Rosiphelee to love is the vision of the punishment she will suffer if she refuses to serve Cupid. It is only after she has the vision – with its emphasis on class consciousness – that she decides to change "hire ferste entente." Rosiphelee does not change her "entente" out of an unmediated or "natural" desire but out of fear of the prospects presented by the vision, and of the "reality" created by Genius. Thus the tale not only depicts a threat to a disobedient daughter, but it actually enacts Genius's authorial and paternal power to control the female body created by himself.

The "Tale of Jephthah's Daughter," which he tells immediately afterwards, also enacts Genius's control over the female body, and in this case Gower's narrator even chastises the daughter's body. Even though Genius mentions that the lesson, which both the "Tale of Rosiphelee" and the "Tale of Jephthah's Daughter" share, also applies to men – the warning quoted above applies to any "kniht" too – it is women (unruly daughters) who become his main object of concern and on whom he inflicts great "peine." Indeed, it is women whom he addresses in his defense of marriage discussed above. His threat of a "grettere peine" is therefore fulfilled on a daughter in the "Tale of

Jephthah's Daughter" (to which the same moral applies). Even though in this tale, unlike the "Tale of Rosiphelee," the plot gives us no indication that the daughter was idle in love, Genius accuses her of idleness and justifies her sacrifice on that basis, punishing her for her "sin." As both author of his tales and voice of social morals, Genius inflicts "a grettere peine" on Jephthah's daughter than he inflicts on Rosiphelee or the maiden in the vision.

The Tale of Jephthah's Daughter

Immediately after the "Tale of Rosiphelee," Genius narrates the "Tale of Jephthah's Daughter" (4.1505–95) as another illustration of the sin of idleness in love. It is a daughter again who is guilty of the sin. Based on Judges 11, although with some significant modifications, Genius's "Tale of Jephthah's Daughter" relates the story of a Jewish duke who went to war against Ammon. He vowed to God that if He granted him victory, he would sacrifice to Him the first person who he would meet on his return home. After winning the battle, the first person he meets when he arrives home is his own daughter. Jephthah laments his bad fortune, and, when his daughter learns the reason for his sorrow, she asks him to keep his oath, but she requests of him that he allow her to mourn for forty days the fact that she is going to die a virgin and childless. Jephthah agrees to her request and, at the end of her mourning period, she "take[th] / Hir deth" (1591–92). Genius ends the tale by remarking that she dies "a wofull Maide" (1593) because of her idleness in love.

The "Tale of Jephthah's Daughter" shares the same moral with the "Tale of Rosiphelee": women should marry soon; otherwise, they will lose their chance to bear children. To quote the moral again:

> Bot what Maiden hire esposaile
> Wol tarie, whan sche take mai,
> Sche schal per chance an other dai
> Be let, whan that hire lievest were.   (1498–1501)

Placed between the two tales, Genius's moral to the "Tale of Rosiphelee" is meant to apply to both Rosiphelee and Jephthah's daughter. But Genius treats each daughter in significantly different ways. While he renders Rosiphelee with some psychological depth – we are given glimpses of what, according to Genius, goes through Rosiphelee's mind and how she develops into a socially dictated acceptance of love – we know very little about Jephthah's daughter's own attitude towards love. Genius tells us about Rosiphelee's past: before she "converted" to love, she had had many suitors, all of whom she had refused: "For so wel coude noman seie, / Which mihte sette hire in the weie / Of loves occupacion" (1255–57). In the case of Jephthah's daughter, however, we do not know what she did or thought about love in the past; we do not even know her age, which would have let us judge whether or not she had "wasted her time." For all we know, she may have been too young to love anyway. Because Genius presents Jephthah's daughter in such a cryptic way, not unlike the version in the Bible, his imposition of the doctrine that he also expounds in the "Tale of Rosiphelee" – that women's main function is to reproduce, and, thus, that they should marry soon – and his subsequent condemnation of the daughter, seems an abuse of power, an attempt to use his power to justify a patriarchal sacrifice that his own version does not manage to justify. Moreover, it also represents a desire to punish the daughter because she dies without offspring and thus fails to follow his own injunction to reproduce.

It is illuminating to compare the "Tale of Jephthah's Daughter" to the "Tale of the Three Questions," discussed in Chapter Two. Although the two tales provide very different outcomes for the daughters, their situations are similar. While in the "Tale of the Three Questions" the daughter saves her father and arranges an advantageous marriage for herself, in the "Tale of Jephthah's Daughter" the daughter saves him through her own death. In both tales an all-powerful father-figure (the king in the "Tale of the Three Questions," and God in the "Tale of Jephthah's Daughter") dominates over another male character who is also a father himself and who has at least one daughter. This daughter allows him to abide by, and respond satisfactorily to, the demands of the more powerful father-figure. Although in the "Tale of the Three Questions" the daughter ultimately advances her own position, while in the "Tale of Jephthah's Daughter" she is destroyed by her father, the pattern in the tales is similar: the daughter redeems her father, and ultimately the father loses her to a father-figure – the king in the case of Rosiphelee's father, God in the case of Jephthah. There is a difference between the two tales, though. In the "Tale of Jephthah's Daughter," Genius seems less interested in the father and hence in the redeeming function of the daughter.

Genius's attitude towards each of these two daughters differs, because their behaviors have different implications. In the "Tale of the Three Questions," the situation seems ideal from Genius's point of view: the daughter actively separates from her father without posing too much of a threat to the dynamic of separation. In the "Tale of Jephthah's Daughter," however, the daughter presents a problem, in Genius's view, because she did not separate soon enough. This problem leads him, as re-creator of his source, to exert his authority over the daughter in an explicit manner. Thus, I will argue, if Jephthah's daughter's end manifests the cruelty of her father, as most traditional interpretations would have it, it also reveals Genius's own cruelty as author of the tale. Finally, the discussion of Genius's literary authority will lead us to the ultimate *auctor* of the whole *Confessio*, the creator of Genius, that is, Gower. By taking on the role of Amans, the one who is taught, Gower positions himself as the one who has to submit to authority. From this detached position, he can comment on Genius's authorial role, and he does so at the end of the "Tale of Jephthah's Daughter."

Although it takes its basic plot from Judges 11, the "Tale of Jephthah's Daughter" differs from it in two main respects. First, the story as it appears in the Bible seems straightforward. There are no side comments about the action on the part of the narrator; neither is there any attempt at conveying an explicit moral, although exegetes and later interpreters have extracted different lessons from it. Genius's version, by contrast, is mainly moralistic, and his moral differs from the lessons one might arguably find in the biblical account. Secondly, even though it seems straightforward, we will see that the version in Judges presents some ambiguities that have given rise to different versions of the plot itself. It is interesting, therefore, to notice that Genius's account presents an unambiguous plot. He erases any possible ambiguities in order to make his point more clearly. By doing so, he departs from his source, in order to stress his vision of a daughter's role in the system of exogamy.

Let us examine first the ambiguities in the biblical version in the light of David Marcus's analysis of the language in the original Hebrew account.[26] The main ambiguity that has given rise to the most significant disagreement among later interpreters has to do with the ending of the story. Most interpreters consider that the daughter is literally sacrificed, that is, killed by her father. This has become the standard version of the sacrifice. Some interpreters, however, according to Marcus, argue that "the daughter was sacrificed only in a metaphorical sense: she was not put to death but had to remain as a virgin, consecrated to God, for the rest of her life" (7). This interpretation, which Marcus calls the "non-sacrificialist" interpretation, seems to have started in the twelfth century with a medieval Jewish exegete, David Kimhi, who noticed, according to Marcus, "the fact that the text does not actually state that Jephthah put his daughter to death" (8). Indeed, both the Hebrew and the Vulgate versions state only that Jephthah fulfilled the vow ("et fecit ei sicut voverat," verse 39 in the Vulgate).[27] If we go back to Jephthah's actual vow in the Hebrew version, we could possibly identify two different parts in it: first, whomever he meets when he comes back from the battle will belong to God, and, second, Jephthah would offer that person to the Lord.[28] Neither the Vulgate nor the original version specify what part of the vow he fulfilled. According to the non-literal interpretation, then, Jephthah simply gave his daughter to God. This non-literal approach, Marcus notes, was adopted by a number of Christian exegetes, "but under the influence of the medieval practice of nunnery, [these exegetes] extended the interpretation of the ending of the story to include consecration at a sanctuary" (9).[29]

---

[26] David Marcus, *Jephthah and His Vow* (Lubbock, TX: Texas Tech UP, 1986).
[27] *Biblia sacra iuxta vulgatam versionem*, ed. Robert Gryson (Stuttgart: Deutsche Bibelgesellschaft, 1994). All other quotations from the Vulgate are taken from the same edition.
[28] Marcus, *Jephthah and His Vow*, translates the Hebrew account as follows: "Whoever goes out from the doors of my house to greet me, when I return safely from the Ammonites, will belong to the Lord, and I will offer him up as an 'olah' " (10). The two possibilities, then, are: giving someone to the Lord (consecrating him or her), and offering someone to God as a sacrifice.
[29] Gower could have known about the non-sacrificial interpretation from Nicholas de Lyra's gloss to this passage in the *Glossa Ordinaria*. Nicholas comments extensively on the

Another problem pointed out by interpreters of Judges 11 is that Jephthah could have tried to avoid sacrificing his daughter. According to Leviticus 27:1–8, Marcus notes, "a human being vowed to God could be redeemed by a monetary payment" (47). Jephthah thus could have saved his daughter and satisfied God by paying a ransom. Later Jewish interpreters have been puzzled by the fact that Jephthah did not try to resort to this possibility, and some of them, according to the *Encyclopaedia Judaica*, attribute "[h]is sinful act of immolating his daughter . . . to his ignorance and false pride."[30] He simply accepts his obligation to kill her and mainly thinks about the effect of her sacrifice on himself. In the Vulgate version he says, "heu filia mi decepisti me et ipsa decepta es / aperui enim os meum ad Dominum / et aliud facere non potero" (v.35).[31] Finally, it is also puzzling that God does not intervene to prevent the sacrifice, as he does in the story of Abraham and Isaac, especially since, as C. A. Brown has observed, "[t]he vow is made to the God of Israel (Judg. 11:30), who categorically opposes human sacrifice (Jer. 19:5)."[32]

The ambiguity surrounding her sacrifice, as Marcus points out, shows that the biblical narrator was more interested in the rashness of Jephthah's vow, as well as his wrongdoing in this respect, than in the fate of his daughter. Throughout the account, the biblical narrator's main focus is the battle between Jews and Ammonites – he provides us with a detailed explanation of its historical causes (Judges 11:1–29). By contrast, the sacrifice of Jephthah's daughter is told in a matter-of-fact tone. There is some lament on the parts of the daughter and the father; and the other maidens mourn the fact that she is a virgin when he fulfills his vow. But the daughter is not given much attention despite, as Brown puts it, the "meaninglessness" of her untimely death.[33] The same silence has prevailed in later Jewish and patristic interpretations of Jephthah: according to Phyllis Trible, "[t]hroughout the centuries patriarchal hermeneutics has forgotten the daughter of Jephthah but remembered her father, indeed exalted him."[34] The main point of the story does not seem to

---

different interpretations. I reproduce here part of his account: "Reuersa est ad Pa[trem] eam interficiendo, & offerendo Domino in holocaustum, secundum quod dicunt expositores catholici. Vnde dicit Hieron[imus] quod fuit indiscretus in vouendo, & impius in adimplendo. Hebraei aperte dicunt, quod ipsam non immolauit, sed uotum eius fuit relaxatum per ipsum Phinees." Quoted from *Biblia sacra cum glossis interlineari, et ordinaria*, vol. 2 (Venice, 1588), p. 47 verso. ("She is returned to the father and he kills her and offers her to God as a sacrifice, according to the Catholic commentators. Jerome says that he was reckless in making his vow, and impious in fulfilling it. The Hebrews say openly that he did not immolate her, but he was released from his vow by Phinehas himself" [my translation.])
30 Quoted from *Encyclopaedia Judaica*, vol. 9 (New York: MacMillan, 1971) 1343.
31 "Alas, my daughter! You have deceived me and you yourself have been deceived; I opened my mouth to God and I cannot do otherwise" (my translation).
32 Cheryl Anne Brown, *No Longer Be Silent: First Century Jewish Portraits of Biblical Women* (Louisville, KY: Westminster/John Knox Press, 1992) 93.
33 Brown, *No Longer Be Silent* 94. As Brown also observes, "[t]he narrator passes over the story without comment" (93).
34 Quoted in Brown, *No Longer Be Silent* 93.

be the daughter's suffering or her "mistake," i.e., not having lost her virginity earlier in her life. As Marcus points out, it is Jephthah's actions and rash vow that the narrator focuses on:

> [T]he ambiguities surrounding Jephthah's daughter serve to blur her fate, but throw something else into sharper relief. This, in my opinion, is Jephthah's rash vow. The daughter, then, would not be the chief focus of the story at all (it will be recalled that she is not even mentioned by her name), rather Jephthah's vow is. (54)

Interestingly enough, in *Handlyng Synne*, Robert Mannyng, Gower's contemporary, does not show a great interest in the daughter either, but develops the lesson implicit in the biblical account about the foolishness of rash vows.[35] Mannyng's version of the story focuses on the rashness of Jephthah's vow, which the English author condemns. His moral is that, first, one should not make foolish vows, especially those that involve slaying a human being, and, second, that even if one makes such a vow, one must not fulfill it:

> Þat y to ȝow dar weyl sey:
> Ȝoure wykkede vowes shal ȝe nat fyll
> Ne make no vow to any yll,
> But change hem to better prow
> And take penaunce for foly vow.[36]

Mannyng's focus, then, is on the father's actions; the daughter is merely the backdrop, and her death is simply the unfortunate and tragic consequence of her father's folly. In largely ignoring the daughter and focusing on the father, Mannyng is thus following traditional interpretations.

Unlike Mannyng and the Bible, Genius, strikingly, focuses on the fate of the daughter, rather than on the father's blame. In his own version, the daughter plays a more important and straightforward role than the father. The "Tale of Jephthah's Daughter" starts with an account of Jephthah's vow and his battle against the Ammonites, but this account only takes eighteen lines. The rest of the tale (seventy-one lines) focuses on the daughter. In the biblical version, more than three-quarters of the story are devoted to the strife between Ammon and the Jews, and to the actual battle, while only one quarter deals with Jephthah's encounter with his daughter. In order to adapt the story to his own moral, Genius shifts the emphasis to the daughter and makes significant changes.

---

[35] Wilbur Owen Sypherd, *Jephthah and His Daughter* (Newark, DE: U of Delaware, 1948), notes that apart from Gower's, Mannyng's, and Peter Abelard's retellings of the Jephthah story, medieval writers do not seem to have been as interested in this story as writers in later periods of Western culture (7–11).
[36] Robert Mannyng, *Handlyng Synne*, ed. Frederick J. Furnivall, EETS o.s. 119 (Oxford: Oxford UP, 1903) 2894–98. All further quotations from *Handlyng Synne* are taken from this edition.

Genius's version, unlike the biblical one, is quite straightforward. From the very beginning, he avoids any of the ambiguities that Judges 11 presents. Jephthah's vow is very specific:

> I schal in tokne of thi memoire
> The ferste lif that I mai se,
> Of man or womman wher it be,
> Anon as I come hom ayein,
> To thee, which art god soverein,
> Slen in thi name and sacrifie.   (1514–19)

Genius specifies that the victim has to be human ("man or womman"), and he discards any possible non-sacrificialist interpretation by insisting upon the blood sacrifice ("Slen in thi name and sacrifie").[37] The focus, then, turns to the daughter. While in Judges 11 we are told only that she came to greet her father with timbrels and dances (v.34), Genius depicts her as a "lusti dowhter" (1525), and describes her joy and desire to see her father in the following terms:

> Sche waiteth upon his cominge
> With dansinge and carolinge,
> As sche that wolde be tofore
> Al othre . . .   (1529–32)

She wants to be the first one "tofore / Al othre" to receive him. Jephthah's reaction upon seeing his daughter is very medieval in its allusion to the instability of fortune ("now, mi lord, al sodeinli / Mi joie is torned into sorwe" [1544–45]). Like the biblical Jephthah, though, he thinks mainly about the effect that the fulfillment of the vow will have on himself, that is, how his daughter's death will affect him. The possibility of trying to break his vow or negotiate some kind of compromise with God does not even enter his mind. In this respect, Genius does not depart from the biblical version.

In a sense, it is the father's aggressive language, his rash vow, that causes the daughter's death. Referring to the biblical version, Brown has remarked that Jephthah's daughter becomes the passive victim of "her father's word."[38] She is even more passive in Genius's tale, for in his version, unlike the Bible or *Handlyng Synne*, the daughter's words are never rendered directly. This is especially striking, since Genius, again unlike the Bible and *Handlyng Synne*, does focus on her. In Judges she speaks in verses 36–37, asking her father to give her leave to lament her virginity before she is killed; in *Handlyng Synne* (2870–76) she has a similar speech in which she also asks to be granted some time to lament her virginity. Genius does tell us that she talks to her father, but he does not render her words directly. That he does not do so is also

---

[37] He emphasizes the same point again in lines 1547–48 when he has Jephthah say: "For I mi dowhter schal tomorwe / Tohewe and brenne in thi servise."

[38] Brown, *No Longer Be Silent* 94.

significant when we compare her characterization with that of the redeeming daughters, analyzed in Chapter Two, who are defined by their female eloquence. When she sees her father's sorrow, Jephthah's daughter, like Peronelle, tries to comfort him; and, like Peronelle too, she offers to save him, in order to help him respond to the demands of the ultimate father-figure, even though for Jephthah's daughter saving him means that she will die. However, unlike Peronelle, who has her own speeches, Jephthah's daughter's words are filtered through Genius's. In contrast, Gower's narrator does render the father's words as direct speeches; they are kept separate and independent from Genius's own language. By denying the daughter her own voice, Genius makes her even more powerless than the biblical daughter, and, more crucially, forecloses any possible suggestion of individuality or independence from himself as narrator and literary father.

Genius's treatment of her death is also significantly different. Marcus notes that in the biblical version it is arguably incongruous that the daughter should bewail her virginity when, in fact, she is going to die.[39] Mannyng shows a similar lack of concern with her death. He is (and he shows Jephthah's daughter to be) more interested in the fact that she will die childless:

> She wepte nat for any outrage
> But for of here com no lynage
> Þat no frute of her myght sprynge
> Þarfore she made here wepynge,
> And for here fadyr hadde chylder no mo.   (2879–83)

Although Genius's main concern is also her virginity, despite his obsession with reproduction (or, perhaps, because of it), Gower's narrator gives us a glimpse of her anguish: "natheless hire herte aflihte / Of that sche sih hire deth comende" (1556–57). Unlike both the narrator in the Bible and Mannyng, Genius infuses her death with some pathos. He does not, though, dwell on it for too long, but quickly diverts our attention from the unfairness of her death to her "mistake" in dying a virgin. The pathos, then, is ultimately counterbalanced by the insistence on her unfruitfulness.

Genius, in fact, does not simply lament that she died a virgin – he even blames her for it, thus displacing the father's blame for her death. Genius's blaming the daughter is quite incongruous, as a comparison with traditional versions of the story shows. According to the biblical account, as we have seen, if anybody is to be blamed, it is Jephthah himself. Mannyng, too, makes this clear and so does another medieval interpretation of the story, Peter Abelard's "Planctus Virginum Israel Super Filia Jeptae Galaditae." In his poem Abelard describes her as "miseranda patris facta victima," the miserable victim of her father's deeds.[40] All these accounts insist on the father's cruelty.

---

[39] Marcus, *Jephthah and His Vow* 31.
[40] First stanza, line 10. Quoted in Sypherd 8.

Such cruelty, according to Boose, is deemed necessary for the proper functioning of the patriarchal system and even becomes an inherent part of it:

> Patriarchal ideology has always imagined that women – and especially the unstructured daughter – pose the ultimate threat to its power. But women may not be the real threat to patriarchy; it may instead be the fathers themselves. To quell the menace of paternal behavior deviating from the authoritarian ideal, the cultural mythmaking apparatus seems continually to have needed to reproduce patterns of dictatorial, resolutely unsentimental fatherhood modeled into father-gods and god-the-fathers. By insinuation, the model is divinely sanctioned. The greatest menace to patriarchy would be the threat of fathers rebelling against the archetypes they inherited.[40a]

The story of Jephthah fits this pattern of unsentimental and dictatorial fatherhood. We should note that in the case of the "Tale of Jephthah's Daughter," Genius understates Jephthah's cruelty. However, in doing so, he carries out another more subtle form of paternal cruelty by insisting that what is pitiful and regrettable about the daughter's sacrifice is not that she dies but that she will never have any offspring.

Jephthah's cruelty is presented as necessary, given the hierarchical organization of the system. This father is faced with a choice: pleasing the Father or saving his daughter. This choice thus involves another crucial relationship in the story, the one between father and son, that is, between God and Jephthah. According to Boose, "[i]n the archetypal father-son structure [unlike the father-daughter relationship], the son's departure is authorized inside a circular pattern that predicts both his inevitable return and the concurrent threat of displacement/usurpation that he will pose" (32). In the "Tale of Jephthah's Daughter," the father-daughter relationship clashes with the father-son relationship; the threat of displacement of the father by the son is in conflict with the threat of separation of father and daughter. Jephthah ultimately has to decide between, on the one hand, fulfilling his vow, and thus not threatening the Father's place as the authority, or, on the other hand, retaining his daughter, and refusing to enact the drama of separation, i.e., disobeying the Father's commands, and in effect displacing Him.[41] In a patriarchal society, the only acceptable and unthreatening outcome to Jephthah's dilemma, obeying his own father or retaining his daughter, is the sacrifice of the daughter. Ultimately, the daughter's father responds to a higher law, the law of the Father, God.

[40a] Boose, "The Father's House and the Daughter in It" 37.
[41] Interestingly enough, the situation in this tale also resembles the one in the "Tale of Canace and Machaire." Jephthah and Machaire are similar in that neither of them challenges his father. By complying with their fathers, they break the "natural" bond with the women, replacing it with the unnatural harshness of patriarchy. Both Jephthah and Machaire disappear at the end, leaving the women to their own fates in the hands of the higher law.

By obeying the Father, Jephthah not only removes the threat of displacement by the son, but also abides by the rules of exogamy. As Boose has noted, "[t]he conflict between separation and retention dominates and spatializes Western culture's father-daughter texts. Essentially, the literary dialectic repeats the exogamy-incest opposition of kinship structures" (32). The retention of the daughter by the father in a sense amounts to an act of incest, i.e., an act that goes against patriarchal rule. By killing the daughter, Jephthah complies with the principle of exogamy, the principle that regulates and governs patriarchal societies.

We should also note, though, that in the very act of sacrificing his daughter Jephthah both separates from her and affirms his incestuous possession of her body. The daughter's sacrifice and her voluntary acceptance of it entails his submission to God, but, more significantly, it also entails the daughter's complete submission both to God *and* to her biological father. The pattern of submission to the father works both at the earthly and at the divine levels. As Boose has observed, "through the father's participation in his daughter's blood, the exogamous model leads back to the incestuous one in which it is anyway implicit" (40). The similarities between Peronelle and Jehphthah's daughter become more evident now, for both reproduce the pattern of submission of Mary to God, of the daughter to the father.

In the "Tale of Jephthah's Daughter," Genius, more so than the father, also ensures that this pattern of submission prevails. He even goes further than the biblical text in his version of this story of unsentimental fatherhood. Instead of recognizing that the reason for the death of Jephthah's daughter is Jephthah's total compliance with an all-powerful divine authority, Genius creates a reason to blame the daughter. He blames her not so much for her death but for the untimeliness of it. Genius's insistence on the daughter's blame is, moreover, ironically incongruous because there is no indication in the tale, unlike in the case of Rosiphelee, that the daughter is responsible for not having married earlier. In fact, Jephthah's daughter's total compliance with her father's and God's will when she accepts her sacrifice suggests the opposite, namely, that she, unlike Rosiphelee – and like her own father – is perfectly compliant with the demands of patriarchal authority. Significantly, Genius's blaming of the daughter in this tale reminds us of Orchamus's blaming of his daughter for suffering Phebus's rape in the "Tale of Leucothoe." In a way, a similar kind of impotence in the face of a higher and more powerful authority (God in the "Tale of Jephthah's Daughter," Phebus in the "Tale of Leucothoe") informs the deflection of the blame onto the victim.

This deflection of the blame is even clearer when we analyze the way the daughter dies in Genius's tale, as opposed to Mannyng's and the Bible's versions. The "Tale of Jepthah's Daughter" is also peculiar in this respect. The narrators of both the Bible and *Handlyng Synne* state explicitly that the father kills the daughter. The narrator in Judges explains that at the end of the two months she returned to her father and he did what he had vowed to do: "Expletisque duobus mensibus reversa est ad patrem suum / et fecit ei sicut voverat" (v.39); while, according to Mannyng, ". . . ryght at þe moneþes ende / Here fadyr dede nat þer of hende, / Þat he hys owne doghter slow" (2885–87). In the *Confessio Amantis*, however, the father disappears towards the end so that he is not explicitly involved in the death of his daughter. Genius describes her moment of death as follows: "hir laste dai / Was come, in which sche scholde take / Hir deth" (1590–92). Although the meaning of "take / Hir deth" is probably that she took her death from someone, rather than that she killed herself, we should notice that the father has disappeared and does not kill her (or Genius omits this detail). Thus Genius insists on the power and authority of the patriarchal system over the individual father's own authority and responsibility.

The changes Genius imposes on the original story show him enacting his own authority over his creation, the tale. I mentioned above that Jephthah is traditionally seen as an unsentimental and cruel father. The same cruelty, I argue, should ultimately be ascribed to Genius himself. First, he tries to ignore the violence of the father and his responsibility for his daughter's death – by noting that she had to kill herself ("sche sholde take / Hir deth"), in effect he washes the father's hands. Then, incongruously, he blames the daughter for not being ready to die rather than pitying her as an innocent victim. (Notice, again, the parallel with Orchamus's reaction to his daughter's rape.) At the same time as the father is erased from the text, Genius, as society's voice and author of the tales, takes control of the situation, assumes authority over the daughter, and himself becomes an autocratic, and even ruthless, father.

Indeed, Amans himself notes Genius's ruthlessness. At the end of the "Tale of Jephthah," Amans points out to Genius that he has noticed how in his treatment of Jephthah's daughter and Rosiphelee, ". . . ye the wommen have noght spared / Of hem that tarien so behinde" (1600–1601). Genius has certainly not "spared" Rosiphelee, who finally seems to submit to textual pressure in view of the threats posed by the vision. Neither has he "spared" Jephthah's daughter. In making her sacrifice even more pointless than in the Bible, since he devises an incongruous reason to blame her, he diverts our attention from the responsibility of the different fathers who act upon her – her biological father and God the Father. Thus he reinscribes patriarchal authority; most significantly, in doing so, he appears as the third father, the father of her fictional existence, and a father who also responds to the pattern of dictatorial and unsentimental fatherhood.

It is significant that it should be Amans who should draw attention to Genius's authorial power. We know that at the beginning and end of the *Confessio*, Gower takes on Amans's persona, even though there is not a straightforward identification of the two – as Olsson puts it, "we cannot be sure, given the multiple personae introduced in the poem, that this character has a single 'identity' at all."[42] Amans's intervention in lines 1600–1601 also

---

[42] Olsson, *John Gower and the Structures of Conversion* 46.

raises the question of the role of the ultimate *auctor* of the poem and all of its characters: John Gower. In identifying himself with Amans, Gower places himself in a subordinate position in a hierarchical relationship of authority. He is the frustrated lover who needs to be taught a moral lesson by Father Genius. But, most importantly, as Amans's observation in lines 1600–1601 indicates, from this subordinate position Gower can examine and comment on the uses and abuses of authority as exercised by Genius. Through Amans, Gower can analyze from a detached point of view the different modes of authority that function in the poem.

This is not to argue that Amans is a reliable source, and, ultimately, the one who has authority in the poem. As various critics have shown, Amans himself is not a reliable reader.[43] Indeed, even his comments at the end of the "Tale of Jephthah's Daughter" reveal that he has difficulty transcending his self-absorption. He cannot see a connection between the women who Genius has not "spared" and men like himself – even though Genius had told him explicitly at the end of the "Tale of Rosiphelee" that the moral lesson also applies to knights (e.g., 1455–59). Amans remarks, "yit it falleth in my minde, / Toward the men hou that ye spieke" (1602–03), and then criticizes Genius for speaking too obscurely: "To speke in words so coverte, / I not what travaill that ye mente" (1606–07).

While the tales analyzed in Chapter Four manifest a critique, or at least a questioning, of excessive fatherly and kingly authority, in the "Tale of Jephthah's Daughter" Genius acts like the abusive and tyrannical fathers and kings in those tales. By blaming the daughter, he ignores the father's responsibility and even replicates "the pattern of dictatorial and unsentimental fatherhood" in the original. The "Tale of Rosiphelee" had already shown that the text can be used as a form of coercion. To quote Wallace again, "[c]ontrol of the text, figured as a woman, facilitates control of woman in society."[44] It only remains to provide final, definitive evidence that Genius figures the text (his text) not just as a woman but as a daughter and that he is thus implicated in the relationships of authority that he tries to regulate. We therefore turn now to the tale of "Pygmaleon and the Statue."

Pygmaleon and the Statue

In his *Ovidius moralizatus* from the early fourteenth century, as I mentioned in the first chapter, Petrus Berchorius allegorizes the story of Pygmalion as an act of confession. Pygmalion is a confessor and the statue is the confessant's soul.

---

[43] As mentioned in Chapter Four, Allen, "Chaucer Answers Gower," has noted "Amans's misguided reading" in her analysis of his reaction to the "Tale of Canace and Machaire" (634). And she continues, "Amans's reception highlights the unreliability of any reader's will" (634). See also Olsson, *John Gower and the Structures of Conversion*, for whom "Amans's short-sighted desire underlies Book 4" (138).
[44] Wallace, *Chaucerian Polity* 277.

Let me quote again from the text: "Per istum factorem imaginum intelligo praedicatores qui animam sciunt sculpere: & pingere correctionibus & virtutibus."[45] In a strikingly pre-Foucaultian view of the creative power of confession, the confessor is compared to Pygmalion: he sculpts and paints a soul with corrections and virtues. Gower seems to have known the *Ovidius moralizatus*; according to Conrad Mainzer, "there is strong evidence to suggest that he was using the *Ovidius moralizatus* in his section on the pantheon in the fifth book of the *Confessio*."[46] Whether Gower was directly inspired by Berchorius's allegorical interpretation or not, his view of Pygmalion as a confessor and in turn of the confessor as a Pygmalion-figure is evident in his version of the myth of the sculptor. Indeed, Gower's Genius identifies with Pygmalion as a confessor/sculptor of souls, and, I will also argue, as an author/creator and father of sorts.

When Gower decided to write his own version of the story of Pygmalion, he had two famous major versions in mind which preceded his, Ovid's version in the *Metamorphoses* (X. 242–99) and Jean de Meun's version in *Roman de la Rose* (20817–21214). Gower's version of the myth thus follows the traditional outline of the story, but, making the story his own, he emphasizes and adds some subtle details. Genius tells us that Pygmalion was a famous sculptor who made a statue of a woman out of ivory. She was so beautiful and lifelike that he fooled himself ("he himself beguileth," 387) and fell in love with her. He lay with her in bed and was distraught because she would not come alive. He therefore prayed day and night until Venus heard him and decided to grant his prayer. One night the image became "full of lif" (423) and thus he won an obedient wife with whom he later had a child. Genius ends his version by emphasizing the power of the word (Pygmalion's prayers) in this story: he tells Amans "That word mai worche above kinde" (438).

Traditionally, the famous story of Pygmalion has been seen as a celebration of creative artistic power, as an exploration of the nature of love, or as an allegory for God's creation of humankind. Recently, J. Hillis Miller has suggested that in Ovid the myth does not only celebrate the power of the artist; it points at the same time to the problematic, even incestuous, self-centeredness involved in the process of artistic creation.[47] While he does not recognize the incestuous connotations of the story, Kevin Brownlee has also seen the story of Pygmalion in Jean's *Roman de la Rose* as a reflection on, and celebration of, his own work as an artist: Jean's modifications of Ovid's Pygmalion story, "serve to call attention to Jean's status as a tranformer of

---

[45] Petrus Berchorius, *Ovidius moralizatus* 152. ("Through this maker of images I perceive preachers who know how to sculpt and paint a soul with corrections and virtues" [translation taken from Reynolds, "The *Ovidius moralizatus*" 355.])

[46] Conrad Mainzer, "John Gower's Use of the 'Medieval Ovid' in the *Confessio Amantis*" *Medium Aevum* 41 (1972): 215.

[47] J. Hillis Miller, *Versions of Pygmalion* (Cambridge: Harvard UP, 1990). See the Proem, "Pygmalion's Prosopopoeia."

Ovid, a self-presentation thereby valorized."[48] Jean de Meun thus uses the story to explore notions of authorship, an exploration that critics have long recognized in the French poem, more so than Gower scholars have usually recognized in the *Confessio Amantis*. Gower's own reworking of the myth suggests that he understood Ovid's and Jean de Meun's versions profoundly and saw that both raise issues of authorship, which he then developed in a significantly different manner.

In the following pages, I will argue that Gower's reworking of the myth elaborates on a paradox also suggested by Jean's and Ovid's version. Inspired by Hillis Miller's analysis of Ovid, I will show that Gower uses Genius's identification with Pygmalion to achieve something paradoxical: at one and the same time, he celebrates the power of the author and problematizes it by hinting at the incestous dimension involved in the authorial relationship between an artist and his creation as it was conceived in the Middle Ages.

In their versions of the story of Pygmalion, neither Gower nor Jean de Meun are interested in the power inherent in any kind of art; they focus, more specifically, on the power of the word, of poetic discourse. Rather than his sculpting abilities, it is Pygmalion's use of language that both versions emphasize. As Brownlee has noted, one of the most striking differences between Ovid's and Jean's versions is that Jean has his Pygmalion deliver no less than four speeches, thus according great importance to his verbal expertise (205). In this way, "the power of (poetic) discourse – a theme vital to the *Rose* – is highlighted by Jean's intertextual exploitation of Ovid" (205). On the basis of this and other considerations, Brownlee sees "a link between Jean de Meun (*qua* poet-author of the *Rose*) and his 'character' Pygmalion (*qua* artist figure)" (207). Gower, I will argue, develops first an identification between Genius and Pygmalion. This identification then points back to himself. The following reading will also help us see that Jean's exploration of the nature of authorship goes a step further than Brownlee implies: his is not a straightforward and uncritical celebration of artistic power. Both medieval authors share with Ovid a certain skepticism about the nature of this power. I will conclude by suggesting that this skepticism helps explain why it is so difficult to locate an authorial voice in both Gower's and Jean's narrative poems. The two authors resist at the same time as they recognize the Pygmalionesque fantasy of total control over their own work.

Gower's reflection on the power of the author needs to be considered in the context of his exploration of the link between discourse and the incest taboo in the *Confessio Amantis*. It is here that Gower departs from Ovid and Jean de Meun. In identifying Genius with Pygmalion, Gower portrays his narrator as an author, a creator of words, who lets himself be led by a kind of desire to control his own discursive creation that responds to the pattern of fathers' desire for their daughters. Genius is thus shown to be implicated in

---

[48] Kevin Brownlee, "Orpheus' Song Re-Sung: Jean de Meun's Reworking of *Metamorphoses*, X," *Romance Philology* 36 (1982): 206.

the kinds of desire that he tries to regulate. Moreover, while he uses his poetic discourse to reinscribe the incest prohibition, he is also at the same time creating incestuous desire through discourse. As Derrida would put it, we can see in Genius's role that "[l]anguage is neither prohibition nor transgression, it couples the two endlessly."[49] Genius's story of Pygmalion in Gower's poem can thus be read as a story that sanctions incestuous desire and reveals the power of discourse to create reality. Ultimately, this tale is also a reflection on Gower's own desire to control his text.

Let us analyze Genius's story of Pygmalion in detail. His version is unusual in several respects. It is one of the few occasions in which Genius uses a tale as an example, not of the consequences of committing a certain sin, but of the advantages of doing the opposite of that sin. Pygmalion is an example of forwardness and constancy in praying and asking for love, opposites of pusillanimity. Rather uncharacteristically also, Genius does not put much emphasis on the marriage of Pygmalion to the statue, a marriage which the sources do mention.[50] This is surprising given Genius's usual defence of matrimony in the *Confessio*, and especially given his outspoken advocacy of it after the "Tale of Rosiphelee," less than a thousand lines later in the same book (1467–1504). "Pygmaleon and the Statue" is also unusual in its attempt to naturalize an action – turning an inanimate object into an animate being – which, Genius himself admits, is "above kinde" (438). In this respect, it resembles the story that follows it immediately, the "Tale of Iphis," in which Cupid turns a girl into a boy to avoid a homosexual relationship between two girls and to make a marriage between the two possible.

"Pygmaleon and the Statue" seems even more peculiar when one realizes that, in his version, Genius makes an interesting omission, an omission that hints at the purpose of his tale. Unlike Gower's, both Jean's and Ovid's stories of Pygmalion mention Myrrha's incest story. Ovid ends his version by first explaining that Pygmalion and Galatea had a daughter named Paphos and then linking this story to the next metamorphosis story: Paphos had a son, Cyniras, who in turn begot a daughter, Myrrha. Myrrha fell in love and committed incest with her father. When Cinyras discovered that he had been sleeping with his own daughter, he tried to kill her, but before he could do so she was transformed into a myrrh tree. Similarly, Jean de Meun notes that Pygmalion begot Paphus and, like Ovid, he mentions the incestuous story of Paphus's (and Pygmalion's) descendants: Cyniras and Myrrha.

Given Genius's interest in incest and in stories of fathers and daughters, it

---

[49] Derrida, *Of Grammatology* 266.
[50] Apart from knowing Ovid's and Jean's version, Gower, as I mentioned above, probably knew Petrus Berchorius's *Ovidius moralizatus* and also the anonymous *Ovide moralisé*. By contrast with all these versions, in which Pygmalion is said to get married after the statue comes to life, Genius's version alludes to the marriage only indirectly, when he notes that Pygmalion "wan a lusti wif" (424). For a discussion of Gower's possible use of the *Ovide moralisé* as well as of other medieval interpretations of Ovid, see Mainzer, "John Gower's Use of the 'Mediaeval Ovid.' "

might seem surprising that he does not tell the famous story of Myrrha at any point in the *Confessio* and, especially, that he does not even allude to it at the end of his version of Pygmalion's story. Such a surprising omission points to Genius's own agenda in the tale. In the following pages, I will show how and why Genius suppresses the incestuous connotations of a story that invites an analysis in terms of father-daughter incest, or the father's desire for his own creation. The metaphor of incest will allow us to understand the relationship between Pygmalion and his statue in Genius's account.[51] It will further support one of my major claims in this analysis: that there is an identification between the two artistic creators, Pygmalion and Genius, and between them and the ultimate artistic creator, John Gower.

The metaphor that presents artistic creation as a kind of procreation, and thus the artistic product as the offspring of the artist, has had a long history, as Gilbert and Gubar have shown. Traditionally, the artist has been seen as a man, and thus a father: "the writer 'fathers' his text just as God fathered the world."[52] The relationship between an author and his text is thus figured as a paternal relationship. In its classical and medieval senses, the Latin word *auctor* carries similar connotations. Scanlon has noted that in classical and late antique Rome the word "[a]uctor could mean author in the modern sense, but it could also mean founder, originator, inventor, or instituter of any sort."[53] Moreover, one of its early senses was that of "father" or "progenitor" (40). These senses of the word *auctor*, Scanlon argues, were later appropriated

---

[51] On the relationship between procreation and artistic creation, see further Brook Thomas, "The Writer's Procreative Urge in *Pierre*: Fictional Freedom or Convoluted Incest?," *Studies in the Novel* 11 (1979): 416–30. Thomas even relates artistic procreation per se with incest. Her explanation of this relation is particularly clarifying for my discussion:
> Artistic procreation is incestuous. The metaphor of incest accounts for both the difference necessary for the creative act and the continual reduplication of personality (repetition) that no artist can avoid, for in incest we make love to someone of the opposite sex in whom we see ourselves mirrored. (422)

I should mention that, although Thomas's definition is problematic because it assumes that incestuous relationships are always heterosexual, it is still useful for my purposes, as my concern centers on a type of relationship, that between father and daughter, which involves two persons of different sexes.

[52] Gilbert and Gubar, *The Madwoman in the Attic* 4. See esp. 3–44. Gilbert and Gubar cite Edward Said's definition of 'authority' and then remark:
> Said himself later observes that a convention of most literary texts is 'that the unity or integrity of the text is maintained by a series of genealogical connections: author-text, beginning-middle-end, text-meaning, reader-interpretation, and so on. *Underneath all these is the imagery of succession, of paternity, or hierarchy*' (italics ours). (4–5)

The metaphor of the writer as the father of his work is also embedded, as they note, in the medieval notion of God as the writer of the Book of Nature (5–6). On this point, see further Ernst Robert Curtius, *European Literature and the Latin Middle Ages*, trans. Willard R. Trask (Princeton: Princeton UP, 1973) 319–26.

[53] Scanlon, *Narrative, Authority, and Power* 39. See further Scanlon's discussion of the medieval notion of *auctoritas* in ch. 3, "*Auctoritas* and *potestas*: a model of analysis for medieval culture."

by Christianity, "which [thus] drew textual and political *auctoritas* definitely together" (45). Indeed, in the Latin Middle Ages, Alastair Minnis has similarly explained, the term *auctor* was thought to derive its meaning from the Latin verbs *agere* ('to act or perform'), *augere* ('to grow'), and *auieo* ('to tie'). Minnis notes that, "an *auctor* 'performed' the act of writing. *He brought something into being*, caused it to 'grow' " (my emphasis).⁵⁴

As the author and "originator" of his statue, the sculptor is also in a sense the *auctor* of his work. He brings something into being. As Kenneth Gross has noted, Ovid's story of Pygmalion "has indeed been read as an essay on the artist's power to create autonomous life in what seems intractable, inanimate matter."⁵⁵ In this sense, his power is god-like. Precisely this reading is found in the *Ovide moralisé*, another popular moralizing interpretation of Ovid from around the beginning of the fourteenth century which, like the *Ovidius moralizatus*, Gower may have known (215). In the *Ovide moralisé* (3585–3777), according to one of the anonymous author's two allegorical interpretations of the story of Pygmalion, the sculptor stands for God and the statue for human nature, created by God:

> Autre sentence i puet avoir.
> . . .
> Li forgierres de tout le monde,
> A sa forme et a sa figure
> Forga nostre humaine nature.⁵⁶

He then points out that the matter to which God gave human form was clay: "La matire fu limonee, / Cui Diex forme humaine a donee" (3594–95). The myth of Pygmalion, therefore, has been perceived as a story about the *auctor*'s power to create, to bring something into being, and to cause it to grow.

The word "forme" in the quotation above is significant. In its Middle English version the notions of "form" and "enfourmacioun" also play fundamental roles in the *Confessio Amantis*, as Simpson has recently shown.⁵⁷ The word "enfourmacioun" contains the notion of 'form': "the primary meaning of 'information' is artistic, or literary (denoting the act of giving form to matter)" (4). Its secondary, pedagogic meaning is connected to God's creation:

> Gower uses the verb 'forme' of God's activity, and expands its implications by the word 'enforme': the pedagogic activity of 'clerkes' imparting knowledge about God's creative information of the world is described as

---

⁵⁴ Minnis, *Medieval Theory of Authorship* 10.
⁵⁵ Kenneth Gross, *The Dream of the Moving Statue* (Ithaca, NY: Cornell UP, 1992) 74.
⁵⁶ *Ovide moralisé*, ed. C. de Boer, Verhandelingen der koninklijke nederlandse akademie van wetenschappen, afdeeling letterkunde 37 (Amsterdam: J. Müller, 1936) 3586, 3589–91. ("There can be another interpretation . . . The forger of all the world, in his shape and in his form, forged our human nature" [my translation]).
⁵⁷ Simpson, *Sciences and the Self*, esp. ch. 1.

itself an 'information' ('as the clerkes us enforme') . . . The role of shaper, or informer, is shared by Genius, since he informs stories to bring them to an ideal, proper form: Genius's literary information is a parallel activity to divine information, since both are designed to bring their objects to a kind of perfection. (4–5)

The sculptor's task is similarly to "inform," to give form to intractable matter. The story of Pygmalion is about Genius's activity, about his work of informing, or shaping the tales as a creative process. Like Pygmalion, Genius tries to create something new out of the matter he has, the earlier versions of the stories.

The metaphor of fathering aptly conveys the notion that the author puts part of himself in his work, thus necessarily mirroring himself in it. As Hillis Miller remarks, "[f]or Pygmalion, the other is not really other. Pygmalion has himself made Galatea. She is the mirror image of his desire" (4). This love of same for same, as Miller also notes, highlights the similarities between Pygmalion's love and that of Narcissus (4–5). There is certainly a narcissistic element in Pygmalion's love, even if Jean's Pygmalion would like us to believe that there is none. In fact, Pygmalion's anxious attempt to distance himself from Narcissus in the *Roman de la Rose* suggests that there is such an element. First, he tries to persuade us (and himself) that, if the texts do not lie, many have loved more foolishly: "se l'escripture ne ment, / Maint ont plus folement amé."[58] Then he mentions Narcissus as an example of foolish love and tells us that he himself is less foolish, "sui je mains fous toutevois" (20887), because, unlike Narcissus, he at least can hold the statue in his arms (20888–90). The sculptor doth protest too much.

Father-daughter incest is indeed a form of narcissism; it is tantamount to self-love – the father falls in love with a reproduction of himself. That Pygmalion's love carries incestuous connotations is suggested by the story of Pygmalion's great-granddaughter, Myrrha, which both Ovid and Jean tell immediately after the story of the sculptor, but Genius significantly omits. Some lines after the story of Pygmalion we learn about the incestuous love of the sculptor's great-granddaughter Myrrha for her father, Cyniras, Pygmalion's own grandson. Hillis Miller has argued that, "[t]he narrative of Myrrha's incestuous love for her father is a retrospective reading of the story of Pygmalion" (10). The metaphorical incest committed by Pygmalion is made literal by his offspring, and it is the offspring who receives the punishment for it. This deferral of the punishment allows Ovid to hint at the problematic self-centeredness of artistic production and, at the same time, to celebrate the power of art (and, consequently, of his own power). Jean de Meun's version of the story of Pygmalion, like Ovid's, also mentions the incest story, encouraging us to reflect back on Pygmalion's love for the statue

---

[58] Guillaume de Lorris et Jean de Meun, *Le Roman de la Rose*, ed. and trans. Armand Strubel (Paris: Librairie Générale Française, 1992) 20878–79. All further quotations from the *Roman* are taken from this edition.

in the light of his great-granddaughter's love for her father. In the *Roman de la Rose*, the poet's account of Pygmalion is a digression from his account of Venus's attack on the Tower of Shame. The poet compares the statue of a maiden in the tower with Pygmalion's statue to point out that Pygmalion's was not even nearly as beautiful as the statue in the Tower of Shame. At the end of his story the poet writes that Pygmalion had a daughter, Paphos, by his statue/wife, and that Paphos had a son Cinyras who was a fine man except for the fact that he committed incest with his daughter unwittingly (21154–64). Myrrha's love for her father points to the tragic irony engendered by Pygmalion's fantasy: his creative act ultimately results in a destructive story of incest. The story of Myrrha and the allusion to Narcissus in the *Roman* suggest that what Brownlee sees as Jean's celebration of artistic power is not a straightforward and uncritical celebration.

The allusion to Narcissus and the story of Myrrha's incestuous love for her father in the *Roman de la Rose* are not the only hints that make us reconsider Pygmalion's story and read it ironically. Significantly, few critics have disagreed concerning the interpretation of the story of the sculptor. They generally see the story as a critique of Pygmalion.[59] Rosemund Tuve, for instance, has argued that Jean's retelling of the story of Pygmalion towards the end of his poem is an appropriate contribution to what she sees as Jean's project in the *Roman de la Rose* – the critique of the narrowing of the meaning of "love" to sexual drive.[60] Tuve argues that the final image in the poem, the seizure of the rose, "is a brilliant satire on the basic pretenses of 'courtly' love," and, referring to the sanctuary within the Tower of Shame that Venus assaults to help the Lover, Tuve adds, "the choice of Pygmalion who *worships* the stone body for comparison with the Lover's own worship of the sanctuary is a masterstroke" (262). Jean de Meun thus leaves the doors open for a negative and ironic interpretation of Pygmalion's love.

In contrast with Ovid and Jean de Meun, Genius seems intent on closing those doors. Again and again, when one looks in his tale for echoes of the incestuous allusions that can be found in his sources, one realizes that Genius has carefully omitted or transformed them. The most obvious omission, as noted above, is that of the story of Myrrha and Cinyras. This particular story does not fit Genius's agenda, because it casts negative and incestuous implications on the story of Pygmalion.

It could be argued that Genius's use of Pygmalion as a good example – an example of the opposite of pusillanimity – is, in a sense, appropriate, since the sculptor's behavior proves his moral: he is an example of constancy and deter-

---

[59] An explanation of some of the different positions taken on Jean de Meun's rendering of the story of Pygmalion can be found in Thomas D. Hill, "Narcissus, Pygmalion, and the Castration of Saturn: Two Mythographical Themes in the *Roman de la Rose*," *Studies in Philology* 71 (1974): 404–26 (see esp. 408–13).

[60] Rosemund Tuve, *Allegorical Imagery: Some Mediaeval Books and Their Posterity* (Princeton: Princeton UP, 1966) 261–62.

mination even in the face of a situation that no human being could have the power to solve. But using the sculptor as a positive example for Amans poses a fundamental problem. While Genius is supposed to "cure" Amans of his love sickness, Pygmalion's story actually encourages Amans to hope that he may win his lady. Olsson has analyzed this problem extensively.[61] He notes that not just in "Pygmaleon and the Statue" but in various tales in Book 4, as, for instance, the "Tale of Iphis," in which a woman is turned into a man so that her love for another woman is made "natural," "[t]he priest encourages Amans to believe that a natural fulfillment of love is possible, no matter how remote, implausible, unnatural, or ridiculous that love appears" (139). And, Olsson continues, "[s]uch advice can only increase the frustration Amans feels and succinctly identifies: 'I seche that I mai noght finde' (4.289)" (139). Instead of showing Amans that his imaginations and fantasies can lead him only to frustration, Genius nourishes Amans's hopes.

Moreover, in presenting Pygmalion in a positive light, Genius forgets the problematic suggestions of idolatry linked to his love for the statue.[62] Even more strikingly, Genius's positive interpretation of Pygmalion's love is not only at odds with traditional interpretations of it but even with his own condemnations of self-love and idolatry at other points in the *Confessio Amantis*.[63] Genius's condemnation of idolatry comes no later than in the following book. His excursus on the world's religions in Book 5, devoted to avarice, takes up more than twelve hundred lines, and, as Olsson argues, "[it] focus[es] on idol-worship and the Pauline teaching that 'avaritia est idolorum servitus' " (153). In a section of the excursus, Genius tells Amans about the origin of idol-worship and describes the idol-worshippers in terms that remind us of Pygmalion. Commenting on the images they make, Genius observes that "the foles to hem knele, / Which is here oghne handes werk" (5.1504–05). Like the idol-worshippers, Pygmalion "made an ymage of entaile" (4.378) with his own hands, and prayed for love from it. Significantly, Genius uses the same phrase to describe the idols: they are "many an image of entaile" (5.1499). The idol-worshippers in Book 5, moreover, "unto suche goddes calle" (5.1515), not unlike Pygmalion himself, who "evere among he axeth grace / As thogh sche wiste what he mente" (4.410–11).

The theme of idolatry surfaces again when, in the context of a discussion on sacrilege, a branch of avarice, Amans tells Genius about his worshipping of his lady in terms that, as Olsson has noted, once again remind us of Pygmalion: "Pygmalion worships and strives to exert 'maistrye' over his creation,

---

[61] Olsson, *John Gower and the Structures of Conversion* 136–40.
[62] For studies of the medieval interpretations of Pygmalion see, Hill, "Narcissus, Pygmalion, and the Castration of Saturn," esp. 410–17, and Annegret Dinter, *Der Pygmalion-Stoff in der europäischen Literatur* (Heidelberg: Carl Winter Universitätsverlag, 1979), esp. 28–47.
[63] We have seen his condemnation of self-love in the "Tale of Albinus and Rosemund," and we have seen it in relation to the themes of incest and father-daughter relations in other tales. I will focus here mainly on his condemnation of idolatry.

and Amans, after his own fashion, does likewise. This worship is, of course, self-worship or idolatry" (152). Amans admits to Genius that,

> ... al mi devocion
> And al mi contemplacion
> With al min herte and mi corage
> Is only set on hire ymage.   (5.7125–28)

This devotion to the image of his lady is like Pygmalion's devotion to the "ymage" he has made with his hands (notice that Genius uses the same word in both cases). Amans continues to confess that he looks at her, while in the church, with the hope of stealing from her "A glad word or a goodly syhte" (5.7138). In the same way, Pygmalion "hire of love preide; / Bot sche no word ayeinward seide" (4.393–94). Despite his confession of idolatry, Amans is not reproved by Genius for his transgression; instead, the confessor simply condemns the fact that Amans tries to steal something from the lady when she is in church as opposed to the "chambre": "The cherche serveth for the bede, / The chambre is of an other speche" (5.7188–89). If we take this reproof in its more apparent sense, we realize that it is perfectly congruent with the section about sacrilege. Nevertheless, it is "curious," as Olsson puts it, that Genius misses here an opportunity to reprove Amans for his idolatry (153). Indeed, Amans's confession in this section shows that he has not learned anything from Genius's previous teachings on idol-worship. But, even more significantly, Genius's silence on this matter also shows that he himself fails to make a connection between his insight into religious idolatry and Amans's courtly idolatry.

Similarly, Genius fails to make a link between religious idolatry and the idolatry of courtly love in "Pygmaleon and the Statue." Olsson has argued that "Pygmaleon and the Statue" is one of the instances in which Genius's advice shows "[t]he failure of the confession to do its work" (139). Indeed, "Pygmaleon and the Statue" is one of those tales in which Genius's overall moralistic purpose is at odds with what his goal as a confessor should be. His moralistic purpose in this tale is to show the power of prayer and constancy. But, by stressing this aspect of Pygmalion's myth, he forgets about the idolatrous implications of the story, thus also conveying the message that idolatry can have its rewards. Such a message cannot help the penitent Amans, who needs precisely to be steered away from the idolatry of courtly love.

It has required a lengthy discussion for me to establish the basis for my argument about "Pygmaleon and the Statue." Let me recapitulate at this point my argument so far. The story of Pygmalion's love for his statue can be read as a story with incestuous connotations in terms of a father-daughter relationship, but Genius seems intent throughout on erasing those connotations. Genius's positive depiction of Pygmalion is at odds with his own views of self-love and idolatry and, especially, with his duty as confessor: to discourage Amans from hoping that he will be rewarded by the same idolatry, and thus to discourage him from sinning. I will demonstrate in the following pages that Genius fails as confessor in this particular tale, because of his identification with Pygmalion. The story of the sculptor suggests that, as narrator, Genius also sees himself as a father and thus participates in the same structures of authority that he tries to delimit in other tales, and even transgresses the boundaries he himself tries to set in those tales.

Critics generally see Amans as the one who is meant to identify with Pygmalion. As I have noted above, there are, indeed, clear parallels between the two lovers, but Gower, following Ovid and Jean de Meun, develops a less obvious, but more original, identification in this tale – that between Genius and Pygmalion. These characters are similar in two fundamental ways. I noted above that Berchorius's allegorical interpretation of Pygmalion sees the sculptor as a confessor. Pygmalion is thus like Genius, who sculpts Amans's soul and tries to recreate it. Even though, as I argued in Chapter One, he ultimately fails, Genius tries to free Amans's soul from its subjection to love in order to fulfill the promise that, according to Foucault, is at the heart of confession. He thus tries to perform what Foucault sees as the confessor's main role, the creation of subjectivity: the "constitution [of men] as subjects in both senses of the word" (60). The second parallel between Genius and Pygmalion is linked to the first one, for the creative power of confession coalesces with the creative power of poetic discourse. Significantly, it is Pygmalion's words, his prayer, rather than his sculpting abilities, that Genius stresses.

Genius's identification with Pygmalion is developed through the emphasis on, and the celebration of, the power of words, a celebration that is also central to the *Roman*'s version. I mentioned above that, as Brownlee has shown, one of the most striking differences between Ovid's and Jean's versions is that Jean has his Pygmalion deliver no less than four speeches, thus according great importance to "the power of (poetic discourse)."[64] The power of poetic discourse is also a central theme in Gower's version. His emphasis on the terms "ymaginacioun" and "ymage" and on the power of words to create become the ground on which his and the sculptor's interests intersect. What leads Pygmalion to sculpture his words and his piece of ivory is his "ymaginacioun." Out of the ivory, Pygmalion forms an "ymage" ("He made an ymage of entaile," 378), and his imagination leads him to love the image:

> ... thurgh pure impression
> Of his ymaginacion
> With al the herte of his corage
> His love upon this faire ymage
> He sette ...   (389–93)

The "ymaginacion" plays a very positive role in the tale of Pygmalion, but we should note that it does not always carry positive connotations in Genius's

---

[64] Brownlee, "Orpheus' Song Re-Sung" 205.

teachings. For instance, in his discussion of pusillanimity prior to the tale, Genius had warned Amans against using imagination as an excuse for not acting: referring to the pusillanimous man, he states that ". . . of ymaginacioun / He makth his excusacioun" (329–30). Moreover, in a preceding tale, that of Ulysses and Penelope (4.147–233), Genius also reflects on the bad effects of the "ymaginacioun" of love. When Ulysses receives Penelope's letter, in which she asks him to return to her because she is being wooed by other men, love seizes his heart "With pure ymaginacioun, / That for non occupacioun . . . He mai noght flitt his herte aside" (211–12, 214). In the case of Ulysses, his "ymaginacioun" does not finally overpower him because he musters "al the wille of his corage" (217) to wait until he can return home. The danger, however, of letting himself be controlled by "ymaginacioun" is still very strongly suggested. We should notice, moreover, that Genius qualifies Pygmalion's love of the statue as "pure impression." In Book 7, however, he uses "impression" in a negative sense, even though the story he tells resembles that of Pygmalion: a man loves a lady, but his lady does not know about his feelings. According to Genius, the lover's "impression" in this case is "[a] fool impression / Of his ymaginacioun" (7.4271–72). Why, then, we should ask, does Pygmalion's "ymaginacioun" play such a positive role, even though his own lady – i.e., his statue – does not know (since she *cannot* know) about his love, either?

Imagination is a fundamental point of connection between the two artists, Genius and Pygmalion; it is also a fundamental element for the courtly poet's work. In his study on medieval imagination, Douglas Kelly argues that "Imagination is a fundamental feature of the conception of art prevalent from the twelfth to the fifteenth century. It is particularly striking in dealing with courtly love."[65] Imagination is a mental faculty: "It governs invention, retention, and expression of Images in the mind; it also designates the artist's Image, projected as it were into matter" (xii). In reference to the *Confessio*, Kelly affirms that "[its] structure and argument are based on the use of Imagination in all its usual senses . . . The principle of Imagination thus relies on memory as a source of exemplary Images suitable to argument" (200). In the *Confessio Amantis*, the narrator, Genius, uses imagination to draw those exemplary images.[66]

In using the faculty of imagination to do his work, Gower's Genius responds to a long tradition that precedes him. This tradition conceives of imagination as a part, not only of the poetic process of creation, but also of the experience of love. The theme of imagination, as Wetherbee has shown, was adopted by twelfth-century poets who saw in the experience of love "an essential coherence, an integrity and harmony which are represented as

---

[65] Douglas Kelly, *Medieval Imagination: Rhetoric and the Poetry of Courtly Love* (Madison: U of Wisconsin P, 1978) xv.
[66] Olsson, *John Gower and the Structures of Conversion*, has similarly pointed out that Genius "relies chiefly on imagination to do his work" (139).

potentially accessible through the fulfillment of human love, or as symbolized by it."[67] Thus, the imagination, so important in courtly poetry, cannot be dissociated from the imagination of courtly love. Or as Kelly puts it, in courtly literature there is "[a] constant union of art of love and art of poetry" (xi).

This synthesis between courtly poetry and sexuality is apparent in Alain de Lille's *De planctu naturae* and also in Gower's Genius. It points, moreover, to the discursive construction of sexuality. According to Wetherbee, in *De planctu* "[Alain] preserv[es] the formal integrity of the lyric of *fin amor* while integrating it with the natural order" (58). In Alain's work the figure of Genius, one of the predecessors of Gower's own Genius, is meant to represent such a synthesis. Traditionally, Wetherbee continues, Genius is a tutelary spirit responsible for instilling in each soul an instinct toward the good, as well as "a creative principle, responsible for uniting matter to form and ensuring that the resulting creature expresses its proper nature" (57). We should ask, though, in the light of Foucault, whether the creature's "proper nature" is not in fact created by Genius, the "creative principle." Significantly, in *De planctu*, Genius is not only a creative principle in the sexual sense. He is also a creative principle in a literary sense: "Genius's posture is that of a lyric poet, his yearning constrained by sin but capable of lyric expression" (58). He thus represents the union of the art of love and the art of poetry. Like his predecessor, Alain's Genius, Gower's own Genius represents this union, and both love and poetry are closely linked with courtly culture and the concept of *fin' amors*. Both the manifestation of *fin' amors* in courtly poetry and *fin' amors* itself, that is, courtly love, share the imagination as an essential faculty.

To give expression to the imagination, moreover, the courtly poet, like the courtly lover, uses words, the poetic discourse. Thus the "proper nature" expressed by Genius's creation cannot be dissociated from Genius's own discourse. In his "Pygmaleon and the Statue," Genius shows that words are more powerful and creative than the art of sculpting itself. Pygmalion and Genius are not just parallel figures with similar powers, one as sculptor, the other one as literary author. Genius suggests that those who work with words have a more radical creative power than those who work with solid matter. Indeed, for his Pygmalion words are the fundamental tool he uses to obtain his desire.[68] While the ivory upon which Pygmalion sculptures his future wife

---

[67] Wetherbee, "The Theme of Imagination in Medieval Poetry and the Allegorical Figure 'Genius' " 50.

[68] Although I agree with his analysis of the significance of 'information' in the *Confessio* and in Genius's version of the story of Pygmalion, Simpson, *Sciences and the Self*, interprets the tale and the importance of imagination differently than I do. Simpson analyzes "imagination" as an integrative, albeit potentially misleading faculty, that helps Amans in his education. In this sense, he sees the story of Pygmalion as an example of "imagination" misleading Amans: "Amans is being encouraged to move from an irascible to a courageously desirous attention to images; in neither case is he moving beyond the (limited) powers of the

constitutes his raw material, it is his words (the prayers he makes "Fro dai to nyht," 417) that effect the desired transformation. These words even acquire something like the materiality of the ivory Pygmalion literally sculpts, when Genius remarks that the sculptor won what he prayed for, because "he hath his word travailed" (428). Working on his words, Pygmalion finally obtains what he desires. Genius's moral to the tale – "That word mai worche above kinde," 438 – emphasizes this point. The word, like the sculpture, is a form of art, but, rather than the art of sculpture, it is the art of the word that acquires the power to "worche above kinde." Similarly, the stories handed down from tradition are Genius's raw material; his own reworking of those words gives expression (gives shape) to his view of those stories. Genius's insistence on Pygmalion's use of words emphasizes the greater power of words and, hence, the links between the two artists as producers of discourse, and thus producers of reality.

There is something particularly striking about "Pygmaleon and the Statue" that serves to emphasize the centrality of discourse. By contrast with Ovid's and Jean de Meun's versions, Genius's lacks any public context; Pygmalion is always in his private study. Neither Ovid's nor Jean de Meun's versions isolate the sculptor from society as much as does Genius. In the *Metamorphoses* seeing the Propoetides is what makes Pygmalion turn away from women (244–45), and when he falls in love with his statue, he participates in the religious life of his community by celebrating the festival of Venus. It is during those festivals that he asks the goddess for help. Similarly, although in Jean de Meun's version there is no reference to the Propoetides, his Pygmalion also participates in the festival of Venus. In contrast, Genius's Pygmalion never goes out, and the social community in which Ovid's Pygmalion lives is not even mentioned. He carves his statue, falls in love, and prays to Venus in his own private home. He is thus represented as a self-sufficient artist, independent from his society. Genius's version, unlike his adaptations of other classical stories, is not turned into an explicitly political story. Pygmalion's desires are fulfilled within his own private world and, unlike other tales, this tale never questions the character's seclusion and separation from the public sphere. Pygmalion creates and lives in his own world.

Genius's identification with Pygmalion, I argue, is one of the reasons he is blind to the structures of authority and the incestuous implications involved in artistic creation. The second crucial reason for his oversight is that, as a kind of father to his tales, he himself is implicated in the relations of power that he tries to delimit in other tales, and, therefore, he himself is bound to transgress those limits. Indeed, as this book argues, and as Genius's story of Pygmalion shows, the power of the authority figure is difficult to delimit because the transgression of boundaries is inherent to the definition of the

---

imagination" (263). I am more interested here in the ways in which the tale suggests the complex and problematic parallel between Pygmalion and Genius as creators and fathers.

authority of the father. As creative principle, Genius is a kind of father-figure of his creation, the tales, which he tries to use to fit his own vision and represent his will and his meaning unequivocally. He would like his tales to mirror his vision as the statue mirrors Pygmalion's desire.

Like Pygmalion, moreover, Genius imagines his creation not only as his offspring but as his female offspring. This female offspring plays a fundamental role in affirming and even constructing the father's masculinity. The law of exogamy necessitates a passive woman who is exchanged and two active men who do the exchanging. An underlying claim in the third chapter of this book is that the "Tale of Albinus and Rosemund" and the "Tale of the False Bachelor" point to the interchangeability of father and son-in-law. The same incestuous side surfaces also in "Pygmaleon and the Statue," but this tale takes this similarity even further. The sculptor falls in love with the image of a woman that he himself has created. Hence, he is a father who, in marrying his daughter, becomes his own son-in-law.

In these three tales, moreover, the father and the husband, who are the same in the case of Pygmalion, exert absolute power over the woman so that she is limited to mirroring the man's desires. The women in the tales become the men's own creations, absolutely ruled by their will. More crucially, their major role is to prove the man's masculinity. In agreeing to marry the young knight, the sultan's daughter submits completely to her father's will in the "Tale of the False Bachelor." Both in this tale and in the "Tale of Albinus and Rosemund," the woman is a passive mirror of the man's desire. Whether she is a daughter or a wife does not make a significant difference. She is there as a necessary foil that proves the man's masculinity. In "Pygmaleon and the Statue," the woman plays a similar role. Let me cite again lines 389–93:

> ... thurgh pure impression
> Of his ymaginacion
> With al the herte of his corage
> His love upon this faire ymage
> He sette ...

Once the statue, or Pygmalion's "ymaginacion," is turned into a woman, she is completely obedient to her male creator. According to Genius, by enacting his manhood ("with al the herte of his corage"), Pygmalion "wan a lusti wif, / Which obeissant was at his wille" (424–25). Genius's remark on her obedience "at his wille" reminds us of the sultan's daughter's complete submission. Pygmalion creates a compliant daughter who also mirrors his desire. The construction of Pygmalion's masculine identity is thus defined in opposition to the feminine, and, even though Pygmalion is not a knight, his approach to love is defined in terms similar to those used for knightly deeds and battles. In the section on pusillanimity that serves to introduce the story of Pygmalion, Genius states that he who is pusillanimous "lacketh bothe word and dede" (322), and "He woll no *manhed* understonde, / For evere he hath drede upon honde: / Al is peril that he schal seie" (325–27 [my emphasis]). The pusillanimous lack "manhed"; and they do not act because they are fearful: they "lacken herte, whan best were / To speke of love, and riht for fere / Thei wexen doumb and dar noght telle" (343–45). (On two other occasions in this section, Genius relates pusillanimity to lack of "herte" or courage [in ll.335 and 349].) To construct their masculinity, Genius's tales imply, men need to construct their creation in gendered terms as passive women. Similarly, male authors' construction of the text as feminine enables them to construct *and* enact their masculinity. Because, as I argued in Chapter Three, the construction of a knight's gender identity depends on the performance of knightly/"masculine" acts, the author, who does not perform knightly deeds, depends on the construction of the text as feminine and on the repetition of masculine acts of control over the text to assert and perform his masculine identity. Genius's identification with Pygmalion, as well as his assertion of authority over Rosiphelee and Jephthah's daughter, reinscribe him as the father/author of his creation.

If Genius is implicated in these relations of power, a question immediately arises: what about Gower? Gower is also implicated in these relations of power; he also sees himself as a fatherly author who desires to control the text. However, I would argue that Genius's role as authority and literary father to the female text enables Gower to examine his own desire to control the text, rather than merely to replicate it. Gower does so by preventing us from identifying him with Genius or any other authoritative voice in the poem. At the beginning of this analysis, I mentioned that critics of the *Roman* generally agree on the importance of Jean's exploration of authorship in the poem. There is great disagreement, though, on the question of where to locate Jean's voice. Is Reason his mouthpiece? Is it the lover? Are we to take their speeches in a straightforward manner? Is Jean being ironic all along? Although he puts this point somewhat differently, Eric Steinle has argued that Jean's voice is to be found everywhere and nowhere, that Jean is interested not so much in one voice but in the contrast among many voices.[69] I argue that Gower's *Confessio* similarly refuses to identify a single authorial voice. Gower's voice is to be located everywhere and nowhere: in Genius, in Amans, in the Latin glosses, in the spaces opened up by the contradictions in Genius's teachings, *and* in none of them. This constant interplay of authoritative voices enables Gower to ask questions about authority. Through the myth of Pygmalion, moreover, both Jean and Gower suggest why they refuse to impose a single authorial voice on their poems. The incestuous connotations in their versions of the myth hint at their ambivalence, even anxiety, towards their own of authority. These connotations remind us that the notion that a work of art will mirror its author's desire, the author's fantasy of

---

[69] Eric M. Steinle, "Versions of Authority in the *Roman de la Rose*: Remarks on the Use of Ovid's *Metamorphoses* by Guillaume de Lorris and Jean de Meun," *Mediaevalia* 13 (1987): 202.

absolute control over its meaning, is, ultimately, a problematic, even if irresistible, Pygmalionesque fantasy.

More crucially, Gower's suggestions about the Pygmalionesque character of the author's power need to be understood in the context of his examination of father-daughter incest. It is as part of his larger exploration of the incest taboo that Gower's version of the story of Pygmalion acquires different implications than Ovid's or Jean de Meun's. My argument throughout this book has been that Gower is interested in the incest taboo as a foundational and originary law at the core of patriarchal society. As foundational and originary, this law has productive power – what Butler has called "the generativity of the taboo."[70] At one point, Butler asks, "[c]an the prohibition against incest that proscribes and sanctions hierarchical and binary gendered positions be reconceived as a productive power that inadvertently generates several cultural configurations of gender?" (72). Through a theoretical argumentation, but without providing specific examples, Butler answers this question in the affirmative. This book has shown that Gower analyzes specific instances of cultural patterns as patterns generated by the incest taboo. His exploration of the theme of incest, specifically of father-daughter incest, enables him to arrive at profound insights with regard to the gendered character of familial, political, and textual relationships of authority because the law of exogamy that prohibits incest between father and daughter is a fundamental and originary law, at the core of patriarchal society, which articulates those other relationships of authority.

The fact that Genius condemns father-daughter incest and also shows a great concern with delimiting the father's power over his daughter in other tales, and yet does not seem concerned with the incestuous implications of Pygmalion's power, does not ultimately represent so much a contradiction, but rather indicates that the transgression of boundaries is inherent to the patriarchal system and the law of exogamy. The law at the same time forbids and produces the father's desire for the daughter. Pygmalion's discursive power, that is, his ability to produce his own reality, his object of desire, through the power of discourse stands for patriarchy's power to create its own reality, hence, to create its own obedient daughters. In the *Confessio Amantis* even as he is concerned with delimiting patriarchal authority in the familial, political, and textual realms, Gower also recognizes the inherent transgressive nature of such authority.

---

[70] Butler, *Gender Trouble* 76.

BIBLIOGRAPHY

PRIMARY SOURCES

Alanus de Insulis. *De planctu naturae.* Ed. Nikolaus Häring. *Studi medievali* 3rd ser. 19 (1978): 797–879.

———. *The Plaint of Nature.* Trans. James J. Sheridan. Toronto: Pontifical Institute of Mediaeval Studies, 1980.

Apollonius of Tyre: Medieval and Renaissance Themes and Variations. Ed. and trans. Elizabeth Archibald. Cambridge: D. S. Brewer, 1991.

Aquinas, Thomas. *Summa Theologiae.* 5 vols. Biblioteca de Autores Cristianos 77, 80, 81, 83, 87. Madrid: Editorial Católica, 1955–58.

———. *The Summa Theologica of Saint Thomas Aquinas.* Trans. Fathers of the English Dominican Province. 3 vols. New York: Benziger Brothers, 1947–48.

Augustine. *The City of God.* Ed. and trans. Philip Levine. Vol. 4. Cambridge: Harvard UP, 1966.

Berchorius, Petrus. *Ovidius moralizatus.* Ed. J. Engels. Utrecht: Institut voor Laat Latijn der Rijksuniversiteit, 1962.

———. "The *Ovidius moralizatus*: An Introduction and Translation." Trans. William Donald Reynolds. Diss. U of Illinois at Urbana-Champaign, 1971.

Biblia sacra iuxta vulgatam versionem. Ed. Robert Gryson. Stuttgart: Deutsche Bibelgesellschaft, 1994.

Boccaccio, Giovanni. *Decameron.* Trans. G. H. McWilliam. Harmondsworth: Penguin, 1984.

The Book of Vices and Virtues: A Fourteenth-Century English Translation of the Somme le Roi of Lorens d'Orléans. Ed. W. Nelson Francis. Early English Text Society, o.s. 217. London: Oxford UP, 1942.

Bryan, W. F., and Germaine Dempster, eds. *Sources and Analogues of Chaucer's Canterbury Tales.* Chicago: U of Chicago P, 1941.

Capellanus, Andreas. *Andreas Capellanus on Love.* Ed. and trans. P. G. Walsh. London: Duckworth, 1982.

Chaucer, Geoffrey. *The Riverside Chaucer.* Ed. L. D. Benson. Boston: Houghton Mifflin, 1987.

Chronicles of the Revolution, 1397–1400: The Reign of Richard II. Ed. and trans. Chris Given-Wilson. Manchester: Manchester UP, 1993.

Fasciculus Morum: A Fourteenth-Century Preacher's Handbook. Ed. and trans. Siegfried Wenzel. University Park, PA: Pennsylvania State UP, 1989.

Genet, Jean-Philippe, ed. *Four English Political Tracts of the Later Middle Ages.* Camden Fourth Series 18. London: Royal Historical Society, 1977.

Godfrey of Viterbo. *Pantheon. Monumenta Germaniae Historica*. Vol. 22. Ed. Georgius Heinricus Pertz. Hannoverae: Impensis Bibliopolii Aulici Hahniani, 1872.

Gower, John. *The Complete Works of John Gower*. Ed. G. C. Macaulay. 4 vols. Oxford: Clarendon, 1899–1902.

———. *The English Works of John Gower*. Ed. G. C. Macaulay. EETS, e.s. 81–82. Oxford: Clarendon, 1900–1901.

———. *John Gower: Mirour de l'Omme (The Mirror of Mankind)*. Trans. William Burton Wilson. East Lansing, MI: East Lansing Colleagues Press, 1992.

———. *The Latin Verses in the* Confessio Amantis: *An Annotated Translation*. Ed. and trans. Siân Echard and Claire Fanger. East Lansing, MI: East Lansing Colleagues Press, 1991.

———. *The Major Latin Works of John Gower*. Trans. Eric W. Stockton. Seattle: U of Washington P, 1962.

Jerome, Saint. *The Letters of St. Jerome*. Trans. Charles Christopher Mierow. Westminster, MD: The Newman Press, 1963.

"Le Lay du Trot." Ed. Margaret Grimes. *The Romanic Review* 26 (1935): 313–21.

Livy, Titus. *The Early History of Rome*. Trans. Aubrey de Sélincourt. Middlesex: Penguin, 1960.

Lorris, Guillaume de, and Jean de Meun. *Le Roman de la Rose*. Ed. and trans. Armand Strubel. Paris: Librairie Générale Française, 1992.

Lydgate, John. *The Fall of Princes*. Ed. Henry Bergen. 4 vols. EETS, e.s. 121–24. Oxford: Oxford UP, 1924–27.

Lyra, Nicholas de. *Biblia sacra cum glossis, interlineari, et ordinaria*. 6 vols. Venice, 1588.

Mannyng, Robert. *Handlyng Synne*. Ed. Frederick J. Furnivall. EETS, o.s. 119, 123. Oxford: Oxford UP, 1901, 1903.

Manuale et processionale ad usum insignis ecclesiae Eboracensis. Ed. W. G. Henderson. Publications of the Surtees Society 63. Durham: Andrews, 1875.

Medieval English Lyrics: A Critical Anthology. Ed. R. T. Davies. Chicago: Northwestern UP, 1964.

Ovid. *Heroides and Amores*. Ed. and trans. Grant Showerman. London: William Heinemann, 1925.

———. *Metamorphoses*. Trans. Mary M. Innes. Oxford: Penguin, 1955.

———. *Metamorphoses*. Ed. William S. Anderson. 2 vols. Leipzig: Teubner Verlagsgesellschaft, 1977.

Ovide moralisé: Poème du commencement du quatorzième siècle. Ed. C. de Boer. 5 vols. Verhandelingen der koninklijke nederlandse akademie van wetenschappen, afdeeling letterkunde 15, 21, 30.3, 37, 43. Amsterdam: J. Müller, 1915–38.

Paulus Diaconus. *Historia Langobardorum*. Ed. G. Waitz. Scriptores Rerum Germanicarum. Hannoverae: Impensis Bibliopolii Hahniani, 1878.

———. *History of the Langoboards.* Trans. William Dudley Foulke. Philadelphia: U of Pennsylvania P, 1907.
Pearl. Ed. E. V. Gordon. Oxford: Clarendon Press, 1953.
Prudentius. *Psychomachia. Aurelii Prudentii Clementis Carmina.* Ed. Johan Bergman. Corpus Scriptorum Ecclesiasticorum Latinorum 61. Vindobonae: Hoelder-Pichler-Tempsky, 1926.
Le Roman de Marques de Rome. Ed. Johann Alton. Tübingen: Bibliothek des Literarischen Vereins, 1889.
Stow, George B., ed. *Historia Vitae et Regni Ricardi Secundi.* Philadelphia: U of Pennsylvania P, 1977.
Trivet, Nicolas. "The Life of Constance." Trans. Edmund Brock. *Originals and Analogues of Some of Chaucer's* Canterbury Tales. Eds. F. J. Furnivall, Edmund Brock, and W. A. Clouston. Chaucer Society Publications 22. London: N. Trübner, 1872.
Trivet's Life of Constance. Ed. Margaret Schlauch in Bryan and Dempster 165–81.
Walsingham, Thomas. *Historia Anglicana.* Ed. Henry Thomas Riley. 2 vols. London: Longman, 1864.

SECONDARY SOURCES

Aers, David, ed. "Masculine Identity in the Courtly Community: The Self Loving in *Troilus and Criseyde.*" *Community, Gender and Individual Identity: English Writing, 1360–1430.* Ed. David Aers. London: Routledge, 1988. 117–52.
———. "A Whisper in the Ear of Early Modernists; or, Reflections on Literary Critics Writing the 'History of the Subject.' " *Culture and History, 1350–1600: Essays on English Communities, Identities and Writing.* Ed. David Aers. Detroit: Wayne State UP, 1992. 177–202.
Alexiou, Margaret, and Peter Dronke. "The Lament of Jephthah's Daughter: Themes, Traditions, Originality." *Studi Medievali* 3rd ser. 12 (1971): 819–63.
Allen, Elizabeth. "Chaucer Answers Gower: Constance and the Trouble with Reading." *English Literary History* 63 (1997): 627–55.
Archibald, Elizabeth. "Fathers and Kings in Apollonius of Tyre." *Images of Authority.* Eds. Mary Margaret Mackenzie and Charlotte Roueché. Cambridge: Cambridge Philological Society, 1989. 24–40.
———. "The Flight from Incest: Two Late Classical Precursors of the Constance Theme." *Chaucer Review* 20 (1986): 259–72.
———. "Incest in Medieval Literature and Society." *Forum for Modern Language Studies* 25 (1989): 1–15.
Arens, W. *The Original Sin: Incest and Its Meaning.* New York: Oxford UP, 1986.
Astell, Ann W. *The Song of Songs in the Middle Ages.* Ithaca, NY: Cornell UP, 1990.

BIBLIOGRAPHY

Atkinson, Clarissa, W. *The Oldest Vocation: Christian Motherhood in the Middle Ages*. Ithaca, NY: Cornell UP, 1991.

Baker, Denise N. "The Priesthood of Genius: A Study in Medieval Tradition." *Speculum* 51 (1976): 277–91.

Barnie, John. *War in Medieval English Society: Social Values in the Hundred Years War, 1337–99*. Ithaca, NY: Cornell UP, 1974.

Batchelor, Patricia. "Feigned Truth and Exemplary Method in the *Confessio Amantis*." Yeager, *Re-Visioning Gower* 1–15.

Beidler, Peter G., ed. *John Gower's Literary Transformations in the* Confessio Amantis: *Original Articles and Translations*. Washington: UP of America, 1982.

Bennett, J. A. W. "Gower's 'Honeste Love.'" *Patterns of Love and Courtesy: Essays in Honor of C. S. Lewis*. Ed. John Lawlor. London: Edward Arnold, 1966. 107–21.

Bennett, Judith M. "Public Power and Authority in the Medieval English Countryside." *Women and Power in the Middle Ages*. Eds. Mary Erler and Maryanne Kowaleski. Athens: U of Georgia P, 1988. 18–36.

Benson, C. David. "Incest and Moral Poetry in Gower's *Confessio Amantis*." *Chaucer Review* 19 (1984): 100–109.

Benson, Larry D. "The Occasion of the *Parliament of Fowls*." *The Wisdom of Poetry: Essays in Early English Literature in Honor of Morton W. Bloomfield*. Eds. Larry D. Benson and Siegfried Wenzel. Kalamazoo: Institute for Medieval Studies, 1982. 123–44.

Bloch, Howard. "Chaucer's Maiden's Head: 'The Physician's Tale' and the Poetics of Virginity." *Representations* 28 (1989): 113–34.

———. *Etymologies and Genealogies: A Literary Anthropology of the French Middle Ages*. Chicago: U of Chicago P, 1983.

———. *Medieval French Literature and the Law*. Berkeley: U of California P, 1973.

———. *Medieval Misogyny and the Invention of Western Romantic Love*. Chicago: U of Chicago P, 1991.

Bloomfield, Morton W. "The Man of Law's Tale: A Tragedy of Victimization and a Christian Comedy." *Publications of the Modern Language Association of America* 87 (1972): 384–90.

Blythe, James M. *Ideal Government and the Mixed Constitution in the Middle Ages*. Princeton: Princeton UP, 1992.

Boase, R. *The Origin and Meaning of Courtly Love*. Manchester: Manchester UP, 1977.

Boehrer, Bruce Thomas. *Monarchy and Incest in Renaissance England: Literature, Culture, Kinship, and Kingship*. Philadelphia: U of Pennsylvania P, 1992.

Boose, Lynda E. "The Father and the Bride in Shakespeare." *PMLA* 97 (1982): 325–47.

———. "The Father's House and the Daughter in It: The Structures of Western Culture's Daughter-Father Relationships." Boose and Flowers 19–74.

Boose, Lynda E., and Betty S. Flowers, eds. *Daughters & Fathers*. Baltimore: Johns Hopkins UP, 1989.

Boswell, John. *Christianity, Social Tolerance and Homosexuality: Gay People in Western Europe from the Beginning of the Christian Era to the Fourteenth Century*. Chicago: U of Chicago P, 1980.

Brewster, Paul G. *The Incest Theme in Folksong*. Helsinki: Sudmalainen Tiedeakatemia, 1972.

Brooke, Christopher N. L. *The Medieval Idea of Marriage*. Oxford: Oxford UP, 1989.

Brown, Cheryl Anne. *No Longer Be Silent: First Century Jewish Portraits of Biblical Women*. Louisville, KY: Westminster/John Knox Press, 1992.

Brown, Emerson, Jr. "What is Chaucer Doing With the Physician and His Tale?" *Philological Quarterly* 60 (1981): 129–49.

Brownlee, Kevin. "Orpheus' Song Re-Sung: Jean de Meun's Reworking of *Metamorphoses*, X." *Romance Philology* 36 (1982): 201–09.

Brundage, James A. *Law, Sex, and Christian Society in Medieval Europe*. Chicago: U of Chicago P, 1987.

Bueler, Lois. "The Structural Uses of Incest in English Renaissance Drama." *Renaissance Drama* 15 (1984): 115–45.

Bullón-Fernández, María. "Confining the Daughter: Gower's 'Tale of Canace and Machaire' and the Politics of the Body." *Essays in Medieval Studies* 11 (1994): 75–85. 24 June 1999 <http://www.luc.edu/publications/medieval/vol11/bullon.html>

———. "Engendering Authority: Father and Daughter, State and Church in Gower's 'Tale of Constance' and Chaucer's 'Man of Law's Tale.'" Yeager, *Re-Visioning Gower* 129–46.

Bullough, Vern, and James Brundage. *Sexual Practices and the Medieval Church*. Buffalo: Prometheus Books, 1982.

Burke, Linda Barney. "Women in John Gower's *Confessio Amantis*." *Medievalia* 3 (1977): 239–59.

———. "Women in the Medieval Manuals of Religious Instruction and John Gower's *Confessio Amantis*." Diss. Columbia U, 1982.

Burrow, John A. *Ricardian Poetry: Chaucer, Gower, Langland, and the Gawain Poet*. London: Routledge & Kegan Paul, 1971.

Burton, Roger V. "Folk Theory and the Incest Taboo." *Ethos* 1 (1973): 504–16.

Butler, Judith. *Bodies that Matter: On the Discursive Limits of "Sex."* New York: Routledge, 1993.

———. *Gender Trouble: Feminism and the Subversion of Identity*. New York: Routledge, 1990.

Camille, Michael. "The Book as Flesh and Fetish in Richard de Bury's *Philobiblon*." Frese and O'Brien O'Keefe 34–77.

Carruthers, Mary. "Reading with Attitude, Remembering the Book." Frese and O'Brien O'Keefe 1–33.

Casey, Kathleen. "The Cheshire Cat: Reconstructing the Experience of

Medieval Women." *Liberating Women's History: Theoretical and Critical Essays*. Ed. Berenice A. Carrole. Urbana: U of Illinois P, 1976. 224–49.

Cesarano, S. P., and Marion Wynne-Davies, eds. *Gloriana's Face: Women, Public and Private in the English Renaissance*. Hertfordshire: Harvester Wheatsheaf, 1992.

Chiarini, G. "Esogamia e incesto nella Historia Apollonii." *Materiali e Discusioni per l' Analisi dei Testi Clasici*. 10–11 (1983): 267–92.

Ciletti, Elena. "Patriarchal Ideology in the Renaissance Iconography of Judith." *Refiguring Woman: Perspectives on Gender and the Italian Renaissance*. Eds. Marilyn Migiel and Juliana Schiesari. Ithaca, NY: Cornell UP, 1991. 35–70.

Cixous, Hélène. "The Laugh of the Medusa." *Signs* 1 (1976): 875–93.

Cleveland, Arthur. "Indictments for Adultery and Incest Before 1650." *Law Quarterly Review* 29 (1913): 57–60.

Coffman, George R. "John Gower in His Most Significant Role." *Elizabethan Studies and Other Essays in Honor of G. F. Reynolds*. University of Colorado Studies, ser. B, 2.4. Boulder: U of Colorado P, 1945. 52–61.

———. "John Gower, Mentor for Royalty: Richard II." *PMLA* 69 (1954): 953–64.

Copeland, Rita. *Rhetoric, Hermeneutics, and Translation in the Middle Ages: Academic Traditions and Vernacular Texts*. Cambridge: Cambridge UP, 1991.

Cormier, Bruno, et al. "Psychodynamics of Father-Daughter Incest." *Canadian Psychiatric Association Journal* 7 (1962): 203–17.

Cottle, Basil. *The Triumph of English, 1350–1400*. London: Blandford, 1969.

Crane, Susan. *Gender and Romance in Chaucer's* Canterbury Tales. Princeton: Princeton UP, 1994.

Curran, Leo C. " Rape and Rape Victims in the *Metamorphoses*." *Arethusa* 11 (1978): 213–41.

Curtius, Ernst. *European Literature and the Latin Middle Ages*. Trans. Willard R. Trask. Princeton: Princeton UP, 1973.

Dean, Ruth. "Nicholas Trevet, Historian." *Medieval Learning and Literature: Essays Presented to Richard William Hunt*. Eds. J. J. G. Alexander and M. T. Gibson. Oxford: Oxford UP, 1976. 328–52.

DeJean, Joan. *Fictions of Sappho, 1546–1937*. Chicago: U of Chicago P, 1989.

Delany, Sheila. *Writing Woman: Women Writers and Women in Literature, Medieval to Modern*. New York: Schocken Books, 1983.

Derrida, Jacques. *Of Grammatology*. Trans. G. C. Spivak. Baltimore: Johns Hopkins UP, 1976.

Dinshaw, Carolyn. *Chaucer's Sexual Poetics*. Madison: U of Wisconsin P, 1989.

———. "Gower's Captive Women." John Gower Society Panel. 24th International Congress on Medieval Studies. Western Michigan University, Kalamazoo. 6 May 1989.

———. "A Kiss Is Just a Kiss: Heterosexuality and Its Consolations in *Sir Gawain and the Green Knight*." *Diacritics* 24 (1994): 205–26.

———. "Straight is the Gate: The Heterosexual Subject of Middle English Literature." Middle English Literature Div. MLA Convention. New York. 28 Dec. 1992.

Dinter, Annegret. *Der Pygmalion-Stoff in der europäischen Literatur*. Heidelberg: Carl Winter Universitätsverlag, 1979.

Donahue, Charles, Jr. "The Canon Law on the Formation of Marriage and Social Practice in the Later Middle Ages." *Journal of Family History* 8 (1983): 144–58.

Donavin, Georgiana. *Incest Narratives and the Structure of Gower's* Confessio Amantis. English Literary Studies 56. Victoria: U of Victoria, 1993.

Duby, Georges, ed. *A History of Private Life: Revelations of the Medieval World*. Trans. Arthur Goldhammer. Vol. 2. Cambridge, MA: The Bellknap Press of Harvard UP, 1988.

———. *The Knight, the Lady and the Priest: The Making of Modern Marriage in Medieval France*. Trans. Barbara Bray. New York: Pantheon Books, 1983.

———. *Medieval Marriage: Two Models from Twelfth-Century France*. Trans. Elborg Forster. Baltimore: John Hopkins UP, 1978.

Durkheim, Emile. *Incest: The Nature and Origin of the Taboo*. Trans. Edward Sagarin. New York: L. Stuart, 1963.

Eberle, Patricia J. "The Question of Authority and The Man of Law's Tale." *The Centre and Its Compass: Studies in Medieval Literature in Honor of Professor John Leyerle*. Eds. Robert A. Taylor, et al. Studies in Medieval Culture 33. Kalamazoo: Medieval Institute Publications, 1993. 111–49.

Echard, Siân. "With Carmen's Help: Latin Authorities in the *Confessio Amantis*." *Studies in Philology* 95 (1998): 1–40.

———. "Glossing Gower: In Latin, in English, and *in absentia*: The Case of Bodleian Ashmole 35." Yeager, *Re-Visioning Gower* 237–56.

Economou, George D. "The Character Genius in Alan de Lille, Jean de Meun, and John Gower." *Chaucer Review* 4 (1970): 203–10.

———. *The Goddess Natura in Medieval Literature*. Cambridge: Harvard UP, 1972.

Elshtain, Jean Bethke. *Public Man, Private Woman: Women in Social and Political Thought*. Princeton: Princeton UP, 1981.

Encyclopedia Judaica Year Book. Vol. 9. New York: MacMillan, 1971.

Engels, Friedrich. *The Origin of the Family, Private Property, and the State*. Ed. and trans. Eleanor Leacock. New York: International Publishers, 1972.

Enright, Michael J. "King James and His Island: An Archaic Kingship Belief?" *Scottish Historical Review* 55 (1976): 29–40.

Esch, Arno. "John Gower's Narrative Art." Trans. Linda Barney Burke. Nicholson, *Gower's Confessio Amantis* 81–108.

Evans, Ruth, and Lesley Johnson. *Feminist Readings in Middle English Literature: The Wife of Bath and All Her Sect*. London: Routledge, 1994.

Fansler, Dean S. *Chaucer and the Roman de la Rose*. New York: Columbia UP, 1914.

Farrell, Thomas J. "Privacy and the Boundaries of the Fabliau in 'The Miller's Tale.'" *ELH* 56 (1989): 773–95.
Federico, Sylvia. "A Fourteenth-Century Erotics of Politics: London as a Feminine New Troy." *Studies in the Age of Chaucer* 19 (1997): 121–55.
Fehrenbacher, Richard. "'Al that which chargeth nought to seye': The Theme of Incest in *Troilus and Criseyde*." *Exemplaria* 9 (1997): 341–69.
Ferguson, Margaret W., Maureen Quilligan, and Nancy J. Vickers, eds. *Rewriting the Renaissance: The Discourses of Sexual Difference in Early Modern Europe*. Chicago: U of Chicago P, 1986.
Ferrante, Joan M. "Male Fantasy and Female Reality in Courtly Literature." *Women's Studies* 11 (1984): 67–97.
Ferrante, Joan M., and George D. Economou. *In Pursuit of Perfection: Courtly Love in Medieval Literature*. Port Washington, NY: Kennikat Press, 1975.
Ferster, Judith. *Fictions of Advice: The Literature and Politics of Counsel in Late Medieval England*. Philadelphia: U of Pennsylvania P, 1996.
——. "O Political Gower." *Medievalia* 16 (1993 [for 1990]): 33–53.
Fisher, John H. *John Gower: Moral Philosopher and Friend of Chaucer*. New York: New York UP, 1964.
Foucault, Michel. *The History of Sexuality: An Introduction*. Vol. 1. Trans. Robert Hurley. New York: Vintage Books, 1990.
Fowler, John Howard. "The Development of Incest Regulations in the Early Middle Ages: Family, Nurturance, and Aggression in the Making of the Medieval West." Diss. Rice U, 1981.
Fox, Robin. *Kinship and Marriage*. Cambridge: Cambridge UP, 1983.
——. *The Red Lamp of Incest*. New York: E. P. Dutton, 1980.
Fradenburg, Louise Olga. *City, Marriage, Tournament: Arts of Rule in Late Medieval Scotland*. Madison: U of Wisconsin P, 1991.
Frese, Dolores Warwick, and Katherine O'Brien O'Keefe, eds. *The Book and the Body*. Notre Dame, IN: U of Notre Dame P, 1997.
Freud, Sigmund. "Mourning and Melancholia." *The Standard Edition of the Complete Psychological Works of Sigmund Freud*. Ed. and trans. James Strachey. Vol. 14. London: Hogarth Press, 1957. 243–58.
——. "The Theme of the Three Caskets." *The Standard Edition of the Complete Psychological Works of Sigmund Freud*. Ed. and trans. James Strachey. Vol. 12. London: Hogarth Press, 1958. 289–301.
——. *Totem and Taboo*. *The Standard Edition of the Complete Psychological Works of Sigmund Freud*. Ed. and trans. James Strachey. 2nd ed. Vol. 13. 1955. Reprint, London: Hogarth Press, 1957. xiii–xv, 1–161.
Gadjnek, R. E. "Death, Incest, and the Triple Bond in the Later Plays of Shakespeare." *American Image: A Psychoanalytic Journal for Culture, Science, and the Arts* 31 (1974): 109–58.
Gallacher, Patrick J. *Love, the Word, and Mercury: A Reading of John Gower's Confessio Amantis*. Albuquerque: U of New Mexico P, 1975.
Gallop, Jane. *The Daughter's Seduction: Feminism and Psychoanalysis*. Ithaca, NY: Cornell UP, 1982.

Gilbert, Sandra, and Susan Gubar. *The Madwoman in the Attic: The Woman Writer and the Nineteenth-Century Literary Imagination*. New Haven: Yale UP, 1979.

Given, James. *State and Society in Medieval Europe: Gwynedd and Languedoc under Outside Rule*. Ithaca, NY: Cornell UP, 1990.

Given-Wilson, Chris. *Chronicles of the Revolution: 1397–1400*. Manchester: Manchester UP, 1993.

———. *The English Nobility in the Late Middle Ages: The Fourteenth-Century Political Community*. London: Routledge & Kegan Paul, 1987.

———. *The Royal Household and the King's Affinity: Service, Politics and Finance in England 1360–1413*. New Haven: Yale UP, 1986.

Goepp, P. H. "The Narrative Material of *Apollonius of Tyre*." *ELH* 5 (1938): 150–72.

Goldberg, Jonathan. "Fatherly Authority: The Politics of Stuart Family Images." Ferguson, Quilligan, and Vickers 3–32.

Goodall, Peter. "John Gower's *Apollonius of Tyre: Confessio Amantis*, Book VIII." *Southern Review* 15 (1982): 243–53.

———. " 'Unkynde Abhomynaciouns' in Chaucer and Gower." *Parergon* n.s. 5 (1987): 94–102.

Goody, Jack. *The Development of the Family and Marriage in Europe*. Cambridge: Cambridge UP, 1983.

Gravdal, Kathryn. *Ravishing Maidens: Writing Rape in Medieval French Literature and Law*. Philadelphia: U of Pennsylvania P, 1991.

Green, Richard Firth. *Poets and Princepleasers: Literature and the English Court in the Late Middle Ages*. Toronto: U of Toronto P, 1980.

Gross, Kenneth. *The Dream of the Moving Statue*. Ithaca, NY: Cornell UP, 1992.

Hallett, Judith P. *Fathers and Daughters in Roman Society*. Princeton: Princeton UP, 1984.

Hanawalt, Barbara. *Chaucer's England: Literature in Historical Context*. Minneapolis: U of Minnesota P, 1992.

Harbert, Bruce. "Lessons from the Great Clerk: Ovid and Gower." *Ovid Renewed: Ovidian Influence on Literature and Art from the Middle Ages to the Twentieth Century*. Ed. Charles Martindale. Cambridge: Cambridge UP, 1988. 83–97.

Harrison, Ann Tukey. "Echo and Her Medieval Sisters." *Centennial Review* 26 (1982): 324–40.

Hatton, Thomas J. "John Gower's Use of Ovid in Book III of the *Confessio Amantis*." *Mediaevalia* 13 (1987): 257–74.

Helly, Dorothy O., and Susan M. Reverby. *Gendered Domains: Rethinking Public and Private in Women's History*. Ithaca, NY: Cornell UP, 1992.

Herlihy, David. "The Making of the Medieval Family: Symmetry, Structure and Sentiment." *Journal of Family History* 8 (1983): 116–30.

———. *Medieval Households*. Cambridge, MA: Harvard UP, 1985.

Herman, Judith Lewis, and Lisa Hirschmann. *Father-Daughter Incest*. Cambridge: Harvard UP, 1981.
Hill, Christopher. "Sex, Marriage and the Family in England." *Economic History Review*. 2nd ser. 31 (1978): 450–63.
Hill, Thomas D. "Narcissus, Pygmalion, and the Castration of Saturn: Two Mythographical Themes in the *Roman de la Rose*." *Studies in Philology* 71 (1974): 404–26.
Hiscoe, David W. "The Ovidian Comic Strategy of Gower's *Confessio Amantis*." *Philological Quarterly* 64 (1985): 367–85.
Holloway, Julia Bolton, Constance S. Wright, and Joan Bechtold, eds. *Equally in God's Image: Women in the Middle Ages*. New York: Peter Lang, 1990.
Hudson, Anne. *The Premature Reformation*. Oxford: Clarendon Press, 1988.
Hutchinson, Harold F. *The Hollow Crown: A Life of Richard II*. New York: John Day, 1961.
Ito, Masayoshi. *John Gower, the Medieval Poet*. Tokyo: Shinozaki Shorin, 1976.
Jacquart, Danielle, and Claude Thomasset. *Sexuality and Medicine in the Middle Ages*. Trans. Matthew Adamson. Princeton: Princeton UP, 1988.
Jed, Stephanie. *Chaste Thinking: The Rape of Lucretia and the Birth of Humanism*. Bloomington: Indiana UP, 1989.
Johnson, H. *The Medieval Tradition of Natural Law*. London: Oxford UP, 1965.
Jones, Richard H. *The Royal Policy of Richard II: Absolutism in the Later Middle Ages*. New York: Barnes & Noble, 1968.
Jordan, Constance. *Renaissance Feminism: Literary Texts and Political Models*. Ithaca, NY: Cornell UP, 1990.
Kaeuper, Richard W. *War, Justice, and Public Order: England and France in the Later Middle Ages*. Oxford: Clarendon Press, 1988.
Kantorowicz, Ernst H. *The King's Two Bodies*. Princeton: Princeton UP, 1957.
Keen, Maurice. *Chivalry*. New Haven: Yale UP, 1984.
Kelley, Donald R. *The Human Measure: Social Thought in the Western Legal Tradition*. Cambridge: Harvard UP, 1990.
Kelly, Douglas. *Medieval Imagination: Rhetoric and the Poetry of Courtly Love*. Madison: U of Wisconsin P, 1978.
Kelly, Henry Ansgar. *Love and Marriage in the Age of Chaucer*. Ithaca, NY: Cornell UP, 1975.
Kelly-Gadol, Joan. "Did Women Have a Renaissance?" *Becoming Visible: Women in European History*. Eds. Renate Bridenthal and Claudia Koonz. Boston: Houghton Mifflin, 1977. 137–64.
———. "The Relation of the Sexes: Methodological Implications of Women's History." *Signs* 1 (1976): 809–23.
Kinneavy, Gerald. "Gower's *Confessio Amantis* and the Penitentials." *The Chaucer Review* 19 (1984): 144–63.
Kolve, V. A. *Chaucer and the Imagery of Narrative: The First Five* Canterbury Tales. Stanford: Stanford UP, 1984.

Kristeva, Julia. "Stabat Mater." *The Female Body in Western Culture*. Ed. Susan Rubin Suleiman. Cambridge, MA: Harvard UP, 1985. 99–118.

Lacan, Jacques. *Feminine Sexuality*. Ed. Juliet Mitchell and Jacqueline Rose. Trans. Jacqueline Rose. New York: Norton, 1982.

———. *The Four Fundamental Concepts of Psycho-Analysis*. Ed. Jacques-Alain Miller. Trans. Alan Sheridan. London: Hogarth Press, 1977.

Leach, Edmund. *Genesis as Myth and Other Essays*. London: Jonathan Cape, 1969.

Leacock, Eleanor. *Myths of Male Dominance*. New York: Monthly Review Press, 1981.

Leicester, Marshall, Jr. *The Disenchanted Self: Representing the Subject in the Canterbury Tales*. Berkeley: U of California P, 1990.

Lévi-Strauss, Claude. *The Elementary Structures of Kinship*. Trans. James Harle Bell, John Richard von Sturmer, and Rodney Needham. Boston: Beacon Press, 1969.

Lewis, C. S. *The Allegory of Love: A Study in Medieval Tradition*. Oxford: Clarendon Press, 1936.

Lochrie, Karma. *Margery Kempe and Translations of the Flesh*. Philadelphia: U of Pennsylvania P, 1991.

Lomperis, Linda. "Unruly Bodies and Ruling Practices: Chaucer's *Physician's Tale* as a Socially Symbolic Act." Lomperis and Stanbury 21–37.

Lomperis, Linda, and Sarah Stanbury, eds. *Feminist Approaches to the Body in Medieval Literature*. Philadelphia: U of Pennsylvania P, 1993.

Macaulay, G. C. "John Gower." *The Cambridge History of English Literature*. Vol. 2. 1908. Reprint, Cambridge: Cambridge UP, 1949. 133–55.

McNally, John J. "The Penitential and Courtly Traditions in Gower's *Confessio Amantis*." *Studies in Medieval Culture*. Ed. John R. Sommerfeldt. Kalamazoo: Western Michigan U, 1964. 74–94.

Mahoney, Dhira B. "Gower's Two Prologues to *Confessio Amantis*." Yeager, *Re-Visioning Gower* 17–37.

Mainzer, C. "John Gower's Use of the 'Mediaeval Ovid' in the *Confessio Amantis*." *Medium Aevum* 41 (1972): 215–29.

———. "A Study of the Sources of the *Confessio Amantis* of John Gower." Diss. Oxford University, 1967.

Maisch, Herbert. *Incest*. Trans. Colin Bearne. London: Deutsch, 1973.

Manzaloui, M. A. " 'Noght in the Registre of Venus': Gower's English Mirror for Princes." *Medieval Studies for J. A. W. Bennett*. Ed. P. L. Heyworth. Oxford: Clarendon, 1981. 159–83.

Marcus, David. *Jephthah and His Vow*. Lubbock, TX: Texas Tech UP, 1986.

Margherita, Gayle. "Historicity, Femininity, and Chaucer's *Troilus*." *Exemplaria* 6 (1994): 243–69.

Masters, R. E. L., and Donald Webster Cory. *Violation of Taboo: Incest in the Great Literature of the Past and Present*. New York: Julian Press, 1963.

Mathew, Gervase. *The Court of Richard II*. New York: Norton, 1968.

Middleton, Anne. "The Idea of Public Poetry in the Reign of Richard II." *Speculum* 53 (1978): 94–114.

———. "War by Other Means: Marriage and Chivalry in Chaucer." *Studies in the Age of Chaucer* 6 (1985): 119–33.

Middletown, Russell. "Brother-Sister and Father-Daughter Marriage in Ancient Egypt." *American Sociological Review* 27 (1962): 603–11.

Miller, J. Hillis. *Versions of Pygmalion*. Cambridge: Harvard UP, 1990.

Millett, Bella, and Jocelyn Wogan-Browne. *Medieval English Prose for Women: The Katherine Group and* Ancrene Wisse. Oxford: Oxford UP, 1990.

Minnis, Alastair J. "De vulgari auctoritate: Chaucer, Gower and the Men of Great Authority." Yeager, *Chaucer and Gower* 36–74.

———, ed. *Gower's* Confessio Amantis: *Responses and Reassessments*. Cambridge: D. S. Brewer, 1983.

———. "John Gower: *Sapiens* in Ethics and Politics." *Medium Aevum* 49 (1980): 207–29.

———. *Medieval Theory of Authorship: Scholastic Literary Attitudes in the Later Middle Ages*. Philadelphia: U of Pennsylvania P, 1984.

———. " 'Moral Gower' and Medieval Literary Theory." Minnis, *Gower's* Confessio Amantis 50–78.

Moi, Toril. "Desire in Language: Andreas Capellanus and the Controversy of Courtly Love." *Medieval Literature: Criticism, Ideology, and History*. Ed. David Aers. New York: Saint Martin's Press, 1986. 11–33.

Morgan, Gerald. "Natural and Rational Love in Medieval Literature." *Yearbook of English Studies* 7 (1977): 43–52.

Nagel, Betty Rose. "Byblis and Myrrha: Two Incest Narratives in the Metamorphoses." *Classical Journal* 78 (1983): 301–15.

Neilson, William Allan. *The Origins and Sources of the* Court of Love. Harvard Studies and Notes in Philology and Literature 6. Boston: Ginn & Company, 1899.

———. "The Purgatory of Cruel Beauties." *Romania* 29 (1900): 85–93.

Newman, Barbara. *From Virile Woman to WomanChrist: Studies in Medieval Religion and Literature*. Philadelphia: U of Pennsylvania P, 1995.

Nicholson, Peter. *An Annotated Index to the Commentary on Gower's* Confessio Amantis. Medieval & Renaissance Texts & Studies 62. Binghamton, NY: Center for Medieval and Early Renaissance Studies, 1989.

———, ed. *Gower's* Confessio Amantis: *A Critical Anthology*. Cambridge: D. S. Brewer, 1991.

Nitzsche, Jane Chance. *The Genius Figure in Antiquity and the Middle Ages*. New York: Columbia UP, 1972.

Oakley, Francis. *The Western Church in the Later Middle Ages*. Ithaca, NY: Cornell UP, 1979.

Olsson, Kurt. *John Gower and the Structures of Conversion: A Reading of the* Confessio Amantis. Cambridge: D. S. Brewer, 1992.

———. "Natural Law and John Gower's *Confessio Amantis*." Nicholson, *Gower's* Confessio Amantis 181–213.

Orme, Nicholas. *Education and Society in Medieval and Renaissance England.* London: Hambledon Press, 1989.

———. *From Childhood to Chivalry: The Education of the English Kings and Aristocracy 1066–1530.* London: Methuen, 1984.

Pantin, W. A. *The English Church in the Fourteenth Century.* Toronto: U of Toronto P, 1980.

Patterson, Lee. *Chaucer and the Subject of History.* Madison: U of Wisconsin P, 1991.

———. "Chaucerian Confession: Penitential Literature and the Pardoner." *Medievalia et Humanistica* 7 (1976): 153–73.

———. "On the Margin: Postmodernism, Ironic History, and Medieval Studies." *Speculum* 65 (1990): 87–108.

———. " 'What Man Artow?': Authorial Self-Definition in the 'Tale of Sir Thopas' and the 'Tale of Melibee.' " *Studies in the Age of Chaucer* 11 (1989): 117–76.

Payer, Pierre J. "Sex and Confession in the Thirteenth Century." Salisbury, *Sex in the Middle Ages* 126–42.

Pearsall, Derek. "Gower's Narrative Art." *PMLA* 81 (1966): 475–84.

———. "The Gower Tradition." Minnis, *Gower's* Confessio Amantis 179–97.

Peck, Russell A. *Kingship and Common Profit in Gower's* Confessio Amantis. Carbondale: Southern Illinois UP, 1978.

Pickles, J. D., and J. L. Dawson. *A Concordance to John Gower's* Confessio Amantis. Cambridge: D. S. Brewer, 1987.

Pitt-Rivers, Julian. "Honour and Social Status." *Honour and Shame: The Values of Mediterranean Society.* Ed. J. G. Peristiany. Chicago: U of Chicago P, 1966. 19–78.

Porter, Elizabeth. "Gower's Ethical Microcosm and Political Macrocosm." Minnis, *Gower's* Confessio Amantis 135–62.

Radcliffe-Umstead, D. *Human Sexuality in the Middle Ages and the Renaissance.* Center for Medieval and Renaissance Studies. Pittsburgh: U of Pittsburgh P, 1978.

Rank, Otto. *The Incest Theme in Literature and Legend: Fundamentals of a Psychology of Literary Creation.* Trans. Gregory C. Richter. Baltimore: Johns Hopkins UP, 1992.

Raybin, David. "Custance and History: Woman as Outsider in Chaucer's Man of Law's Tale." *Studies in the Age of Chaucer* 12 (1990): 65–84.

Reynolds, William Donald. "The *Ovidius Moralizatus* of Petrus Berchorius: An Introduction and Translation." Diss. U of Illinois at Urbana-Champaign, 1971.

Rivière, Joan. "Womanliness As a Masquerade." *Formations of Fantasy.* Eds. Victor Burgin, James Donald, and Cora Kaplan. London: Methuen, 1986. 35–61.

Robertson, Elizabeth. *Early English Devotional Prose and the Female Audience.* Knoxville: U of Tennesee P, 1990.

Robins, William. "Romance, Exemplum, and the Subject of the *Confessio Amantis*." *Studies in the Age of Chaucer* 19 (1997): 157–81.

Rubin, Gayle. "The Traffic in Women: Notes on the 'Political Economy' of Sex." *Toward an Anthropology of Women*. Ed. Rayna R. Reiter. New York: Monthly Review Press, 1975. 157–210.

Rubin, Rick, and Greg Byerly. *Incest: The Last Taboo. An Annotated Bibliography*. New York: Garland, 1983.

Salisbury, Joyce. *Medieval Sexuality: A Research Guide*. New York: Garland, 1990.

———, ed. *Sex in the Middle Ages: A Book of Essays*. New York: Garland, 1991.

Scala, Elizabeth. "Canacee and the Chaucer Canon: Incest and Other Unnarratables." *Chaucer Review* 30 (1996): 15–39.

Scanlon, Larry. *Narrative, Authority, and Power: The Medieval Exemplum and the Chaucerian Tradition*. Cambridge: Cambridge UP, 1994.

———. "The Riddle of Incest: John Gower and the Problem of Medieval Sexuality." Yeager, *Re-Visioning Gower* 93–127.

Scattergood, V. J. "Literary Culture at the Court of Richard II." *English Court Culture in the Later Middle Ages*. Eds. V. J. Scattergood, J. W. Sherborne and J. A. Burrow. New York: St. Martin's Press, 1983. 29–43.

Schibanoff, Susan. "Worlds Apart: Orientalism, Antifeminism, and Heresy in Chaucer's Man of Law's Tale." *Exemplaria* 8.1 (1996): 59–96.

Schlauch, Margaret. *Chaucer's Constance and Accused Queens*. New York: New York UP, 1927.

———. "The Man of Law's Tale." *Sources and Analogues of Chaucer's Canterbury Tales*. Ed. W. F. Bryan and G. Dempster. Chicago: U of Chicago P, 1941. 155–206.

Schmitz, Götz. "Gower, Chaucer and the Classics: Back to the Textual Evidence." Yeager, *John Gower* 95–111.

———. *'the middel weie': Stil- und Aufbauformen in John Gowers* Confessio Amantis. Bonn: Bouvier Verlag Herbert Grundmann, 1974.

Sedgwick, Eve Kosofsky. *Between Men: English Literature and Male Homosocial Desire*. New York: Columbia UP, 1985.

———. *Epistemology of the Closet*. Berkeley: U of California P, 1990.

Shell, Marc. *The End of Kinship: Measure for Measure, Incest, and the Ideal of Universal Siblinghood*. Stanford: Stanford UP, 1988.

Shoaf, R. A. "'Unwemmed Custance': Circulation, Property, and Incest in the Man of Law's Tale." *Exemplaria* 2.1 (1990): 287–302.

Simpson, James. *Sciences and the Self in Medieval Poetry: Alain of Lille's* Anticlaudianus *and John Gower's* Confessio Amantis. Cambridge: Cambridge UP, 1995.

Soliday, Gerald L., et al. *History of the Family and Kinship: A Select International Bibliography*. Millwood, NY: Kraus-International Publications, 1980.

Spearing, A. C. "Canace and Machaire." *Mediaevalia* 16 (1993 [for 1990]): 211–21.

Stallybrass, Peter. "Patriarchal Territories: The Body Enclosed." Ferguson, Quilligan, and Vickers. 123–42.
Stanbury, Sarah. "The Voyeur and the Private Life in *Troilus and Criseyde*." *Studies in the Age of Chaucer* 13 (1991): 141–58.
———. "Women's Letters and Private Space in Chaucer." *Exemplaria* 6 (1994): 271–85.
Steinle, Eric M. "Versions of Authority in the *Roman de la Rose*: Remarks on the Use of Ovid's *Metamorphoses* by Guillaume de Lorris and Jean de Meun." *Mediaevalia* 13 (1987): 189–206.
Stiller, Nikki. *Eve's Orphans: Mothers and Daughters in Medieval English Literature*. Contributions in Women's Studies 16. Westport, CT: Greenwood Press, 1980.
Stillwell, Gardiner. "John Gower and the Last Years of Edward III." *Studies in Philology* 45 (1948): 454–71.
Stollreither, Eugen. *Quellen-Nachweise zu John Gowers* Confessio Amantis. *I. Teil*. Munich: Kastner & Lossen, 1901.
Stone, Lawrence. *The Family, Sex, and Marriage in England 1500–1800*. New York: Harper & Row, 1977.
Stow, George B. "Richard II in John Gower's *Confessio Amantis*: Some Historical Perspectives." *Medievalia* 16 (1993 [for 1990]): 3–31.
Strohm, Paul. "Form and Social Statement in the *Confessio Amantis* and the *Canterbury Tales*." *Studies in the Age of Chaucer* 1 (1979): 17–40.
———. *Hochon's Arrow: The Social Imagination of Fourteenth-Century Texts*. Princeton: Princeton UP, 1992.
———. *Social Chaucer*. Cambridge: Harvard UP, 1989.
Swanson, R. N. *Church and Society in Late Medieval England*. Oxford: Basil Blackwell, 1989.
Sypherd, Wilbur Owen. *Jephthah and His Daughter*. Newark, DE: U of Delaware P, 1948.
Tavormina, Theresa M. *Kindly Similitude: Marriage and Family in* Piers Plowman. Cambridge: D. S. Brewer, 1995.
Thomas, Brook. "The Writer's Procreative Urge in *Pierre*: Fictional Freedom or Convoluted Incest?" *Studies in the Novel* 11 (1979): 416–30.
Thorpe, Lewis. "A Source of the *Confessio Amantis*." *Modern Language Review* 43 (1948): 175–81.
Thrupp, Sylvia. *The Merchant Class of Medieval London*. Chicago: U of Chicago P, 1948.
Tierney, Brian. *The Crisis of Church and State, 1050–1300*. Toronto: U of Toronto P, 1988.
Tinkle, Theresa. *Medieval Venuses and Cupids: Sexuality, Hermeneutics, and English Poetry*. Stanford: Stanford UP, 1996.
Tuck, Anthony. *Richard II and the English Nobility*. London: Edward Arnold, 1973.
———. *Crown and Nobility, 1272–1461: Political Conflict in Late Medieval England*. Totowa, NJ: Barnes & Noble Books, 1985.

Tuve, Rosemund. *Allegorical Imagery: Some Mediaeval Books and Their Posterity.* Princeton: Princeton UP, 1966.
Ullmann, Walter. *Principles of Government and Politics in the Middle Ages.* London: Methuen, 1961.
Verducci, Florence. *Ovid's Toyshop of the Heart:* Epistolae Heroidum. Princeton: Princeton UP, 1985.
Wack, Mary F. *Lovesickness in the Middle Ages: The 'Viaticum' and Its Commentaries.* Philadelphia: U of Pennsylvania P, 1990.
Wallace, David. *Chaucerian Polity.* Stanford: Stanford UP, 1997.
Warner, Marina. *Alone of All Her Sex: The Myth and the Cult of the Virgin Mary.* New York: Vintage Books, 1983.
Wetherbee, Winthrop. "Constance and the World in Chaucer and Gower." Yeager, *John Gower* 65–93.
———. "Genius and Interpretation in the *Confessio Amantis.*" *Magister Regis: Studies in Honor of R. E. Kaske.* Ed. Arthur Groos. New York: Fordham UP, 1986. 241–60.
———. "The Theme of Imagination in Medieval Poetry and the Allegorical Figure 'Genius.'" *Medievalia et Humanistica,* n.s. 7 (1976): 45–64.
White, Hugh. "Nature and the Good in Gower's *Confessio Amantis.*" Yeager, *John Gower* 1–20.
Wilbern, David. "*Filia Oedipi*: Father and Daughter in Freudian Theory." Boose and Flowers 75–96.
Wilcox, Helen. "Private Writing and Public Function: Autobiographical Texts by Renaissance Englishwomen." Cesarano and Wynne-Davies 47–62.
Wilks, Michael. "Chaucer and the Mystical Marriage in Medieval Political Thought." *Bulletin of the John Rylands Library* 44 (1962): 489–530.
———. *The Problem of Sovereignty in the Later Middle Ages.* Cambridge: Cambridge UP, 1963.
Wilson, Katherine, and E. M. Makowski. *Wykked Wyves and the Woes of Marriage: Misogamous Literature from Juvenal to Chaucer.* Albany: SUNY, 1990.
Wogan-Browne, Jocelyn. "The Virgin's Tale." *Feminist Readings in Middle English Literature: The Wife of Bath and All Her Sect.* Eds. Ruth Evans and Lesley Johnson. London: Routledge, 1994. 165–94.
Woolf, Rosemary. "Moral Chaucer and Kindly Gower." *J. R. R. Tolkien, Scholar and Storyteller.* Eds. Mary Salu and Robert T. Farrell. Ithaca, NY: Cornell UP, 1979. 221–45.
Yeager, Robert F., ed. *Chaucer and Gower: Difference, Mutuality and Exchange.* English Literary Studies. Monograph Series 51. Victoria: U of Victoria, 1991.
———, ed. *John Gower: Recent Readings.* Kalamazoo: Medieval Institute Publications, 1989.
———. "John Gower and the Exemplum Form: Tale Models in the *Confessio Amantis.*" *Mediaevalia* 8 (1982): 325–30.

———. "John Gower and the Uses of Allusion." *Res Publica Litterarum* 7 (1984): 201–13.

———. *John Gower's Poetic: The Search for a New Arion*. Cambridge: D. S. Brewer, 1990.

———. "Learning to Speak in Tongues: Writing Poetry for a Trilingual Culture." Yeager, *Chaucer and Gower* 115–29.

———. "The Poetry of John Gower: Important Studies, 1960–1983." *Fifteenth-Century Studies*. Ed. Robert F. Yeager. Hamden, CO: Archon Books, 1984. 3–28.

———, ed. *Re-Visioning Gower: Current Work*. Asheville, NC: Pegasus Press, 1998.

Ziolkowski, Jan. *Alan of Lille's Grammar of Sex: The Meaning of Grammar to a Twelfth-Century Intellectual*. Cambridge: The Medieval Academy of America, 1985.

INDEX

Abelard, Peter   193n, 195
absolutism *see* tyranny
Aers, David   3n, 8n, 103n, 109–10, 114, 182, 184n
Alain de Lille   7–8, 170, 178, 185, 211
Albinus   40, 102–04, 115–29
Allee   80, 81, 83–84
Allen, Elizabeth   4n, 7n, 11n, 46n, 50n, 53, 57, 58n, 75n, 76, 77, 78, 92n, 159n, 161n, 199n
Amans   46, 53, 137–38, 160–62, 176, 207–10, 214; as confessant   7–8; and Genius   25, 35–36, 122n, 174, 187, 198; and subjectivity   7–8
Andreas Capellanus   183, 184n
anger *see* wrath
Annunciation   71, 137, 140
Antiochus   2, 42–43, 46–54, 56–57, 59–61, 62, 68, 92, 97, 149, 160
Antiochus's daughter   42–43, 46–49, 55, 57, 59–60, 68, 97
Apius Claudius   145–57
Apollonius   2, 25, 42–64, 68
Aquinas, Thomas   10–11, 13, 17–18, 24, 102–03, 162–63
Archibald, Elizabeth   10, 75n
Aristotle   26, 162
Artestrathes   46–47, 50–52, 62
Astell, Ann W.   92n
auctor (*see also* authority; authorship)   35, 36, 41, 176, 188, 190, 199, 203–04
Augustine, St.   10–11, 13, 24
Augustine of Canterbury, St.   95
authority (*see also* gender; Genius; Gower; incest)   1–3, 10, 32, 36, 38, 42, 87, 94, 95, 101, 136, 176, 199, 214–15; in author-text relationship   2, 17, 33–38, 40–41, 61, 129, 130, 168–69, 173–74, 176–77, 187, 200–201, 203, 212–15; clerical   36–37, 39, 75, 79, 86–88; confessor as   6–10; in father-daughter relationship   2, 17, 18, 21, 25–29, 33, 36–38, 40–41, 61–64, 67–68, 73–74, 77, 90–91, 102–04, 106, 111–16, 118, 125, 129, 130–33, 136–37, 142, 144–46, 148, 151–53, 155–61, 164, 167, 170, 173–76, 181, 188, 190, 194, 196–98, 209, 212–15; in father-son relationship   167, 196; God's   64, 87, 90, 196–98; in husband-wife relationship   25–26, 28, 44–45, 47, 76, 81, 91, 102, 111–12, 116, 118, 125, 128, 213; in king-subject relationship   2, 4, 5, 17, 20–29, 31, 33, 38, 40, 44, 46–49, 61–64, 67–68, 73–74, 89, 90, 95, 97, 99, 102–03, 105–06, 123, 129, 130–33, 135–36, 142–49, 152–53, 155–60, 162, 164, 173, 215; lay   36–37, 39, 75, 79, 86–88; limits of   2, 5, 10, 19–23, 26–28, 31–33, 36–38, 39–41, 44–45, 47–48, 61–64, 67, 96, 100–101, 104, 129, 130–33, 136–37, 140–41, 143, 145–46, 148, 153, 155–56, 162, 164, 209, 212–15; poetic   5, 33, 36–38, 40–41, 176–78, 214–15
authorship (*see also auctor*; authority)   201, 214; and incest   176–77, 201, 214–15
avantance   120–21, 123–29
avarice (*see also* stealth)   207

Batchelor, Patricia   36n
Bennett, J. A. W.   52n, 180, 185n
Bennett, Judith M.   32n, 185n
Benson, C. David   146, 158n, 161n, 168
Benson, Larry D.   1n, 11n
Berchorius, Petrus   6, 199–200, 202n, 204, 209
Bergen, Henry   146n
Bergman, Johan   163n
Bible, Judges.   189–96, 198
Bloch, R. Howard   95n, 136, 138n, 178–79, 182, 185n
Bloomfield, Morton W.   88
Blythe, James M.   26
boasting *see avantance*
Boccaccio, Giovanni: *Decameron*   183–84
body: daugther's   40, 130–33, 136, 139, 141, 144, 148, 153, 155–60, 164, 167, 170–72, 188, 197; politic   159–60,

INDEX

162–63; and privacy 132–33; woman's 27
Boer, C. de 204n
Boehrer, Bruce Thomas 22–25, 57, 59, 118
Book of Vices and Virtues 163–64
Boose, Lynda E. 3n, 20, 125, 160, 166–67, 170, 174, 196–97
Boswell, John 56n
Brown, Cheryl Anne 192, 194
Brown, Emerson, Jr. 151
Brownlee, Kevin 200–201, 206, 209
Brundage, James A. 19
Bryan, W. F. 80n
Burke, Linda Barney 74
Butler, Judith 3n, 9–10, 13–15, 40, 43, 59, 61, 72–73, 78, 82, 86, 103, 106n, 108, 110, 215

Camille, Michael 173n
Canace 40, 51n, 130–34, 155, 157, 158–72
Carruthers, Mary 173n
Cesarano, S. P. 149n
chambre 131–32, 136–37, 139–41, 143, 165–66, 208
chastity *see* virginity
Chaucer, Geoffrey (*see also* Gower): and private/public distinction 30–33, 133, 165; *Canterbury Tales*, Franklin's Tale 73; General Prologue (Knight's Portrait) 108; Knight's Tale 50, 105, 117n; Man of Law's Prologue and Tale 1–2, 16, 19, 75–76, 79, 80–81, 84–85, 86, 87, 88, 89n, 94, 98; Melibee 66n; Pardoner's Tale 6n; Physician's Tale 29n, 136, 138n, 146–48, 150–52, 155; Squire's Tale 73; *Legend of Good Women* 117n; *Parliament of Fowls* 179–80, 186; *Troilus and Criseyde* 10n, 11n, 13n, 29n, 109, 131n, 182
chivalry 40, 103–11, 114–23, 126–29, 214
Christ *see* Mary, Virgin
Christianity (*see also* God; Church) 2, 80, 82, 86–87, 94, 95, 100
Church (*see also* authority): and spiritual power 79, 90–100; and State 39, 75, 79, 86–100; and temporal power 5, 79, 90–100
Ciletti, Elena 74n
Cixous, Hélène 172

comune 22–23, 25, 29, 64, 153–54, 156–57
comune profit 37, 116, 133, 148, 162
confession (*see also* Genius) 175, 200; and subjectivity 5–10, 200, 209
Constance 38–39, 42–45, 54, 55, 63, 69, 74–101, 151
Constantine (Constance's father) 42–45, 76, 78, 79, 80, 83–86, 92, 93, 95, 97–100, 151
Constantine, Donation of 87, 99–100
Copeland, Rita 35
court of love 175, 178, 183–84, 186–88
courtly love poetry 167–68, 172, 178–79, 209–15
Crane, Susan 73
creativity: artistic 6, 200, 203; literary 160, 169–72, 174, 201, 211–12
Cupid 177, 182, 185, 188
Curran, Leo C. 138
Curtius, Ernst 203n
daughters (*see also* body; desire; father-daugther relationships; female eloquence; incest; sexuality) 37–38, 42–45, 48, 77, 79, 100, 144; exchange of 14, 26–28 (*see also* exchange); as individuals 26, 32, 70, 77–78, 81, 83, 86, 133, 156, 158, 161, 164–65, 167–70, 180–81, 187–88, 195; as property 14, 26, 40, 130, 132–33, 153; as redeemers of fathers 38–39, 44–45, 48, 63–64, 66–67, 74, 100, 190, 195
Davies, R. T. 139n
Dean, Ruth 75n
Decameron see Boccaccio
DeJean, Joan 158n
Delany, Sheila 89n
Dempster, G. 80n
Derrida, Jacques 3n, 16–17, 86, 202
desire (*see also* sexuality): author's 174, 202, 211–15; daughter's 3, 43, 66, 74–75, 77, 79, 81, 84–86, 112–14, 170, 181–83; father's 3, 18–19, 39, 47, 97, 112–13, 203; female 14, 183–84; male 109, 113, 134, 136, 149, 211, 213; sexual 134–35, 138, 140, 142–45, 161, 179, 182, 185
Dinshaw, Carolyn 3n, 7, 14n, 37–38, 75n, 78, 85n, 89n, 105–06, 109n, 111n, 113n, 173n
Dinter, Annegret 207n
discourse (*see also* incest) 5–17, 19–21, 77, 78, 160, 172, 175, 181, 212; of

INDEX

courtly love 177–78, 182–84, 187, 211; poetic 201–02, 209, 211–12
Dodd, William G. 45n
Donavin, Georgiana 1n, 3, 11n, 43, 65–66, 68, 71n, 73, 75n, 98
Duby, Georges 131–32, 153

Eberle, Patricia 75n, 87, 95, 99
Echard, Siân 36n, 94
Edward II 22, 146, 154
Edward III 116, 121n, 146
Elpidio, Alexander de S. 90
Elshtain, Jean Bethke 32, 166
enformacioun see information
Engels, Friedrich 30n, 31n, 57, 59–61
envy 55, 82, 100, 104
Eolus 53, 130–34, 141n, 144, 149, 158–72
Esch, Arno 77, 81n, 181, 185n
Evans, Ruth 145n
exchange (*see also* incest) 13–15, 18–20, 23, 26, 37–38, 39–40, 42–45, 48–51, 54, 66–70, 72, 73, 77–80, 82, 85, 101, 102–04, 111, 114, 118, 129, 135, 160, 164, 174–75, 179, 190–91, 213, 215
exogamy *see* incest; exchange

False Bachelor 102–04, 111, 112, 114
family (*see also* incest) 3–4, 14, 26–29, 42, 47–48, 57, 58, 63, 69, 79, 96, 97, 100–101, 102–03, 105–06, 116, 129, 130–31, 152–53, 164, 170, 178–80, 215
Fansler, Dean S. 168
Farrell, Thomas J. 30n
fathers (*see also* desire; authority) 27, 39, 47, 61, 67, 100; authors as 173, 203; and sons-in-law 39–40, 102, 104, 106–07, 111–12, 115–16, 124–29, 150, 213
father-daughter relationships (*see also* incest; authority) 1–3, 14, 18–19, 38–41, 42–64, 66–70, 73, 75–79, 82–85, 89, 94, 96, 98, 131
Federico, Sylvia 28–29
Fehrenbacher, Richard 10n, 11n, 13n
female eloquence (*see also* silence) 32, 43, 64, 66, 68, 70, 72–74, 76–79, 82–83, 85, 134, 195
femininity *see* gender; women
Ferguson, Margaret W. 27n
Ferster, Judith 3, 4n, 145n, 154, 156
Fisher, John H. 4n, 8n, 65n

Foucault, Michel 5–10, 175, 200, 209, 211
Foulke, William Dudley 118n
Fradenburg, Louise Olga 118, 121n, 126
Francis, William Nelson 163n
Frese, Dolores Warwick 173n
Freud, Sigmund 13n, 114, 160–61
Furnivall, Frederick J. 193n

Gallacher, Patrick J. 65, 71n, 76n, 137n
Gallop, Jane 18–19, 112
Gawain and the Green Knight 106
gender (*see also* performance; performativity; women): and authority 18, 41, 42, 44, 47–48, 89–96, 102–04, 106, 129, 131, 136, 144–45, 213; and body 27, 40; and family 3, 26–28; femininity 66, 72, 103, 110, 114, 213–14; and identity 108, 111, 114, 126; masculinity 40, 103–15, 213–15; and politics 26–28, 79, 89–96; and private/public 14, 29–33, 50–51, 157 (*see also* private; public); social/cultural construction of 15, 215
Genius (*see also* Amans; authority; Gower): as author 6, 33–36, 40–41, 44–45, 72, 83, 119–20, 129, 130, 133, 134–35, 148, 157, 159, 160, 167–68, 170–72, 173–74, 176, 188, 190, 198, 200, 209–15; as authority 33–36, 40–41, 174–76, 180, 187–88, 190, 198–201, 209, 214–15; as Christian priest 8, 175–76; as confessor 5–10, 35–36, 173, 200, 208–09; as creator 6, 168, 170–72, 176, 187, 190, 200, 203, 205, 210–11; as father 6, 36, 41, 72, 133, 160, 167, 168, 172, 173–76, 187–88, 195, 198–205, 209, 212–15; and incest 10–17, 39, 59–62, 104, 212–15; and marriage 180, 186, 202; as moralist 8, 15–16, 33–36, 39–41, 44–45, 48, 65–66, 74, 128–29, 134, 148, 151, 156–57, 174–75, 188, 191, 197–98, 208, 212; as poetic principle 16–17, 170; as priest of Venus 7–8, 15–16, 175, 185; as promoter of love and reproduction 8, 16, 62, 85, 122, 170–72, 175, 180, 183–86, 190, 195; in Alain de Lille's *De planctu naturae* 7–8, 170, 185; in Jean de Meun's *Roman de la Rose* 7–8, 185
Gilbert, Sandra 168–69, 203
Giles of Rome 26n

INDEX

Given-Wilson, Chris 3n, 21n
Glossa ordinaria see Nicholas de Lyra
glosses, Latin *see* Gower
God (*see also* authority) 48, 64, 125, 140, 176, 190–92, 200, 204; and Mary 2–3, 39, 45, 66–67, 71, 74, 97–100, 139, 197
Godfrey of Viterbo: *Pantheon* 115, 118–20, 123–24, 127n, 128
Goldberg, Jonathan 26n
Goodall, Peter 58n, 75–76
Gordon, E. V. 139n
governance 4, 21, 115, 128–29, 146, 162
Gower, John (*see also* authority): and Amans 34–36, 190, 198–99, 214; as author 36, 37, 168, 190, 199, 201, 203, 214–15; as authority 5, 33, 36–38, 40–41, 187, 214–15; and Chaucer 1–2, 88–89, 165; and Genius 33–36, 187; and private/public distinction 29–33; as textual father 37–38, 168, 172, 173, 176, 201–03, 214–15; *Confessio Amantis*, Latin glosses 36, 94, 115, 140, 176, 187, 214; Latin epigrams 36, 104–05, 176; tales of: Aeneas and Dido 170n; Albinus and Rosemund 39, 101, 102–04, 115–29, 179, 207n, 213; Amon and his Sister 1, 12, 17; Apollonius of Tyre 1–2, 9, 16, 17, 20, 39, 42–64, 68, 75–76, 78, 82, 85, 92, 96, 97, 147; Caligula and his Three Sisters 1, 17; Calistona 135n; Canace and Machaire 1–2, 40, 45, 53, 97, 130–34, 142, 145–46, 151n, 155, 158–72, 196n; Capaneus 117; Chastity of Valentinian 142–43; Constance 2–3, 18, 39, 42–45, 73, 74–101, 139, 182; Constantine and Silvester 86, 100; Donation of Constantine 91; False Bachelor 39, 101, 102–15, 121, 122n, 129, 179, 213; Florent 69n; Galba and Vitellius 27, 122–23; Geta and Amphitrion 104; Iphis 15–16, 202, 207; Jephthah's Daughter 2, 41, 67, 173–75, 177, 188, 189–99; Leucothoe 40, 130–45, 146–47, 155, 162, 171–72; Lot and his Daughters 1, 17, 45, 160; Narcissus 15–16, 126, 183; Nectanabus 137; Neptune and Cornix 135n; Pope Boniface 91, 104; Prologue 5, 9, 37–38; Pygmaleon and the Statue 6, 41, 157, 173, 176, 177, 199–215; Rape of Lucrece 147; Rosiphelee 41, 173–75, 177–89, 199, 202; Tereus 134n, 135n; Three Questions 3, 39, 42–45, 64–74, 78, 85, 139, 190; Ulysses and Penelope 210; Virginia 40, 67, 130–34, 145–57, 158, 162, 166, 171–72; *Cronica Tripertita* 23, 142–43; *Mirour de l'Omme* 4, 8, 36, 70–71; *Vox lamantis* 4, 8, 28, 36
Gratian 10n
Gravdal, Kathryn 135n
Gregory, St. 70–71
Groos, Arthur 187n
Gross, Kenneth 204
Gryson, Robert 191n
Gubar, Susan 168–69, 203
Gurmond 115–16, 121–24, 126

Handlyng Synne see Mannyng, Robert
Harrison, Ann Tukey 15n
Hatton, Thomas J. 162n
Helly, Dorothy O. 30, 31n, 131n
Henderson, W. G. 85
Henry IV 28n, 37n, 143
Henry VIII 24–25
heterosexuality *see* sexuality
Hill, Thomas D. 206n, 207n
Historia Apollonii regis Tyri 50, 51, 56
homosexuality *see* sexuality
honor 105, 118, 126
Hudson, Anne 91n, 99n
humility 39, 65–67, 70–74, 76
husbands and wives *see* authority
Hutchinson, Harold F. 21n, 132n, 163n, 164

identity (*see also* gender) 105, 110, 111, 127; daughter's 112–13; and chivalry 103–12, 117–18, 126
idlenesss 177, 181, 185, 189
idolatry 207–08
imagination 209–11, 213
incest 1–4, 24, 28–29, 45, 147; and discourse 5–17, 19–20, 43–44, 48–49, 55–61, 70, 72, 77, 78, 86, 201–202; father-daughter 1–4, 10, 13n, 14, 17–21, 26–29, 42–64, 68, 74–79, 84–86, 89, 91–92, 96–101, 118, 125–27, 155, 159–62, 164, 166–67, 171–72, 174, 176, 197, 201–03, 205–09, 212–15; and kingship 22–29, 37, 40, 79, 96, 99; and law 2, 5–17, 25, 41, 43–44, 86, 215; and law of

exogamy 10, 13–14, 22–23, 41, 60–61, 197; mother-son 17–18; and nature 11–17, 18, 57–61, 86; prohibition 19–20, 39, 43, 47, 57–61, 86, 174, 215; and reason 11–13; sibling 1–2, 10–13, 13n, 17, 45, 158–59, 164–65, 167, 172; and text 33–38, 176–77, 201, 214–15
information 176, 204–05, 211n
Innes, Mary M. 135n
Ito, Masayoshi 168

Jean de Meun: *Roman de la Rose* 7–8, 38, 43, 68, 146, 150, 152, 155, 185, 200–202, 205–06, 209, 212, 214–15
Jed, Stephanie 38n
Jephthah 173–75, 189–99
Jephthah's daughter 35, 173–75, 189–99, 214
Jerome, St. 140
Johnson, Lesley 145n
Jones, Richard H. 21n, 22n, 163–64

Kaeuper, Richard W. 3n, 116, 117, 118, 121n
Kantorowicz, Ernst. H 23n, 25n, 162n
Keen, Maurice 69n, 120–21
Kelley, Donald R. 31n, 133n
Kelly, Douglas 210–11
Kelly-Gadol, Joan 26, 31n
Kimhi, David 191
kinde 12–13, 16, 58–61, 133, 157, 171, 202
kingship (*see also* authority; governance; incest; tyranny) 4–5, 21– 29, 40, 44, 49, 50, 54, 67, 87, 95, 96, 100, 103, 115, 116–17, 123, 125–29, 130–33, 136, 142–49, 153, 159–60, 163–64, 215; and the law 21–29, 163–64
Kinneavy, Gerald 10n
knighthood *see* chivalry
Kolve, V. A. 88
Kristeva, Julia 92, 94–95

Lacan, Jacques 72
law *see* incest; *kinde*; nature
Lay du Trot 183–84
Leacock, Eleanor 31n
lechery *see* lust
Leicester, Marshall, Jr. 105
Leucothoe 40, 130–45, 171–72
Lévi-Strauss, Claude 13–16, 18, 70, 77, 78, 82, 125, 135

lineage 80–81, 85, 95, 113–14, 175, 178–79, 181
Livy (Titus Livius) 29, 146–47, 149–50, 152–53, 155, 156
Lollards *see* Wyclif
Lochrie, Karma 139
Lomperis, Linda 147–48, 155n, 156, 159
love 7, 43, 46, 53, 68, 109–10, 115, 119–23, 127, 142, 154, 160–62, 172, 177–90, 205–11
Lucrece 29, 38n
lust 10, 45, 47, 49, 146–49
Lydgate, John 146n

Macaulay, G. C. 7n, 23n, 45n, 50, 71n, 108n, 118, 168, 170n, 183n
Machaire 158–60, 165–66, 196n
McWilliam, G. H. 183n
Mahoney, Dhira B. 37n
Mainzer, Conrad 200, 202n
Mannyng, Robert 193–95, 197
Manuale et processionale 85
Marcus, David 191–93, 195
Margherita, Gayle 31n
marriage 11–12, 18, 20, 66, 80, 98, 113–14, 118, 125, 145, 175, 179–82, 185–90, 202
Mary, Virgin (*see also* Annunciation; God) 65–67, 71–73, 80, 92, 96, 137, 139–40; and Jesus 92, 98
masculinity *see* gender
melancholy 53–54, 159–65
Metamorphoses see Ovid
Middleton, Anne 37, 153–54
Mierow, Charles Christopher 140n
Miller, J. Hillis 200–201, 205
Millett, Bella 145n
Minnis, A. J. 4n, 34, 35, 147n, 187n, 204
Moi, Toril 184n
mothers (*see also* incest) 18, 55, 79, 80–81, 83, 91, 92–100
Myrrha 202–03, 205–06

narcissism 120–21, 125–26, 205–06
Narcissus 126, 205–06
natural law *see kinde*; nature
nature (*see also kinde*; incest) 12–13, 59–61, 110, 136–37, 180; Dame Nature in Chaucer's *Parliament of Fowls* 180, 186; natural order 136–37
Neilson, William Alan 183n
Newman, Barbara 144

INDEX

Nicholas de Lyra 191n
Nicholson, Peter 33n

Oakley, Francis 93
Ockham, William of 26n
O'Keefe, Katherine O'Brien 173n
Olsson, Kurt 6n, 12n, 33, 56, 57n, 58n, 98n, 134–35, 138, 185n, 198, 199n, 207–08, 210n
Orchamus 130–36, 141–45, 149, 155, 159, 171–72, 197, 198
Ovid: *Heroides* 158–59, 165–67, 169; *Metamorphoses* 134, 138, 140n, 141, 143, 144, 200–206, 209, 212, 215
Ovide moralisé 202n, 204
Ovidius moralizatus see Berchorius, Petrus

Pantheon see Godfrey of Viterbo
Pantin, W. A. 88, 91n
Patterson, Lee 3n, 6n, 8n, 22n, 117, 121n, 127
Paul the Deacon (Paulus Diaconus) 118–19, 128
Payer, Pierre J. 10n
Pearl 139
Pearsall, Derek 187
Peck, Russell 4n, 50, 66n, 86, 121, 147
performance 40, 103–04, 106, 108, 111, 120, 214
performativity 40, 103–04, 106, 110, 114–15, 214
Peronelle 38–39, 42–45, 54, 63, 64–74, 76, 77, 78, 79, 80, 85, 86, 100, 195, 197
Petro 42–45, 64, 67–70, 72–74
Phebus 130–44, 197
Philomela 134
Pitt-Rivers, Julian 118n
Planctu naturae, De see Alain de Lille
Porter, Elizabeth 4n, 31–32,
power (*see also* authority; women) 4, 6, 22–23, 26–28, 29, 31–32, 36, 38, 41, 64, 79, 86–101, 102, 121, 127, 128, 130, 136, 148–53, 190, 197, 201–02, 209, 213–15
pride *see avantance*
private (*see also* chambre; public) 29–33, 40, 44–45, 47–56, 62, 68–69, 73, 76–77, 79–83, 112, 116–17, 126–28, 130–36, 138, 141, 144–49, 152–59, 162, 165–66, 172, 212
procreation (*see also* creativity) 11–12, 16, 81, 113–14, 160, 169–70, 175, 203

property (*see also* private) 30–33, 69–70, 130, 132–33, 135–38, 144, 148, 164
Prudentius: *Psychomachia* 163
public (*see also* private) 29–33, 40, 44–45, 47–56, 62, 66, 68, 70, 73, 76–77, 79–83, 110, 126–28, 131–34, 136, 141, 145–49, 152–59, 162, 165–66, 172, 212
pusillanimity 202, 210, 213–14
Pygmalion 6, 36, 38, 173, 176, 199–215

querele 43, 83–84, 117, 181–82

rape 27, 122–23, 131–32, 134–39, 141–44, 147
Raybin, David 89
redemption *see* daughters
Reverby, Susan 30, 31n, 131n
Reynolds, William Donald 6n, 200n
Richard II 21–23, 25, 29–33, 37–38, 103, 117, 132–33, 136, 142–44, 146, 163–65, 179
Richard de Fournival: *Conseils d'Amour* 183–84
Rivière, Joan 66, 72–73
Robertson, Elizabeth 140n
Robins, William 4n, 7n, 9, 46n, 58n, 62, 77, 175
Roman de la Rose see Jean de Meun
Roman de Marques de Rome 107, 110n, 111, 113
Roman knight 102–15, 213
Rosemund 102–04, 115–16, 118–19, 121–29, 179, 213
Rosiphelee 35, 69, 79, 84, 177–89, 197, 198, 214
Rousseau, Jean Jacques 16–17, 57–59, 61, 86
Rubin, Gayle 13–14
Runacres, Charles 45n

sacrilege 112n, 208
Said, Edward 168, 203n
Salut d'Amor 183–84
Scala, Elizabeth 75n
Scanlon, Larry 1, 3n, 4n, 5, 8n, 11n, 12n, 20, 24, 34, 36, 46n, 48n, 50n, 54, 56, 57n, 60, 87, 91, 97, 142n, 147n, 154n, 203–04
Scattergood, V. J. 28n
Schibanoff, Susan 89n
Schlauch, Margaret 75n, 76–77, 78, 80n, 97

Schmitz, Götz 58n, 170n
self *see* subjectivity
self-restraint 87, 136–37, 142–44, 164
sexuality 10–13, 14, 28–29, 56–57, 81, 86, 142, 178, 211; daughter's 26–28, 40, 155, 172, 181; female 26–28, 29, 55, 175, 186; heterosexuality 15–16, 43, 61; homosexuality 15–16, 202; male 186
Shell, Marc 19, 58
Shoaf, R. A. 75n
silence 57; female 57, 59, 77–79, 82–84, 86, 134–35, 137–38, 142–44
Simpson, James 170–71, 176, 204–05, 211n
sloth 174n, 177, 181
Spearing, A. C. 159n, 161, 169
Stallybrass, Peter 27n
Stanbury, Sarah 30–33, 131n, 132–33, 147n, 153, 156, 159, 165
State (*see also* Church; kingship) 3–4, 25–29, 47–48, 63–64, 155, 159, 164, 180–81; and family 3–4, 26–28, 41, 44, 63, 106, 155–57, 158–59, 179–81
stealth 132, 134–35, 137–38, 143–44
Steinle, Eric M. 214
Stockton, Eric W. 24, 143n
Stone, Lawrence 26–28
Stow, George B. 4n
Strohm, Paul 27n, 28, 42, 67, 74, 162–63
Strubel, Armand 205
subjectivity (*see also* confession) 77, 78; and discourse 5–10, 48, 62–64, 77, 178
supplantation 39–40, 67, 101, 102–07, 111–16, 150
Swanson, R. N. 88n, 96
Sypherd, Wilbur Owen 193n, 195n

temporalia see Church; authority
text (*see also* authority) 3–4, 33–38; gendered feminine 16, 37–38, 173, 177, 184–85, 199, 214–15
Thaise 2, 38–39, 42–49, 52–61, 63–64, 68, 69, 74, 76, 77, 78, 85, 86, 100, 134
Thomas, Brook 203n
Thorpe, Lewis 107n
Tierney, Brian 87, 88n, 89
Tinkle, Theresa 4n, 176
Trask, Willard R. 203n

Trible, Phyllis 192
Trivet, Nicholas 75n, 79, 84, 92, 93–94
Tuck, Anthony 3n, 21–23
Tuve, Rosemund 206
tyranny 2, 21–25, 35, 91, 97, 99–100, 143–49, 152–58, 160, 163–64, 199

Ullman, Walter 87, 88n

Venus (*see also* Genius) 2, 18, 34, 35, 84, 135, 138–39, 142, 177, 182n, 212
Verducci, Florence 158n
violence 128; chivalric 117–19, 126
Virginia 40, 130–34, 145–57, 166, 171–72
Virginius 51n, 130–34, 144, 145–57, 159, 166, 171–72
virginity 55, 132, 135–45, 149–50, 155, 192–95

Wack, Mary Frances 53, 160–61
Wallace, David 8n, 22n, 25, 32, 66n, 102, 117n, 162n, 184, 199
Walsingham, Thomas 24, 29, 132–33, 162
war 103–10, 115, 122–23
Warner, Marina 65n, 92n
Wenzel, Siegfried 179n
Wetherbee, Winthrop 16, 76, 80, 98, 159n, 170, 187, 210–11
White, Hugh R. B. 12n
Wilbern, David 114
Wilcox, Helen 149
Wilks, Michael 88n, 90
Wilson, William Burton 71
Wogan-Browne, Jocelyn 144–45
women (*see also* authority; daughters; female eloquence; gender; mothers): female power 67–68, 70, 72–74, 78, 83, 89–90, 91, 95, 96, 168; and land 122–23; and state 27–30, 44
wrath 53, 141n, 149, 155, 159–65, 171
writing *see* authority; text
Wyclif, John 91, 99n
Wynne-Davies, Marion 149n

Yeager, R. F. 8n, 12, 34n, 45n, 46n, 65n, 118n, 120, 123, 127n, 159

Ziolkowski, Jan 178